WITHDRAWN

RELATING SKILLS:
A PRACTICAL GUIDE TO EFFECTIVE
PERSONAL RELATIONSHIPS

Richard Nelson-Jones

CASSELL

Cassell
Wellington House   127 West 24th Street,
125 Strand   New York
London WC2R 0BB   NY 10011

British Library Cataloguing-in-Publication Data

Nelson-Jones, Richard, 1936-
  Relating skills : a practical guide to effective personal
  relationships. − New ed.
  1. Interpersonal relations
  I.Title II. Human relationship skills
  302

ISBN 0-304-33420-0

Typeset by York House Typographics Ltd, London.

Printed and bound in Great Britain by Redwood Books, Trowbridge, Wiltshire.

Contents

Exercises

List of tables

List of figures

Preface

Welcome to *Relating Skills: A Practical Guide to Effective Personal Relationships*. Following are answers to some questions you may have about the book.

What is this book's purpose?

This is a practical 'how to' relationship education book. The book's main purpose is to assist you to improve your personal relationships. I aim to help you gain greater relationship satisfaction and prevent unnecessary distress and pain. Relating skills are viewed as sequences of choices in various skills areas that you can make well or poorly. You can either support or oppress yourself and one another by the choices you make. This book assists you to make affirming rather than destructive choices in your relationships.

For whom is this book intended?

This book is intended for the following audiences.

• Lecturers running relationship education courses in colleges and universities, schools, adult education centres and in non-educational settings.

• Students in colleges, universities and adult education centres taking human relations and human communication courses.

• Students on marriage preparation and relationship education courses run by voluntary and church-related agencies.

• Students in the final years of secondary school.

• Students training for the helping services: for instance, as psychologists, counsellors, social workers, nurses, personnel officers, teachers and pastoral care workers.

• Helping service professionals and voluntary agency counsellors for reference and for recommending to clients.

• Singles and couples interested in improving relating skills and relationships by means of self-help.

Though strongly supporting family values, I do not intend this book for those wishing to learn more about family and parenting skills. Nevertheless, I hope the book indirectly results in happier families and children.

What are this book's contents?

Part 1 of the book, entitled 'Introduction', contains four chapters. The first chapter stresses the importance of relationships. The chapter also provides evidence that, at some stage of their lives, many people experience major relationship difficulties. Chapter 2 introduces the relating skills approach, with its emphasis on feelings, thoughts and actions. Chapter 3 explores how you learned and now maintain relating skills strengths and deficits. Chapter 4 reviews what you bring to relationships: for instance, your sexuality, fears, values and cultural background.

Part 2 of the book, entitled 'Skills' contains 14 chapters. I devote 13 chapters to the skills of: disclosing, listening, showing understanding, managing shyness, choosing a partner, trust, caring, intimacy, companionship, sexual relating, assertion, managing anger, and solving relationship problems. The final chapter examines how to maintain and develop your relating skills. To help further develop your knowledge and skills, I provide a 40-book annotated bibliography along with extensive further references.

What features does this book possess?

• *Lifeskills emphasis*. This book is based upon my lifeskills counselling approach, which I regard as humanistic-existential with a cognitive-behavioural face. Do not worry if you do not understand what I mean, because I direct this comment at those who either work as or train as voluntary or professional helpers. Throughout the book, I use the term relating skills rather than lifeskills.

• *Comprehensiveness*. I offer a comprehensive coverage of the skills you require for effective personal relationships. In addition to skills like assertion and managing anger, I include the gentler, softer skills of trust, caring, intimacy and companionship. Also I break the sexual silence of most texts on relating skills by devoting a lengthy chapter to this important topic.

• *Emphasis on traditional as well as on newer values*. The book emphasizes traditional relationship values such as loyalty, cooperation, compassion and gentleness as well as the newer values of equality, openness, assertion and fun.

• *Emphasis on mental cultivation*. The book emphasizes personal responsibility, courage and mental discipline. Nowhere do I encourage you to think that relating well is always easy.

• *Anglo-Australian emphasis*. Unlike most relationship education texts which are American, this book draws on British and Australian demographic data, books, articles and research findings.

• *Practical exercises*. The book includes 88 practical exercises to help you as singles, partners or in groups develop your knowledge and skills.

- *User-friendly format*. Each chapter follows the same user-friendly format: chapter questions, text, chapter highlights and exercises.

- *Readability*. I have endeavoured to write the book in clear, simple English.

With a little help from my friends

In order to improve this book's quality and to guard against unintentional male bias, I asked four female reviewers to preview Chapters 9 to 17. Each reviewer read two or three chapters. I sincerely appreciate the helpful comments of Associate Professor Di Bretherton, Director of the International Centre for Conflict Resolution, School of Behavioural Science, Melbourne University; Ms Meredith Fuller, a private practice psychologist specializing in mid-life and vocational counselling and in organizational consultancy; Professor Marita McCabe, Coordinator of the Masters in Clinical Psychology training programme and Director of the Sexual Behaviour Clinic at Deakin University's Burwood Campus in Melbourne; and Ms Margaret Robertson, Director of Student Counselling at the Royal Melbourne Institute of Technology's City Campus. Also, I thank the editorial and production staff of my British publishers, Cassell, for commissioning and producing the book.

A final word

In his book of sermons entitled *Strength to Love*, American civil rights leader, Martin Luther King, encouraged Christians to go forth with a tough mind and a tender heart. I have tried to write a tough-minded, tender-hearted, sensitive and humane book so that you may have happier and more fulfilled relationships. Of the books I've authored, this is the one about which I care most deeply. I hope the book articulates a vision of how to relate that resonates with you. Good luck and, above all, good skills!

Richard Nelson-Jones

In Memoriam
Patris Mei
Nelson
1903–1995
Medicinae Doctoris
Aegrorum Curatoris

PART ONE

Introduction

ONE
Importance of Relationships

United we stand, divided we fall.

Aesop

CHAPTER QUESTIONS

- *What are relationships?*
- *Why are relationships important?*
- *What are some ways of looking at distress in relationships?*
- *What are some values for effective relationships?*
- *What is the challenge of relationships?*

Relating skills are the skills involved in human connection. People need people. Relationships are a central part of human existence. Whether you be the royal family in Britain or Kevin and Leanne in outback Australia, the quality of your relationships is vitally important. Relationships can be for good or ill, for pleasure or pain. Relationships come with no guarantee of happiness. However, the more skilled you are in relating, the greater is the likelihood that you will both maximize your own and others' happiness and also contribute less to the sum of human pain and misery.

We all like our relationships to be rewarding. Following are examples of people relating in *rewarding* ways.

> On his girlfriend Rachel's birthday, Martin cooks a special dinner for her and some of their close friends.
> After the ceremony in which she receives her bachelor's degree, Sally tells her parents, Ken

and Nancy, how much she appreciates their love and support.

Sharon has just been made redundant from her job as middle manager in an accounting firm. Jim, her husband listens sympathetically as she shares her pain, anger and confusion.

After a period of emotional withdrawal, Kim and Maria state their commitment to each other and make the effort to discuss their differences cooperatively.

Following are examples of people relating in *unrewarding* ways.

When Carolyn comes home late from work one evening, her partner Tim aggressively shouts at her that she does not care for him.

Guy, a teenager, tells Simon, his father, that he is gay. Simon tells Guy that he should spend more time with girls.

Alice gets jealous because she thinks her husband Bob is leaning over too close as he converses with Nina at a party. Later she accuses him of flirting. Alice angrily rebuffs Bob's explanation that he was trying to hear Nina who spoke quietly.

Theo aggressively tells his wife Helen that he thinks her best friend, Anna, is an interfering bitch.

In each of these examples, people used varying degrees of relating skills. Those giving and getting rewards in their relationships effectively used their relating skills to attain these ends. Those behaving in unrewarding ways were deficient in the relevant relating skills.

WHAT ARE RELATIONSHIPS?

Connection is the essential characteristic of relationships. People in relationships exist in some connection or association with each other, be it marriage, kinship, friendship, acquaintance, service provider or work colleague. Isolation, being alone or placed apart from others, is the opposite of relationship. The Elizabethan John Donne wrote in his seventeenth Meditation: 'No man is an *Island*, entire of it self; every man is a piece of the *Continent*, a part of the *main*.' In short, humans are social animals who cannot avoid relationships. We are condemned not only to exist, but to relate. However, in an existential sense, humans are also condemned to isolation: for example, no person can die another's death for them (Yalom, 1980). Out of their existential separateness humans strive to relate.

Though relationships can be very brief, the term generally implies a longer time frame. Argyle and Henderson (1985) write: ' "Relationships", "personal relationships" or "long-term relationships" refer to regular social encounters with certain people over a period of time...together with the expectation that this will continue for at least some time in the future' (p. 4). Feelings of attachment, commitment and obligation can run very deep in such relationships.

Interdependence is a characteristic of many relationships: for instance in families, work environments, and shopping centres (Callan, Gallois, Noller, & Kashima, 1991). People relate to meet common or complementary goals. Relationships also involve the use of resources, be they: physical – a kiss; emotional – offering sympathy; intellectual – sharing ideas; or financial – giving or receiving money (Lake, 1981).

Inevitably relationships involve change. Over time, all people change in varying degrees. For instance, they age and frequently develop different interests. Also, how partners relate to each other can contribute to changes in them, such as greater or less self-confidence. In addition, change can be deliberately initiated within relationships, for example buying a flat or having a baby. Sometimes external circumstances precipitate change, for instance unemployment or an inheritance. Relationships need to accommodate changes. Given the imperative in life of change and challenge, relationships can grow and develop or wither and die. Litvinoff (1992) observes: 'A good relationship is a creative developing *partnership*... The best relationships can meet almost any challenge and use the experience positively' (p. 11).

Levels of relationships

When two people relate, they do so on differing levels. First, there is the *intrapersonal* level. Each individual has a relationship with himself or herself. As a simple illustration, shut your eyes for 30 seconds and try to think of nothing. You will soon become aware that you are talking to yourself. People's relationship to themselves can be of varying levels of psychological wellness. For instance, some people may be quite isolated from themselves. Such isolation may stem from a mixture of their biological make-up and unfortunate early learning experiences that psychologically they have not moved beyond. The results may be insufficient sense of identity and poor access to feelings and thoughts. People also relate to themselves not just in terms of their pasts, but also in terms of their presents and futures: for instance, they think and feel about current and future relationships with others. The inner game of relating is another term for the intrapersonal level of relationships. As described in the next chapter, people's thinking skills form a central part of how well or poorly they relate to themselves.

Second, there is the *interpersonal* level of relationships. This is the level of relationships alluded to in the above discussion on connection. People outwardly relate to each other in terms of their thoughts, feelings, physical reactions and actions. In all relationships, people have roles, for instance, spouse, parent, child, manager or worker. A distinction exists between role relationships and person relationships (Hendrick &

Hendrick, 1992). Role relationships tend to be heavily influenced by traditional expectations of behaviour. Person relationships allow for spontaneity, flexibility and individual differences. Though a simplification, in varying degrees as relationships progress people move beyond relating as they should be (their roles) to relating as they are (as persons).

Third, there is the *social context* level of relationships. All relationships take place within social contexts. For instance, the social contexts of two people contemplating marriage include: their families, friends, acquaintances, cultures, social class, race, religions, places of employment and so on. The arenas in which relationships take place provide important social contexts: for instance, homes, schools, work places and recreational facilities. An important aspect of such social contexts is that they provide rules and expectations about what is appropriate and inappropriate behaviour.

Relationships as perceptions

All individuals exist in the subjective world of their perceptions (Rogers, 1951, 1959). Your perceptions are your reality. The Chinese proverb states: 'Two-thirds of what we see is behind our eyes.' Relationships do not exist independent of people's perceptions of them. People in the same relationship will perceive and experience it differently. Thus within a marital relationship, there can be *her* and *his* relationship as well as *our* relationship. Your perceptions influence your intrapersonal relationship, for example not seeing some of your own negative attributes; your interpersonal relationships, for example seeing only good qualities in someone to whom you are attracted; and how you relate within your social context, for example the importance you attach to behaving according to your culture.

Two of you in a relationship do not just relate to each other. Instead you relate to your perceptions of yourselves, each other and of your relationship. These perceptions are of varying degrees of accuracy. Another way of stating this is that in relationships each of you develops a *personification* of yourself and of the other person (Sullivan, 1953). These personifications – literally meaning making up or fabricating a person – are the mental maps that guide your relationship journeys. In distressed relationships, misunderstandings start and are maintained by partners developing and holding on to distorted pictures or personifications of each other and of themselves (Beck, 1988).

WHY ARE RELATIONSHIPS IMPORTANT?

Why are relationships important? What are the benefits of relationships? Beyond the obvious biological reason of reproducing the species, the following are some sources of benefit from relationships.

Meaning

Humans require meaning in their lives. Austrian psychiatrist Viktor Frankl views the will to meaning as the fundamental human motivation (Frankl, 1963, 1988). Throughout their lives people search for meaning. Though other sources of meaning exist, for instance work and religion, personal relationships provide a central purpose in most people's lives. Frankl regards people as most human when they can transcend themselves. Mature love is a source of meaning involving transcending oneself to understand or grasp the inner core of another person's personality. Many people feel incomplete, 'half rather than whole', when not in a close couple relationship.

Happiness and contentment

Most humans regard being happy as their main priority. Happiness has many meanings ranging from pleasure and fun to quiet contentment. Happy people balance short-range hedonism with long-range hedonism. Relationships can greatly contribute to people's perceptions of the quality of their lives. For instance, the majority of both males and females considered getting married or engaged, falling in love, making a new friend, and having friends visit or staying with friends as positive life events (Argyle & Henderson, 1985). In a large-scale study of what gave them happiness, single women and men both ranked 'friends and social life' and 'being in love' within their first three most important items. For married women, 'being in love', 'marriage' and 'partner's happiness' were ranked as the three most important items. Married men ranked the same items as second, third and fifth, respectively (Freedman, 1978). In another American survey, 35 per cent of married males and 41.5 per cent of married females reported themselves as 'very happy'. The corresponding figures were for single males and females 18.5 per cent and 25.5 per cent, respectively, and for divorced males and females 18.5 and 15.5 per cent, respectively (Veroff, Douvan, & Kukla, 1981).

Showing altruism

Altruism is a source of happiness in relationships. People can show concern not only for their own but for another's welfare and happiness. They can participate in the joy of giving as well as of receiving. Caring can reap its own rewards. Argyle (1991) points out that most research on love and other close relationships has been based on the economic or social exchange assumption that each party tries to maximize his or her own rewards. He makes a strong case that humans have innate as well as socially learned tendencies to cooperation, helping and altruism. He writes that 'in love and close relationships there is great concern for the needs and welfare of the other' (p. 6). Such concern is inappropriately described as simply seeking individual rewards.

Maslow (1971) suggested that many people are inhibited in expressing their higher potentials. He observed that: 'Repression, denial, reaction formation and probably all the Freudian defence-mechanisms are available and are used against the highest within ourselves just as they are mobilised against the lowest within ourselves' (p. 338). These higher values include truth, beauty, goodness, justice and simplicity. Though not cited in Maslow's list of higher values, they also include altruism and a sympathetic identification with the human species. The tragedy of many relationships is that partners inhibit, lose touch with and fail to continue expressing altruistic feelings towards each other.

Belonging

Most humans prefer to belong. They want to be members of families, participate in friendships and interact in clubs and other groups. They prefer to be parts of larger units rather than remain in isolation. They like to reach out to others and for others to reach out to them. Rather than be alone they may even remain in unrewarding relationships, since receiving some social recognition seems preferable to no recognition at all.

Intimacy

Most people prefer not only to be part of social and friendship networks, but also to have a few deep relationships. Marriages and other partner relationships, friendships and parent–child relationships may each provide close attachments. In partner relationships, intimacy may be characterized by depth of mutual disclosure, sexual contact and a high degree of caring and commitment to each other's happiness and well-being. Eric Berne, the originator of Transactional Analysis, defined intimacy as 'a candid, game-free relationship, with mutual free giving and receiving and without exploitation' (Berne, 1972, p. 25).

Learning lifeskills

At all stages of their lives, relationships can provide people with opportunities to learn lifeskills. Some of this learning is by means of conditioning, or the rewards that people receive or fail to receive in their relationships. Much learning is through observing how others relate and the rewards they receive for their behaviour (Bandura, 1986). Some learning is through instruction and self-instruction. People who have not had access to adequate relationships often have significant gaps in information about how to live effectively. In addition, sometimes they possess considerable mis-information about how to relate (Lazarus, 1992).

Healing

People enter close relationships in varying degrees of prior emotional deprivation. Even recipients of good parenting skills may still have emotional scars and areas of vulnerability. Others, who have not worked through deeply felt rejections from destructive relationships in their pasts, enter close relationships feeling and thinking that '*no* one can love *all* of me. The core of me is dark and unlovable' (Rogers, 1973, p. 107). In healthy relationships, partners can feel free to risk revealing their fears, vulnerabilities and perceived weaknesses safe in the knowledge of each other's underlying love and acceptance of them as persons. Rogers gives the moving example of Irene who at first did not let her partner Joe see 'this little black, rotten, ugly ball I have buried down inside that's really me, that's unlovable and unacceptable' (Rogers, 1973, p. 100). Gradually, Irene peeled off and shared layers of her ugly black ball and each time obtained a real reaction from Joe, who never left her. Joe's trust in Irene's potential and his acceptance of all aspects of her contributed to a healing and growth-promoting relationship.

Identity and growth

Throughout their lives, people can have their identity, or sense of who they are, developed and crystallized through their relationships. As with Irene, they may receive feedback that they are valuable and worthwhile. In addition, people may try out roles and different ways of behaving and observe their effects. In healthy relationships, partners are both separate and together. They can encourage each other as they develop and change, even though such changes may require accommodations and adjustments on their parts. Growth-enhancing relationships help people develop the confidence and belief in themselves to take calculated risks and to persist in difficult, but worthwhile endeavours (Bandura, 1986). Thus, each partner's sense of identity becomes firm, yet still flexible enough to deal appropriately with newly emerging information and situations.

Health

The presence and quality of people's relationships affects their health. The widowed and divorced become more susceptible to illness than those still married or who have stayed single. They are ill more and see their doctors more frequently. Furthermore, for many fatal illnesses, their death rates average one and a half to two and a half times as high as those for married people. In addition, the divorced and separated are more likely either to be or to become mentally ill. Widowed males are particularly susceptible to suicide (Argyle, 1991; Argyle & Henderson, 1985).

Support

Relationships can provide people with social and emotional support. The adage 'A problem shared is a problem halved' suggests that supportive relationships enhance people's ability to cope with life's stresses and burdens: for example bereavement, divorce or other loss of attachments, loss of job and illness or accidents to family members. People may feel supported by their family, friends, work colleagues and through membership of clubs and groups. In general, females appear to be more skilled than males both at asking for support and at providing it for others (Argyle, 1991). Support can include such activities as listening, companionship, offering sympathy, providing information, doing shopping and cooking meals and offering help in other ways.

Security

Relationships are sources of security. Survival is the primary human imperative, even before happiness. Cooperative relationships help alleviate people's underlying anxiety that they will be unable to meet their survival needs: for instance, for basic physio-logical needs such as food, water and shelter. Frequently, financial security is a primary motive for people staying in otherwise unsatisfactory relationships.

Sharing tasks

In relationships, people can cooperate to share tasks to their mutual benefit. Sometimes this sharing involves people doing the same tasks either simultaneously or in rotation: for instance, cooking, washing up, shopping and cleaning the house. Sometimes partners may decide on a division of labour: for instance, one being the breadwinner and the other being the house-person. Also, partners can adjust the sharing of tasks to accommodate each other: for instance, if one has a particularly busy period at work, the other can ease his or her load in the home.

Companionship

One of the main benefits of relationships is companionship. Close relationships may be viewed as continuing conversations. Relationships can provide having somebody around to talk to, eat with and, possibly, sleep with. Many shared activities involve not only the activity but also opportunity for communication before, during and afterwards. Activities that can be done in isolation may be more fun if done jointly, for instance, going for a walk, seeing a movie or eating in a restaurant. Others are joint activities by their very nature: for instance, playing team games, playing games that require an opponent, dancing and playing in a musical group.

Broadening horizons

Relationships with people who differ from you in significant characteristics can be sources of greater understanding of both them and yourself. For example, getting to know people from different cultures can give you insight into their ways of acting in and perceiving the world. In addition, such relationships can challenge your view that the only and best way is how things are done in your culture. Age, social class and sexual orientation are some other characteristics where you may interact with people different from you to your mutual benefit.

Career success

This book's main focus is on personal rather than work relationships. Nevertheless, the two overlap in many significant ways. Most jobs involve considerable interaction with others. Good personal relationships with work colleagues and with customers can increase productivity, sales and job satisfaction. In addition, people who relate well possess a vocational skill that contributes to employability and promotion and reduces the likelihood of redundancy. Furthermore, since work offers people one of their main avenues for meeting others, many find spouses and partners at work.

RELATIONSHIP DISTRESS

The preceding discussion on the importance of relationships focused on the positive benefits of relationships. However, relationships are also important because they can be sources of considerable suffering, pain and misery. All of the items listed in the previous section have a potential 'downside'. Relationship distress can occur in many forms. Relationships can be sources of meaninglessness, unhappiness, selfishness, isolation, psychological distance, learning lifeskills deficits, continued emotional scarring, identity confusion, ill-health, lack of support, insecurity, conflict over sharing tasks, lack of real companionship, narrowing of horizons and career difficulties. Loneliness and marital breakdown are two specific illustrations of relationship distress.

Loneliness

Loneliness, defined by Yalom (1980) as interpersonal isolation, is a common form of relationship distress. Loneliness can be contrasted with being alone. People can be alone out of choice and the need for privacy. Most people require space for themselves as well as time with others. Loneliness is a subjective state of feeling alone. Loneliness can involve feeling rejected by others, though not necessarily so. People may feel lonely on their own, in relationships or when with groups of people. Though many lonely people are in social contact with others, these relationships may lack sufficient intimacy or depth. People's perceptions of their loneliness tends to be a function of gap between their desired and actual level of social intimacy.

Middle-aged men with jobs tend to be the least lonely, though they may have few friends (Argyle & Henderson, 1985). In a British survey (MORI, 1982), people likely to feel lonely once a month or more were single parents (38 per cent), the widowed (36 per cent), the divorced (29 per cent), people living alone aged 16–59 (27 per cent), the 65 plus age group (20 per cent), women (18 per cent) and the 15–24 age group (18 per cent).

Many factors can contribute to loneliness. Personal factors include insufficiently good relating skills for initiating contact and developing intimacy. Shy people can be crippled by fear of rejection. Some people may be heavily conflicted about intimacy, for instance yearning for closeness but fearing being emotionally engulfed or legally trapped.

Social factors also contribute to loneliness and the development of what has been called the lonely society (Derlega & Chaikin, 1975). People are increasingly nomadic, changing their home addresses many times during their lives (Johnson, 1993). Related to this has been a decline in local communities with their extended families, churches and neighbourhood shops. Big city living can be very impersonal, with little attention paid to neighbours. In addition, technological advances like television mean that people's leisure is often passive and solitary. The quickening of the pace of work life and increased materialism also contribute to many people allocating limited time to developing friendships and intimate relationships.

The growth of individualism provides another reason why many people are lonely. Arguably, there has been a shift from people viewing themselves in communal terms to viewing themselves in individual terms. Seligman (1991) talks of the waxing of the self and the waning of the commons. He asserts that the new self has an 'absorbing concern for its gratifications and losses' (p. 283). Seligman considers that individualism has contributed to America's tenfold increase in depression.

Marital breakdown

Increase in cohabitation

In Britain, there are trends towards a decline in marriages and an increase in cohabitation. In 1993, the number of marriages in England and Wales fell to its lowest level for 50 years at just under 300,000. The fall in the number of first marriages has been particularly striking: from a peak of 340,000 in 1970 to 182,000 in 1993. In the early 1990s, approximately 70 per cent of first marriages were preceded by premarital cohabitation compared with approximately 10 per cent in the early 1970s. For those first marrying in the 1990s and the 1970s, the median (midpoint in a set of scores) duration of premarital cohabitation was about two years and one year, respectively. In 1993, over 20 per cent of non-married men and women were cohabiting, compared with under 15 per cent in the mid-1980s, continuing a persistent trend towards cohabitation. In addition, growing proportions of men and women are living outside a partnership. The youngest age groups, particularly those in their twenties, show the greatest changes in patterns of marriage and cohabitation (Haskey, 1995).

In the 1986 Australian Census 6 per cent of all couple-families identified themselves as being in marriage-like but informal relationships (Harrison, 1993). British trends indicate that these figures grossly underestimate the current level of cohabitation in Australia.

Though the section below is on marital distress, distress and breakdown can also occur in cohabiting partnerships. Also, the ending of cohabiting partnerships contributes to the rising incidence of lone parenthood.

Marital distress

Most people enter marriage expecting it to be permanent. However, as Shakespeare wrote 'The course of true love never did run smooth.' In both Australia and Britain the divorce rates are high and rising. In 1961 in England and Wales, overall there were 25,400 divorces. The *Divorce Reform Act* of 1969, making divorce easier to obtain, became operative on 1 January 1971 and, that year, there were 74,400 divorces. In 1981 overall there were 145,700 divorces and, in 1991, 158,700 divorces. In 1991, the average age at divorce was 37 for men and 34 for women. An increasing number of remarriages (second or later marriages) are ending in divorce: 1961, 1900; 1971, 5200; 1981, 18,100; and 1991, 29,000 (Office of Population Census and Surveys, 1994). Population projections by marital status indicate that, between 1985 and 2000, the number of divorced people in England and Wales is expected to rise by 64 per cent, from 1.9 million to 3.2 million (Haskey, 1988).

In Australia, the percentage of marriages ending in divorce rose from 14 per cent in 1971 to 35 per cent in 1986 (McDonald, 1988). Perhaps the most important factor in this increase was the *Family Law Act* of 1975 that defined irretrievable breakdown as the sole ground for dissolution of marriage. This legislation provided faster and easier access to divorce for either party by both removing the need to prove fault and also reducing the separation period from five years to one year. By 1991, about 40 per cent of marriages ended in divorce (Australian Institute of Family Studies, 1993a). At time of divorce, the average ages of men and women were 38.4 and 35.5 years respectively. The average duration of marriages was 7.4 years between marriage and separation, and 10.3 years between marriage and divorce.

In 1971, one or both partners was remarrying in 14 per cent of Australian marriages; by 1986, this figure had more than doubled to 33 per cent. Divorce rates were a little higher for remarriages of divorced persons than for persons in their first marriages (McDonald, 1988). Though most people still want to marry, in recent years there has been a decline in the rate of marriage from 7.8 per thousand in 1976, to 7.2 in 1986, to 6.6 in 1991.

The divorce figures underestimate the extent of marital breakdown and distress. If figures for the separated population were added to those of the divorced population to form a 'dissolution index', the statistics for marital breakdown and distress would be considerably higher. Moreover, for numerous reasons – including concern for children, financial insecurity, fear of going it alone and religious beliefs – many couples remain unhappily married. Add these people to the 'dissolution index' and it could be argued that many more marriages end up being unhappy than happy.

Frequently partners leaving relationships have numerous painful experiences. Some may end up wishing that they had never left (Litvinoff, 1993). Most will suffer a loss of confidence and self-esteem. Many will experience financial hardship and loneliness. All will need to build new lives.

Divorce also involves children. Though divorce is not the only cause of single parent families, it is a major contributor. In 1984, there were approximately 940,000 such families in Great Britain and by 1991 this figure had risen to 1.3 million (Haskey, 1986, 1993). About one in five families with dependent children was a single parent family, the vast majority headed by lone mothers.

In Australia, in 1991 approximately 54 per cent of the divorces granted were to couples with dependent children under 18, totalling 46,467 children (Harrison, 1993). In the 1986 Australian Census there were nearly 325,000 single parent families or 8 per cent of all families. By June 1993, there were 416,200 one-parent families, of which 88.5 were headed by women (Australian Institute of Family Studies, 1993b).

Though divorce may be better than living with an high level of parental conflict, it can negatively affect children. Hendrick and Hendrick (1992) stress that the child's relationship with each parent is a more critical factor in their adjustment than the parents' relationship to each other. Negative effects of divorce on children can show up in increased depression, self-blame for the parental split, conflicting loyalties and anxiety over their future (Goldenberg & Goldenberg, 1990). Also, children of divorce may need to make more adjustments than children from intact families: for example, moving house, moving school, visiting a non-custodial parent, mother starting a new job and a parent remarrying (Seligman, 1991).

Reasons for marital breakdown

The reasons for marital breakdown are both personal and social. Partner alcoholism and violence are mainly female reasons for wanting to separate. Other reasons are more evenly divided among the sexes: for instance, relationship problems, infidelity, perceptions that 'things won't change', growing apart and external pressures, such as work and in-laws (Australian Institute of Family Studies, 1993a). In addition, relating skills deficits increase the chances of marital breakdown.

Social reasons for marital breakdown include the fact that obtaining a divorce is easier and less socially stigmatized than in the past. In addition, with the increased emphasis on individuals getting their needs met, there has been a rise in expectations regarding marital happiness. Higher expectations have a higher chance of being unmet. The increased participation of women in the work-force means that they are less dependent on their husband's incomes and so freer to leave. Furthermore, the decline in the influence of the church lowers another psychological barrier to divorce.

VALUES FOR EFFECTIVE RELATIONSHIPS

Schwartz (1992) defines values as 'the criteria people use to select and justify actions and to evaluate people (including the self) and events' (p.1). Another way Schwartz defines values is as 'guiding principles in the individual's life' (p. 17). Values in themselves are neutral – their value rests on the weightings given to them. Some values may be more preferable as guiding principles for relationships than others. If so, virtue lies in trying to attain them, not just in successful attainment. Increasingly, I have become disturbed by a hardening of the values of contemporary relationships. Sometimes the current emphasis on individualism, materialism and outer success seems at the expense of the softer aspects of relationships, such as sharing, caring and forgiving. Here, at risk of seeming naive and idealistic, I state in lay person's terms some values of this book conducive to effective relationships. The remainder of this book attempts to translate these values into their component relating skills.

A simple distinction can be made between traditional and newer or emergent values in relationships (Bennett, 1993; Spindler, 1963). Traditional and newer values overlap and reflect differing emphases rather than separate categories. Effective relating in contemporary society requires a blending of the best of both sets of values. Sources of traditional values include: religions like Christianity and Buddhism, and wisdom passed down through generations. Sources of newer values include counselling and personality theories, popular psychology, and 'movements' such as women's liberation, men's liberation and gay liberation.

Following are some traditional relationship values.

• *Commitment and loyalty*. Partners can rely on and trust each other. They respect each other and attempt to avoid behaving in ways that might endanger that respect.

• *Cooperation and compromise*. Partners work together for the sake of their relationship. Each person values the relationship and is prepared to make concessions to keep it healthy and intact.

• *Acceptance and tolerance*. Partners do not expect to change each other in major ways. They not only accept each other as persons, but within reason are also prepared to tolerate specific uncongenial behaviours, 'mistakes' and idiosyncrasies. Partners incorporate forgiveness and resilience into how they relate.

• *Caring and compassion*. Partners treat each other with altruism and kindness. In pursuit of such values, American psychiatrist Aaron Beck advises 'cultivate the tender, loving part of your relationship: sensitivity, consideration, understanding, and demonstrations of caring' (Beck, 1988, p. 11).

• *Gentleness*. In this context, gentleness means being moderate and avoiding unnecessary harshness. Such gentleness is based on equanimity and inner strength. Gentle strength does not require that people be meek and self-effacing.

Following are some newer relationship values.

• *Equality*. Though traditional male and female roles both had advantages and disadvantages, power tended to be unevenly divided in favour of the male who was 'head of the house'. This book advocates equality in all couple relationships, be they heterosexual or gay. Real friendship is only possible on the basis of equality.

• *Openness*. Perhaps in previous times, there may have been greater tendency than nowadays to act out roles in relationships rather than to engage in genuine person-to-person relationships. Partners and close friends need to be willing and unafraid to reveal themselves deeply to each other.

• *Assertion*. Meanings of assertion include the capacity to show caring in ways that are appropriate. In addition, assertion includes being willing to: take initiatives and make suggestions, offer opinions, stand up for rights, set limits, request changes in behaviour and confront issues in the best interests of the relationship. Assertion neither means 'sweeping things under the carpet' nor 'coming on too strong'.

• *Fun*. In the past, many people worked very hard for very little. Life was to be endured rather than enjoyed. With rising material affluence, increasingly people look to relationships for enjoyment and fun. The question that American-based psychologist Arnold A. Lazarus always asks when someone dies is, 'Did this person have enough fun on this earth?' (Dryden, 1991, p. 14). If not he considers they have had wasted lives.

• *Personal and relationship growth*. Partners and friends are concerned with their own and each other's personal development as separate, yet interdependent people. They are also interested in strengthening their relationship both in good and bad times.

People differ in the values they consider important in their relationships. For example, the religiously inclined are influenced by the values of their respective religions. Also, values may differ by culture and social class. The above list represents a blend of ten traditional and newer values that may increase the probability of making your relationships work.

THE CHALLENGE OF RELATIONSHIPS

Although the focus of this chapter has been on personal relationships, serious relationship difficulties are frequently found at work and in other settings outside the home. The challenge of relationships is that many of them are extremely difficult. You are faced with coping with your own and others' deficiencies, vulnerabilities and frailties and required to rise above them. Each of you has a huge capacity for effective relating. You have many strengths already. I hope that this book helps you build on these strengths.

CHAPTER HIGHLIGHTS

• Relationships involve people in connection with others, often over long periods of time. Characteristics of relationships include: attachment, commitment, interdependence, use of resources and change.

- People relate on different levels. The intrapersonal level is their relationship with themselves. The interpersonal level is their relationship with others. The social context level is the broader arena in which their relationships take place.

- Relationships are important because they are sources of: meaning, happiness and contentment, showing altruism, belonging, intimacy, learning lifeskills, healing, identity and growth, health, support, security, sharing tasks, companionship, broadening horizons and career success.

- Relationships can be sources of considerable suffering, pain and misery. Loneliness and marital breakdown are two forms of relationship distress.

- People's perception of their loneliness tends to be a function of the gap between their desired and actual level of social intimacy.

- Personal factors, such as poor relating skills, and social factors, such as greater mobility, contribute to loneliness. The growth of individualism provides another reason why many people are lonely.

- In Britain – and probably in Australia – especially among young people, trends exist towards increasing cohabitation prior to or instead of marriage.

- In both Australia and Britain over a third of marriages end in divorce. Frequently marital breakdown involves children.

- The reasons for marital breakdown include: legal reform making divorce easier; personal factors, such as poor relating skills and alcoholism; and social factors, such as the increased financial independence of women.

- Values for effective relationships can be loosely divided into traditional and newer values. Traditional values include: commitment and loyalty, cooperation and compromise, acceptance and tolerance, caring and compassion and gentleness. Newer values include: equality, openness, assertion, fun and personal and relationship growth.

- The challenge of relationships is to cope with and rise above your own and others' deficiencies, vulnerabilities and frailties.

EXERCISES
EXERCISE 1.1
WHAT ARE MY RELATIONSHIPS?
Instructions

Complete this exercise on your own. Then, if appropriate, share your diagram and discuss your answers with your partner, another or others.

On a piece of paper, draw a version of the boxes diagram shown here.

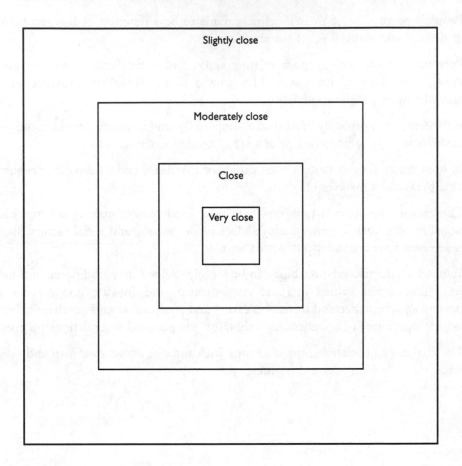

Figure 1.1 Identifying the closeness of my relationships

Fill in your diagram as follows:

• *Very close*. In the centre box fill in the first name(s) of the people you care for most and to whom you feel you have the strongest bonds.

• *Close*. In this box fill in the names of people, such as friends and relations, with whom you feel comfortable and with whom you have strong bonds.

• *Moderately close*. In this box, fill in the names of people whose company you like and with whom you have moderately strong bonds.

• *Slightly close*. In this box, fill in the names of acquaintances with whom you have fairly regular superficially pleasant contacts and only slightly strong bonds.

Further questions

1. Identify any people in your diagram with whom you should be getting in contact to maintain your relationship.

2. Identify any people in your diagram with whom you would like to deepen your relationship.

3. Identify any people in your diagram with whom you would like to weaken or break your relationship.

4. Identify the people in your diagram to whom you would most prefer to turn to for support during a difficult period in your life.

5. Identify any people not in your diagram with whom you would like to start a relationship.

6. Looking at your diagram do you notice any differences between females and males in the quantity and closeness of your relationships.

EXERCISE 1.2
WHAT DO I WANT FROM MY RELATIONSHIP(S)?
Instructions

This exercise may be done *either* by focusing on a specific relationship *or* in regard to relationships in general. Either way, first make your ratings on your own. Then, if appropriate, discuss your answers with your partner, another or others.

Using the following scale, rate the importance of each of the following sources of benefit you would like from your relationship(s):

5 Extremely important
4 Very important
3 Important
2 Moderately important
1 Slightly important
0 Of no importance

Your rating

_____ meaning
_____ happiness and contentment
_____ showing altruism
_____ belonging

_____ intimacy
_____ learning lifeskills
_____ healing
_____ identity and growth
_____ health
_____ support
_____ security
_____ sharing tasks
_____ companionship
_____ broadening horizons
_____ career success
_____ other sources not mentioned above
(specify and rate each separately)

Summarize the main benefits you want from your relationship(s). To what extent are you getting what you would like?

EXERCISE 1.3
MY EXPERIENCE OF BENEFITS AND DISTRESS IN RELATIONSHIPS

Instructions

First answer the following questions on your own. Then, if appropriate, discuss your answers with your partner, another or others.

Previous relationship

Look at an important relationship that you had when you were growing up. This could be with a parent, sibling or friend.

1. Specify what were the main benefits you experienced in the relationship.

2. Assess both your and the other person's contribution to the benefits you experienced.

3. Specify areas in which you experienced distress and emotional pain in the relationship.

4. Assess both your and the other person's contribution to the distress you experienced.

5. Assess the overall balance of benefits and distress in the relationship.

Current or recent relationship

Look at an important current or recent relationship of yours. This could be a partner relationship, a friendship or a work relationship.

1. Specify what are/were the main benefits you experience(d) in the relationship.

2. Assess both your and the other person's contribution to the benefits you experience(d).

3. Specify areas in which you experience(d) distress and emotional pain in the relationship.

4. Assess both your and the other person's contributions to the distress you experience(d).

5. Assess the overall balance of benefits and distress in the relationship.

EXERCISE 1.4
VALUES IMPORTANT IN MY RELATIONSHIPS
Instructions

This exercise may be done *either* by focusing on a specific relationship *or* in regard to close relationships in general. Either way, first make your ratings on your own. Then, if appropriate discuss your answers with your partner, another or others.

Using the following scale, rate the importance to you of each of the following values in your relationship(s):

5 Extremely important
4 Very important
3 Important
2 Moderately important
1 Slightly important
0 Of no importance

Your rating

Traditional values

_____ commitment and loyalty
_____ cooperation and compromise
_____ acceptance and tolerance
_____ caring and compassion
_____ gentleness
_____ other traditional values not mentioned above (specify and rate each separately)

Newer values

_____ equality
_____ openness
_____ assertion
_____ fun

_____ personal and relationship growth
_____ other newer values not mentioned above (specify and rate each separately)

Additional questions

1. Summarize the main values that are important in your relationship(s).

2. If you are in a close relationship, to what extent and how do your relationship values differ from those of your spouse/partner? What are the consequences of any differences?

3. What were the main values in your parents' (or main parental) relationship? To what extent was there value similarity or value dissimilarity and how did this help or harm their relationship?

4. Is the distinction between traditional and newer relationship values a useful one? Provide reasons for your answer.

EXERCISE 1.5
GROUP DISCUSSION: IMPORTANCE OF RELATIONSHIPS
Instructions

This is intended as a group exercise, though it may be done individually or in pairs. For each part:

1. spend 10–15 minutes answering the question in groups of three or four,

2. each group shares its answers with the whole group,

3. then the whole group ranks the six most important points from the most important to the least important.

Part A
Sources of benefit

List the six most important sources of benefit that people can derive from relationships.

Part B
Relationship distress

List the six most important outcomes of relationship distress.

Part C
Relationship values

List the six most important values for effective personal relationships.

TWO
A Relating Skills Approach

Avoid evil, do good, purify the mind!
Chief of all Buddhist teachings

CHAPTER QUESTIONS

- *What is skills language?*

- *How are relating skills defined?*

- *What are action skills?*

- *What are thinking skills?*

- *What are feelings?*

- *How are actions, thoughts and feelings related?*

- *What are some reservations about a relating skills approach?*

- *What does assuming personal responsibility for your relating skills mean?*

How can you enhance your likelihood of happy relationships and minimize your chances of relationship distress? The simple answer is to develop your relating skills. Relationships are the connections that you make between others. Relating skills are the processes or 'hows' of connecting.

SKILLS LANGUAGE

To talk about how to relate requires a common language in which to do so. Skills language provides such a framework.

What are skills?

One meaning of the word skills pertains to *areas* of skill. For instance, albeit overlapping, broad areas of skills include: work skills, study skills, leisure skills, health skills and relating skills. As demonstrated in subsequent chapters, relating skills can be further broken down into areas such as rewarding listening, overcoming shyness, caring, assertion, managing anger and solving relationship problems. A second meaning of the word skills refers to *level of competence* or expertise. For instance, in a specific skills area you can be skilled, unskilled or a mixture of the two.

The third meaning of the word skills is less common. This meaning relates to the knowledge and *sequence of choices* entailed in implementing a skill. The main way that I can help you to acquire, develop and maintain satisfactory levels of competence in specific skills areas is by training you in their required sequences of choices.

The concept of relating skills is best viewed not in either/or terms in which you either possess or do not possess a skill. Rather, in any skills area, it is preferable to think of yourself as possessing *skills strengths*, or *skills deficits*, or a mixture of the two. If you make good choices in a skills area, for instance either in listening or in talking about yourself, this is a skills strength. If you make poor choices in a skills area, this is a skills deficit. In all relating skills areas, in varying degrees you are likely to possess both strengths and deficits. For instance, in the skills area of listening, you may be good at understanding talkers but poor at showing them you actually have understood. The object of working on your relating skills is, in one or more areas, to help you shift the balance of your strengths and deficits more in the direction of strengths. Put another way it is to help you affirm yourself and others more by becoming a *better chooser*.

What is skills language?

Skills language means consistently using the concept of skills to describe and analyse people's behaviour. In regard to relating, skills language means thinking about how you relate in terms of skills strengths and deficits. A distinction exists between everyday or descriptive language and skills language. Below is an example of Paddy who shows caring to his wife Tessa by massaging the area round her neck when she is stressed. Tessa likes this very much.

> *Paddy thinking in everyday language:*
> 'When I notice that Tessa is stressed I massage
> the area round her neck.'

> *Paddy thinking in skills language:*
> 'I use my noticing when Tessa is stressed skills
> and then, if she seems stressed, I use my mas-
> saging the area round her neck skills.'

The above is a simple example of the use of skills language. More sophisticated uses of skills language involve identifying specific thinking and action skills strengths that help people deal with relationship problems and specific thinking and action skills deficits that maintain their problems. You may consider it artificial to translate how you relate into skills terms. Many people are brought up to think in skills language when learning how to drive a car or play a sport. However, probably you have not learned to apply skills language to how you relate.

Why, then, do I advocate thinking in skills language? First, skills language requires you to identify the specific skills you require for your relationships. Second, skills language provides you with a relatively simple way that you can analyse and work on problems. You now have the tools with which to break problems down into the skills deficits that contribute to maintaining them. Third, many of you may find it less threatening to look at your problems in terms of the skills you need to work on them rather than having to admit personal inadequacy or blame. Fourth, my assumption is that many of your relationship problems repeat themselves. Consequently you may need not only to deal with current problems, but also to prevent future similar problems. Skills language lends itself to self-instructing not only now but in the future. As such, it provides a practical language for continuing self-helping.

Public and private uses of skills language

Skills language can be used in public and private talk. Public talk is where people use skills language when conversing with others. On many occasions, you may consider it too cumbersome to use skills language. However, there can be occasions where talking out loud in skills language is useful. Such occasions include: when learning the different relating skills, when instructing others in relating skills and when talking about relationship problems.

As in the above example of Paddy, skills language can also be used privately in how you think, without being spoken out loud to others. Thinking involves self-talk. A distinction exists between *aware* self-talk and *automatic* self-talk (Beck, 1988). With aware self-talk, you are conscious of what you are thinking. Thus, you can consciously think in skills language. Automatic self-talk exists at a pre-conscious level. Such self-talk is below your level of awareness, but is retrievable if needed.

Learning and implementing specific relating skills can involve three steps. First, public use of skills language between trainers and learners. Second, aware private use of skills language self-talk on the part of learners. Third, automatic use of skills language self-talk as learners gain fluency in using the skill. An analogy is that of learning to drive a car: first the instructor tells you what to do, then you are aware of instructing yourself, and lastly your self-instructions become automatic. During this process, your use of driving skills moves from feeling awkward to feeling natural. The same feelings can occur as you learn and then gain fluency in implementing specific relating skills.

Repertoire of relating skills

For your various relationships you require a *repertoire* of relating skills. Sometimes you may not have a particular skill in your repertoire: for instance, the ability to say no to an unreasonable request. Other times you may want to strengthen a particular skill: for instance, expressing appreciation to a loved one. With some skills, you may also want to strike a more appropriate balance: for example, neither depending too much nor too little on others. Some relating skills deficits you should eliminate altogether: for instance, physical or sexual abuse. Your repertoire of relating skills comprises your strengths and deficits in each skills area.

Defining relating skills as lifeskills

Elsewhere I distinguish between biological and psychological life (Nelson-Jones, 1995). The two concepts overlap. Psychological existence takes place within biological life. Biological life influences psychological life, for instance the association between fatigue and irritability, and psychological life can influence biological life, an extreme example being suicide.

Following are some important distinctions between biological and psychological life. First, the primary focus of psychological life is the mind and not the body. Second, whereas the main goals of biological life are survival and good physical health, the main goal of psychological life is attaining human potential. Psychological life concerns people's ability to use their minds for the purposes of enhancing the quality of their existence by fulfilling their unique potentials. Third, there is no concept of cure in psychological life. Psychological life is reversible in that people can go backwards as well as forwards in ability to make choices. Because maintenance of psychological life cannot be assumed, the skills required for effective living need be regarded as self-helping skills.

Apart from such obviously biological functions such as breathing, I view virtually all human behaviour in terms of lifeskills. Lifeskills are sequences of choices that people make in specific skills areas pertinent to psychological life. As lifeskills, relating skills can be defined both neutrally and positively. The neutral definition does not assume a level of skilfulness – you can have deficits as well as strengths. The positive definition implies skilful use of skills. In the appropriate contexts, both definitions are useful. Following are neutral and positive definitions of the term relating skills.

• *Neutral definition.* Relating skills are the specific lifeskills by which you affirm and/or negate your own and one another's psychological life in your relationships.

• *Positive definition.* Relating skills are the specific lifeskills by which you affirm your own and one another's psychological life in your relationships.

THE INNER AND OUTER GAMES OF RELATING

If you are to control how you relate, you need to think and act effectively. A simple way to highlight the distinction is to talk about the inner and outer games of relating. The inner game refers to what goes on inside you, how you think and feel or your thinking skills and feelings. The outer game refers to what goes on outside you, how you act or your action skills. Thinking and feeling are covert, action is overt.

Outer game: Your action skills

Action skills involve observable behaviours. Action skills refer to what you do and how you do it rather than what and how you feel and think. These skills vary by area of application: for instance, relating, studying, or working.

There are five main ways that you can send relating skills, and indeed any other, action messages.

- *Verbal messages.* Messages that you send with words. For example, saying 'I love you' or 'I hate you.'

- *Voice messages.* Messages that you send through your voice: for instance, through your volume, articulation, pitch, emphasis and speech rate.

- *Body messages.* Messages that you send with your body: for instance, through your gaze, eye contact, facial expression, posture, gestures, physical proximity, and clothes and grooming.

- *Touch messages.* A special category of body messages. Messages that you send with your touch: for instance, through what part of the body you use, what part of another's body you touch, how gentle or firm you are and whether or not you have permission.

- *Action messages.* Messages that you send when you are not face to face with others: for example, sending flowers or a legal writ.

Inner game: Your thinking skills

You can use how you think to support yourself and others or to oppress yourself and others. Below are brief descriptions of 12 thinking skills areas derived from the work of leading psychiatrists and psychologists, such as Aaron Beck and Albert Ellis. Rather than describe the skills in detail here, I illustrate their use throughout this book.

- *Owning responsibility for choosing.* You assume personal responsibility for your life. You are aware that you are the author of your existence and that you can choose how you think, act and feel. You are aware of the limitations of existence, such as your death.

- *Understanding the relationship between how you think, feel and act.* You possess insight into how you can influence how you feel and act through how you think. You are aware that your feelings and actions in turn influence your thoughts.

- *Getting in touch with your feelings.* You acknowledge the importance of getting in touch with how you feel. You are able to access significant feelings, for instance your wants and wishes, and accurately state them as thoughts.

- *Using coping self-talk.* Instead of talking to yourself negatively before, during and after specific situations, you can make coping self-statements that calm you down, coach you in what to do and affirm the skills strengths and support factors you possess.

- *Choosing realistic personal rules.* Your unrealistic personal rules make irrational demands on yourself, others and the environment: for instance, 'I must be liked by everyone', 'Others must not make mistakes' and 'Life must be fair'. Instead you can develop realistic rules: for instance, 'I prefer to be liked, but it's unrealistic to expect this from everyone.'

- *Choosing to perceive accurately.* You avoid labelling yourself and others either too negatively or too positively. You distinguish between fact and inference and make your inferences as accurate as possible.

• *Explaining cause accurately*. You explain the causes of events accurately. You avoid assuming too much responsibility by internalizing, 'Its all my fault', or externalizing, 'It's all your fault'.

• *Predicting realistically*. You are realistic about the risks and rewards of future actions. You assess threats and dangers accurately. You avoid distorting relevant evidence with unwarranted optimism or pessimism. Your expectancies about how well you can relate are accurate.

• *Setting realistic goals*. Your short-, medium- and long-term goals reflect your values, are realistic, are specific and have a time frame.

• *Using visualizing skills*. You use visual images in ways that calm you down, assist you in acting competently to attain your goals and help you to resist giving in to bad habits.

• *Realistic decision-making*. You confront rather than avoid decisions and then make up your mind by going through a rational decision-making process.

• *Preventing and managing problems*. You anticipate and confront your problems. You assess the thinking and action skills you require to deal with them. You state working goals and plan how to implement them.

Inner game: Your feelings

To relate effectively, you require the ability to experience, express and manage your feelings. Though fundamental to relationships, feelings represent your animal nature and are not skills in themselves. Dictionary definitions of feelings tend to use words like 'physical sensation', 'emotions' and 'awareness'. All three of these words illustrate a dimension of feelings. Feeling as *physical sensations* represent your underlying animal nature. People are animals first, persons second. As such you need to learn to value and live with your underlying animal nature. Also, to get it working for rather than against you. The word *emotions* implies movement. Feelings are processes. You are subject to a continuous flow of biological experiencing. *Awareness* implies that you can be conscious of your feelings. However, you may also deny and distort them. Table 2.1 provides a list of words that describe feelings.

Table 2.1 List of feelings words

accepted	dependent	involved	supported
adventurous	depressed	irresponsible	suspicous
affectionate	discontented	jealous	tense
aggressive	embarrassed	joyful	tired
ambitious	energetic	lonely	trusting
angry	envious	loved	unambitious
anxious	excited	loving	unappreciated

apathetic	fit	optimistic	unassertive
appreciated	free	outgoing	unattractive
assertive	friendly	pessimistic	underconfident
attractive	frightened	powerful	uneasy
bored	grieving	powerless	unfit
carefree	guilt-free	rejected	unfriendly
cautious	guilty	relaxed	unloved
cheerful	happy	resentful	unsafe
competitive	humiliated	responsible	unsupported
confident	hurt	sad	unwanted
confused	indecisive	secure	uptight
contented	independent	shy	vulnerable
cooperative	inferior	stressed	wanted
daring	insecure	strong	weak
decisive	interested	superior	worried

Interrelationships between feelings, thoughts and actions

In varying degrees, most relating skills comprise thinking, feeling and action elements. Thinking, feeling and action influence each other. Thinking and acting often accompanies or results from feelings at various levels, for instance wishes are the parents of thoughts and actions. Conversely, thoughts can influence feelings and actions, for instance the way you perceive another's behaviour mediates how you feel and what you do about it. Also, actions can influence thoughts and feelings. For instance, succeeding at a feared task can lead to feeling more confident and thinking you can succeed again next time. Figure 2.1 depicts the interrelationships between feeling, thinking and acting.

Figure 2.1 Interrelationships between feeling, thinking and acting

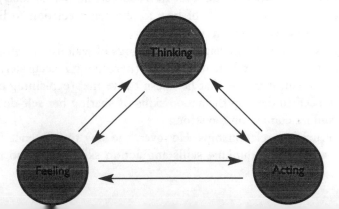

Interrelationships between thinking skills, action skills and feelings

Three areas in relationships, albeit overlapping, where feelings are important are experiencing feelings, expressing feelings and managing feelings, Below I illustrate each area with a brief example.

Experiencing feelings

> Robyn, 19, finds it very difficult to experience feelings of anger in her relationship with her boyfriend Russell.

Expressing feelings

> Sandy, 39, is in a marriage heading for the rocks. He has always had great difficulty expressing his positive feelings towards his wife, Babs. She sees him as far too negative and critical.

Managing feelings

> Daphne, 28, is very jealous of her husband Jim. She gets upset and angry when he talks to other women and afterwards picks fights with him. She has no evidence that Jim has ever been unfaithful.

In the above examples, Robyn, Sandy and Daphne need to experience, express and manage their feelings more effectively. To do this, they need to identify the thinking skills and action skills that maintain their feelings difficulties and work on them. For instance, Robyn may inhibit her angry feelings because of thinking skills deficits such as: 'Women must never show anger' (unrealistic personal rule) or 'If I show anger, I will automatically be abandoned' (unrealistic prediction). She may also inhibit her feelings of anger because she lacks the action skills to express her anger assertively and to cope with Russell if he returns her anger.

Sandy may have difficulty expressing positive feelings because of thinking skills deficits such as: 'Babs should know that I love her' (unrealistic personal rule) and insufficiently acknowledging what Babs does for him (perceiving inaccurately). Sandy may also need to develop the action skills of how to show appreciation to Babs with his verbal, voice, body, touch and action messages.

Daphne may have difficulty managing her feelings of jealousy because of thinking skills deficits such as: 'I'm insufficiently lovable' (perceiving inaccurately) and 'If Jim talks to another woman, it means that he doesn't love me' (explaining cause inaccurately). She may need to develop the action skills of sharing her self-doubts tactfully with Jim and avoiding coming on too strong.

Feelings are crucial to relationships. However, the way to influence feelings is by working on the appropriate thinking skills and action skills. In sound relationships, partners cooperate to build not only their own but one another's relating skills. In the above examples, Robyn and Russell, Sandy and Babs, and Daphne and Jim could help each other with what are problems not only for one of them but for their relationship together.

RESERVATIONS ABOUT A RELATING SKILLS APPROACH

Some of you may have reservations about viewing relating in skills terms. Here I answer some common reservations.

Reservation: The approach is unnatural

Answer: You may consider that you have been born with a style of relating and do not wish to have this interfered with by acquiring artificial skills. Underlying this reservation is the issue of nature versus nurture. In addition to your biological sex, your genetic make-up influences how you relate in numerous ways. People differ in temperament: for example some are extroverts whereas others are introverts. They also differ in physical appearance, for example, how tall, what sort of body structure, what eye colour, what hair colour, what race and so on. In addition, intelligence contains a large genetic component. However, high intelligence is no guarantee of relating intelligently. Also, people with below average IQs can be above average in how they relate.

Whether or not skills language is used, the main point is that how people relate largely reflects learning or nurture rather than nature. Unlike non-human animals whose instinctual programming is strong, humans only possess weak instinct remnants (Maslow, 1970, 1971). Humans are not programmed with strong genetic messages telling them what to do. Behaviour that has become learned habit may seem natural to you, but this does not mean that you did not learn it in the first place. Furthermore, you maintain the behaviour because you have learned to think about it in certain ways: for instance, 'It is good or bad to behave like this' or 'I am more likely to get what I want if I do this'. The explanation that your behaviour is natural can lead you to remain stuck in unproductive patterns of relating, since you may erroneously think that you cannot change your 'nature'.

Reservation: The approach pays insufficient attention to feelings

Answer: Some of you may think that a relating skills approach is too analytic and may interfere with your being a real person with real feelings. Being in touch with your feelings is very important in such areas as: acknowledging liking and attraction, being spontaneous and being sensual. If you are out of touch with your feelings you are alienated from the core of your personhood. As indicated in the previous section on the relationship between thinking skills, action skills and feelings, a relating skills approach does not ignore feelings. Rather the approach regards feelings as so important that they cannot be left to chance. Everybody needs to be in touch with their capacity to feel.

Carl Rogers, in particular, stressed that a feature of modern life was that all people, in varying degrees, were out of touch with their inner valuing process (Rogers, 1961, 1980). A relating skills approach can assist you to get in touch with what you feel about situations rather than reacting unthinkingly on the basis of your previous conditioning. By identifying the thinking skills and action skills deficits that interfere with genuine feeling and spontaneity, the approach can assist you to become a more, not a less, feeling person.

In addition, expressing feelings and managing unwanted feelings are too important to be left to chance. Again, a relating skills approach addresses rather than ignores these important concerns.

Reservation: The approach is mechanistic

Answer: You may feel that breaking down your skills strengths and deficits in different relating areas erodes your humanity by treating you like a machine. Additionally, you may fear that the over-examined life leads to 'the paralysis of analysis.' There are many dehumanizing features of modern life stemming from industrialization, computerization and materialism. A misunderstanding of a relating skills approach may lead people to treat themselves and others and objects rather than as human beings. Proper application of the relating skills approach is neither cold nor dehumanizing. Rather the approach aims to combine the gentleness and softness of humanistic approaches to psychology with the technical incisiveness of behavioural and cognitive approaches. In addition, the relating skills approach heavily emphasizes the existential notion of choice.

Reservation: The approach is manipulative

Answer: The reservation about a relating skills approach being manipulative concerns people using skills to get what they want regardless of others' interests. People can use knowledge of relating skills in shrewd and unfair ways against others. The fact that a relating skills approach can be abused is not a reason for abandoning it. You can use a relating skills approach to counter manipulation in two important ways. First, the more genuinely skilful you are at relating, the less likely you are to manipulate others. Reasons skilful people are less manipulative include: having other skills to get what they want, having some skills with which to work on their own manipulative tendencies and being more understanding and respectful of the rights of others. The second way you can use a relating skills approach to counter manipulation is by developing specific skills to deal with and not be 'sucked into' others' manipulative skills deficits and games (Berne, 1964; Glasser, 1984; Steiner, 1981).

Reservation: The approach is superficial

Answer: The opposite to superficiality is depth. The reservation about the relating skills approach being insufficiently deep is on a number of dimensions. One dimension echoes the manipulative and mechanistic reservations in that people can go through the motions of skilled relating without having genuine contact. Even in their closest relationships, they are inclined to treat others in 'I-it' rather than in 'I-thou' ways

(Buber, 1970). Treating others as objects rather than as persons reflects relating skills deficits rather than relating skills strengths.

Yalom (1980) distinguishes between an archaeological definition of depth, where depth means first, and an existential definition, where depth means thinking deeply about existential concerns. Unlike psychoanalysis, a relating skills approach pays little attention to infantile sexuality and the clash between ego and instinctual sexual and aggressive drives. The approach does not ignore the past, but attends to it mainly in so far as it illuminates the present and future.

Regarding confronting existential concerns, people relate at varying levels of depth. In quality relationships, partners are likely to think deeply about and talk about existential ultimate concerns, such as death, suffering, freedom, isolation and meaninglessness. Relating skills, for instance the ability to listen sensitively to one another, can assist you to confront and deal openly with rather than avoid such issues.

Differing levels of consciousness constitute a further dimension of depth. A relating skills approach acknowledges that humans repress into their unconscious much that is important: for instance, altruistic tendencies and anxiety about death (Maslow, 1971; Yalom 1980). However, the relating skills approach mainly focuses on material that is either conscious, in awareness, or pre-conscious, moderately easily accessible to awareness. This is because most relating skills can be learned and most relationship issues addressed by working with these levels of consciousness.

ASSUMING PERSONAL RESPONSIBILITY FOR YOUR RELATING SKILLS

A fundamental value of this book is that ultimately you are personally responsible for your survival, happiness and fulfilment (Nelson-Jones, 1984). To use President Truman's expression: 'The buck stops here.' Now, what does this stark existential truth mean?

Defining personal responsibility

When you are being personally responsible you are in the process of making the choices that maximize your happiness and fulfilment, but not at the expense of others. Personal responsibility is a positive thinking skill whereby you are responsible *for* your well-being and making your *own* choices. It contrasts with a common meaning of responsibility, namely that of responsibility *to* others, including living up to their standards. Though the thinking skill of assuming personal responsibility can be far from easy, adopting it as a basic attitude towards living liberates you to concentrate on how you can be most effective. It entails neither focusing on other people's faults nor thinking that you need say 'my fault' all the time.

Are you always responsible for your choices? The answer is 'yes', but with qualifications. The first qualification is that there was a maturational lag in that your capacity for reasoning as a child developed later than your need to make some of the choices that would help you live most effectively. Consequently, one way in which you acquired skills deficits was through not having the early reasoning power to make good choices. Your poor initial choices may then have developed into poor relating skills habits. A second and related qualification is that the thinking skill of personal responsibility and the ability to make effective choices are mainly learned. If your childhood learning was deficient, this puts you at a disadvantage. Third, many social factors may make it more difficult for you to assume personal responsibility. Adverse conditions like poor housing, urban over-crowding, unemployment, poverty, racial discrimination and poor educational opportunities may each militate against your learning to make and continue making the choices that serve you best.

Below some self-talk to remind you about assuming personal responsibility for your relating skills.

> I am personally responsible for the way I think, feel and act in my relationships. Adverse past and present circumstances may make it more difficult for me to be an effective chooser. Nevertheless, I am still responsible for making my life through the quality of my choices. For the sake of my own and others' future happiness and fulfilment I have much to gain by working hard to acquire, maintain and develop my relating skills.

The courage to relate

Assuming responsibility for relating skills involves courage. The work courage is derived from the Latin word *cor*, meaning heart. Paul Tillich in his inspiring book *The Courage to Be* (1952) wrote: 'The courage to be is the ethical act in which man affirms his own being in spite of those elements of his existence which conflict with his essential self-affirmation' (p. 3). May, a long-standing friend of Tillich's, distinguished between physical, moral, social and creative courage (May, 1975).

Here I distinguish between three different, yet overlapping kinds of courage. First, there is the courage to confront and relinquish your relating skills deficits. Though relating skills deficits may offer the illusion of security, by definition they constrict psychological life. It can take courage to acknowledge your human frailty. Second, there is the courage to acquire relating skills strengths. Acquiring relating skills strengths frequently occurs despite the many factors that make it hard to do so. Such 'despite' factors include the work involved and anxieties about learning and change. Third, there is the courage to maintain and further develop your relating skills. There is no magic or concept of cure. Nor is there any automatic 'pat on the back' for good use of relating skills. Instead you need to work hard on the skills of having the courage to be a 'centred' and authentic person. Inner strength is another term to describe the sort of courage to which I refer.

Mental cultivation

Assuming responsibility for your relating skills requires you to train your mind. In your relationships you will be constantly challenged to exercise self-discipline.

Training your mind entails taming your mind. Traditional religions, like Christianity and Buddhism, stress the need to curb the self. Indeed Buddhism moves beyond curbing selfishness to advocate the concept of *anatta* or no-self, the non-existence of a permanent self (Roscoe, 1994). Whether or not you are religiously inclined, you require mental cultivation so that you can place limitations on your ego or self.

People who relate effectively possess a balance between involvement and detachment. They possess emotional awareness and the ability to step back and think about their thinking and behaviour. Earlier I listed many thinking skills or habits of thought in which you possess both strengths and deficits. You can cultivate your mind to exercise self-discipline in two important ways. First, even when the going is smooth, you can work on developing and maintaining your thinking skills so that you possess more inner strength. Second, when faced with differences and difficulties in your relationships, you can further strengthen yourself by resisting your thinking skills deficits and by applying and refining your thinking skills strengths. I mention practical approaches to cultivating your mind at various stages throughout this book.

Mental cultivation can be approached at varying levels of depth. You can cultivate individual thinking skills deeply: for instance, changing unrealistic into realistic rules. Here the word depth means thoroughness and persistence. Even better is persistently attempting to cultivate all the main thinking skills as a way of life. This level of depth should translate into greater freedom to make affirming choices in your relationships. Working on one or more thinking skills superficially is usually insufficient for change and for maintaining change.

Some added values

In Chapter One, I listed some traditional and newer values for effective relationships. Now I add three further values. First, *personal responsibility* for developing your relating skills. Second, the *courage* to acknowledge relating skills deficits, make changes, and maintain and develop relating skills strengths. Third, *mental cultivation* or training your mind to resist thinking skills deficits that lead to egocentricity and develop thinking skills strengths that place appropriate limits on your ego or self.

Much of the current self-help literature, especially that emanating from North America, seems to encourage excessive pre-occupation with getting what you want out of relationships in rather superficial ways. With its imbalance on getting rather than giving, such literature may contribute to rather than alleviate relationship distress. Effective relationships involve both partners in possessing a compassionate concern for one another's welfare.

CHAPTER HIGHLIGHTS

• Skills are sequences of choices in which people can have strengths, deficits or a mixture of both.

• Skills language means consistently using the concept of skills to describe and analyse people's behaviour.

• Relating skills are lifeskills. A positive definition of relating skills is that they are the specific lifeskills with which humans in their relationships affirm their own and others' psychological life.

• A simple distinction is that between the inner and outer games of relating. The inner game refers to thoughts and feelings, whereas the outer game refers to observable actions.

• Five ways that you can send action skills messages are by verbal, voice, body, touch and action messages.

• Thinking skills areas include: owning responsibility for choosing; understanding the relationship between how you think, feel and act; getting in touch with your feelings; using coping self-talk; choosing realistic personal rules; choosing to perceive accurately; explaining cause accurately; predicting realistically; setting realistic goals; using visualizing skills; realistic decision-making; and preventing and managing problems.

• To relate effectively, you require the ability to experience, express and manage your feelings. You can influence how you feel by means of your thinking skills and action skills.

• Reservations about a relating skills approach include that the approach: is unnatural, pays insufficient attention to feelings, is mechanistic, is manipulative, and is superficial. These reservations reflect abuses of rather than the skilful use of the approach.

• You need to assume responsibility for your relating skills. This involves courage and a willingness to cultivate and discipline your mind.

EXERCISES

EXERCISE 2.1
TRANSLATE EVERYDAY INTO SKILLS LANGUAGE
Instructions

This exercise may be done in relation to either a specific partner or another close relationship. Either way, first do the exercise on your own. Then, if appropriate discuss your answers with your partner, another or others.

Questions

1. Using your usual everyday language, list ways that you show caring to your partner/close friend.

2. Using your usual everyday language, list ways that your partner/close friend shows caring to you.

3. From each of the above lists, translate at least one way of showing caring from everyday language to skills language:
(a) me to my partner or close other
(b) my partner or close other to me

As a guide, here is the example of Paddy and Tessa used in the text: *Paddy's everyday language*. 'When I notice that Tessa is stressed I massage the area around her neck.'
Paddy's skills language. 'I use my noticing when Tessa is stressed skills and then, if she seems stressed, I use my massaging the area round her neck skills.'

4. How positively or negatively do you react to the idea of using skills language? Provide reasons for your answer.

EXERCISE 2.2
SEND ACTION SKILLS MESSAGES
Instructions

This exercise may be done in relation to either a specific partner or another close relationship. Either way, first do the exercise on your own. Then, if appropriate, discuss your answers with your partner, another or others.

1. In each of the categories below, identify specific action skills messages by means of which you show caring to your partner/close friend.
a. Verbal messages
b. Voice messages
c. Body messages
d. Touch messages
e. Action messages

2. In each of the categories below, identify specific action skills messages by means of which your partner/close friend shows caring to you. In particular, emphasize caring action skills messages that are different to the messages you send.
a. Verbal messages
b. Voice messages
c. Body messages
d. Touch messages
e. Action messages

EXERCISE 2.3
ASSESS MY THINKING SKILLS
Instructions

First do the exercise on your own. Then, if appropriate, discuss your answers with your partner, another or others.

Using the rating scale below, assess how skilled you are at using each of the following thinking skills in your relationships. Leave a blank for any thinking skill you do not understand.
5 Extremely skilled
4 Very skilled
3 Skilled
2 Moderately skilled
1 Slightly skilled
0 Unskilled

Your rating

_____ owning responsibility for choosing
_____ understanding the relationship between how I think, feel and act
_____ getting in touch with my feelings
_____ choosing realistic personal rules
_____ choosing to perceive accurately
_____ explaining cause accurately
_____ predicting realistically
_____ setting realistic goals
_____ using visualizing skills
_____ realistic decision-making
_____ preventing and managing problems

Summarize your main thinking skills strengths and deficits in your relationships. To what extent is how you think harming or helping you to relate effectively?

EXERCISE 2.4
RESERVATIONS ABOUT A RELATING
SKILLS APPROACH
Instructions

First do this exercise on your own. Then, if appropriate, discuss with your partner, another or others.

1. What do you think about each of the following reservations about taking a skills approach to how people relate?

a. It is unnatural.

b. It pays insufficient attention to feelings.

c. It is mechanistic.

d. It is manipulative.

e. It is superficial.

2. Can you think of other reservations about a relating skills approach? If so, list and provide reasons.

3. What are some strengths of taking a skills approach to how people relate?

EXERCISE 2.5
ASSESS MY PERSONAL RESPONSIBILITY, COURAGE
AND MENTAL CULTIVATION
Instructions

First do this exercise on your own. Then, if appropriate, discuss your answers with your partner, another or others.

1. To what extent do you currently assume personal responsibility in your relationships in each of the following areas (provide reasons for your answers):

a. how I think?

b. how I feel?

c. how I act?

2. Assess how courageous you are in each of the following areas:

a. confronting and relinquishing my relating skills deficits

b. acquiring relating skills strengths.

c. maintaining and further developing my relating skills strengths.

3. Do you consider that cultivating your mind and thinking skills is necessary for relating effectively? Provide reasons for your answer.

EXERCISE 2.6
GROUP DISCUSSION:
A RELATING SKILLS APPROACH
Instructions

This is intended as a group exercise, though it may be done individually or in pairs. For each part:

1. spend 10–15 minutes answering the question in groups of three or four,

2. each group shares its answers with the whole group,

3. then the whole group ranks the six most important points from the most important to the least important.

Part A
Disadvantages of a relating skills approach

List the six most important actual or potential disadvantages of viewing relationships and how you relate in relating skills terms.

Part B
Advantages of a relating skills approach

List the six most important advantages of viewing relationships and how you relate in relating skills terms.

THREE
Learning Relating Skills

I am simply a human being, more or less.
Saul Bellow

CHAPTER QUESTIONS

- *What is the difference between acquiring and maintaining relating skills strengths and deficits?*

- *How do people learn relating skills from examples?*

- *How do people learn relating skills from consequences?*

- *What is the role of supportive relationships?*

- *What is the role of instruction and self-instruction?*

- *What is the role of information and opportunity?*

- *What is the role of anxiety and confidence?*

- *Does insufficient use of skills language maintain relating skills deficits?*

- *How do thinking skills deficits contribute to maintaining relating skills deficits?*

- *How do unchanged environmental circumstances contribute to maintaining relating skills deficits?*

This chapter aims to raise your awareness of how you learned, have maintained and currently maintain your relating skills strengths and deficits. Each of you brings a learning and maintenance history into your relationships. For instance, if you marry aged 25, you will be 50 before you have lived as much time inside as outside your marriage. Just as people bring learning and maintenance histories into marriages, so you bring them into all other relationships, whatever the degree of intimacy.

HOW YOU LEARNED YOUR RELATING SKILLS

Unlike other animals whose behaviour is programmed by instincts, most human behaviour is learned. The human animal is distinguished from other animals by its capacity for self-awareness and conscious thought. Consequently, not only is human behaviour learned in the first place but then humans keep regulating it by the way they think (Bandura, 1986).

Acquiring and maintaining relating skills

A useful distinction is that between *acquiring* relating skills and *maintaining* them. In a sense each one of you has at least two learning histories for every skill: acquiring the skill in the first place, which is the traditional definition of learning, and then improving, diminishing or maintaining your initial level of skill. It is an important distinction because changing or improving a skill entails changing what is *maintaining* the skill at a lower level than desirable in the present and future. It is impossible to go back and change how a skills weakness was first *acquired*.

For example, Mae Ling, 17, initially learned to be shy because her parents had 'a children should be seen and not heard' rule. She maintained her shyness throughout her childhood and adolescence partly because her parents continued not to encourage her to talk about herself. Right now you cannot change how she became shy. Also, it is uncertain whether her parents' behaviour, which plays an important part in maintaining her shyness, can be changed. However, Mae Ling can work to acquire self-helping skills of being more outgoing. Also, if necessary, she can seek professional help, for instance from school or college counsellors. Thus, she can create a third or *change* learning history by making new choices to overcome skills deficits both acquired and maintained previously.

A further reason for distinguishing between acquisition and maintenance is that, even when you possess good relating skills, you still have to maintain them. There is no magical concept of cure, just daily diligence and effort.

Sources of influence

From the moment of birth numerous people give you messages that influence the development of your relating skills. Some messages help you relate more effectively whereas others weaken your effectiveness. Sometimes these messages are consistent. At other times they may be contradictory, not just to the extent of different messages from different people but also from the same person. Children are easily influenced in acquiring relationship skills strengths and deficits. They are physically and emotionally dependent on others and also intellectually immature.

Let us now look at the kinds of people who may have influenced and may still influence the choices you make in your relationships. Such people include:

- *Parents*. These include step-parents and other substitute parents.

- *Brothers and sisters.* They may be influential especially if older, but not too old to be out of frequent contact.

- *Grandparents.* Your grandparents reared your parents and consequently their influence lives on through others as well as through themselves, if alive.

- *Aunts and uncles.* Like grandparents, aunts and uncles may be important. However, greater geographic mobility than previously within families may sometimes lessen their importance.

- *Older friends.* Friends of the family who visit fairly frequently.

- *Community leaders.* People in church, medical, sporting and other visible positions.

- *Peer groups.* People of roughly your own age, outside your immediate family, with whom you play and study.

- *Teachers.* Contact with teachers may be either in class or in extracurricular activities, for instance games, music.

- *Famous people.* Such people may be well-known sports or entertainment personalities. Some may be historical and religious leaders.

- *Fictional people.* Characters portrayed in books, on TV and in movies.

- *Advertising.* People behaving in specific ways with the purpose of influencing purchasing decisions.

Supportive relationships

Children require supportive relationships. Bowlby (1979) talks of the concept of a secure base, otherwise referred to as an attachment figure. He notes accumulating evidence that humans of all ages are happiest and most effective when they feel that standing behind them is a trusted person who will come to their aid should difficulties arise. Rogers also stressed the need for supportive parent–child relationships characterized by high degrees of respect, genuineness and empathic understanding whereby children can feel sensitively and accurately understood (Rogers, 1951, 1959). Supportive relationships can be provided by many people other than parents: for instance, relatives and teachers. When growing up, most people seem to need at least one primary supportive relationship.

Many reasons exist why presence of supportive and absence of unsupportive or hostile relationships can help children develop relating skills strengths. First, supportive relationships provide children with the security to engage in exploratory behaviour and risk trial-and-error learning. Such exploratory behaviour represents a series of personal experiments in which children collect information about themselves and their environments. Second, supportive relationships help children listen better to themselves. By feeling prized and accurately understood, children can get more in touch with their wants, wishes and personal meanings. Third, children may feel freer to bring out into the open and show others emerging relating skills without risk of ridicule. Fourth, instruction in specific relating skills is frequently best conducted in the context of supportive relationships in which the anxiety attached to learning is diminished. Fifth, the presence or absence of supportive relationships can either affirm or negate children's sense of worth. They may either be helped to become confident or they may become inhibited, withdrawn and afraid to take risks. Alternatively, they may mask their insecurity by excessive attention–seeking.

Learning from examples

'Monkey see, monkey do' is one way of viewing learning from examples. Learning from examples is a major way in which people acquire relating skills strengths and deficits (Bandura, 1986). How to think, feel and act can be learned from others' examples. Below are two examples of parents demonstrating relating skills deficits.

> Darren and Andrea, find it very hard to show positive feelings to their children Rachel, 14, and Brett, 11. They find it easier to criticize rather than to praise. Also, apart from a brief goodnight kiss, Darren and Andrea rarely touch Rachel and Brett.
>
> The style of managing conflict in the Robinson family is one of competitive combat. Each parent has to be right, has 'legitimate' reasons for anger, and shouts and finger points. They do not listen to each other. Blame is the name of the game. Their children, Nancy, 10, Cindy, 8, and Jon, 5, observe and absorb how their parents fight.

A number of points are implicit in the above examples. Demonstrating how to feel, think and act may be unintentional as well as intentional. Observers may remain unaware that they are learning from example. In families, it is all too easy for children to adopt what their parents do without conscious choice. They learn relating skills strengths and deficits along with eating their breakfast cereal. A consequence of this is that each of you may not only have absorbed some relating skills deficits, but you may have the added barrier of remaining unaware that you have done so.

Learning from consequences

Observational learning is frequently intermingled with learning from rewarding or unrewarding consequences. For example, parents poor at showing emotions may also be poor at receiving children's emotions. In addition, children learn from observing the consequences of behaviour for others rather than always having to experience them first hand.

When as a child you were naughty, your parents may well have said 'bad girl' or 'bad boy'. When you behaved well, your parents were more likely to say 'good girl' or 'good boy'. In each instance, your parents were granting or withholding the reward of their approval. As a child you not only learned from the consequences of your behaviour provided by others but also from the consequences or feedback given you by your feelings. For instance, if teasing one of your friends was pleasurable, this was likely to increase the probability of future teasing of that person. A major internal consequence provided by your feelings was whether your actions produced pleasure or pain for you.

Sometimes a conflict may have occurred in that behaviours that were pleasurable for you were disapproved by your parents. If your parents' reaction was very strong you may have buried your true feelings and owned your parents' feelings *as if* they were your own (Rogers, 1951). People tend to talk about themselves as though they have access to their own feelings without distortion. However, frequently their feelings are the result of their parents' examples and rewards rather than what they would truly feel given a more accepting upbringing. Below is an example.

> When Frank was a child he would cry easily both when he got into fights with other children and when he saw something sad on television. When Frank cried during a fight, other children were quick to put him down as a 'sissy' and a 'cry baby'. Charlie, Frank's father, was afraid his son might become a homosexual. Charlie told Frank how wet he was to cry when watching television and that he was behaving like a little girl. After a time, Frank began to think of crying in boys and men as a sign of weakness.

When growing up, many people provided positive and negative consequences for your relating skills behaviour. Your relating skills strengths and deficits may have been *either* rewarded, *or* discouraged and possibly punished, *or* ignored. The basic idea is that behaviour that has resulted in positive consequences for you has a higher probability of being repeated than that resulting in negative consequences.

However, you do not just receive consequences, you think about the past consequences you have received, the present consequences you are receiving and then make rules and predictions that guide your future behaviour (Bandura, 1986). Thus, your thinking may strengthen, weaken or otherwise alter the impact of rewarding consequences. In addition, there are biological differences in people's propensity to be conditioned by rewarding consequences: for example, introverts being more conditionable than extroverts.

Instruction and self-instruction

Psychologists researching animal behaviour stress the importance of learning from example and consequences. However, humans possess the capacity for symbolic thought and communication. Consequently, instruction is a major transmitter of relating skills strengths and deficits. Much informal relating skills instruction takes place in the home. Some of this instruction is very basic: for instance, asking children to say 'please' and 'thank you'. Often instruction at home is insufficiently systematic. Also, few children are instructed in how to think effectively.

In addition, much informal relating skills instruction takes place in schools and colleges. However, systematic attempts to train children in a range of relating skills are probably still more the exception than the rule. Nevertheless a range of relating skills programmes may be offered in educational settings inside or outside the formal curriculum: for instance, making friends, managing anger and being assertive.

Instruction can be for better or worse. Relating skills deficits as well as strengths may be imparted. Frequently, instruction contains sex bias: for instance teaching only girls cooking and parenting skills. In addition, relating skills may not be communicated clearly enough for young people to instruct themselves afterwards. If learners are unable to talk themselves through the relevant sequences of choices, relating skills have been inadequately imparted and/or learned.

Information and opportunity

You require adequate information to develop relating skills. For example, keeping children in ignorance about basic facts of sexuality and death impedes self-awareness and emotional responsiveness. Intentionally or unintentionally, adults often relate to children on the basis of lies, omissions of truth and partial truths (Steiner, 1974). Furthermore, necessary information may not be readily available outside the home. For instance, schools differ greatly in the adequacy of sex and relationship education they provide.

Children, adolescents and adults alike need available opportunities to test out and to develop their relating skills. Ideally, such opportunities are in line with your maturation and state of readiness. You may have different opportunities on account of sex, race, culture, social class, physical disability, financial position and schooling, to mention but some potential barriers. Furthermore, you may be fortunate or unfortunate in having parents who open up or restrict learning opportunities. Children and adults also have a role in seeking out opportunities. Some of you have better skills at this than others.

Anxiety and confidence

Children can grow up having both helpful and harmful experiences for developing the self-esteem required for effective relating. The fortunate acquire a level of anxiety that both protects against actual dangers and also motivates them towards realistic achievements. Those less fortunate may acquire debilitating anxieties through faulty role modelling, instruction and provision of consequences. Even parents who communicate carefully can bruise children's fragile self-esteem. Far worse are parents who communicate aggressively and then become defensive. Here children's feelings and perceptions are doubly discounted: first, by the initial aggression and, second, by being subject to further aggression when they react. However, children differ both biologically in the extent to which they are vulnerable to negative parental behaviour and also in terms of the coping skills they possess.

Relating skills deficits resulting from as well as manifesting debilitating anxiety include: unwillingness to take realistic risks; a heightened tendency to say and do the wrong things; unnecessary aggression; and excessive approval seeking. Inadequate performance in the various relating skills may further raise anxiety and make future learning even more difficult.

HOW YOU MAINTAIN YOUR RELATING SKILLS

Once acquired, you can maintain both relating skills strengths and deficits. Here I focus on maintaining deficits rather than strengths. Especially for children, acquiring relating skills deficits is more a matter of 'what the environment does to me' than 'what I do to myself'. Frequently young people are at the mercy of their elders. However, maintaining relating skills strengths and deficits is a different matter. Here, partly because relating skills are maintained into adulthood, cause shifts more in the direction of 'what I do to myself' than 'what the environment has done or does to me'.

A contributing factor to people maintaining relating skills deficits is that they insufficiently think about their behaviour in skills terms. You can go round in circles talking about your relationship problems in everyday or descriptive language rather than breaking them down into skills terms.

Thinking skills deficits

Thinking skills deficits play a major part in people maintaining poor relating skills. Below are some illustrative thinking skills deficits that help people stay stuck in self-defeating patterns of behaviour.

Negative self-talk

Negative self-talk contrasts with coping self-talk (Meichenbaum, 1986; Meichenbaum & Deffenbacher, 1988). Negative self-talk statements can inhibit you from working on a range of relating skills deficits. Such negative statements include: 'I'm never going to be able to change', 'I'm starting to feel anxious and this is a signal that things may get out of control' and 'I'm no good at this.'

Coping self-talk has three main functions: calming, coaching and affirming. A sample calming self-instruction might be: 'Keep calm.' A sample coaching self-instruction might be: 'Speak slowly and clearly.' A sample affirming self-instruction is: 'I have some skills to deal with this situation.' Frequently, calming, coaching and affirming self-instructions are combined: 'Keep calm. Speak slowly and clearly. I have some skills to deal with this situation.'

Unrealistic personal and relationship rules

Personal rules are the 'dos' and 'don'ts' by which you lead your life. Each person has an inner rulebook of standards for themselves and for others with whom they relate. Sometimes these standards are realistic and appropriately flexible. On other occasions the standards may be unrealistic and inappropriately rigid. Ellis has coined the term 'musturbation' to refer to rigid personal rules characterized by 'musts', 'oughts' and 'shoulds' (Ellis, 1980, 1989). Below are illustrations of musturbatory *personal rules* in different relating skills areas.

Self-disclosing	'Men must not show their feelings.'
Showing affection	'My partner must always know what I want.'
Sex	'I must always perform at a high level.'
Assertion	'Women must not be assertive.'
Solving relationship problems	'My partner must make the first move.'

Partners can develop unrealistic rules for their relationships (Lazarus, 1985). Sometimes these joint rules are more covert than overt. Following are some musturbatory *relationship* rules.

Sharing activities	'Couples must do everything together.'
Marital satisfaction	'The relationship must fulfil all our dreams.'
Marital distress	'Marriages must never break up, however unhappy everyone may be.'
Solving relationship problems	'Good relationships must not have conflict.'

People as individuals or as couples can also possess unrealistic rules about change – that it must always be easy, effortless and painless. Such rules contribute to low tolerance of the frustrations entailed in changing, which in turn contributes to their maintaining relating skills deficits (Ellis, 1988).

Perceiving inaccurately

You can erroneously maintain relating skills deficits if you rigidly perceive your skills to be better or worse than they are. You may find it difficult to accept contrary feedback if you overestimate how intelligent, affectionate, competent in the kitchen or good in bed you are. Also, you can misperceive positive feedback to sustain a negative self-picture as well as negative feedback to sustain a positive self-picture (Rogers, 1959). An example of misperceiving positive feedback is belittling any compliments you receive. Frequently, when relationships start turning sour, people magnify the negative and minimize the positive qualities of one another. Such inaccurate perceptions contribute to both partners staying stuck in unproductive hostility.

'Defence mechanisms', 'defences' or 'security operations' are terms for the ways that people operate on incoming information that differs from their existing self-pictures (Freud, 1936; Rogers, 1959; Sullivan, 1953; Yalom, 1980). Defensive processes involve people diminishing awareness for short-term psychological comfort. Defensive processes range from denying incoming information, for instance 'How could anyone say that about me?', to distorting it in various ways: for example rationalizing, making excuses when your behaviour causes you anxiety, or projecting, externalizing thoughts and feelings on to others rather than owning them.

Explaining cause deficits

Following are possible explanatory errors that may sustain relating skills deficits. A common theme is that these explanations of cause tend to convert partial truths into whole truths by missing out relevant aspects of personal responsibility.

• *'It's my nature.'* Such biological or genetic explanations inadequately acknowledge the large learned component in most relating skills.

• *'It's my unfortunate past.'* For people who have left home, explanations of inadequate pasts are largely irrelevant to how they maintain relating skills deficits in the present.

• *'It's my bad luck.'* People often make their luck by developing relevant skills.

• *'It's my poor environment.'* Many people have learned to overcome relating skills deficits contributed to by poor environments. Also, sometimes people can influence their environments for the better.

• *'It's all your fault.'* The problem is my partner or some other person. Why bother to change when negative events are someone else's fault?

• *'It's all my fault.'* Quite apart from being inaccurate, overinternalizing cause may erode the confidence you need to deal with relationship problems.

Unrealistic predictions about change

Once acquired, relating skills deficits can become well-established habits resistant to change (Ellis, 1987). Following are possible areas for unrealistic predictions about change.

• Fear of the unknown.

• Fear of the discomfort in making the effort to change.

• Fear of losing the payoffs from existing relating skills deficits.

• Fear of inner conflict between the old and the emerging self.

• Fear of making mistakes.

• Fear of conflict with others arising from changed relating skills.

• Fear of rejection.

• Fear of the consequences of success (for instance, starting your first serious relationship).

• Fear of commitment and of losing independence.

• Fear of being taken advantage of.

Especially if unrealistic, a major prediction that blocks change can be lack of confidence about your ability to enact the level of skilful performance needed to achieve a desired relationship outcome (Bandura, 1986). Many people either fail to try out changed relating skills or, if tried, fail to persist in them in face of setbacks. All learning involves giving up the safety of the known to develop new or different skills. Some people are better able to confront fears about change and setbacks than others. Some of the thinking skills mentioned earlier – for example, perceiving accurately and using coping self-talk – can help you to manage rather than to avoid change.

In relationships, both partners can make self-defeating predictions about the possibility of change. Such self-defeating predictions include: 'my partner is incapable of change', 'nothing can improve our relationship', 'things will only get worse', 'people are set in their ways and cannot change', 'too much damage has already been done', and 'it only postpones the inevitable' (Beck, 1988, p. 197). Such predictions can erode each partner's willingness to work on improving their individual relating skills for the benefit of their joint relationship.

Unchanged environmental circumstances

Relating skills deficits are usually maintained both by how you think and also by how the environment constrains you. Most factors mentioned in the section on how you learned relating skills can help to maintain your skills deficits. You may continue to have insufficiently supportive relationships. You may still be exposed to examples of poor thinking and action skills. You may continue to receive inappropriate rewarding consequences, for instance receiving rewards for dependent behaviour. You may fail to receive or find adequate relating skills instruction and also continue instructing yourself in skills deficits. In addition, you may still be exposed to insufficient or faulty information and lack suitable opportunities to develop your skills and human potential.

CONCLUDING COMMENT

If anything this chapter has focused more on the acquisition and maintenance of relating skills deficits than strengths. The processes that contribute to you acquiring relating skills strengths are the reverse of those leading to deficits: for example, supportive rather than unsupportive relationships and good rather than poor examples. Also, the processes that help you maintain relating skills strengths are the reverse of those maintaining deficits: for example, effective rather than ineffective thinking skills. Often, learning and maintenance of relating skills is more complex than presented above. For instance, you can concurrently acquire and then maintain both strengths and deficits in one or more relating skills areas.

CHAPTER HIGHLIGHTS

• An important distinction exists between initially acquiring relating skills strengths and deficits and then maintaining them.

• Influences on learning your relating skills include: parents, brothers and sisters, grandparents, aunts and uncles, older friends, community leaders, peer groups, teachers, famous people, fictional people and advertising.

• The presence or absence of supportive relationships is important in helping children develop relating skills strengths or deficits.

• Learning from examples is a major way that people acquire relating skills. Frequently, people remain unaware of the full impact of what they have learned.

• Observational learning is frequently intermingled with learning from rewarding or unrewarding consequences. People think about the consequences provided for their behaviour and develop rules and predictions that guide future behaviour.

• People also learn relating skills strengths and deficits from instruction and self-instruction.

• Adequate information and opportunities are important to developing relating skills strengths.

• Poor parental relationships may cause children to possess debilitating anxiety which in turn may interfere with their acquiring relating skills strengths and make it easier for them to acquire relating skills deficits.

• A contributing factor to people maintaining relating skills deficits is that they insufficiently think about their behaviour in skills terms.

• Thinking skills deficits that help people stay stuck in self-defeating patterns of behaviour include: negative self-talk, unrealistic personal and relationship rules, perceiving inaccurately, explaining cause deficits and unrealistic predictions about change.

• Unchanged environmental circumstances can also contribute to people maintaining relating skills deficits.

EXERCISES
EXERCISE 3.1
MY PAST EXPERIENCES OF SUPPORTIVE RELATIONSHIPS
Instructions

First do this exercise on your own. Then, if appropriate, discuss your answers with your partner, another or others.

Select the two most important childhood relationships you had with parents or other significant adults. For each relationship, specify behaviours that supported or hindered you in acquiring relating skills strengths.

1. Details of relationship _____

_____

_____

Supportive behaviours _____

_____

Unsupportive behaviours _____

_____

2. Details of relationship _____

_____

_____

Supportive behaviours _____

_____

Unsupportive behaviours _____

_____

3. Based on your answers to questions 1 and 2, rank order supportive behaviours, listing the most supportive behaviour first.

4. Based on your answers to questions 1 and 2, rank order unsupportive behaviours, listing the most unsupportive behaviour first.

EXERCISE 3.2
LEARNING RELATING SKILLS FROM PARENTAL EXAMPLES

Instructions

First do this exercise on your own. Then, if appropriate, discuss your answers with your partner, another or others.

1. What were the examples set by your parents in each of the following relating skills areas? In most instances 'parents' refers to your biological parents. However, if a step-parent or surrogate parent has been more important to you, answer in respect of him or her.

Sender skills	Your mother	Your father
Talking about their experiences		
Showing their feelings		
Standing up for themselves		

Receiver skills	Your mother	Your father
Paying attention		
Understanding another person's communications		
Showing under-standing of another's communications		

Solving relationship problems skills	Your mother	Your father
Managing anger constructively		
Confronting problems assertively		
Working for rational solutions		

2. Summarize the effects on your current relating skills strengths and deficits of your parents' examples in each of the following areas: (a) sending information, (b) receiving information, and (c) solving relationship problems.

EXERCISE 3.3
LEARNING RELATING SKILLS FROM PARENTAL CONSEQUENCES

Instructions

First do this exercise on your own. then, if appropriate, discuss your answers with your partner, another or others.

1. Indicate the extent to which you were rewarded by your parents for each of the following behaviours by putting an M in the box that best describes your mother's reaction and an F in the box that best describes your father's reaction. Also, try to give one or two specific examples of the consequences they provided for you. If answering in terms of a biological parent is inappropriate, answer for a step-parent or surrogate parent.

Reward from parents

Your behaviour	Much	Little	None	Punished	Examples(s)
Expressing affection to him/her					

Your behaviour	Much	Little	None	Punished	Examples(s)
Expressing anger to him/her					
Expressing your opinions on current affairs					
Expressing negative feelings about yourself (e.g. depression)					
Expressing positive feelings about yourself (e.g. happiness)					
Saying you wish to be left out of parental disagreements					
Being prepared to listen to him/her					
Responding help-fully to him/her					
Requesting participation in decisions involving you					
Wanting to discuss a conflict between you					

Your behaviour	Much	Little	None	Punished	Examples(s)
Stating your position in the conflict					
Trying to under-stand his/her position					
Placating and giving in to him/her					
Working for a rational solution to a conflict with him/her					

2. Summarize the effects on your current relating skills strengths and deficits of the consequences provided for your behaviour by your parents.

EXERCISE 3.4
HOW I MAINTAIN A RELATING SKILLS DEFICIT
Instructions

First do this exercise on your own. Then, if appropriate, discuss your answers with your partner, another or others.

1. Select a specific action skills relating deficit that you are currently maintaining

_____

_____

2. Assess the contribution of each of the following thinking skills deficits to maintaining your action skills relating deficit.

Negative self-talk _____

_____

Unrealistic personal and relationship rules _____

_____

Perceiving inaccurately _____

_____

Explaining cause deficits _____

_____

Unrealistic predictions about change _____

_____

3. Specify ways and assess the extent to which unchanged environmental circumstances contribute to maintaining your action skills relating deficit

_____

_____

_____

You may repeat this exercise for another action skills relating deficit.

EXERCISE 3.5
GROUP DISCUSSION:
LEARNING RELATING SKILLS
Instructions

This is intended as a group exercise, though it may be done individually or in pairs. For
each part:

1. spend 10–15 minutes answering the question in groups of three or four,

2. each group shares its answers with the whole group,

3. then the whole group ranks the six most important points from the most to the least
important.

Part A
Acquiring relating skills

List the six most important ways or processes by which people acquire relating skills
strengths and/or deficits.

Part B
Maintaining relating skills

List the six most important ways or processes by which people maintain relating skills
strengths and/or deficits.

FOUR
What You Bring to Relationships

There is no hope of joy except in human relations.
Saint-Exupéry

CHAPTER QUESTIONS

- *How emotionally responsive are you?*

- *How confident are you?*

- *What anxieties and fears do you possess?*

- *What is your physical health?*

- *What is your sexuality?*

- *What sex-role identity and expectations do you possess?*

- *What are your values?*

- *What culture and cross-cultural skills do you bring?*

- *What race and racial skills do you bring?*

- *What social class and social class skills do you bring?*

Relationships do not start from scratch. You bring your thinking skills and action skills to your relationships. In addition, you bring numerous other personal characteristics. This chapter explores some of them.

YOUR CAPACITY TO FEEL

Seeing's believing, but feeling's the truth.
Thomas Fuller

You bring to your relationships your capacity to experience your feelings. There are a number of dimensions to how emotionally responsive you may be to yourself and to others.

Inhibiting and repressing feelings

As people grow up they learn, in varying degrees, that it is unsafe to acknowledge, experience and express all feelings. Consequently, an editing process takes place about which you may remain unaware. Some people find it difficult to express any feelings. They are emotionally flat and lifeless. In all families people learn permissions and inhibitions regarding how to feel, though change is possible. For instance, different families may inhibit or dilute the experiencing of specific emotions like sensuality, anger, sadness or death anxiety. In addition, families vary in the extent to which they encourage children to experience and show altruistic feelings. Furthermore, families can influence the degree to which children inhibit wants and wishes. Following is a brief example of how parents can foster sexual repression.

> Sean grew up in a home where it was taboo to talk about sex. Neither of his parents ever acknowledged that they were sexual beings to him. When small, his parents stopped him when he played with his penis. When an adolescent, they banned girlie magazines in the house. Also, they disparaged open shows of affection on television. Sean's father particularly disliked the way footballers hugged each other when goals were scored.

People also learn permissions and inhibitions according to their social characteristics. For instance, females and males may find it easier to express affectionate and competitive feelings, respectively. If anything, male conditioning is more likely to lead to emotional inexpressiveness than female conditioning. The 'strong, silent' type is a male stereotype. Culture also influences the degree to which feelings are experienced and expressed: for instance, the British 'stiff upper lip' contrasts with southern European emotional expressiveness. Social class is another influence on which feelings get acknowledged and how they are expressed.

Internalizing others' feelings as if your own

How many of your feelings are truly your own and how many are 'hand-me-downs' from your parents and culture? Especially where parental affection has been conditional, children may internalize the feelings of significant others as if they were their own. Carl Rogers gives the example of a child who enjoys hitting his baby brother learning to deny his feelings of enjoyment. Rogers writes: 'The accurate symbolisation would be: "I perceive my parents as experiencing this behaviour as unsatisfying to them." The distorted symbolisation, distorted to preserve the threatened concept of self, is: "I perceive this behaviour as unsatisfying" ', (Rogers, 1951, p. 500). The main thrust of Rogers' person-centred therapy is to assist clients to experience their own inner valuing process rather than to deny and distort their feelings.

Homosexual feelings provide an example where many people deny and distort what they truly feel. Many gay people go through a process of acknowledging and coming to terms with their gayness. This process can be more difficult because of the internalized loathing about homosexuality that they may have learned and may still face from both parents and culture.

> When as an adolescent, Alice noticed that she was attracted to other girls, she did her best not to take any notice of these feelings. Instead, to affirm her heterosexuality, she engaged in an active social life of dating boys. Hard as she tried to be affectionate, Alice's heart was not in these relationships. Then Alice became friendly with a slightly older girl, Marsha. When they kissed and embraced, Alice felt so guilty that she told Marsha it was wrong and she could no longer be her friend. Alice is now in her late 20s and still feels ambivalent about being a lesbian. She has 'come out' to a few close friends, but has yet to tell her parents who wonder why she is not married.

In relationships, it can be important for partners to work through what they really feel and think as contrasted to what they have been taught to feel and think. Many conflicts originate in partners internalizing the feelings of significant others in their pasts as if they were their own and then not examining their validity in light of present circumstances.

Carrying around unfinished business

Many people transfer significant unfinished emotional business from past relationships into present relationships. For example, children who have had their integrity consistently attacked by inadequate and manipulative parents may grow up with a backlog of insufficiently expressed hatred and resentment. Such feelings may be kept in check through courtship and honeymoon phases of relationships only to surface later. Related to feelings of anger are deep insecurities about unlovableness. Partners whose self-acceptance on entering their relationships is low can become very clinging, jealous and demanding.

> Josh grew up in a family where his father was physically violent to his mother, his older sister and himself. He became an angry adolescent and, later, an angry young man. Josh restrained his anger when courting Beth. However, now married, Josh hits Beth when she argues strongly with him. Beth is on the verge of leaving the relationship.

Another way that people can carry round unfinished business is to transfer feelings about significant people in their pasts into their existing relationships. The term *transference* is used in psychoanalysis to describe this phenomenon. Transferred feelings can be positive as well as negative. However, the fact that the feelings are transferred may create problems if the feelings are inappropriate to current circumstances. For example, when dating, both males and females can distort the reality of girlfriends and boyfriends through creating conscious and unconscious similarities with their parents of the opposite sex. Similarly, people can erroneously transfer feelings about previous lovers and partners to current ones.

> Julie had always been her father's favourite child. He called her 'Princess' and spoiled her. Julie's repertoire of getting what she wanted from her father included playing the cute little girl and, if necessary, crying. Julie was bitterly disappointed when her boyfriend Graham did not always allow her to get her way.

Listening to your feelings

In your relationships you are constantly required to listen to your feelings. This does not mean that you ignore others' feelings. Being sensitively attuned to your own feelings gives you an excellent basis for tuning into theirs. Listening to your feelings ideally means that these feelings are appropriate to the 'here-and-now' rather than residual feelings from your childhood or other relationships. Listening to past feelings in a present context lessens the relevant information available for you to meet your preferences and needs now.

As you read the above paragraphs you may have thought, 'What, me? It surely applies only to others that, often without realizing it, they drag their past agendas and feelings inappropriately into the present.' If so, the news is that it probably applies to you, to a greater or lesser degree, as well. Most humans are subject to *illusions* of *autonomy* and *rationality*. They consider that they act independently and rationally most of the time without distracting interference from the residues of childhood and other learning experiences. Such illusions may block you from working to alter your thinking so that you can release your full capacity to feel.

YOUR SENSE OF WORTH AND ANXIETIES

No one can make you feel inferior without your consent.

Eleanor Roosevelt

You bring into your relationships your feelings of security or insecurity and your fears and anxieties. Vulnerability can be an attractive quality. It helps others feel that you and they are part of the human race. It provides the opportunity for caring and being cared for. You can share your own and your partner's vulnerability in ways that enhance and deepen your relationship. Mutual sympathy and liking develop from sensitive understanding of each other's vulnerabilities as much as from appreciation of strengths. Also, if you are unable to acknowledge your own fears and anxieties you are likely to lack responsiveness to other people's.

Your sense of worth

Insecurities and fears, if not confronted and managed, can be the breeding ground for hatred and distress in relationships. Nobody's upbringing is perfect. In varying degrees you have learned to feel 'Not OK' as well as 'OK', even though these 'Not OK' feelings may be difficult for you to acknowledge. Robert Carkhuff (1987) categorizes families into two main groupings, facilitative and retarding. The members of facilitative families help each other become persons. The members of retarding families are in process of becoming non-persons. In facilitative families, parents are likely to have a secure sense of their own worth which is transmitted to their children. In retarding families, either or both parents feel insecure. Lacking a true sense of their own worth, they send messages that undermine the sense of worth of their children.

Intentionally or unintentionally when people communicate they send two broad categories of messages. One set is specific, having to do with the ostensible purpose of the communication. The other set of messages may be more general and less intentional. These give the receivers messages pertaining to their worth as persons as well as revealing how high or low the senders value themselves. Children need the security of positive messages about their unique loveableness. Unfortunately many parents fail to realize that they often send messages that undermine the tender self-esteem of those they love. Sometimes this can have devastating results. This is especially true if parents compound their initial communication error by not hearing and understanding the pain their children suffer. Life can be very unfair. Children whose parents mostly send retarding messages are less likely to be heard, even though their need for understanding may be much greater than that of children whose parents mostly send facilitative messages.

Your fears and anxieties

The late American psychiatrist Harry Stack Sullivan reportedly said that 90 per cent of human communication was specifically designed not to communicate. Anxiety on the part of both senders and receivers distorts much communication. It can be a powerful enemy of relating effectively. Ultimately the fear of death and of non-being is the underlying fear from which all other anxieties are derived (May & Yalom, 1989; Yalom 1980). I prefer the term survival anxiety. Anxiety can be both helpful and harmful. It has a survival value in that it alerts you to realistic dangers to your existence. Unfortunately all people suffer in varying degrees from anxiety that is higher than that required to cope specifically with life's challenges. Their sense of danger becomes disproportionate and debilitating rather than facilitating (Alpert & Haber, 1960; Beck & Emery, 1985).

The words anxiety and fear are often used interchangeably. Anxiety may be defined as your fears about your capacity to cope adequately with the future. This may either be a general *trait* of yours or a *state* that applies mainly to specific situations. There is a close connection between your sense of worth and feelings of anxiety. Insecurity both manifests and engenders anxiety. People who feel worthwhile are relatively free from debilitating anxieties.

Adults are children grown up, more humorously expressed as 'Adults are children with mortgages.' One way of looking at loving another person is that the intuitive little child in you feels comfortable with and cares for the little child inside the adult exterior of the person you love. However, children carry their psychological wounds and scars into adulthood, especially if they not have developed the skills to manage them. Adults are often full of fears and anxieties. Sometimes these are acknowledged and obvious to all concerned. On other occasions they may not be acknowledged and their insidious effects on communication go largely unrecognized.

Below is an illustrative list of just a few of the anxieties that people may bring into their relationships. These fears represent their subjective rather than objective reality. However, often they are exaggerated and result in self-defeating feelings and actions. Sometimes you may be more afraid of getting what you want than not getting it. Consequently, I group fears into three categories, albeit overlapping, fear of failure, success and change. Since, in the previous chapter, I discussed fear of change, here I provide examples of fear of failure and of success.

Fear of failure	*Fear of success*
Fear of rejection	Fear of intimacy
Fear of feeling unlovable	Fear of inability to maintain
Fear of being truly known	success
Fears about physical	Fear of being happy
attractiveness	Fear of others' envy
Fears about being boring	
Fears about sexual performance	
Fears about making mistakes	
Fear of hurting another emotionally	
Fears about being engulfed	
Fear of abandonment	
Fear of loneliness	
Fear of being unhappy	
Fear of not coping with the other sex	

Fear of showing strong emotions
Fear of what others think
Fear of giving in too much
Fear of getting your way too little
Fear of adjusting to another
Fear of being unable to cope with your partner's changing

Along with your fears and anxieties, you bring into your relationships your skills strengths and deficits in coping with them. Also, you bring your skills strengths and deficits in coping with one another's insecurities and anxieties.

YOUR PHYSICAL HEALTH

When in a close relationship you cannot help becoming very aware of one another's physical health. Though biology and psychology overlap, below are just a few physical health considerations that people can bring to relationships.

• *Energy level.* How much physical and mental energy do you have? To what degree do you possess vitality or seem apathetic? How physically resilient are you? If your energy level is very low, check with your doctor for possible medical explanations.

• *Fitness.* People differ greatly in how fit they are and how well they look after their bodies. Also, they differ in how much they expose themselves to health risk factors, such as obesity, smoking, alcoholism and drug abuse.

• *Sickness and sickliness.* People may bring their sickness into a relationship. For instance, in the British play and film *Shadowlands* the heroine's terminal cancer was a relationship-deepening factor. In addition, people differ in how prone they are to various ailments, be they minor or more serious.

• *Managing stress skills.* People differ in how good their skills are at acknowledging and managing stress. Some people are very poor at listening to the signals that their body is over-stressed. At worst, poor managing stress skills can result in terminal heart attacks. Also, poor managing stress skills can result in increased relationship distress, for instance through heightened irritability and conflict.

• *Physical disability.* To what degree are you physically disabled, for instance with impairments of vision, hearing or mobility? If physically disabled, your thinking and actions skills strengths and deficits in coping with your disability become very important.

• *Fertility.* People differ in the extent to which they are fertile. Though usually undiscovered until partners unsuccessfully try to conceive, infertility can be an extremely important biological factor with huge psychological ramifications that people can bring into relationships.

• *Mental illness.* Some mental problems have a biological component to them, for instance schizophrenia and manic-depression (American Psychiatric Association, 1994). Again, people bring their attitude towards their mental illness and skills of coping with it into their relationships.

You not only bring your physical health into your relationships, you also bring your attitude and skills in coping with your partner's level of physical health. In addition, in long-term relationships, partners need to come to terms with changes in each other's health, including possibly the dying and death of one of them.

YOUR SEXUALITY

All humans are sexual from birth. However, you have a choice concerning how much of your sexuality you bring into your relationships. Sexuality is at once both simple and complex. On the one hand, nothing can feel simpler than being attracted to someone and wanting to hold them in your arms. On the other hand, your sexuality consists of a complex interplay of physiological, health, psychological, social and cultural influences.

Sex and love are often confused. Your sexuality can be a powerful force for bridging your separation from others by making and maintaining contact with them. However you can love people, for instance parents and friends, without being sexually attracted to them. Also, given the ambiguity of human nature and your capacity for choice, you can have affectionate relationships with varying degrees of sexuality implicit in them.

Your sexual feelings

People bring into relationships their level of sexual energy or libido. Also, they enter relationships with preferences for how, when and how many times they like to have sex. Furthermore, they bring their prior sexual experiences. In a large-scale British survey, conducted in 1990–1, of sexual behaviour of 16–59 year olds, for both females and males aged 16–24 the median (midpoint in a set of scores) age of first intercourse was 17. This was four years earlier than the median age of first intercourse for 55–9 year old women and three years earlier than that for 55–9 year old men (Wellings, Field, Johnson & Wadsworth, 1994).

Despite the strength of their sexual urges, people differ in their capacity to experience themselves as sexual beings. This is partly because humans need to learn how to express their sexuality. You bring into your relationships the fruits of your sexual learnings, for good or ill. Hopefully your attitude towards your sexuality is healthy and loving. However, ignorance and poor thinking skills may interfere with your effectiveness. There is probably less ignorance about sex now than previously. Nevertheless, people enter into their relationships with skills deficits in respect to: knowledge about their own bodies, how to express tender feelings, how to give and receive pleasure and how to handle contraception. Despite the so-called sexual revolution, children's opportunities to learn about integrating sexuality into loving relationships often leave much to be desired. Many parents feel uncomfortable about discussing sexuality with their children and some lack adequate knowledge. Gourlay (1995) observes: 'Generally, friends are nominated by people as their most common source of information about sexuality…yet for most, parents and schools were actually their preferred sources of information' (p. 41).

Faulty thinking can lead people to either underemphasize or overemphasize their sexuality. Children can pick up their parents' inhibitions about being sexual. A major area for therapists working with sexually dysfunctional couples is that of helping either or both partners work through thoughts interfering with performance, for instance 'Sex is dirty' or 'Sharing sexual fantasies is wrong.' In addition, many people have counter-productive fears about their bodies: for instance that either their breasts or penises are too small. Especially for males poor thinking skills may lead to an exaggerated emphasis on sexual performance. They may boast about their sexual conquests to their peers and treat women as objects rather than persons. Fears underlie both inhibited and exaggerated sexuality. These fears include: acknowledging the strength of sexual feelings; fears about physical attractiveness; performance fears; and fears about being seen to be sufficiently 'masculine' or 'feminine'.

Your sexual orientation

Are you straight, gay or in-between? You bring your sexual orientation to your relationships. I use the term sexual orientation rather than sexual preference. Many, if not most, predominantly gay people's sexual orientation is a fact of life, based on genetics and social learning, and not a preference, based on free choice. The word homosexual is derived from the Greek word *homo*, meaning same. Researchers experience difficulty obtaining accurate data on the extent of homosexual attraction and experience. If anything, the amount of homosexuality gets under-reported. Until 1967 male homosexuality was a criminal offence in Britain. At time of writing, homosexuality is still a criminal offence in some Australian states, for instance Tasmania. Only as recently as 1974 did the American Psychiatric Association remove homosexuality from its list of psychiatric disorders. In Western societies there is still widespread stigma attached to being gay. Consequently, gay people may select themselves out of survey samples. Once in samples, some gay people may be inhibited from revealing full details of their behaviour. Also, some survey respondents may find it difficult to acknowledge consciously any homosexual attraction or experience and, if they do, can find it easy to forget afterwards.

In the late 1940s and early 1950s pioneering studies on American sexual behaviour were conducted by Alfred Kinsey and his colleagues (Kinsey, Pomeroy & Martin, 1948; Kinsey, Pomeroy, Martin & Gebhard, 1953). They found that in the large, predominantly white, middle-class population that they surveyed, 4 per cent of males and between 1 to 3 per cent of females were exclusively homosexual. Furthermore, 10 per cent of males were more or less exclusively homosexual for at least three years between ages 16 and 65, and 37 per cent had participated in at least one homosexual experience which led to orgasm. Though heterosexuality was very much the predominant sexual preference for both males and females and exclusive homosexuality very much the minority preference, there was a considerable amount of bisexuality.

More recent data exist regarding homosexual attraction and experience in Britain. Wellings and her colleagues (1994) found that, in face to face interviews, of their large sample of 16–59 year olds, 5.5 per cent of men and 4.5 per cent of women admitted to having been *attracted* to a person of the same sex. In addition, 5.2 per cent of men and 2.7 per cent of women reported some homosexual *experience*. Sexual experience was defined as 'any kind of contact with another person that you felt was sexual (it could be just kissing or touching, or intercourse or any other form of sex)' (p. 181).

Wellings and her colleagues also collected data from a self-completion booklet. Based on booklet responses, 6.1 per cent of men reported some homosexual experience and 3.6 per cent genital contact with a man. The corresponding figures for women were 3.4 per cent and 1.7 per cent, respectively. These British findings for men are similar to American data which estimate lifetime prevalence of male homosexual experience within the range 4.8 per cent to 4.9 per cent (Rogers & Turner, 1991).

Homosexual experience and homosexual self-concept are not always synonymous. For instance, many male-to-male prostitutes in Thailand – and possibly in Britain and Australia too – play an active role in commercial encounters that does not threaten their heterosexual self-concept (Allyn, 1992). It would be a different matter if they allowed themselves to be penetrated.

Though heterosexuality is very much the predominant orientation, many females and males are confronted with choices about how to handle gay feelings, whether to engage in gay sex and whether to admit their gay feelings openly. Kinsey and his colleagues considered that, if social constraints and taboos had not been so strong, there would have been a much higher incidence of homosexual response.

People not only bring their sexual orientation to their relationships, but they also bring their fears about their sexual orientation. Heterosexuality as well as homosexuality may be repressed. For example, a young man who experiences attraction to another man may wrongly label himself as gay rather than a bisexual who is predominantly heterosexual. Especially among males, there is much anxiety about being gay. For some males the exaggerated emphasis on heterosexual performance is an attempt to gain reassurance about their masculinity. It is preferable to acknowledge rather than deny any gay feelings. You can then make a conscious choice as to how to handle them. Though this book primarily emphasizes heterosexual relationships, gay people have a perfect right to fulfilling emotional and sexual relationships. However, heterosexual relationships have the added importance of producing and rearing children, though some mainly gay people do both too.

YOUR SEX-ROLE IDENTITY AND EXPECTATIONS

There was, I think, never any reason to
believe in any innate superiority of the male,
except his superior muscle.

Bertrand Russell

A fundamental value of this book is that of equality between females and males. Equality between the sexes means that both females and males should have the same opportunity to develop their potential and express their humanity. Apart from realistic constraints stemming from biological differences, both sexes should have the same opportunity to exercise choice in their lives. Equality between the sexes is an ideal towards which progress is being made in Western societies. In the past females and males have related both to their own sex and to the other sex in traditional ways that needlessly constricted choice. You are in a transitional period now where perhaps females especially, but also many males, are challenging conventional wisdoms about sex-related attitudes and behaviours. This poses threats and risks as well as exciting opportunities. Gender is now on the agenda in all but the most unaware of male–female relationships.

Defining terms

Below I stipulate some definitions of basic terms relevant to your exploring the sex-role expectations that you bring to relationships.

• *Sex*. In this context sex refers to biological differences between males and females: for instance, differences in genitals, reproductive functions, bone structure and size.

• *Gender*. Gender refers to the social and cultural classification of attributes, attitudes and behaviours as 'feminine' or 'masculine'.

• *Sex-role identity*. Your sex-role identity is how you see yourself on the dimensions of 'masculinity' and 'femininity'.

• *Sex-role expectations*. These are your thoughts and feelings about how you and others should think, feel and behave on account of differences in your biological sex. They are your personal rules in this area.

• *Sexism*. Individual sexism relates to any feelings, thoughts and actions that assume the superiority of one sex over the other. Institutional sexism relates to institutional structures that discriminate and devalue a person on the grounds of sex.

Masculinity, femininity and androgyny

In Western societies, certain psychological characteristics have been traditionally viewed as either 'feminine' or 'masculine'. Feminine characteristics have included being: affectionate, gentle, sensitive to the needs of others, tender and warm. Masculine characteristics have included being: aggressive, ambitious, assertive, analytical and dominant (Bem, 1974). The predominant traditional roles of women have been those of the nurturer and social harmonizer within the home. Men's traditional roles have focused on being the breadwinner outside the home and the enforcer of discipline within the home.

Because of their sex-role learning, males and females develop different relating skills strengths and deficits. Argyle (1984) states that the research evidence suggests that there are a number of areas where females may be more socially competent than males. These include: being better at sending and receiving body language; being more rewarding and polite; and disclosing more and forming closer friendships. However, he notes that being assertive is an area where women appear to have more problems than men. Both masculine and feminine sex-roles may have costs. The traditional feminine sex-role has created problems for many women in such areas as expressing anger, being autonomous and obtaining power and status (DeVoe, 1990). The traditional masculine role has created problems for many men through excessive concern with success, power and competition, being emotionally inexpressive, and restricting affectionate behaviour between men (Good, Dell & Mintz, 1989).

Underlying the 'femininity-masculinity' dimension is the issue of nature versus nurture. Moir and Jessel (1989) review research indicating that from birth males and females are different. The main behavioural difference is the natural, innate aggression of men. Moir and Jessel observe that the sexes are different because their brains are different and observe: 'To maintain that they are the same in aptitude skill or behaviour is to build a society based on a biological and scientific lie' (p. 5). On the other hand, some social scientists consider that humans have weak instinctual remnants towards either a male or a female sex-role identity and that such biological predispositions may be easily overwhelmed by the strength of their learning experience (Oakley, 1972).

There are two interesting possibilities in how the nature nurture controversy can be positively resolved. One possibility is that 'masculinity' and 'femininity' become outmoded concepts because further research indicates that the sexes are biologically similar. The second possibility is that further research supports Moir and Jessel's position that the sexes possess important biological differences and they manage to utilize each other's strengths for everyone's benefit.

Related to the issue of nurture or nature is the increasing popularity of the concept of psychological androgyny. The androgynous male or female 'is flexibly masculine or feminine as circumstances warrant' (Bem, 1981, p. 362). Thus, females and males can be brought up with the capacity to express a range of characteristics independently whether they have traditionally been viewed as 'masculine' or 'feminine'. For instance, men can be tender and women assertive.

So long as males and females increasingly adopt the strengths rather than the deficits of the other sex's gender characteristics, androgyny offers much promise for improving and enriching people's relating skills. This is true for gay as well as for heterosexual relationships. Already there are many of both sexes who, in varying degrees are flexible in exhibiting masculine and feminine characteristics. Hopefully, there will be a continuing trend towards bringing up and encouraging more people to acknowledge and share the full range of their psychological characteristics. Such sharing is likely to lessen the amount of loneliness and alienation in Western countries.

Changing patterns of sex-role expectations

The increasing emphasis in equality of choice, where possible, between the sexes is becoming manifest in changes in expectation regarding specific aspects of male–female relationships. Below are some possible *emergent* personal rules in the areas of dating, sex, marriage and family that treat the sexes more similarly than *traditional* rules. Ultimately each individual and each couple has to choose the rules for themselves and for their relationship that work best for them.

• *Dating*. It's OK for either sex to initiate a relationship. The expenses of going out together are to be shared.

• *Sex*. Mutuality and sensitivity to each other's pleasure is important. It's OK for both females and males to initiate sex and to show enjoyment of it.

• *Marriage*. Marriage is a relationship between separate, equal and interdependent partners. The roles that males and females play within marriage are to be decided by agreement rather than by tradition.

• *Family.* Child care is the responsibility of both parents. Both male and female children should be accorded the same educational opportunities.

One of the most important areas in which sex-role expectations are changing concerns the place of women in the world of work. In Australia, historically women had low participation in the labour force, with rates between 20 to 25 per cent up until 1947. By 1991 the labour force participation rate of women had increased to 51 per cent reflecting changing attitudes to the role and status of women, trends towards smaller family size and the emergence of part-time work (Castles, 1993) The change in labour force participation has been even more dramatic for married women. In the 1930s, marriage meant an end to the working careers of most women, but by 1991, two-thirds of married women in the peak labour force ages of 25–54 were working. In June 1993, 43.2 per cent of married women with dependent children were employed full time (Australian Institute of Family Studies, 1993b).

The role of women in the Australian and British workforces is changing. In Australia, between 1989 and 1994, the number of women in professional and managerial jobs rose by 23 per cent. During this period women took 80 per cent of the net growth in managerial jobs and, by 1994, held 26 per cent of non-farm managerial jobs. In 1994, women made up 43 per cent of all professionals: 69 per cent of school-teachers, 52 per cent of other teachers, 43 per cent in the arts, 42 per cent in medicine (excluding nursing), 35 per cent in social professions (including clergy and welfare workers), 32 per cent in business professions such as accounting, and 29 per cent of natural scientists. The building professions, such as engineering, were the major professional area where women were outsiders. About 97 per cent of building professionals were male, unchanged from 1989 (Colebatch, 1994). Women are also increasing their share of managerial and professional jobs in Britain.

If American experience is a guide, an increasing number of British and Australian women are becoming entrepreneurs. In 1960, women started one in ten new American businesses; in 1985, they started one in five. The figure for 1995 was projected to be one in two (Bloom, 1986).

As women increase their choices in relation to work, there are likely to be more opportunities for men to make choices traditionally restricted to women. These choices include spending more time on home-making and children. Furthermore, a second income allows some husbands to find more fulfilling lower paid full-time or part-time work.

The changing role of women in the workforce may be associated with the increase in divorce over the same period. The growing financial independence and willingness of women to seek fulfilment outside as well as inside the home may make many less willing to stay in unhappy marriages. Furthermore, the fact that a high percentage of first marriages in Britain and Australia end in divorce may reinforce women in wanting to develop their own careers as an insurance policy for being on their own. If people are increasingly going to stay in marriages because they *want* to be in them and not because they *have* to be in them, this puts more pressure on females and males to develop relating skills, both for their own and for their children's sakes.

Sex differences in communication

The area of sex differences in communication is a vast one. Differences, as well as similarities, are pervasive in the ways males and females communicate within their sex and with the other sex (Henley, 1977; Eakins and Eakins, 1978). Sex differences in communication cannot be adequately covered in a book such as this. However, at points in subsequent chapters I draw attention to some of the different relating skills strengths and deficits of males and females. This is not to imply that all males and all females possess the same strengths and deficits: individual differences abound.

YOUR VALUES

In Chapters One and Two I mentioned some values or guiding principles for effective relating. However, you may also bring other values to your relationships. Your values influence how you interact with others. Also, you may be subject to value conflicts both within your values and between your and another's values.

A prominent measure of Western values is the Rokeach Value Survey (Rokeach, 1967). Rokeach saw values as conceptions of the desirable means and ends of action. The Rokeach Value Survey distinguishes between terminal values, or the ultimate end-goals of existence, and instrumental values, or the behavioural means for achieving such end goals. Between 1968 and 1981, American terminal values were highly stable. In 1981 the six most highly ranked terminal values were: a world at peace, family security, freedom, happiness, self-esteem and wisdom. Rokeach last surveyed American instrumental values in 1971, when the six most highly ranked values were being: honest, ambitious, responsible, forgiving, broad-minded and courageous (Rokeach and Ball-Rokeach, 1989).

Schwartz is another prominent researcher in the area of values (Schwartz, 1992; Schwartz and Bilsky, 1990). Schwartz classified values into ten types: power, achievement, hedonism, stimulation, self-direction, universalism, benevolence, tradition, conformity and security. Based on information from 20 countries in six continents, Schwartz (1992) confirmed each of the ten values was found in at least 90 per cent of the countries he surveyed, suggesting that his value types are near universal. Feather (1994) used the Schwartz Value Survey types in a study of Australian university students. He found that identification with Australia was positively related to the importance attached to the hedonism, security and achievement value types.

You can view yourself as possessing a profile of values or guiding principles for your life. This profile is composed of your values and the importance you attach to each. Below are some values that you and others, consciously or otherwise, bring to your relationships (Allport, Vernon and Lindzey, 1951; Holland, 1973; Maslow, 1970; Rokeach and Ball-Rokeach, 1989; Schwartz, 1992).

• *Survival.* Biological survival is the primary instinctive value, though other values sometimes override it, for example, patriotism or religious belief.

- *Love*. Loving and being loved; appreciating others for what they are and not just for what they do.

- *Friendship*. Being joined to others outside your family by mutual intimacy and interests.

- *Family life*. Having and being part of a family; valuing parenthood.

- *Religion*. Acknowledging the need for connectedness to some ultimate and superhuman power.

- *Achievement*. Being ambitious; valuing success, status and influence.

- *Materialism*. Valuing the accumulation and control of money.

- *Security*. Valuing financial security and social order.

- *Aesthetics*. Appreciating beauty and good taste, with special reference to the arts such as music, literature and painting.

- *Intellect*. Valuing analytical and rational pursuits.

- *Social interest*. Helping others; being benevolent and showing social concern.

- *Hedonism*. Valuing fun, pleasure and having a good time.

- *Excitement*. Valuing being daring and a varied and stimulating life.

- *Conformity*. Being obedient; respecting and honouring parents and authority figures.

- *Tradition*. Appreciating the status quo; accepting your position in life.

- *Career*. Valuing having a career and the work entailed.

- *Practical*. Valuing practical pursuits and, where practical matters are concerned, self-reliance.

- *Nature*. Appreciating and valuing being outdoors and in communion with nature.

- *Health*. Valuing being healthy and engaging in pursuits conducive to good health.

- *Self-direction*. Valuing autonomy, choosing your goals, and personal freedom.

- *Personal growth*. Being committed to personal development.

YOUR CULTURE AND CROSS-CULTURAL SKILLS

You bring cultural rules and assumptions to your relationships. Culture refers to the predominant pattern of a given group during a given period. Culture pervades every aspect of living: values, ethics, religion, language, food, table manners, music, clothing, attitudes towards democracy, sporting activities, family structures and relations, social relations and body language – to mention only some. Ho (1995) distinguished between internalized culture, the culture operating in the individual through enculturation, and the external culture or cultural group membership. Especially in a multicultural migrant country like Australia, your internalized culture may be influenced by parents who came from a different culture as well as by Australian culture.

Examples of cultural differences abound. For example, Ho (1985) observes that important Western values include emphasis on youth, assertiveness, independence and competition, whereas the corresponding Eastern values emphasize maturity, compliance, interdependence and cooperation.

Your cultural and ancestral roots

What are your cultural and ancestral roots? In Britain, there is a majority British culture, though there are many sub-cultures within it as well as many ethnic minority groups. The 1991 British census showed that the non-white ethnic minority population was just over 3 million or 5.5 per cent of the total population of 54.9 million. The largest individual ethnic minority group was Indian, constituting 1.5 per cent of the total population, or 27.9 per cent of the ethnic minority population as a whole. Pakistanis formed 0.9 per cent of the total population, 15.8 per cent of the ethnic minority population. Three black categories – Black Caribbean, Black African and Black other – combined formed 1.6 per cent of the total population, 29.5 per cent of the total ethnic minority population. Bangladeshis and Chinese each formed 0.3 per cent of the total population (Teague, 1993).

The 1991 Australian census found 265,000 people who identified as being of Aboriginal or Torres Strait Islander origin out of Australia's total population of 17.28 million. Though Australia's population is still primarily Anglo-Celtic, the census counted 3.8 million overseas-born people who were classified to 224 countries. A further 3.3 million people had one or both parents born overseas. Between 1947 and 1991, the proportion of the population born overseas increased from 10 per cent to 23 per cent. In the period 1947 to 1961, there was more than a sevenfold increase in migrants from continental Europe, while the number from the UK and Ireland increased by less than half.

More recently, there has been an increase in immigration from other countries, especially New Zealand, Viet Nam, China and the Philippines (Castles, 1993). In 1994, there were 77,490 permanent (settler arrivals) in Australia, of whom 19 per cent were born in Southeast Asia (Malaysia, Philippines, Viet Nam), 11 per cent in Northeast Asia (China, Hong Kong, Taiwan) and 8.2 per cent in Southern Asia (India, Sri Lanka) (Australian Bureau of Statistics, 1995). Asians are now the main migrant group, which reflects Australia's geographic location. In 1994, only 12.3 per cent of permanent (settler) arrivals were born in the United Kingdom. The Australian Bureau of Statistics estimated that, at the end of 1994, the resident population of Australia was nearly 18 million people.

Settler New Zealand culture also has its origins in Anglo-Celtic culture. New Zealanders are sometimes called the 'Poms of the Pacific.' However, Maoris constitute about 10 per cent of New Zealand's population of approximately 3.5 million. In 1994, 11.5 per cent of Australian permanent (settler) arrivals came from New Zealand.

Your cross-cultural awareness and skills

The message from the above figures is simple, Though there are undoubtedly national characteristics common to most Britishers, Australians and New Zealanders, awareness of cultural differences and the ability to build bridges across them are important relating skills. How aware are you of the extent and ways in which how you think, feel and behave has been conditioned by your cultural upbringing? You may possess cultural tunnel vision without knowing it.

You bring your cultural assumptions to your relationships with people from different cultures. The culture-deficit model assumes that the rules and values of the dominant or mainstream culture are normal. Variations observed in minorities are deficits (Rogoff and Morelli, 1989). The culture-sensitive model advocates respect for cultural differences and the positive features of cultural variation are emphasized.

You also bring your cross-cultural skills to your relationships. How good are you at helping people from different cultures share their cultural differences with you? Cross-cultural skills include: understanding the cultural meaning of verbal, voice and body messages; giving others permission to talk about their culture; and helping others work through cross- cultural mistrust and alienation.

YOUR RACE AND RACIAL SKILLS

You also bring your race to your relationships – whether you are Caucasian, Aboriginal, African, Asian, Polynesian or of mixed race. The 1991 British census showed that 94.5 per cent of the population were Caucasian, with the remaining 5.5 per cent being predominantly Asian and African (Teague, 1993). Though the majority of Australians are Caucasian, with immigration the proportion of Asians steadily increases. This development points to the possibility of Australia having a Eurasian future. New Zealanders are also predominantly Caucasian. However, the Maoris are Polynesian.

Your racial attitudes and skills

When you relate outside your racial group, you bring your attitudes towards your own and other races. You may have a racial learning history in which you have acquired negative thoughts and feelings about your own or other races or both. In Western societies, the main kind of racism is the belief in white genetic superiority over other racial groups. Racist assumptions and behaviours by whites can contribute to second-order racism whereby members of oppressed minority groups react with simplistic racial stereotypes of whites, for instance calling them 'Potatoes'.

Frequently, racial differences are highlighted by cultural differences. Much behaviour labelled racist stems from cultural rather than solely from racial differences. On the other hand, racial differences can disguise cultural similarities, as in the case of second and third generation Asian-Australians, sometimes known as 'Bananas' (yellow on the outside and white on the inside). In multiracial societies, it is important that you possess race-sensitive as well as culture-sensitive skills: for instance, giving people permission to share their views on the role of race in their lives and in their relationship with you.

YOUR SOCIAL CLASS AND SOCIAL CLASS SKILLS

Every society throughout the globe has its pecking order or status system. These are open to varying degrees of vertical mobility. Many people migrated to the Antipodes to get away from what they perceived as the stultifying traditional social class systems of Europe based on old money, landed estates, titles, schooling and accent.

Income, educational attainment and occupational status are currently three of the main measures of social class in Britain, Australia and New Zealand. Other indicators include schooling, accent, clothing, manners, nature of social networks, and type and location of housing. The social class into which you are born and raised influences: your chances of surviving at birth, your educational and occupational opportunities, whom you are likely to meet and to marry, how much money you are likely to make, how well your health is looked after and the quality of your funeral.

Social class can be an important consideration in starting and maintaining personal relationships. Those born on the 'wrong' or the 'right' side of town can feel awkward about going out with or marrying someone from the opposite side. Moreover, often families exert pressure on children to develop close relationships only within their own social class or a higher one.

Each of you brings your social class to your relationships. You also bring your sensitivity to the effect of others' social class on you and your social class on them. If you are insufficiently skilled, social class considerations may create unnecessary barriers between yourselves and others. An important social class thinking skill is to eliminate any feelings of inferiority or superiority on account of your social class. A useful social class action skill is the ability to handle resistances and negative messages resulting from others' social class insecurities.

CHAPTER HIGHLIGHTS

• You bring to your relationships your capacity to experience feelings. Dimensions of this capacity are: inhibiting and repressing feelings, internalizing others' feelings as if your own, carrying round unfinished business and listening to your feelings.

• You bring your sense of worth to your relationships. Also, you bring some debilitating anxieties along with some realistic ones. Debilitating anxieties include fears of failure, success and change.

• Aspects of physical health that people bring to relationships include: energy level, fitness, sickness and sickliness, managing stress skills, physical disability, fertility and mental illness.

• People differ in the strength of their sexual feelings, their capacity to experience them, their sexual likes and dislikes and their prior sexual experience.

• Survey results may underestimate the incidence of homosexuality. In a large-scale British survey 6.1 per cent of men and 3.4 per cent of women reported some homosexual experience.

- Your sex-role identity is how you see yourself on the dimensions of 'masculinity' and 'femininity'. Though nurture plays a large part in gender differences, the extent of innate biological differences between the sexes is an important research area.

- There is increasing emphasis on equality of choice and opportunity between the sexes and people's sex-role expectations are changing accordingly. Increases in women's labour force participation and work status provide evidence of changed sex-role expectations.

- You bring your values or philosophy of life to your relationships. You may be subject to value conflicts both within your values and between your and another's values.

- You bring your culture and cross-cultural skills to your relationships. You can either see minority cultures as inferior to the mainstream culture or value cultural diversity.

- Britain has a non-white racial population of 5.5 per cent. Australia is predominantly Caucasian, though the proportion of Asians steadily increases.

- Indicators of social class include: income, educational attainment, occupational status, schooling, accent, clothing, manners, nature of social networks and type and location of housing. You can develop skills of surmounting barriers to communication based on differences in social class.

EXERCISES

EXERCISE 4.1
HOW I LEARNED TO FEEL WORTHWHILE:
HELPFUL AND HARMFUL EXPERIENCES

Instructions

First do this exercise on your own. Then, if appropriate, discuss your answers with your partner, another or others.

This exercise aims to help you explore how you learned to feel either worthwhile or worthless as a person and how this effects you now. Think back over what you saw and experienced when you were growing up that influences the degree of self-esteem that you bring to your current relationships. Some of these experiences were helpful and constructive whereas others were harmful and destructive.

1. Take a piece of paper and head it LEARNING MY SENSE OF WORTH. Draw a line down the centre underneath this heading. At the top of the left-hand column write HELPFUL EXPERIENCES, at the top of the right-hand column write HARMFUL EXPERIENCES.

2. List five experiences that you consider were *helpful* in developing your sense of worth and capacity to love and that you would like to *repeat* with your children.

3. List five experiences that you consider were *harmful* in developing your sense of worth and capacity to love and that you would like to *avoid* with your children.

4. Summarize how secure and confident a person you feel now and how this affects your capacity to relate to others effectively.

EXERCISE 4.2
ASSESS MY RELATIONSHIP FEARS AND ANXIETIES

Instructions

First do this exercise on your own. Then, if appropriate, discuss with your partner, another or others.

Answer the following questions.

1. What fears and anxieties do you bring into your relationships in each of the following areas (if they apply to you):

- fear of failure,

- fear of success, and

- fear of change?

2. What fears and anxieties have you noticed other people bringing into their relationship with you?

3. What do you consider the effects of your own and others' anxieties have been on the quality of your relationships?

EXERCISE 4.3
ASSESS MY SEXUALITY
Instructions

First do this exercise on your own. Then, if appropriate, discuss with your partner, another or others.

Answer the following questions.

1. To what extent are you satisfied or dissatisfied with your capacity to experience and express your sexuality?

2. Think of your body image. To what extent are you satisfied or dissatisfied with your body from the viewpoint of sexual relating?

3. What is your sexual orientation and how do you know? If you are bisexual, identify the extent to which you are heterosexual or homosexual.

4. Do you bring any fears and anxieties about your sexuality into relationship(s) where sex may form a part? If so, be as specific as possible in identifying them.

5. Take a piece of paper and at the top write HOW I LEARNED ABOUT MY SEXUALITY. At the top of the left-hand column write HELPFUL EXPERIENCES and at the top of the right-hand column write HARMFUL EXPERIENCES. List important experiences that have helped or harmed you to express your sexuality effectively.

EXERCISE 4.4
HOW I LEARNED MY SEX-ROLE IDENTITY
Instructions

First do this exercise on your own. Then, if appropriate, discuss with your partner, another or others.

The way you think of yourself as 'masculine' or 'feminine' has been largely learned. Think back over your experiences as you were growing up and answer the following questions.

1. Did you get different toys on account of your sex? Illustrate with examples.

2. Did you get different clothes, including their colour, on account of your sex? Illustrate with examples.

3. What roles did your mother and father play in caring for you as a child?

4. Who did the following household tasks in your family?
Vacuum cleaning
Dusting
Shopping for food
Cooking meals
Washing dishes
Making beds
Polishing furniture
Washing clothes
Ironing
Mending clothes
Changing a fuse
Interior decoration
Exterior decoration
Mowing the lawn
Looking after the car

5. Either in your home or amongst your friends were you ever called a 'sissy' or a 'tomboy'? If so, provide an example.

6. Which of the following psychological characteristics do you consider each of your parents either encouraged you or discouraged you to show:
being analytical
gentleness
ambition
dominance
showing feelings of vulnerability
concern with your clothes
competitiveness
being nurturing
career orientation
home orientation

7. Did the books and magazines you read when growing up show males and females as having different psychological characteristics, interests and activities? Provide examples.

8. Did the TV programmes you watched when growing up show males and females as having different psychological characteristics, interests and activities? Provide examples.

9. Did the advertising you saw when growing up show males and females as having different psychological characteristics, interests and activities? Provide examples.

10. Which of the following activities were you encouraged to participate in at elementary school?
Football
Netball
Cooking
Needlework
Cricket

11. If you went to a co-educational elementary school, did your teachers treat girls and boys differently?

12. If you went to a co-educational secondary school, do you think boys and girls were encouraged differently in relation to choosing the following subjects?
Physics
Home economics
Computer studies
Languages
Mathematics

13. In your secondary school, assuming it was mixed, did boys and girls obtain (a) popularity and (b) high status from their peer group for the same or for different reasons? If different, specify in what ways.

14. Do you consider that your choice of occupation either has been or is being influenced by your sex? If so, specify how.

15. Summarize how you see your current sex-role identity. To what extent does it work either for or against you?

EXERCISE 4.5
ASSESS MY SEX-ROLE EXPECTATIONS
Instructions

First do this exercise on your own. Then, if appropriate, discuss with your partner, another or others.
   Answer the following questions

Part A
Taking initiatives

Below are a number of areas in female–male relationships where either or both of you may take the initiative:
Asking for a date
Ordering a meal
Paying the bill after eating out
Arranging to go to a movie
Arranging a vacation
Driving
Verbally expressing affection
Touching
Making love
Asking for support

1. To what extent are you prepared to take the initiative in each of the above areas?

2. To what extent do you have a double standard between yourself and the other sex in regard to taking initiatives in each of these areas?

Part B
Female–male roles

1. What do you think about equality of the sexes in each of the following areas?
Being the breadwinner
Having a career
Nurturing children
Disciplining children
Doing housework
Looking after the garden
Looking after the car(s)
Sexual behaviours
Explaining the facts of life to girls and boys
Showing feelings
Offering emotional support
Being able to dress in many colours
Getting custody of children after divorce
Engaging in professional and managerial work
Engaging in manual work, for example repairing roads
Being conscripted into the forces in time of war

Part C
Assess my sex-role expectations

1. Make a summary statement of the sex-role expectations that you bring to female–male relationships with people roughly your own age.
2. Do you think your current sex-role expectations help you or harm you in relating effectively with the other sex?

EXERCISE 4.6
ASSESS MY VALUES
Instructions

First do this exercise on your own. Then, if appropriate, discuss with your partner, another or others.

Using the following seven-point scale, rate the importance of each of the following values AS A GUIDING PRINCIPLE IN MY LIFE.

Rating scale

Of supreme importance	5
Very important	4
Important	3
Moderately important	2

Slightly important	1
Not important	0
Opposed to my values	−1

My rating   *Value*

_____ Survival

_____ Love

_____ Friendship

_____ Family life

_____ Religion

_____ Achievement

_____ Materialism

_____ Security

_____ Aesthetics

_____ Intellect

_____ Social interest

_____ Hedonism

_____ Excitement

_____ Conformity

_____ Tradition

_____ Career

_____ Practical

_____ Nature

_____ Health

_____ Self-direction

_____ Personal growth

1. Group your values according to your ratings.

2. To what extent are you satisfied with your values?

3. Are there any significant areas of conflict within your values?

4. If in a relationship, to what extent are your values compatible with those of your partner?

EXERCISE 4.7
ASSESS MY CULTURE, RACE AND SOCIAL CLASS
Instructions

First do this exercise on your own. Then, if appropriate, discuss with your partner, another or others.

Answer the following questions

Part A
Culture

1. Other than your national culture, from which ancestral culture(s) are you?

2. What behaviours and expectations do you possess that are related to your ancestral culture(s)?

3. What are the main problems that you experience in your relationships with people from different cultures?

4. Assess your skills strengths and deficits at relating to people from different cultures.

Part B
Race

1. From which race(s) are you?

2. What behaviours and expectations have you learned that are related to your race(s)?

3. What are the main problems that you experience in your relationships with people from different races?

4. Assess your skills strengths and deficits at relating to people from different races.

Part C
Social class

1. To what social class do you belong?

2. What behaviours and expectations do you possess that you related to your social class?

3. What are the main problems that you experience in your relationships with people from different social classes?

4. Assess your skills strengths and deficits at relating to people from different social classes.

EXERCISE 4.8
GROUP DISCUSSION: WHAT YOU BRING
TO RELATIONSHIPS
Instructions

This is intended as a group exercise, though it may be done individually or in pairs. For each part:

1. spend 10–15 minutes answering the question in groups of three or four,

2. each group shares its answers with the whole group,

3. then the whole group ranks the six most important points from the most important to the least important.

Part A
Most important characteristics

List the six most important characteristics that people bring to relationships.

Part B
Characteristics most difficult to influence

List the six characteristics that people bring to relationships in order of how difficult each is to change.

PART TWO

SKILLS

FIVE
Disclosing Skills

They do not love that do not show their love.
William Shakespeare

CHAPTER QUESTIONS

- *What are some skills for sending effective verbal messages?*
- *What are some dimensions of appropriate self-disclosure?*
- *What are some skills for sending effective voice messages?*
- *What are some skills for sending effective body messages?*
- *What are some considerations in touching another person?*
- *Why can actions speak louder than words?*
- *Why is it important to disclose by sending consistent messages?*

This chapter on disclosing yourself focuses on how you send action skills messages, sometimes intentional and sometimes unintentional, to others (Jourard, 1964). In relationships, being an effective sender of messages can have at least four important functions. First, you create and define yourself. Second, you influence how others respond to you. Third, you may help others to reveal themselves. Fourth, you reduce the chances of misunderstanding and increase the chances of working through genuine differences. In chapter 2, I divided action skills messages into five types: verbal, voice, body, touch and action messages. Here I elaborate on each of these ways of sending messages. In addition, I discuss sending genuine and consistent messages.

All relationship messages are encoded by senders and then decoded by receivers (Argyle, 1983). Mistakes can be made at both ends. Senders may not send the messages they wish to send. Much human communication is either poor or unintentional. Also, senders sometimes intentionally seek to deceive. At the receiving end people with poor listening skills may decode even the clearest of messages wrongly. However, you are much more likely to be misunderstood if you have poor disclosing skills.

The notion of social rules is important for both how you encode and decode messages (Argyle, 1991; Argyle & Henderson, 1985). Every group, however large or small, establishes rules for the expected behaviour of its members. Thus all your relationship behaviour – be it friendship, dating, copulating, being married, raising a family, working, pursuing leisure interests – is likely to be influenced by a network of social rules and expectations. In Britain and Australia, some rules apply to everyone: for example, saying 'hello', 'hi', 'good day' or 'G'day' on meeting someone. Other rules differ according to your sex: for instance, it is more OK for women to wear skirts than men and it may be more OK for men to interrupt than women. Still others vary according to your culture, for example, the greater emphasis both on face-saving and also on respect shown to older people in Asian cultures. In your relationships you have a choice as to whether you stick to the rules or, if necessary, establish ones that work better for you. For instance, Jock, 18, did not care for the rule that men should not show 'feminine' feelings, like caring. Consequently, he decided to become very emotionally literate regarding expressing, where appropriate, the full range of his feelings.

VERBAL MESSAGES

Verbal messages are messages you send with words. How skilled are you at using words? Are you able to find the right words for the right occasion or are you at a loss for words? Below are examples of people with *deficits* in their verbal message, or using words, skills.

> Sandra, 17, is very shy. She discloses little about herself and has few friends. People say she is too hard to get to know.

> Bob, 42, always seems to be promoting himself by stressing his accomplishments. His wife, July, 40, finds his boasting a turn-off, even though privately she acknowledges his ability.

> Steven, 24, has trouble getting on with people. He teases his colleagues and discusses other people negatively in their absence. His work-mates feel wary of his sharp tongue as does his partner Julia, 22.

Below are some examples of people with *strengths* in their skills of sending verbal messages.

> Naomi, 58, was told by her doctor that she needed a heart bypass operation. She was

able to talk about her situation and her fears to her husband, Col, family and close friends and was warmed by their support.

Anita, 26, had been wanting to have a chat with Paul, 29, for some time. Eventually, she found the courage to phone him. By the end of the phone call, they had arranged a date.

When a boy, Ross, 21, had been sexually abused by a close family friend. Ross thinks that his relationship with Ruth, 20, has deepened as a result of his sharing this 'secret'.

Sending 'I' messages

One verbal message skill is to take clear responsibility for speaking for yourself. Thomas Gordon (1970), in his book *Parent Effectiveness Training*, makes a useful distinction between 'You' messages and 'I' messages. 'You' messages focus on the other person and can be judgemental: for example, 'You don't love me' or 'You're selfish to ask me to play with you when I've only just got home'. 'I' messages are centred in you as the sender: for example: 'I do not feel loved by you' or 'I don't feel like playing with you just after I've got home.' When sending an 'I' message you clearly own your message.

You communicate more openly and honestly in relationships if you speak for yourself. A method of doing this is to send messages starting with the word 'I' when you choose to disclose feelings, thoughts and actions. Starting with the word 'I' has a number of advantages. First, you acknowledge that 'I' and 'You' are separate people and what I think or feel about you is my perception and not necessarily what you are. Second, you may feel better when you assume responsibility for what you say than when you do not. Third, you are less likely to get others' backs up. 'I' messages tend to cause less defensiveness than 'You' messages, with their connotations of blame. Fourth, if said directly, positive statements such as 'I love you' sound much more as though they come from your heart rather than from your head.

Disclosing yourself entails talking for yourself. Ways in which you may avoid sending 'I' messages include starting messages with words like 'You', 'People', 'We', 'They' and 'It'. Below are some examples of 'I' messages that are disguised and are not sent 'loud and clear'.

'Would you like the salt?'
'It just happened that my girlfriend got pregnant.'
'Would you like us to buy that painting?'
'You never help around the house.'
'Are you thick?'
'You're boring me.'

'A lot of people find you attractive.'
'You made me drive too quickly.'
'We're uneasy about your speech.'
'They want me to stand for public office.'

You can either send or fail to send 'I' messages in regard to your feelings, thoughts and actions. Here are some examples.

• *Owning a feeling.* Wendy and Denis are having a fight. Denis's non-'I' message is: 'You are the limit.' Denis's 'I' message is: 'I feel hurt and angry.'

• *Owning a thought.* Dawn and Stuart go to an art gallery and Dawn falls in love with a picture that she wants them to buy. Dawn's non-'I' message is: 'What did you think about that picture?' Dawn's 'I' message is: 'I really love that picture and want us to buy it.'

• *Owning an action.* Eddie scratched the side of the family car in the supermarket parking lot. Eddie's non-'I' message is: 'The side of the car got scratched in the supermarket parking lot.' Eddie's 'I' message is: 'I scratched the side of the car in the supermarket parking lot.'

I do not suggest that you never send non-'I' messages. You require flexibility. Nevertheless, when you wish to define yourself by sending messages about your feelings, thoughts and actions, usually you communicate more clearly when starting with the personal pronoun 'I'.

Disclosing personal information

Parent: 'Where have you been?'
Adolescent: 'Out.'
Parent: 'What did you do?'
Adolescent: 'Nothing.'

Michael Argyle

Think of yourself as an information database. From, birth you have been storing personal information about yourself. Therefore, one broad area of personal information you may choose to reveal or conceal concerns various aspects of your past. You also store a considerable amount of information about your present. In addition, you store information about your goals and dreams for the future.

Paraphrasing the 'To be or not to be?' dilemma raised by Shakespeare's Hamlet: 'To reveal or to not to reveal? That is the question.' All the time you choose what information to send about yourself. How skilled are you at letting others know you? All humans in varying degrees lead secret lives. Sometimes, even in long-standing marriages, partners know relatively little about one another. People can be highly concealing as well as revealing. Sometimes, they deliberately lie. Also, they may silently omit to tell any of the truth or economize on how much of it they tell.

Following are some reasons why good self-disclosure skills are fundamental to effective relationships.

• *Defining yourself.* Disclosing personal information lets you be known to others. If you do not define yourself, misunderstandings are more likely to occur. Another person may define you anyway, on their own rather than on your terms.

• *Knowing yourself.* As you talk about yourself you can get deeper insights and understandings about the sort of person you are. Also, you give others the opportunity to provide feedback.

• *Reaching out.* Talking about yourself, and letting others talk about themselves, gives each of you the chance to break out of your separateness and make contact. Each is given the opportunity to share and receive.

• *Developing intimacy.* A sharing of yourself is at the heart of intimacy. As you embark towards a deeper level of mutual disclosure: trust may be enhanced, misunderstandings cleared up, and each of you may become more comfortable about being open.

Appropriateness of disclosure

Derlega and Chaikin (1975) provide the following report of a college student commenting on another student who discloses too much personal information: 'There's this girl on my floor in the dormitory who's really weird – she tells people she's just met about really personal things, like all these guys she's sleeping with. Everyone tries to avoid her. I think she really needs help.' (p. 10). Underdisclosing and overdisclosing may each be skills deficits. Both extremes put others off. By concealing you are hard to get to know. You give little or nothing of yourself to others. By 'letting it all hang out' people know too much about you too soon. You impose on their goodwill and interest rather than revealing an amount that is comfortable for both of you.

Following are considerations relevant to the appropriateness of disclosing personal information.

• *Your goals.* What do you want from this stage of the relationships? What impression do you wish to make on the other and what reaction do you seek? Is revealing particular items of personal information likely to help you or harm you in attaining your goals?

• *Sensitivity to the receiver.* What is in it for people who listen to your disclosures? You need to balance respect for the wishes of listeners with your right to define yourself.

• *Topic area.* Topic areas are those in which you can reveal personal information. Taylor and Altman (1966) have suggested 13 broad areas for disclosure: religion; own marriage and family; love, dating and sex; parental family; physical condition and appearance; money and property; government, politics, current events and social issues; emotions and feelings; interests, hobbies and habits; relationships; attitude values, ethics and self-evaluation; school and work; and biographical characteristics. An additional area might be how you perceive your relating skills strengths and deficits!

• *Amount*. The quantity of personal information you reveal. For instance, within a given topic area you might reveal one, a few or many items of information.

• *Breadth*. The range of topic areas in which you reveal personal information. Also, the breadth of information you reveal within any single topic area.

• *Depth*. The degree of intimacy of your revelations. Here intimacy may be defined as your own and the other's perception of the amount of risk or personal threat attached to your disclosures.

• *Reciprocity*. If you follow another's disclosure with one of your own, does your intimacy match his or hers by being neither too shallow nor too deep?

• *Centrality*. How central or important is the personal information you reveal to your view of yourself.

• *Positive/negative*. Items of personal information you like and dislike about yourself.

• *Timing*. Revealing personal information in a relationship is a process in which timing is important. Timing can also refer to whether or not your disclosures are interrupting someone who is trying to disclose to you.

• *Accompanying messages*. How you frame or back up your disclosures of personal information by sending voice, body touch and/or action messages.

• *Target person(s)*. The person or persons to whom you reveal.

• *Social context*. The occasion or social context, with its accompanying rules, in which you reveal information.

Fears about disclosure

There are both risks and gains to revealing personal information (Nelson-Jones & Dryden, 1979). Earlier I suggested some gains. The risks, sometimes more imagined than real, include: being rejected; being misunderstood; lack of confidentiality; and disclosing too much too soon and having your disclosures used against you. You may also be afraid of the positive consequences of your disclosures: people may start liking you; you may be in a position of having to choose amongst girlfriends or boyfriends; and you might be entering your first intimate relationship and think: 'Help, how do I handle this?'

What items of personal information do people consider most negative? Stanley Strong and I asked 150 British undergraduates to rate 120 items on a positive/negative scale 'if this item were true for me' (Nelson-Jones & Strong, 1977). The 12 most negatively rated items were:

> 'I hate myself'
> 'I have attempted suicide'

'I am violent'
'I have suicidal thoughts'
'I am a homosexual/lesbian'
'I am dull'
'I often hurt people I care about'
'I am erotically attracted by some men (male question)/women (female question)'
'I pity myself'
'I am a hypocrite'
'I am generally uninteresting'
'I have a "fear" of the opposite sex'

In general males and females evaluated these characteristics much the same. Differences existed in how people responded to the same item: for instance, gayness can be a source of pride or shame. Furthermore, the fact that people rate a characteristic of themselves very negatively it does not necessarily mean that they are going to be so hard on others who disclose it to them.

The difference between what you think of your personal characteristics and how others react to your disclosures may be even more pronounced if you reveal what you like about yourself. Revealing positive characteristics risks being viewed as self-promotion and boasting. It can threaten others. You run less risk if you intermingle negative with positive disclosures than if you consistently extol your virtues (Nelson-Jones & Strong, 1976). Many people, with some justification, have fears about revealing positive personal information.

Cultural and sex-role considerations

Many broader contextual considerations influence how much and in what ways people reveal themselves. With over a third of British and Australian first marriages ending in divorce people feel less inhibited in talking about their own or their parents' divorces than previously. There are also differences between cultures. For example, British female undergraduate students have been found to disclose less than their American counterparts (Jourard, 1971). Furthermore differences have been found between the sexes, with women tending to be more revealing than men (Argyle, 1991; Cozby, 1973, Jourard, 1971). This may partly be because there are dissimilar expectations regarding the appropriateness of males' and females' levels of disclosure. The 'strong silent' role may be perceived as more likeable for males, whereas females may be more favourably evaluated when they are expressive and revealing (Chelune, 1976). Loneliness, through skills deficits in revealing personal information, appears to be more a problem for males than it is for females. However, females may also feel lonely if and when males fail to reciprocate the intimacy of their disclosures. Again, I stress that there are individual differences amongst both males and females. Any generalizations based on sex must be treated cautiously.

VOICE MESSAGES

It ain't what you say, but how you say it.

Anon

When talking about yourself, you communications consist of voice and body *framing* messages which may or may not match your verbal messages, the *literal* content of what you say. These framing messages are extremely important. Your voice and body framing messages can either correspond to, heighten, lessen or contradict the intention of your verbal messages. For instance, Pattie may be saying 'Everything is all right in my relationship with Jeffrey' at the same as time talking with a choked voice and frowning. Here, it does not take an expert decoder to surmise that everything is not all right. Before going on his first date with Emma, Todd says 'I'm feeling pretty confident' in a quick, shallow voice and with a nervous smile. How both Pattie and Todd fame their verbal messages speaks more loudly than what they actually say.

If you can control your voice messages, you have acquired a very useful skill in dealing with others. Your voice messages can speak volumes about what you truly feel and how emotionally responsive you are to others' feelings. You can avoid your voice messages communicating differently to how you would like: for instance, sending mildly angry verbal messages too harshly.

Your voice messages can give skilled observers insight into your capacity to experience your feelings. Often people out of touch with their feelings speak in flat and monotonous ways, even though using words expressing strong feelings. Others show their anxiety by coming on far too loud and strong. Below are examples of people communicating feelings by means of voice messages.

> When he goes on dates Bill, 16, feels scared and speaks very quickly.
>
> When talking on the phone with her mother Tiffany, 35, is nervous and speaks quietly and with many pauses.
>
> Alison, 57, feels very depressed and speaks in a slow and monotonous voice.
>
> Ray, 23, is mad as hell with Carolyn, 23, and screams and shouts at her.
>
> Linda, 19, is bored with Guy, 18, and says with little emphasis 'I still love you'.

Following are five dimensions of voice messages. They form the acronym VAPER – volume, articulation, pitch, emphasis and rate.

• *Volume*. Volume refers to loudness or quietness. You need to disclose at a level of audibility that is comfortable and easy to hear. Some people let their voices trail away at the end of sentences. Some unnecessarily quieten their voices to match other people's voices. Though a booming voice overwhelms, speaking too quietly may communicate that you are a 'wimp'. A firm and confident voice is a good starting point from which you can make variations as appropriate, for instance by speaking more gently or more loudly.

• *Articulation*. Articulation refers to the clarity of your speech. You are easier to understand if you enunciate words well. People who possess excessively nasal, guttural or throaty voices might consider speech therapy. If repeatedly misunderstood, people with strong regional or overseas accents should consider modifying them.

• *Pitch*. Pitch refers to the height or depth of your voice. An optimum pitch range includes all the levels at which a pleasing voice can be produced without strain (Kruger, 1970). Errors of pitch include either being too high pitched or too low pitched.

• *Emphasis*. It is important that your voice is expressive when sharing your feelings and feelings nuances and also when responding to others' feelings. You may use too much emphasis and seem melodramatic or too little emphasis and come across as wooden. In addition, you may use emphasis in the wrong places.

• *Rate*. Often speech rate is measured by words per minute. Your speech rate depends not only on how quickly you speak words, but on the frequency and duration of pauses between them. If you speak very quickly, you may appear anxious and others may have difficulty understanding you. On the other hand, too ponderous a speech rate can be boring.

BODY MESSAGES

Both when speaking and listening you disclose yourself through your body message skills. For instance, whether speaking or listening, if you continue looking out of the window without good reason, you send a negative message. Following are some of the main forms of body messages.

• *Availability*. Woody Allen is reported to have joked that 'Ninety per cent of life is just turning up.' You need be physically present according to the rules of your different relationships. In addition, you should send clear messages about your availability. Unintentionally, you may send messages that either distance others or invite unwanted intrusions.

• *Facial expression*. Facial expressions are perhaps the main vehicle for sending body messages. Ekman, Friesen and Ellsworth (1972) have found that there are seven main facial expressions of emotion: happiness, interest, surprise, fear, sadness, anger and disgust or contempt. Your mouth and eyebrows can convey much information: for instance, 'down in the mouth' and 'raised eyebrows'. There are display rules which indicate which facial expressions can be shown when: for instance, at funerals down-turned mouths are more appropriate than up-turned ones – even for people who are only at the funeral to make sure that the corpse is really dead!

• *Gaze and eye contact.* Gaze, or looking at other people in the area of their faces, is both a way of showing interest and also a way of collecting facial information. Speakers look at listeners about 40 per cent of the time and listeners look at speakers about 70–75 per cent of the time (Argyle, 1992). Argyle observes: 'Gaze is closely coordinated with speech: speakers look just before the end of utterances, and at major grammatical breaks, in order to collect feedback on listener reactions' (1992, p. 11). Women are more visually attentive than men in all measures of gaze (Henley, 1977; Argyle, 1983, 1991).

There are cultural differences in gaze. In the 'contact cultures' of the Arab world, Latin America and Southern Europe, the amount of gaze is high. Too little gaze is seen as impolite and insincere. However, 'in non-contact' cultures like North America, Northern Europe and Asia, a high amount of gaze may threaten (Watson, 1972). In fact, the Japanese when conversing may gaze at the neck rather than at the face (Pease, 1981).

Eye contact is a more direct way of sending messages, be they of interest, anger or sexual attraction. Seeing 'eye to eye' is better than having 'shifty eyes'. The dilation of pupils is another source of eye messages: dilated pupils can indicate 'bedroom eyes' or sexual interest, while undilated pupils may get decoded as 'beady little eyes'.

• *Gestures.* Gestures are physical movements that can frame or illustrate words coming before, during or after what is being said. Gestures may have no meaning on their own. Argyle (1983) suggests four functions of gestures that accompany speech: displaying the structure of the utterance by enumerating elements or showing how they are grouped; pointing to people or objects; providing emphasis; and giving illustrations of shapes, sizes or movements, particularly when these are difficult to describe in words. An example of a gesture used to show an emotion, with or without words, is the clenched fist for aggression.

Gestures can also take the place of words: for example, nodding your head either up-and-down or sideways for saying 'yes' or 'no', respectively. As an experiment that highlights the power of your conditioning, alternate between shaking your head sideways as you say 'yes' and nodding your head up and down as you say 'no'. How did you feel and what did you think about doing that?

Gestures, have different meanings in different cultures. In Greece, people toss their heads back to say 'no'. The 'A-Okay' sign in North America of thumb-and-forefinger-in-a-circle means in France and Belgium, 'You're worth nothing', and in Southern Italy either 'You arsehole' or signifies that you desire anal sex (Ekman, Friesen and Bear, 1984). In addition, how you gesture can vary according to your sex. Eakins and Eakins (1978) suggest that men's gestures are larger, more sweeping and forceful, while women's gestures are smaller and more inhibited.

• *Posture.* Your posture may convey various messages. If you are confident you may 'walk tall'. When feeling less confident you may not stand so erect, put your chest out, or square your shoulders. Height tends to be associated with status: for instance, you 'talk down to' or 'talk up to' someone. Children and women may be at a disadvantage unless another's body posture is changed: for instance, by either crouching to be at the same level as children or sitting down. Turning your body towards someone is more encouraging than turning away from them. Also, whether you lean forwards or backwards may indicate interest or disinterest.

Posture may also communicate how anxious you are: for instance, sitting with your arms and legs tightly crossed suggests that you are emotionally as well as literally uptight. However, especially if you are female, you may appear too relaxed: males may mistakenly perceive uncrossed and open legs as a sign of sexual availability whether the woman wears a skirt, trousers or jeans. Such perceptions manifest a double standard in how people decode body messages.

• *Clothing and grooming.* If clothes do not make the woman, man or child, they certainly send many messages about them. These messages include: social and occupational standing, sex-role identity, ethnicity, conformity to peer group norms, rebelliousness, how outgoing you are and your sexuality. Often, people dress for effect. They wish to influence others' impressions of them. A young man who goes to a party in a sober blue suit defines himself very differently to a young 'stud' in tight jeans that outline his genitals. Children, also, are quick to decode clothing cues. In one study of fourth- and sixth-grade children, they attributed different personalities to other children depending upon what jeans they wore; the options being a designer brand, a medium-price traditional brand and an inexpensive brand (Solomon, 1986).

Your personal grooming also provides important information about how well you take care of yourself and how you wish others to see you. For instance, you may be clean or dirty, tidy or untidy and smelly or fresh. Additionally, the length, styling and care of your hair sends messages about you.

• *Proximity.* The degree of physical proximity that is comfortable for Britons, Australians and North Americans is generally the same (Hall, 1966; Pease, 1981). The zones vary according to the nature of the relationship.

1. *Intimate zone* (between 6 to 18 inches). Here it is easy to touch and be touched. This zone is reserved for spouses, lovers, close friends and relatives.

2. *Personal zone* (between 18 and 48 inches). This zone is appropriate for less close friends and for parties and other social gatherings.

3. *Social zone* (between 4 to 12 feet). This zone is comfortable with shopkeepers, tradespeople and for people not known at all well.

4. *Public zone* (over 12 feet). This is the distance for addressing public gatherings.

People stand or sit closer to those whom they like. Men may be readier to enter a woman's space than the reverse and women more ready to move out of the way (Eakins and Eakins, 1978). There are also large cross-cultural differences: for instance, Arabs and Latin Americans stand very close. Physical distance is also used in starting and ending conversations: for instance, you go up to someone to start a conversation and edge away as a signal to finish one.

TOUCH MESSAGES

You disclose yourself through your touch skills. In touching another you are in their close intimate zone. Touch connects humans in a most fundamental way. In parent-child relationships touch offers security, tenderness and affection. Touch is a major way in which adults can demonstrate protection, support and caring for each other. These are numerous social rules and taboos regarding who may touch, which parts of the body, when. Females may feel freer to touch other females than males to touch other males (Jourard, 1971).

Touch messages can be positive or negative. Positive touch messages are those which the recipients appreciate. Affection and tenderness may be expressed through: a light touch on the hand, arm or shoulder; holding hands; walking arm in arm; an arm over the shoulders; a caress on the side of the face; a semi-embrace; a warm hug; and a kiss on the cheek or mouth, to mention but some ways.

Negative touch messages are those which, with varying degrees of severity, violate another's physical and psychological well-being. Women, men and children can be the victims of negative touch messages. Though occasionally males are raped by females (Timnick, 1983), the vast majority of rapes are done by males. Sexual harassment is almost entirely a problem for females being crudely and insensitively treated by males, though this may change somewhat as women get more power. Most child sexual abuse, be it of girls or boys, is perpetrated by males. Though wives may sometimes punch, scratch and throw things at their husbands, acts of domestic physical violence are mainly committed by males. Within their own sex, males more than females, are likely to send negative touch messages by pushing, shoving and hitting. In short, blatant negative touch messages are predominantly male skills deficits. However, there are other negative touch messages, like hurtful and aggressive pushing away of affection, that are the preserve of both females and males. Also, sometimes both sexes send mixed touch messages and require skills of accentuating the positive and eliminating the negative.

ACTION MESSAGES

Actions speak louder than words.

Anon.

In today's slang, your actions are 'the bottom line'. Here action messages are defined as what you do when not in the presence of another. Action messages are crucial in the development of trust. If you say you are going to do something, do you actually do it? People have differing levels of skill at sending action messages. For instance, if you go overseas and want to maintain a relationship with someone at home while you are away, you can send action messages through letters and phone calls. If you fail to do so, your relationship may suffer.

Promises, promises, promises. A good definition of a 'phoney' is someone whose action messages fall far short of their verbal, voice and body messages. The importance of sending good action messages in initiating, developing and maintaining effective relationships cannot be over-emphasized. Below are a few illustrations of people's actions not matching their words.

> Martin, 48, tells his son, Chris, 18, that he will back him whatever career he chooses. When Chris declares he wants to train as a ladies' hairdresser, Martin refuses to offer him any financial or moral support.
>
> Gina, 24, has repeatedly told her partner Greg, 26, that she is no longer prepared to wash the dishes all the time. Every time Greg breaks his agreement to do his share of the washing up, Gina ends up washing the dishes herself.
>
> Shirley, 39, is a university lecturer who has just published a book stressing the importance of family life and loyalties. She is married with two young children. Gradually it emerges that, when writing the book, she was conducting an affair with Glenn, 28, another staff member in her department.
>
> Fred, 22, says he believes in equality of the sexes. However, when he goes out on a date, he always insists on paying.

Each of the above vignettes illustrates a major theme where actions can contradict words.

• *Control.* You may talk respect for the individuality of your loved ones and yet act in possessive and controlling ways towards them.

• *Lack of assertion.* Assertion entails, where appropriate, backing up your words with your actions.

• *Infidelity.* Being faithful to someone's trust in you entails keeping your formal and informal contracts or else openly attempting to renegotiate them.

• *Inequality.* Equality means that both sexes may have to alter some of their traditional behaviours that influence the balance of power in their relationship.

GENUINENESS: SENDING CONSISTENT MESSAGES

Things are seldom what they seem,
Skim milk masquerades as cream.
Externals don't portray insides,
Jekylls may be masking Hydes.

Sidney Jourard

Since humans can send messages in so many different ways, genuineness becomes important. Above I gave illustrations of people with skills deficits in having their actions match their words. When sending messages you can be deceiving others, yourself or both (Ekman & Friesen, 1969). However, human communication is often more complex than this and involves shades of grey. If you have good skills of sending messages 'loud and clear', your voice and body messages match your words. Also, if relevant, so do your touch and action messages. If you fail to send consistent verbal, voice and body messages, you make it harder for listeners to decode your communications accurately. Also, you increase their chances of perceiving you as insincere.

The skill of disclosing genuinely requires you to send honest and consistent messages. When growing up you may have learned to mask many of your thoughts and feelings by choosing not to express them with either your words, voice or body. However, sometimes you deceive yourself more than others since the meaning of your words points in one direction and your body and voice messages point in another.

Below is an example of Ted, 41, who has good disclosing feelings skills talking about the recent death of his mother. His sadness is communicated consistently by means of his verbal, voice, and body messages.

- *Verbal messages.* Words Ted uses include: 'I feel sad, low, miserable, unhappy, depressed.' Phrases he uses include: 'I feel really low', and 'I feel a huge gap in my life'.

- *Voice messages.* Ted's voice messages include speaking slowly and quietly.

- *Body messages.* Ted's body messages include turning down the corners of his mouth and looking tearful.

CHAPTER HIGHLIGHTS

- All relationship messages are encoded by senders and decoded by receivers.

- You possess skills strengths and deficits at disclosing yourself through verbal or word messages.

- When you send 'I' messages you speak for yourself. 'I' messages can own feelings, thoughts or actions.

- Disclosure of personal information can be about your past, present or future.

- Considerations in appropriateness of disclosing personal information include: your goals, sensitivity to the receiver, topic area, amount of disclosure, breadth, depth, reciprocity, centrality, positive/negative, timing, accompanying messages, target person(s) and social context.

• People can have realistic and unrealistic fears about disclosing both negative and positive personal information.

• You can have voice message skills strengths and deficits in the following areas: volume, articulation, pitch, emphasis and speech rate.

• Important body message skills include: availability, facial expression, gaze and eye contact, gestures, posture, clothing and grooming and proximity.

• Touch messages, which can be positive or negative, are a special kind of body message. Negative touch messages include rape, sexual abuse and physical violence.

• Action messages may or may not match other kinds of messages. If your actions do not match your words, this can seriously undermine trust.

• Lack of genuineness means that you are sending messages that deceive others, yourself or both.

• Genuine disclosure requires skills of sending honest and consistent messages. Your voice and body messages match your words. Also, if relevant, so do your touch and action messages.

EXERCISES

EXERCISE 5.1
SEND 'I' MESSAGES
Instructions

This exercise may be done either on your own or with your partner, another or others.

1. Change each of the following non-'I' message statements into 'I' message statements.
'Would you like the salt?'
'Would you like us to buy that painting?'
'Are you thick?'
'A lot of people find you attractive.'
'It just happened that my girlfriend got pregnant.'
'You never help around the house.'
'You're boring me.'
'You made me drive too quickly.'
'They want me to stand for public office.'

2. Assess your strengths and deficits in the skill of sending 'I' messages.

3. Make and implement a plan to improve your sending 'I' message skills.

EXERCISE 5.2
DISCLOSE PERSONAL INFORMATION
Instructions

Part A
Assessment

1. Assess your skills strengths and deficits in revealing personal information.

2. Think of either a personal or a work relationship that might be improved by your disclosing more personal information.

3. Use the following rating scale. Rate how threatening it would be for you in this relationship to reveal each item of personal information listed below.

4	Impossible, much too threatening
3	Very threatening
2	Moderately threatening
1	Slightly threatening
0	Not threatening at all
N/A	Not applicable

Rating Personal information areas

_____ Positive thoughts/feelings about my parents

_____ Negative thoughts/feelings about my parents

_____ Positive thoughts/feelings about the other person

_____ Negative thoughts/feelings about the other person

_____ Problem areas in our relationship

_____ Feelings of loneliness

_____ Feelings of inadequacy

_____ Feelings of depression

_____ Failures in my work

_____ Successes in my work

_____ Work habits

_____ Successes in my personal relationships

_____ Failures in my personal relationships

_____ Things I like about my body

_____ Things I dislike about my body

_____ Leisure interests

_____ Feelings about death

_____ Religious beliefs

_____ Political preferences

_____ Past sexual experiences

_____ Sexual fantasies

_____ Masturbation behaviours

_____ Homosexual tendencies

_____ Intellectual ability

_____ Musical preferences

_____ Financial position

_____ Times I have lied/cheated

_____ Things that make me happy

_____ Things that make me miserable

_____ Things that make me angry

_____ Things that make me afraid

_____ My goals in life

_____ My central values

_____ How worthwhile I feel

_____ The people I love

_____ The people I hate

_____ My peak experiences in life

Part B
Practice – Disclose personal information in a group

1. *Pairs exercise.* Work with a partner. First Partner A, using 'I' statements such as 'I am intelligent', spends a prearranged period of time, say two minutes, describing himself/herself to Partner B so that Partner B can get to know him/her. Then, reverse roles. Be conscious of how you choose to define yourself by what you reveal and conceal.

2. *Group exercises*
(a) An extension of the above pairs exercise is for partners to introduce themselves or each other to the group.
(b) Each person stands up in front of the group, say for 90 seconds or two minutes, and introduces themselves. They may then have a set period of time for answering questions.
(c) Group members can fill out a yellow 'post-it' sheet with information about themselves. They pin or stick their information on their fronts. Then they circulate and hold brief conversations with as many people in the group as they can within a set period, say 15 minutes.

Part C
Practice – Disclose personal information in a relationship

1. State as specifically as possible the change or changes you wish to make in how much you disclose in the relationship you chose in Part A.

2. Plan how you will disclose this information, for instance when and how you will do so.

3. Indicate the specific consequences for yourself and the other person that you predict will follow from disclosing this additional personal information.

4. Implement your plan to disclose more.

5. Assess the positive and negative consequences for yourself and the other person of disclosing more personal information. Have your predictions been confirmed or negated? Has this exercise taught you something about how you can strengthen your disclosing personal information skills? If so, what?

EXERCISE 5.3
DISCLOSE THROUGH VOICE MESSAGES
Instructions
Part A
Assess my voice messages

1. Assess the strengths and deficits of your voice message skills in the following areas. You may wish to cassette record and play back your speech for evidence.

MY VOICE MESSAGES

Area	Skills strengths	Skills deficits
Volume		
Articulation		
Pitch		
Emphasis		
Speech rate		

2. Ask at least two people who know you well to give you feedback on whether and how your voice messages could be improved.

3. Summarize the strengths and deficits in your voice message skills. Then specify voice message skills that you wish to change.

Part B
Practice – Develop my voice messages in a group

1. *Pairs exercise*. Each person targets a specific voice message skill that they wish to improve. Members work on developing their targeted voice message skills.
2. *Group exercise*. Members get into a larger group and each has a turn in which he/she identifies his/her targeted voice message skill, makes a few 'I' statements to the group using that skill and then gets feedback from the group.

Part C
Practice – Develop my voice messages in a relationship

1. Identify a specific relationship in which you could improve your voice message skills.

2. State as specifically as possible the change or changes you wish to make in your voice messages: for instance, 'Speaking much louder'.

3. Plan how you implement the change(s) in your voice messages, for instance when and in what situations.

4. Indicate the specific consequences for yourself and the other person that you predict will follow from your change in voice messages.

5. Implement your plan to change your voice messages.

6. Assess the positive and negative consequences for yourself and the other person of changing your voice messages. Have your predictions been confirmed or negated? Has this exercise taught you something about how you can strengthen your voice message skills? If so, what?

EXERCISE 5.4
DISCLOSE THROUGH BODY MESSAGES
Instructions

Part A Assess my body messages

1. Assess the strengths and deficits of your body message skills in the following areas.

MY BODY MESSAGES

Area	Skills strengths	Skills deficits
Availability		
Facial expression		

Area	Skills strengths	Skills deficits
Gaze and eye contact		
Gestures		
Posture		
Clothing and grooming		
Proximity		

2. Ask two people who know you well to give you feedback on your strengths and deficits in sending body messages.

3. To what extent do you think your body messages are affected by your cultural and sex-role conditioning?

Part B
Practice – Develop a body message skill in a group

1. *Pairs exercise.* Each person picks a particular body message skill they want to improve, specifies a behaviour change goal, and rehearses their targeted skill.

2. *Group exercise.* Group members take turns in demonstrating their targeted body message skills and getting feedback.

Part C
Practice – Develop my body messages in a relationship

1. For a specific relationship, identify one or more body message skills that you wish to change.

2. Specify one or more behaviour change goals that are attainable.

3. Rehearse your targeted body message skill(s) either on your own or with a third party.

4. Implement your changed body message behaviour(s) in the relationship and evaluate how successful you were. If appropriate, modify your behaviour(s) in light of feedback.

EXERCISE 5.5
DISCLOSE FEELINGS THROUGH VERBAL, VOICE, BODY, TOUCH AND ACTION MESSAGES

Instructions

First, do this exercise on your own. Then, if appropriate, discuss with your partner, another or others.

1. For each of the following feelings write down:

a. verbal messages

b. voice messages

c. body messages

d. touch messages (if appropriate)

e. action messages (if appropriate)

which a partner could use to express the feeling genuinely in a close personal relationship.

Love
   verbal messages
   voice messages
   body messages
   touch messages
   action messages

Anger
Fear
Happiness
Boredom
Shame
Depression

2. Are there some feelings you find easier to disclose genuinely than others? Specify which feelings are easy and which feelings are difficult for you to disclose.

3. Assess your strengths and deficits in the skills of disclosing your feelings genuinely and consistently.

EXERCISE 5.6
GROUP DISCUSSION:
DISCLOSING SKILLS

Instructions

This is intended as a group exercise, though it may be done individually or in pairs. For each part:

1. spend 10–15 minutes answering the question in groups of three or four,

2. each group shares its answers with the whole group,

3. then the whole group ranks the six most important points from the most important to the least important.

Part A
Disclosing yourself

List the six most important ways that people can disclose themselves in their relationships.

Part B
Identifying insincerity

List the six most important ways that people can identify another's insincerity in their relationships.

SIX
Listening Skills

The reason why we have two ears
and only one mouth is that we may
listen the more and talk the less.
Zeno of Citium

CHAPTER QUESTIONS

- *What is rewarding listening and why is it important?*

- *What does it mean to possess an attitude of respect and acceptance?*

- *How can you tune in to another's internal viewpoint?*

- *How can you send good voice messages?*

- *How can you show interest through body messages?*

- *How can you use opening remarks, small rewards and open-ended questions?*

In distressed relationships, common cries are: 'You don't understand me' and 'You never listen.' The next two chapters focus on rewarding listening skills. Listening is one of the most powerful psychological rewards that you can give. However, with how many people can you be open and share the secrets of your heart? Some readers may answer none. Most people are short of confidants who genuinely listen. Varying degrees of unrewarding listening are widespread. Occasionally not being listened to may create mild psychological pain; often not being listened to, moderate pain; and mostly not being listened to, severe pain. Never being listened to is like a psychological death penalty.

Defining rewarding listening

A distinction may be made between hearing and listening. *Hearing* involves the capacity to be aware of and to receive sound. *Listening* involves not only receiving sounds but, as much as possible, accurately understanding their meaning. However, you can listen accurately without being a rewarding listener. *Rewarding listening* entails not only accurately understanding speakers' communications, but showing and, where necessary, clarifying your understanding. As such, rewarding listening involves both receiver and sender skills.

Four kinds of listening take place in any two-person conversation. Listening takes place both between persons and within each of them (Gendlin, 1981; Nelson-Jones, 1986). Indeed the quality of your inner listening, or being appropriately sensitive to your own thoughts and feelings, may be vital to the quality of your outer listening. If you listen either poorly or too much to yourself, you listen less well to others. Conversely, if you listen well to others, this may help the quality of their inner listening. Following is a saying of Lao-Tse that beautifully illustrates this point:

> *It is as though he/she listened*
> *and such listening as his/hers enfolds us in a silence*
> *in which at last we begin to hear*
> *what we are meant to be.*

Importance of rewarding listening

Following are some reasons why it is important that you work to develop and maintain your rewarding listening skills.

• *Making contact.* Often the people you meet are shy and anxious. Trust may not come easily. If you listen well to them, you increase the chances that they will feel comfortable, safe and understood by you. Your skills help them to disclose personal information and share their thoughts and feelings. If you use poor listening skills, you set up blocks to starting relationships. Perhaps the major find from research into self-disclosure, is that intimacy levels of disclosures tend to be matched (Cozby, 1973). Your gradually telling your secrets and my gradually telling you mine is a process that depends on us being willing to listen to each other as well as to disclose. Trust is built as much from acceptance of our disclosures as from our willingness to disclose.

• *Knowing another.* Erich Fromm in *The Art of Loving* states that there are common elements in all forms of love: care, responsibility, respect and knowledge. Relating closely to another person involves knowing their separateness and prizing it. You know them on their terms. In close relationships such knowledge 'does not stay at the periphery, but penetrates to the core' (Fromm, 1956, p. 27). Rewarding listening allows another to feel safe and to strip away the social masks that they wear for protection. You no longer need make so many assumptions about what they think and feel since they tell you anyway. Also, no one can know the weight of another's burden unless told.

• *Knowing yourself.* Listening effectively to others provides you with valuable information about yourself. Though you may not always like what you hear, remaining open to feedback gives you the opportunity to change. Also, if others listen well to you, it gives you the opportunity to experience and explore your thoughts and feelings.

• *Maintaining relationships*. Once you start a relationship, skilled listening and disclosing helps maintain it. Relationships are ongoing conversations. Happy couples are skilled at taking an interest in one another's lives. They use their listening skills to transcend their narcissism and show their respect and concern for each other. Many of their conversations are mutually satisfying.

In addition, rewarding listening builds trust and stability by helping partners prevent and manage problems. If partners are able to say what they think and feel, misunderstandings are less likely to occur. Furthermore, if partners listen well to each other, they stand a much better chance of resolving difficulties to their mutual satisfaction.

Poor listening skills interfere with relationship maintenance. Defensiveness or tuning out information that clashes with your picture of yourself corrodes a relationship as does switching off to your partner. You and your partner may replace an *open* communication system, in which you share what you think and feel, with a *closed* communication system. Here you may tiptoe around each other's fragile egos at the expense of honesty. During this process, you can become progressively alienated from yourselves and one another through not having the courage to provide and listen to feedback.

• *Bridging differences*. Every person has a potential set of blinkers depending upon her or his circumstances. How can you know what it is like to be old, dying, female, male, gay, physically disabled, an immigrant, White, Black, Asian, Aboriginal or Maori…if the description does not fit you? However, if you relate to someone with a different set of life's circumstances, she or he can greatly assist you to understand them if you use good listening skills. Similarly, if she or he listens skilfully to you, together you build bridges and not walls.

REWARDING LISTENING: A TEN-SKILLS APPROACH

The remainder of this and most of the next chapter describe ten key skills of being a rewarding listener. Some of the skills overlap. Each of these skills requires you to make choices. The skills are not presented in any rigid order of importance.

Skills of rewarding listening

Skill 1. Possess an attitude of respect and acceptance.

Skill 2. Tune in to the speaker's internal viewpoint.

Skill 3. Send good voice messages.

Skill 4. Send good body messages.

Skill 5. Use opening remarks, small rewards and open-ended questions.

Skill 6. Paraphrase.

Skill 7. Reflect feelings.
Skill 8. Clarify by questioning.
Skill 9. Clarify by challenging.
Skill 10. Avoid listening blocks.

SKILL 1
POSSESS AN ATTITUDE OF RESPECT AND ACCEPTANCE

An accepting attitude involves respecting others as separate human beings with rights to their own thoughts and feelings. Fromm (1956) notes that respect comes from the Latin word *respicere* meaning to look at. Respect means the ability to look at others as they are and to prize their unique individuality. Respect also means allowing other people to grow and develop on their own terms without exploitation and control.

The extent to which you are able to respect and accept yourself is reflected in the level of acceptance and respect, and hence the listening skills, you can offer another. Table 6.1 depicts the relationship between your level of self-acceptance and how much you can accept others on their terms. The table is a simplification because in close personal relationships you will be put to the test when in conflict. Unless you discipline yourself, the acceptance that underlies skilful listening can be the first casualty of an angry conflict. Consequently, self-acceptance should be extended to mean accepting yourself enough to control your temper and stay tuned in to another when the going gets rough.

Table 6.1 Relationship between level of self-acceptance and ability to accept others

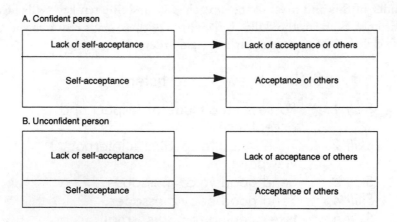

BARRIERS TO AN ACCEPTING ATTITUDE

An accepting attitude involves respecting others as separate and unique human beings. This does not mean that you agree with everything they say. However you are secure enough in yourself to respect what they say as their versions of reality. You do not need to use barriers and filters to protect you from listening to the full range of their messages. These barriers can be internal and external. Internal barriers operate on, distort and filter out certain elements of the messages you receive. At worst you may deny or block out the whole message. External barriers manifest themselves in subtle and not so subtle voice and body cues to others that they should edit what they say. Barriers also manifest themselves in the more obvious verbal blocks to being a rewarding listener, listed in Chapter 7.

What are some of the main barriers and filters that act as sources of interference to your receiving another loud and clear? All of them are related to your sense of worth and to how much debilitating anxiety you possess. The stronger you are emotionally, the less need is there for you to use barriers and filters, so the more open you are to others. Barriers to accepting attitude include the following.

• *Strong feelings*. Experiencing strong positive or negative feelings can interfere with your listening. Earlier I mentioned how hard it can be to stay open to another when in an angry conflict. Strong positive feelings can also contribute to your not adequately hearing another. Sexual harassment and date rape are instances where negative messages are not heeded.

> Barry, 23, was very attracted to Nancy, 22, whom he had just met. After their first dinner date, Nancy drove him home and accepted his invitation to come up for a coffee. During coffee, despite Nancy's protestations, Barry came on increasingly strongly about wanting sex with her. Nancy walked out and stopped seeing Barry.

• *Unfinished business*. You may have unfinished emotional business that interferes with your listening skills. For instance, if you come home after a row with someone at work you may be less ready to listen to your partner who wants to discuss his or her day. Also, if you have strong feelings about a past occurrence in your relationship, until you have processed this you may listen less well. In addition, you may transfer unfinished business from previous relationships into present ones.

> Nina and Brad are a couple in their early thirties. Nina has just come out of a relationship with Tom. At times she finds herself getting upset with Brad as though he were Tom, even though Brad treats her much better.

• *Trigger words and phrases.* Trigger or 'red flag' words and phrases are those that you perceive to be emotionally-charged 'put-downs'. Each individual has their own triggers. Many of these are 'You' messages: for example, 'You're weak', 'You stuffed it up', and 'Can't you do anything right?' Children can switch off when adults make comments starting with 'When I was your age' or 'Be a man/woman.' Adjectives like 'thoughtless', 'clumsy' and 'effeminate' can also act as trigger words. Much of the power of trigger words and phrases comes from the negative voice and body messages that accompany them.

> Matt, 39, and Stephanie, 38, argue a lot about how much time to spend with his mother, Joyce, 66. When Stephanie shouts 'You care for Joyce more than me', Matt thinks 'What's the use!' and tells Stephanie to 'F... off.'

Positive words and phrases can also trigger feelings that interfere with your listening. For example, flattery like 'Gee, you're wonderful Mr/Ms Murgatroyd...I really admire you' may contribute to your not hearing other less flattering feedback.

• *Anxiety-evoking people.* There may be specific people or categories of people with whom you feel anxious and, hence, do not listen to them well. These may include: your parents, your relatives, friends of the same or other sex, strangers and authority figures.

> Anne, 17, tends to get anxious when males in authority give her instructions. She is afraid that she will not be able to follow the instructions adequately and thus creates a 'self-fulfilling prophesy'. However, Anne does not get nearly so anxious when older females or people her age or younger of both sexes give her instructions.

• *Anxiety-evoking topics.* For reasons connected with how you were brought up, certain topic areas may be anxiety-evoking. You may either not like discussing them at all or get defensive when others state different opinions.

> Catherine, 19, was brought up in a home where sex was not openly discussed. Catherine gets very nervous when in a group of other women who share some details of their sex lives.

• *Anxiety-evoking situations.* Anxiety and threat are present to a greater or lesser degree in all situations. Below are some common situations where people may feel vulnerable and hence their own agendas may preclude fully listening to others.

> Going on your first date with a different person.
>
> Going to a party where you do not know anyone.
>
> Meeting for the first time your girlfriend/boyfriend's parents.
>
> Having to answer questions after a public talk you have given.
>
> Going for a job interview.
>
> Being teased on a sensitive topic.
>
> Making love for the first time.

Many of the above illustrations involve coping with new situations. However, even when you have either been for a number of job interviews or fielded questions after a number of talks, you may still experience some debilitating anxiety that interferes with your listening skills.

• *Prejudices*. Again for reasons connected with your upbringing, you may tune out to people who are different to you by reasons of, amongst others, their age, sex, sexual orientation, culture, race, social class, physical disability and intelligence level.

> Megan, 26, dislikes old people. She does not seem to realize that they were young once too. Also, that they have thoughts and feelings that merit respect just as much as her own. She treats old people coldly and maintains her distance from them.

• *Information differing from your self-picture*. You may find it hard to keep assuming an accepting attitude when the information you receive differs from your picture of yourself. People differ in their thresholds for being open to such information. Positive as well as negative information can be denied and distorted.

> Felicity, 43, is a powerful and narcissistic primary school headmistress. She is quick to notice others' failings. She discourages honest feedback about herself and dismisses any negative remarks as 'trouble-making'.
>
> Bruce tells Tracey he finds her very intelligent. Tracey looks shy and replies 'Oh, not really'.

• *Physical barriers*. Physical considerations may contribute to your being less accepting of others than you might be. For instance, fatigue, illness, the discomfort of being too hot or too cold, and external noise may all affect how well you listen. The stresses of your life may contribute to your being depressed, irritable and tense. None of these feelings are conducive to your being open and accepting of another person.

Rosa, 36, and Noel, 34, live in a small flat with three children under the age of ten. Due to fatigue, constant noise and interruptions, they find it hard to create the physical and psychological space required to discuss important 'you–me' issues in their relationship.

SKILL 2
TUNE IN TO THE SPEAKER'S INTERNAL VIEWPOINT

Don't judge any man until you have
walked two moons in his moccasins.
American Indian proverb

If people are to feel that you receive them loud and clear, you need the skills to 'get inside their skins' and 'see the world through their eyes.' At the heart of rewarding listening is a basic distinction between 'you' and 'me', between 'your view of you' and 'my view of you' and between 'your view of me' and 'my view of me.' Now 'your view of you' and 'my view of me' are both inside or internal viewpoints, whereas 'your view of me' and 'my view of you' are both outside or external viewpoints. Rewarding listening is based on your choosing to acknowledge the separateness between 'me' and 'you' by getting into the other's internal viewpoint rather than remaining in your own external viewpoint.

If I respond to what you say in a way that shows an accurate understanding of your viewpoint, I am responding *as if* I am inside your internal viewpoint. If however I chose not to show an understanding of your viewpoint, or lack the skills to do so, I respond from my external viewpoint. In short, if I respond to you as if inside your internal viewpoint, I respond to you from where you are. If I step outside your internal viewpoint, I respond in an external way that reflects more where I am or think you should be than where you are.

Following are examples of responses by listeners from their *external* viewpoints.

'Don't talk to me like that.'
'Stop crying. You should be a brave boy/girl.'
'Let me tell you about a similar experience to yours.'
'You're not still going on about that, are you?'

Tuning into speakers' internal viewpoints involves understanding them on their terms. You listen carefully and allow them the psychological space to say what they want. In addition, you need to decode their messages, taking into account voice and body as well as verbal messages.

Following are examples of responses by listeners as if in speakers' *internal* viewpoints.

'You feel betrayed by Alex.'
'You have mixed feelings about accepting the job.'
'You're delighted that she phoned.'
'You're frustrated that Helen does not pull her weight cleaning the flat.'

SKILL 3
SEND GOOD VOICE MESSAGES

The emotional atmosphere you provide when you listen can be greatly enhanced by your voice messages. Talkers need to feel that you are responsive to their feelings. One of the main ways you can do this is by sending voice messages that neither add nor subtract emotional meaning and emphasis. Below I look at the voice messages mentioned in Chapter 5 in terms of listening.

- *Volume*. You need to respond at a level that is comfortable and easy to hear.

- *Articulation*. Poor enunciation can interrupt the speaker's train of thought. Heavy accents can be very difficult to listen to, especially if accompanied by poor use of grammar and language. Again, this may interfere with speaker's train of thought.

- *Pitch*. High pitched and shrill voices can disconcert. A harsh tone can threaten.

- *Emphasis*. It is important that your voice is expressive in accurately picking up the major feelings and feeling nuances of speakers. Speaking in a weak and diffident voice may indicate that you have problems and deter the speaker. Speaking too firmly overwhelms.

- *Rate*. You create a more relaxed atmosphere if you do not talk too fast when you respond. Your use of pauses and silences can enhance your capacity to be a rewarding listener. To make it easy for speakers to tell their stories, you can pause after each utterance to see if they wish to continue. Also, good use of silences can both allow speakers more psychological space to think things through before speaking and to get in touch with their deeper feelings.

SKILL 4
SEND GOOD BODY MESSAGES

Following are some of the main body message skills that demonstrate interest and attention (Argyle, 1992; Egan, 1994; Ivey, 1994). In varying degrees, they provide non-verbal rewards for talking.

- *Availability*. People always off to the next events in their busy lives may not find time to listen adequately to those to whom they relate. Close relationships require an investment of quality time. If this is not forthcoming, sooner rather than later either or both partners are likely to feel that they are being inadequately listened to. If you are rarely or never available to listen, you have withdrawn much of your interest and attention from the other person.

• *Facial expression*. A friendly relaxed facial expression, including a smile, initially demonstrates interest. However, as the other talks, your facial expressions need to show that you are tuned into what they say. For instance, if another is serious, weeping or angry, adjust your facial expression to indicate that you observe and hear what they communicate.

• *Gaze and eye contact*. Good gaze skills indicate your interest and enable you to receive important facial messages. In addition, gaze can give you cues about when to stop listening and start responding. However, the main cues used in synchronizing conversations are verbal and voice messages rather than body messages (Argyle, 1983). Good eye contact skills involve looking in the other's direction so that you allow the possibility of your eyes meeting reasonably often. There is an equilibrium level for eye contact in any relationship depending upon: cultural and social rules, the degree of anxiety in each partner, the nature and state of development of the relationship and the degree of attraction involved. Staring at another threatens. Looking down or away too often may indicate that you are tense or uninterested.

• *Gestures*. The head nod is perhaps the most common gesture in listening 'small ones to show continued attention, larger and repeated ones to indicate agreement' (Argyle, 1992, p. 11). A head nod can be viewed as a reward to talkers. On the negative side, head nods can also be powerful ways of controlling speakers. Then unconditional acceptance becomes conditional acceptance. Arm and hand gestures can also be used to show responsiveness to speakers. However, listeners who gesture either too little or too much with their heads and arms can discourage. Other negative gestures include: tightly crossed arms and legs that act as barriers, hands clenched together, finger drumming, fiddling with your hair, your hand over your mouth, ear tugging and scratching yourself, to mention but some.

• *Posture*. Postural skills include physical openness, being relaxed, degree of trunk lean and postural similarity. Physical openness means facing the speaker not only with your face but with your body. You need to be sufficiently turned towards the other person so that you can receive all their significant facial and body messages. A relaxed body posture, provided you do not sprawl, conveys the message that you are emotionally accessible. If you do sit in a tense and uptight fashion, the listener may either consciously consider or intuitively feel that you are too bound up with your personal agendas and unfinished business to be fully accessible to them.

Your trunk lean may be forwards, backwards or sideways. If you lean too far forward you look odd and others may consider that you invade their personal space. If you lean far back, others may find this distancing. A slight forward trunk lean can both encourage talkers and avoid threat, especially at the start of relationships. Some research suggests that postural similarity, where two people take up mirror-image postures, is perceived as a sign of liking (Argyle, 1992).

• *Proximity*. In Chapter 5 I mentioned the various zones of intimacy for different kinds of conversations. Rewarding listening entails respecting these zones. If you move too quickly into another's personal space, they may both feel uncomfortable and move away. If you are physically too far away, not only do they have to talk louder but they may perceive you as emotionally distant. The most comfortable height for conversations is if your heads are at the same level. If you persist in standing when someone seated talks to you, this is likely to feel awkward for them. When seated, listeners' and speakers' chairs should be at the same level, though this becomes less important when people become comfortable with each other.

• *Touch*. When people date there may be high levels of touch as they listen to and get to know one another. Their body contact may include: holding hands, a semi-embrace, and sitting close so that their legs touch. In many relationships, touch can be an effective way of showing concern for someone who is hurting and in pain. Demonstrations of concern include touching another's hands, arms, shoulders and upper back. The intensity and duration of touch should be sufficient to establish contact and yet avoid creating discomfort. Part of being a rewarding listener includes picking up messages about the limits and desirability of your use of touch.

Both *within* your body messages and also *between* your body messages and your voice and verbal messages, consistency increases the chances of your being perceived as a rewarding listener. For instance, you may be smiling and at the same time either fidgeting or tapping your foot. Your smile may indicate interest, your foot-tapping impatience, and your overall message may appear insincere.

SKILL 5
USE OPENING REMARKS, SMALL REWARDS AND OPEN-ENDED QUESTIONS

Opening remarks, small rewards and open-ended questions all require the use of a few words as well as of good voice and body messages. They each make it easier for the speaker to talk.

Opening remarks

Opening remarks, openers or permissions to talk are brief statements indicating that you are prepared to listen. Such remarks can occur at any time in a relationship. The message contained in all opening remarks is: 'I'm interested and prepared to listen. I'm giving you the opportunity to share what you think and feel.' A good time to use an opening remark can be when you sense something is bothering another and she or he requires encouragement to share it. Such an opener may be a response to another's body messages. Here are some examples of opening remarks.

'How are you?'
'How was your day?'

'You look really happy.'
'You seem tense today.'
'What's the matter?'
'Is there something on your mind?'
'Would you like to talk about it?'
'I'd like to know what you think?'

When using opening remarks, you must be sensitive to others' reactions. They may not be ready to talk or consider you are not the right person to talk to. They probably do not want information dragged out of them. However, sometimes you rightly sense that others want to talk, but have difficulty doing so. In such situations follow-up remarks – for instance, 'It's pretty hard to get started' or 'Take your time' – may further help the speaker open up. Poor body messages can totally destroy the impact of an opening remark. For example, a husband who looks up and says 'What's on your mind, dear?' and then continues reading the newspaper discourages his wife from telling him.

Small rewards

Small rewards are brief verbal expressions of interest designed to encourage speakers. The message they convey is: 'I am with you. Please go on.' Small rewards can be used for good or ill. On the one hand they can reward people for talking to you from their internal viewpoint. On the other hand, they may range from crude to subtle attempts to take others out of their internal viewpoint by shaping what they say. For instance, you may say 'Tell me more' whenever someone says what you want to hear, yet remain silent when they do not. Below are some examples of verbal small rewards, though perhaps the most frequently used, 'Um-hmm', is more vocal than verbal.

'Um-hmm'	'Sure'
'Please continue'	'Indeed'
'Tell me more'	'And'
'Go on'	'So'
'I see'	'Really'
'Oh'	'Right'
'Interesting'	'Ah'
'Then'	'Yes'
'I hear you'	'You're not kidding'

Another kind of small reward is to repeat the last word someone has said:

Speaker: I'm feeling nervous.
Listener: Nervous.

Open-ended questions

You may use questions in ways that either help speakers to elaborate their internal viewpoints or lead them out of their viewpoints, possibly into yours. Open-ended questions allow speakers to share their internal viewpoints without curtailing their options. Open-ended questions include 'Tell me about it?'; 'Please elaborate?' and, slightly less open-ended, 'How do you feel about that?' Open-ended questions may be contrasted with closed questions that curtail speakers' options: indeed they often give only two options, 'yes' or 'no'.

> **Open-ended question:** How do you feel about your relationship?
> **Closed question:** Is your relationship good or bad?

Closed questions may have various negative outcomes. You may be perceived as leading and controlling the conversation. You may block another from getting in touch with and listening to themselves and responding from their internal viewpoint rather than to your external viewpoint. You may set the stage for an interrogation. Since closed questions can be disincentives to talking, they can create silences in which the stage is set for further closed questions. I do not mean to imply that you never use closed questions. It depends on the goals of your listening. They are useful if you wish to collect information. However, show restraint if you wish to help others share their worlds. You may also need to use open-ended questions sparingly.

CHAPTER HIGHLIGHTS

• Rewarding listening entails not only accurately understanding speakers' communications, but showing them that you have understood.

• In two-person conversations, listening takes place both between persons and also within each of them.

• Reasons for the importance of developing rewarding listening skills include: making contact, knowing another, knowing yourself, maintaining relationships, and bridging differences.

• Listeners should possess an attitude of respect and acceptance towards speakers as separate human beings with rights to their own thoughts and feelings.

• Barriers to an accepting attitude include: strong feelings; unfinished business; trigger words and phrases; anxiety-evoking people, topics and situations; prejudices; information differing from your self-picture; and physical barriers.

• Tuning into speakers' internal viewpoints involves understanding them on their terms and not yours.

• You require skills of sending good voice messages when responding to speakers: for instance, comfortable volume and appropriate variations in emphasis.

• When listening, you can reward speakers by showing interest through body messages including your: facial expression, gaze and eye contact, gestures, posture, proximity and touch.

• You need a repertoire of opening remarks that communicate that you are available to listen.

• Small rewards are brief verbal messages you can use to encourage speakers to continue: for instance, 'Go on', 'Then' and 'I hear you'.

• Open-ended questions, unlike closed-ended questions, allow speakers to share their internal viewpoints without curtailing their options.

EXERCISES
EXERCISE 6.1
ASSESS MY BARRIERS TO AN ACCEPTING ATTITUDE WHEN I LISTEN
Instructions

First do this exercise on your own. Then, if appropriate, discuss your answers with your partner, another or others.

1. Assess yourself in terms of how much each of the following barriers interferes with your possessing an attitude of respect and acceptance when you listen.

Barrier	My assessment
Strong feelings	
Unfinished business	
Trigger words and phrases	
Anxiety-evoking people	
Anxiety-evoking topics	
Anxiety-evoking situations	
Prejudices	
Information differing from my self-picture	
Physical barriers	
Other(s) (please specify)	

2. Summarize the extent to which you see yourself possessing an attitude of respect and acceptance when you listen to:

a. your spouse/partner/girlfriend/boyfriend, and

b. your friends.

EXERCISE 6.2
TUNE INTO ANOTHER'S INTERNAL VIEWPOINT
Instructions

Part A
Identify another's internal viewpoint

Part A of this exercise asks you to identify whether the listener has responded as if from the speaker's internal viewpoint. Some responses may seem artificial since they have been devised to make the point of the exercise clear. Answers for the exercise are provided at the end of the chapter. Below are some statement-response excerpts from different relationships. Three responses have been provided for each statement. Write IN or EX by each response according to whether it represents the speaker's internal viewpoint or comes from an external viewpoint.

Example

> Husband to wife
>
> Husband: 'I'm worried about the kids. They always seem to be out late these days and I'm beginning to feel that I scarcely know them.'
>
> Wife
> EX a.   'If you took a bit more interest you would know them better.'
> IN b.   'You're concerned that you're becoming distant from the kids because you see so little of them.'
> EX c.   'You're a good dad and deserve better than this.'

Statements and responses

> 1. *Wife to female friend*
>
> Wife: 'My husband is overly critical of me.'
>
> Friend
> _____ a. 'Mine is too.'

_____ b. 'Why don't you tell him he's not so great either!'

_____ c. 'You feel unfairly attacked by your husband.'

2. Child to mother

Child: 'Mum. I got my grades today and I'm really excited because I came first in my class.'

Mother

_____ a. 'You've got your mother's brains.'

_____ b. 'You're really pleased to be number one.'

_____ c. 'Dad will be glad.'

3. Friend to friend

Friend A: 'I'm finding it difficult to stay interested in my studies.'

Friend B:

_____ 'You're struggling to stay motivated to study.'

_____ 'What are you going to do if you drop out?'

_____ 'Your course sounds pretty boring to me.'

Part B
Practice – Summarizing another's internal viewpoint

Work with a partner.

1. Person A talks for at least two minutes about what he/she considers important in a close relationship (Person A's internal viewpoint). Person B does not interrupt.

2. When Person A finishes, Person B summarizes the main points of what Person A was saying. Person A does not interrupt.

3. When Person B finishes summarizing, Person A comments on how accurate Person B was in understanding his/her internal viewpoint. Person B can respond to this feedback.

4. Then reverse roles and repeat 1, 2 and 3 above.

EXERCISE 6.3
HOW REWARDING ARE MY VOICE MESSAGES WHEN I LISTEN?
Instructions

First do Part A of this exercise on your own. Then, if appropriate, discuss your answers with your partner, another or others.

Part A
Assess my voice messages

Assess your strengths and deficits at sending body messages when you listen.

Voice message	My assessment
Volume	
Articulation	
Pitch	
Emphasis	
Rate	

Identify specific skills deficits in your voice messages when listening and set goals for change.

Part B
Practice – Using terrible and good voice message skills when listening

Work with a partner and hold a conversation on a topic of mutual interest.

1. First two minutes: both of you converse normally.

2. Second two minutes: use terrible voice message skills as you show your partner you listened to his/her utterances.

3. Third two minutes: use good voice message skills as show your partner you listened to his/her utterances.

4. Evaluation period: discuss what it felt like receiving and sending terrible and good voice messages. Your evaluation session may be more educational and fun if you play back a cassette of your six-minute conversation.

5. Then reverse roles and repeat 2, 3 and 4 above.

EXERCISE 6.4
HOW REWARDING ARE MY BODY MESSAGES WHEN I LISTEN?

Instructions

First do Part A of this exercise on your own. Then, if appropriate, discuss your answers with your partner, another or others.

Part A
Assess my body messages

Assess your strengths and deficits at sending body messages when you listen.

Body message	My assessment
Availability	
Facial expression	
Gaze and eye contact	
Gestures	
Posture	
Proximity	
Touch	

Identify specific skills deficits in your body messages when listening and set goals for change.

Part B
Practice – Using terrible and good body message skills when listening

Work with a partner and hold a conversation on a topic of mutual interest.

1. First two minutes: both of you converse normally.

2. Second two minutes: remaining silent, use terrible body message skills when listening as your partner talks.

3. Third two minutes: still remaining silent, use good body message skills when listening as your partner talks.

4. Evaluation period: discuss what it felt like receiving and sending terrible and good body messages. Your evaluation session may be more educational and fun if you play back a video of your six-minute conversation.

5. Then reverse roles and repeat 2, 3 and 4 above.

EXERCISE 6.5
GROUP DISCUSSION: LISTENING SKILLS
Instructions

This is intended as a group exercise, though it may be done individually or in pairs. For each part:

1. spend 10–15 minutes answering the question in groups of three or four,

2. each group shares its answers with the whole group,

3. then the whole group ranks the six most important points or skills from the most important to the least important.

Part A
Advantages of rewarding listening

List the six main advantages of rewarding listening in personal relationships.

Part B
Voice message skills

List the six main voice message skills for rewarding listening in personal relationships.

Part C
Body message skills

List the six main body message skills for rewarding listening in personal relationships.

ANSWERS TO EXERCISE 6.2 (Part A)

1.   a. EX   b. EX   c. IN
2.   a. EX   b. IN   c. EX
3.   a. IN   b. EX   c. EX

SEVEN
Showing Understanding Skills

Understanding is the beginning of approving.
André Gide

CHAPTER QUESTIONS

- *What is active understanding?*
- *How can you use paraphrasing skills?*
- *How can you use reflecting feelings skills?*
- *How can you use questioning skills?*
- *How can you use challenging skills?*
- *What are some skills for avoiding blocking speakers from talking?*

The first part of this chapter presents some skills of actively showing understanding of another's internal viewpoint. The second part of the chapter looks at clarifying understanding by questioning and confronting skills. The chapter ends by examining some common blocks to showing understanding.

SHOWING UNDERSTANDING

In this book I use the term *active understanding* as a shorthand term for showing understanding by responding as if in the speaker's internal viewpoint. Active understanding entails tuning in to and reflecting with your verbal, voice and body messages the crux of the meaning contained in the verbal, voice and body messages of another. Here are a couple of brief examples.

Friend to friend

> *Friend A:* 'When I first heard I'd got terminal cancer, my world fell apart. I'm still pretty shaken and frightened at the thought of death.'

> *Friend B:* 'You feel scared about dying and are still reeling from the news of your cancer.'

Husband to wife

> *Husband:* 'With the children nearing the end of their education I want develop my own interests more. I don't want to keep sacrificing this much of myself when it no longer becomes necessary.'

> *Wife:* 'You feel boxed in and want more freedom when the financial pressures ease off.'

When assessing an active understanding response, think of a three-link chain: first statement – active understanding response – second statement. Good responses allow the opportunity for another's second statement to be a continuation of the train of thought contained in their first statement. Bad responses do not.

Uses of active understanding

When people are first introduced to the skills of active understanding they frequently express reservations: for instance, 'It's so unnatural', 'People will just think I'm repeating everything they say' or 'It gets in the way of my being spontaneous.' When learning any new skill, from driving a car to driving a golf ball, there is a period where you are likely to have to concentrate extra hard on making the correct sequence of choices that make up the skill. Active understanding is no exception. If you work and practise at a skill, you ultimately are likely to own it as a 'natural' part of you. It is natural to the extent that it feels natural.

Active understanding should not be used all the time, but flexibly incorporated into your repertoire of responses. Following are some occasions where using active under-standing skills may help you to relate more effectively.

- When another struggles to understand himself or herself.

- When another requires help in expressing thoughts and feelings.

- When another is trying to manage a personal problem or make a decision.

- When you need to be clear about another's position in a disagreement.

- When you wish to ensure that the responsibility for a decision or course of action in his or her life rests with the other person.

However, on other occasions you may gain from either not using active understanding or using it sparingly.

• When you consider someone talks too much and it is time communication became more two-way.

• When you wish to match the level of intimacy of another's disclosures.

• When you are aware that you are listening as a means of avoiding defining and asserting yourself.

• When you feel too tired or hassled to listen properly.

• When you consider another's solution might damage either yourself and/or him or her.

SKILL 6
PARAPHRASE

Along with reflecting feelings, paraphrasing is one of the component skills of active understanding. It is important that you paraphrase because you drive people crazy if you parrot them. As a frustrated husband once said to his wife: 'If I had wanted someone to repeat everything I said after me, I would have married a parrot.' Paraphrasing means rewording speakers' verbal utterances. However, it excludes showing understanding of their voice and body messages.

When you paraphrase, you may sometimes use the speakers' words, but sparingly. You try to stay close to the kind of language they have used. Here are a few basic examples.

Wife to husband

> *Wife:* 'Go to hell.'
>
> *Husband:* 'You're mad at me.'

Partner to partner

> *First partner:* 'I've got the blues.'
>
> *Second partner:* 'You feel really low.'

Divorcee to friend

> *Divorcee:* 'It's painful for me that all the friends we knew as a couple now seem to want to see only Jim (her ex-husband).'
>
> *Friend:* 'You're very hurt that your mutual friends only keep in contact with Jim.'

A good paraphrase can provide a response often clearer and more succinct than the original utterance. If so, speakers may comment 'That's it' or 'You've got me'. A simple tip for paraphrasing is to start your responses with the personal pronoun 'you' to indicate that you reflect speakers' internal viewpoints. Another tip is not to speak too quickly – this gives you more time to think. A good memory and a large vocabulary also help. To become confident, flexible and fluent in the skill requires much practice.

SKILL 7
REFLECT FEELINGS

Reflecting feelings is the main skill of actively showing understanding. Reflecting feelings entails responding to speakers' music and not just to their words. It may be viewed as feeling with a speaker's flow of emotions and experiencing and being able to communicate this back. When you reflect feelings, you give another the opportunity to listen more deeply to their own feelings.

There is a risk that if you constantly reflect speakers' feelings, you can just encourage self-pity. For instance, Mark may persist in feeling sorry for himself when discussing his relationship with Maria, which is not going well. You need to use your judgement in how much and when to reflect feelings. For instance, you might use reflecting feelings responses to allow Mark to express his feelings and to show that you understand them. Then, possibly, you could ask a question like 'Well, is there anything you can do to improve the situation?'

Pick up feelings words and phrases

Let's start with the obvious. A good but not infallible way to discuss what another feels is to listen to their feelings words and phrases. Sometimes people ask: 'Well, what did you feel?' just after they have already been told. Sometimes feelings words are not the central message. For instance, Vanessa may say 'It's just great' that, after the break-up of a relationship, she is living on her own again, at the same time as her voice chokes, her face looks sad and the corners of her mouth are turned down. Also, sometimes people say 'I feel' when they mean 'I think'. For example, 'I feel that equality between the sexes is essential' describes a thought rather than a feeling. On the other hand, 'I feel angry about sex discrimination.' describes a feeling. It is important that you distinguish between speakers' thoughts and feelings, if you wish to be skilful at picking up feelings accurately.

In Table 2.1 I listed many feelings words. Feelings phrases are colloquial expressions used to describe feelings words. For instance, 'I'm over the moon' is a feelings phrase describing the emotion of joy. Incidentally, it is cumbersome, when reflecting feelings always to put 'You feel' before feelings words and phrases. Sometimes 'You're' is sufficient: for example, 'You're delighted' instead of 'You feel delighted.' The following is an example of someone using feelings words and phrases that communicate clearly what he means. Randy says to Alicia: 'I really enjoyed our date last night. It was just great. Even after so little time I feel there is something special between us. When can we meet again?' Randy's feelings words and phrases are 'really enjoyed', 'just great', 'something special between us' and 'can we meet again?'

Skilful reflection of feelings words and phrases requires attention to the following areas.

- *Strength.* Try and understand the strength of speaker's feelings. For instance, after a row, the speaker may feel 'devastated' (strong feeling), 'upset' (moderate feeling), or 'slightly upset' (weak feeling).

- *Multiple and mixed feelings.* Sometimes people use many words to describe their feelings. The words may cluster around the same theme, in which case you may chose to reflect the crux of the feeling. Alternatively, speakers may verbalize varying degrees of mixed feelings ranging from simple opposites, for instance 'happy/sad' to more complex combinations, such as 'hurt/anger/guilt'. Good reflections pick up all key elements of feelings messages as in the following example.

> *Girlfriend:* 'It's great when we're together, but I don't want to be around him all the time.'
>
> *Friend:* 'You enjoy Bob's company, but want your own space too.'

- *Assisting labelling of feelings.* Sometimes you can assist speakers to find the right way to express their feelings. Here reflecting feelings involves helping others choose feelings words that resonate for them.

> *Andy:* 'I don't know how to express my reaction to the way my father treated me...possibly angry...upset, no that's not quite it...bewildered.'
>
> *Rita:* 'Hurt, anxious, confused...do any of these words strike a chord?'

Pick up voice and body messages

Much information about speakers' feelings comes from their voice and body messages. Frequently, people's voice and body are inconsistent with their verbal messages. Speakers may struggle to express what they truly feel in face of their conditioning about what they should feel. Also, in relationships, it takes time to develop the trust that leads to more open communication.

If you are unclear about speakers' real or underlying feelings, you can check with them. For instance, you may make comments like 'I think I hear you saying (state feelings tentatively)' or 'I want to understand what you're feeling, but I'm still not altogether clear'. Another option is to reflect back the mixed message: for instance, 'On the one hand you are saying you don't mind. On the other hand, you seem tearful.' After a pause you might add: 'I'm wondering if you are putting on a brave face?' A further consideration in picking up feelings is to understand whether and to what extent speakers possess insight into their feelings: for example, being able acknowledge to themselves that they feel hurt.

Sender skills for reflecting feelings

When you've decoded speakers' feelings messages to the best of your ability, how do you actively show that you understand them? Here are a few guidelines for reflecting feelings.

1. *Reflect the crux of the message.* Whatever else you do, communicate back the speaker's main feeling. Even though speakers may not start with their main feeling, they may feel better understood by you if you reflect their main feeling at the front of your response.

> *Damien:* We just argue and argue and don't seem to get anywhere. I don't know what to do. It's so frustrating. I wish I knew the answer. I don't seem able to handle our relationship.
>
> *Tara:* You're extremely frustrated with constant unproductive arguments and not knowing how to improve matters.

2. *Keep your responses simple.* Use simple and clear language. Avoid unnecessary words and qualifications. However, be prepared to state different parts of multiple and mixed messages.

3. *Use voice and body messages to add expressiveness to your verbal messages.* You are not just talking about feelings, you are reflecting feelings. For instance, if a hypothetical suicide-prone friend says 'I'm at the end of my tether', you can adjust your voice and facial expression to mirror, to some extent, a sense of despair.

4. *Where appropriate, reflect feelings and reasons.* Sometimes you can reflect speakers' feelings and the reasons they offer for them. A simple way of doing this is to make a 'You feel...because...' statement that mirrors their internal viewpoint. Reflecting back reasons does not mean that you make an interpretation or offer an explanation from your external viewpoint.

> *Pete:* We're having difficulty keeping up with mortgage payments, and the flat is now worth less than our mortgage. We feel anxious about our future and in a real bind.
>
> *Rashiv:* You feel worried and trapped because you've got a negative mortgage that you're struggling to make payments on.

5. *Check your understanding.* You respond to speakers' utterances with differing degrees of tentativeness depending on how clearly they have communicated and how confident you are about receiving their messages accurately. However, all your reflections of feelings should contain an element of checking the accuracy of your understanding. Sometimes you check by slight voice inflections. On other occasions, you check by asking directly: for instance, 'Do I understand you properly?'

EXPANDING UNDERSTANDING

So far I have focused on being a rewarding listener so that you make it easy for another to share their internal viewpoint. However, at times you may help to expand another's understanding by asking questions and challenging them. Questions and challenges come from your internal and the speaker's external viewpoint. You can use questioning and challenging skills to take another beyond his or her existing internal viewpoint. Depending upon how you use these skills, the focus of the conversation can remain on another or change to you.

SKILL 8
CLARIFY BY QUESTIONING

Questions can show another you are interested in what they say. Questions can also help or hinder another in managing problems. Let's take the example of Bill who has a problem at work that he wishes to discuss with his partner Kerry. There are two extremes to how Kerry might question Bill. Kerry could use questions to take control of Bill's problem and come up with solutions for him. Alternatively, Kerry could use questions to help Bill come to his own solutions. Underlying, these two ways of questioning is the issue of who owns the problem, Kerry or Bill? When Kerry asks controlling questions for her purposes, she owns Bill's problem. However, if Kerry asks questions that help Bill to cope with the problem on his terms, she allows the ownership of the problem to remain with him (Gordon, 1970). If Kerry uses good questioning skills she can help Bill to explore, clarify and enlarge his internal viewpoint.

Types of questions

Listeners need to choose from among various types of questions, including the following.

• *Open-ended versus closed-ended questions.* Open-ended questions give speakers considerable choice in how to respond, whereas closed-ended questions restrict choice (see Chapter 6, pp. 118–19).

• *Specific detail questions.* You can use specific detail questions to collect concrete information about an issue or problem.

> 'How did you actually behave?'
> 'When did it start?'
> 'Where does it happen?'
> 'Describe a specific instance of his/her doing that.'

• *Elaboration questions.* Elaboration questions are open questions that give speakers the opportunity to expand on what they have said.

> 'Would you care to elaborate?'
> 'Tell me more.'

* *Eliciting personal meanings questions*. The information speakers provide often has personal or symbolic meaning for them. For example, whenever her husband would come home late without having called her, his wife would think he did not care about her (Beck, 1988). Eliciting personal meaning questions should be tentative, since speakers may need to think before answering.

> 'I'm wondering about the meaning of...for you?'
> 'What do you make of that?'
> 'Why is it so important for you?'

* *Checking understanding questions*

> 'When you say...what do you mean?'
> 'Sounds to me you're saying...'
> 'Can I check that I've understood you properly?'

* *Solution focused questions*

> 'What are your options?'
> 'What are you planning to do?'
> 'How can you change your behaviour?'

Enlarging another's internal viewpoint

I do not advocate that you always ask questions for another's benefit and not yours. However, since this is a chapter on rewarding listening, I focus on questioning that help speakers understand themselves better. Below are some skills of collaborating with another when asking questions.

1. *Intersperse active understanding with questions.* Speakers feel interrogated if you ask a series of questions in quick succession. You can soften your questioning if you pause to see if another wants to continue responding and then reflect each response before asking another question. Following are two brief conversations between Kerry and Bill about his work problem.

Kerry owning the problem:

> *Bill:* 'I'm having difficulty getting on with my boss.'
>
> *Kerry:* 'Why do you always have problems with people at work?'

> *Bill:* 'I have this large project to finish and he refuses to let me have more help.'
>
> *Kerry:* 'Why aren't you being more assertive with him?'
>
> *Bill:* 'I've tried to talk to him, but I don't seem to make any impression.'
>
> *Kerry:* 'If I were you, I'd tell him to stop making unrealistic demands and realize how hard you work.'

Kerry allowing Bill to own the problem:

> *Bill:* 'I'm having difficulty getting on with my boss.'
>
> *Kerry:* 'You're worried about this conflict. What do you think is going on?'
>
> *Bill:* 'I have this large project to finish and he refuses to let me have more help.'
>
> *Kerry:* 'You feel stressed because he's not backing you up. Is there anything you think you can do about it?'
>
> *Bill:* 'Last time I talked with him, I did not explain clearly how many different angles there are to the project. Perhaps, I could sit down with him and try to negotiate some limits on it.'

Though these are only short excerpts, in the first one Kerry dominates Bill, whereas in the second Kerry uses questions to help Bill enlarge his internal viewpoint and do his own work. Also, in the second excerpt Kerry shows active understanding of Bill's feelings.

2. *Ask follow-on questions.* Avoid jack-rabbiting in which you quickly hop from one topic to another. Listen carefully to what another has just said. Frequently, your next question follows on from and encourages speakers to enlarge upon their last response. Questions linked logically to speakers' previous responses help show your understanding.

3. *Carefully observe how questions are answered.* Much of the skill of questioning lies in decoding another's answers. Speakers send messages by what is left unsaid or only partially said and by voice and body messages. Skilled listeners tune in finely to subtle messages. They sensitively pick up another's anxieties, confusions and vulnerabilities and take them into account in whether and how they ask their next question.

SKILL 9
CLARIFY BY CHALLENGING

The skill of challenging sometimes is sometimes called confronting. My emphasis here is on using challenging, when listening, to help another expand and explore their perceptions (Egan, 1994). The starting point is his or her internal viewpoint rather than yours. There may be other occasions in your relationships, for instance confronting a conflict, when the starting point may be your viewpoint. This is covered in a later chapter.

You can challenge another's existing perceptions so that they can work with more and better information. Each of you lives in the world of your own perceptions. Sometimes a challenge or confrontation from an external viewpoint can broaden and deepen the speaker's internal viewpoint. In relationships, challenges can be invitations to consider other ways of viewing matters. Needless to say, the skills you use when challenging are very important.

Challenging inconsistencies and possible distortions of reality are two of the main skills of challenging that you can include in your repertoire of relating skills.

Challenging inconsistencies

When someone talks to you, you can experience inconsistencies in the messages they send you. Such inconsistencies may include the following.

• *Inconsistency between verbal, voice and body messages.* 'On the one hand you say that you are fine, but on the other I catch a note of pain in your voice and see you looking tearful.'

• *Inconsistency between words and actions.* 'You say you love your children from your former marriage, but you rarely try to see them and are behind on your maintenance payments.'

• *Inconsistency between past and present statements.* 'You now say you hate her, but a week ago you were saying how much you loved her.'

• *Inconsistency between your view of you and my view of you.* 'You say that you see yourself as unattractive, but I genuinely do not see you that way.'

• *Inconsistency between your view of you and others' views of you.* 'You see yourself as pulling your weight in doing the chores, but you seem to be getting a lot of messages that other members of the family don't agree.'

How do you challenge inconsistencies? A common response here is: 'On the one hand you say..., but on the other hand...' – for example, 'On the one hand you say that you are fine, but on the other hand I catch a note of pain in your voice.' This response is often shortened to 'You say..., but...' – for example, 'You say that you are fine, but I catch a note of pain in your voice.'

Challenging possible distortions of reality

When another talks to you he or she may make statements like the following: 'I have no friends', 'I'm a poor father', 'I'm no good with women/men', 'He/she doesn't love me any more', 'I'm no good at anything', 'They made me do it' and 'He/she never says anything positive.' All these statements are possibly faulty perceptions that harm rather than help. One way you could respond is to reflect the speaker's internal viewpoint. Another way is to challenge the speaker's version of reality. People often jump to conclusions on insufficient evidence and then treat their conclusions as facts (Beck & Freeman, 1990; Beck, & Weishaar, 1995). You require judgement as to whether you continue listening within the internal viewpoint or you challenge possible distortions of reality.

How do you challenge possible distortions of reality? A good response for challenging distortions is 'You say…, but what's the evidence?' – for example, 'You say that you have no friends, but what's the evidence?' Such a response reflects the speaker's internal viewpoint and then invites them to produce evidence to support it. The speaker may then make a remark like: 'Well, Kathryn never phones me up any more?' Then you may challenge them again with a question such as 'Is there any other way of looking at that?' With the questions 'What's the evidence?' and 'Is their any other way of looking at that?' you invite speakers to produce their own evidence to confirm or negate their versions of reality rather than doing it for them. On other occasions you may suggest that they consider some evidence from your viewpoint.

Some guidelines for challenging

Following are some guidelines for how to challenge.

1. *Start with active understanding*. Always start your response by showing that you have heard and understood the speaker's message. Then build on this with your challenging response. This way you are more likely to keep the speaker's ears open to what comes from your viewpoint.

2. *Where possible, help speakers to challenge themselves*. By reflecting inconsistencies, you allow speakers to draw their own conclusions about them. Similarly, by asking speakers to search for evidence to back their statements, you help them to challenge themselves. Often assisting speakers to challenge themselves leads to less resistance than if you challenge them directly from your external viewpoint.

3. *Do not talk down*. Keep your challenges at a democratic level. Make your challenges invitations for exploration rather than papal pronouncements. Avoid 'You' messages. A major risk in challenging others is that they perceive you are putting them down rather than being helpful.

4. *Use the minimum amount of 'muscle'*. Only challenge as strongly as required to achieve your goal. Heavy challenges can create resistances. Though sometimes necessary, they are generally to be avoided.

5. *Avoid threatening voice and body messages*. Try to avoid threatening voice and body messages, like raising your voice and glaring.

6. *Leave the ultimate responsibility with the speaker.* Allow speakers to decide whether your challenges actually help them to move forward in their exploration. Many of your challenges, if well timed and tactfully worded, are unlikely to elicit much defensiveness.

7. *Do not overdo it.* Nobody likes being challenged persistently. With constant challenges, you create unsafe emotional climates for speakers. You can help others move forward with skilled challenges; but you can block them and harm your relationship if you challenge too often and too clumsily.

BLOCKING UNDERSTANDING

We're all of us sentenced to solitary confinement
inside our own skins for life.

Tennessee Williams

You cannot and should not listen to others all the time. However, if you care for people, you try to help them out of their solitude. You endeavour to avoid responses that close them up rather than help them to unfold and blossom. Many characteristic ways in which people respond to others in everyday conversation can block them from sharing their internal viewpoint. A distinction is sometimes made between a counselling conversation, where the counsellor listens carefully to the client, and a social conversation, cynically described as 'two people taking turns to exercise their egos.' Counsellors are trained to make the listening choices that help clients to feel safe and accepted. This includes avoiding the kinds of blocking responses prevalent in everyday conversations.

SKILL 10
AVOID LISTENING BLOCKS

Just as you can tune in to others, so you can tune out to them. If people are going to give you the gift of revealing themselves, they need psychological safety and space. Such safety and space is both quantitative and qualitative. If you are either not physically available or, when present, you monopolize the conversation or keep interrupting, you are scarcely giving another the *quantity* of safety and space they need. However, you can also preclude them from having the *quality* of safety and space they need by choosing to respond in ways that show lack of respect for the importance of their internal viewpoint. This not only makes it more difficult for others to talk to you, but it also interferes with their listening to themselves. A tragedy in many close relationships is that often, unintentionally through their skills deficits, friends, partners and lovers block each other when they listen. You may wish to express caring by helping your friends or partner. However, instead you may communicate that they are not absolutely free to talk about and to be themselves.

Some blocks to rewarding listening follow (Gordon, 1970; Litvinoff, 1992; McKay, Fanning & Paleg, 1994). Some of these blocks you should never use; others might be appropriate, depending on the circumstances. All the blocks below focus on verbal responses; but as we have seen discouraging voice and body messages can be just as devastating.

- *Interrupting*. Interrupting means not allowing the other person to finish what they are saying. In heated arguments, partners may cease listening because they are so busy trying to prove their point. Frequently, even in normal conversations, people interrupt each other. Beck observes that interruptions can evoke many negative thoughts in people cut off such as: ' *"He's not listening to me," "She doesn't think much of what I have to say," "He's only interested in hearing himself talk"* ' (Beck, 1988, p. 289).

- *Monopolizing*. When you monopolize the conversation, you are so busy talking about what interests you that others have little chance to speak. Once that happens you have little opportunity to listen. You can hold forth at great length and be impervious to the effect you have on others.

- *Rehearsing*. You can be so busy rehearsing what you plan to say next that you inadequately listen to speakers. You may be more interested in sparring or debating than hearing. For instance, rather than listening carefully, when Sally and Isaac discuss their vacation plans each rehearses how they can counter the other's suggestions and argue their case.

- *Switching off*. You can tune out altogether when the other person sends messages you do not want to receive. For instance, Gerry had a manipulative mother who used to control him with her tears. Now, even at age 40, Gerry switches off whenever his wife Angie cries as she criticizes him. Often this behaviour intensifies Angie's crying and Gerry emotionally withdraws even more.

- *Part-listening*. You can listen with just part of your attention as you read the newspaper, watch the telly, think of whom next to talk with at a party, daydream or preoccupy yourself with private thoughts. Sometimes when people part-listen, they try to cover it by faking attention: for instance, with comments like: 'How interesting!' and 'Oh, really'. Possibly part-listening is more common in established relationships, where people may be more inclined to take each other for granted, than in the earlier stages of relationships.

- *Mind-reading*. Mind-reading involves discounting what another actually says and inferring something different. In distressed relationships couples may be more willing to read negative intentions into each other's minds than in happier relationships: for example, they may think: 'Although you say you didn't mean to hurt me, I know that you really did.'

- *Being right*. Being right involves only listening to information that confirms your view of yourself. Anything that goes against your view of yourself is denied or filtered. Being right can also mean not listening properly to information that negates your view of others. For instance, wives who need to see their husbands as strong may not listen to information that suggests otherwise (Litvinoff, 1992).

- *Changing the subject*. When you do not want to keep listening, you can literally change the subject to another topic. Sometimes people change the subject to their favourite topic, themselves – for instance, 'You think you have problems, let me tell you mine.' Possibly, a more subtle way of changing the subject is to alter the emotional temperature: for example, by making a joke out of a serious concern of your partner's.

- *Intimidating*. You can use responses like anger, criticism and threats to control people and stop them from saying what they truly think and feel. These are power-plays whose purpose is to control others (Steiner, 1981). For instance, when Italian-Australian Maria brings up the subject of developing a relationship with Lon, from a Vietnamese background, her parents get very angry and say they never want Lon to set foot in their house.

- *Placating*. You are too quick to agree. You can be so nice and supportive that you do not give the other person time to truly share what they think and feel. For instance, a coping strategy that Dick uses to stop his mother, Irene, expressing her anger is to become very apologetic and keep saying 'I'm sorry…I will not do it again.'

- *Reassuring*. You can try to make others feel better by reassuring and humouring them. Often, reassurance is more for people's own sake than for that of speakers who may be blocked from sharing their true feelings. Illustrative reassuring comments are: 'We all feel like that sometimes', 'You'll get by', and 'Look, I've made you laugh. It can't be that bad.' Reassurance can involve infantilizing people rather than treating them as adults.

- *Advising*. As illustrated in the earlier example of Kerry and Bill, people can take over ownership of others' problems. You may barely listen to what another has to say before you come up with what they should be doing. Your style of responding implies 'I know what is best for you.'

- *Judging*. You can make judgemental statements about people's thoughts, feelings and actions indicating that speakers fall short of your standards: for example, 'You should respect your parents', 'You shouldn't be feeling depressed', and 'You are not very good at communicating with your kids.'

- *Interrogating*. You can ask people a series of questions that stops them from listening to themselves and gets them responding to you. Also, you can use questions in such a way that others feel threatened by unwanted probing: for instance, 'How often do you have sex? What are your favourite sexual activities? What are your erotic fantasies?'

- *Breaking confidences*. Each social interaction has implicit or explicit rules about confidentiality. Breaking confidences indicates that you have not listened adequately to the degree of trust in your discretion placed in you by speakers. If found out, you will be perceived as much less safe to talk to in future.

You bring your thinking skills strengths and deficits to listening. All the listening blocks just mentioned reflect poor thinking skills. For example, you may possess realistic or unrealistic rules about yourself and others. You may use self-talk in ways that create anxiety of calm you down. You may perceive speakers and their reactions to you either accurately or inaccurately. The need for all people to think effectively in their relationships pervades this book.

CHAPTER HIGHLIGHTS

• Active understanding is a shorthand term for listeners showing understanding by responding as if in speakers' internal viewpoints. You need to use active understanding flexibly.

• Paraphrasing, rewording speakers' verbal utterances, is one of the component skills of active understanding.

• Reflecting feelings is the main skill of actively showing understanding. Reflecting feelings entails showing understanding of speakers' verbal, voice and body messages. In addition, listeners can reflect the reasons speakers provide for their feelings.

• Questions can help clarify and expand speakers' internal viewpoints. Questioners can still allow speakers to continue owning their problems and issues.

• Types of questions include: open-ended versus close-ended; specific detail; elaboration; eliciting personal meanings; checking understanding; and solution-focused questions.

• Questioning skills include: interspersing active understanding with questions, asking follow-on questions and carefully observing how questions are answered.

• When listening, you can challenge or confront speakers to help them expand and explore their perceptions. You can challenge speakers' inconsistencies and possible distortions of reality.

• Skills for challenging include: starting with active understanding, assisting speakers to challenge themselves and avoiding threatening voice and body messages.

• Listeners should avoid responding in ways that block speakers from having sufficient psychological safety and space to reveal themselves.

• Listening blocks include the following: interrupting, monopolizing, rehearsing, switching off, part-listening, mind-reading, being right, changing the subject, intimidating, placating, reassuring, advising, judging, interrogating and breaking confidences.

• All listening blocks reflect thinking skills deficits.

EXERCISES

EXERCISE 7.1
DEVELOP MY PARAPHRASING SKILLS

Instructions

Part A
On your own

1. Paraphrase once the content of each of the following statements into clear and simple language. Use 'you' or 'your' where the speaker uses 'I' or 'Me'. Remember there is no single correct answer.

a. 'It bothers me when you don't respond.'
b. 'I appreciate the help you've given me.'
c. 'I shall miss my girlfriend when she's away.'
d. 'I couldn't help laughing when he screwed up.'
e. 'You're having me on.'

2. Think of at least three different ways of paraphrasing the following statements.

a. 'I've always been shy in social situations.'
b. 'I feel shut out by her and don't know why.'

Part B
Practise in pairs and in a group

1. *In pairs*. You 'feed' each other statements. Listeners paraphrase speakers' statements and speakers provide feedback on their reactions to each paraphrase.

2. *In a group*. Members take turns in making statements – they may write them on whiteboards or blackboards. After each statement, all group members formulate a paraphrase and then share them with the group.

EXERCISE 7.2
DEVELOP MY REFLECTING FEELINGS SKILLS

Instructions

Part A
Identify and paraphrase feelings words and phrases

For each of the following statements: (a) identify the words and phrases the speaker has used to describe how he or she feels; and (b) paraphrase these words and phrases to reflect accurately how the speaker feels.

1. Tony to Wayne: 'I find being without a job depressing. I'm young and want to get ahead. Right now my prospects look bleak.'

Tony's feelings words and phrases: _____

_____

Paraphrases of feelings words and phrases: _____

_____

2. Eileen to Tricia: 'I'm determined to be my own woman. Its exciting to think I could have a successful career.'

Eileen's feelings words and phrases:_____

_____

Paraphrases of feelings words and phrases:_____

_____

Part B
Reflect feelings and reasons

For each of the following statements formulate a 'You feel…because…' response that reflects the speaker's main feeling or feelings and states their explanation for it/them.

1. Maureen to Vince: 'I hate being teased. I just hate it. I'm no different from the other girls and yet they seem to enjoy ganging up on me. It makes me feel so angry and lonely.'

You feel _____

because _____

_____

2. Ian to Sally: 'I get annoyed when people don't understand my relationship with Tom. Sure we are emotionally very close, but what's wrong with that? Some people can't understand intimate friendships between guys.'

You feel _____

because _____

_____

Part C
Practise in pairs and in a group

1. *In pairs.* Each of you takes turns to be speaker and listener. When listening, help your speaker to talk about his/her feelings by reflecting them accurately. Pay attention to voice and body as well as verbal messages.

2. *Group exercises*

a. The group picks a feeling. Then members identify and demonstrate the verbal, voice and body messages required to express that feeling mildly, moderately and strongly. Repeat the exercise for other feelings.

b. This exercise may be done with a beach ball or tennis ball. Members sit in a circle. The member holding the ball (the speaker) expresses a feeling by means of verbal, voice and body messages. He/she pauses to allow all members to formulate a reflection of feeling response and then throws the ball to one member (the listener) who attempts to reflect the feeling accurately. Then the listener becomes the speaker and so on.

c. One member sits in front and acts as a speaker who is trying to share and explore his feelings on a topic. The remaining group members sit in a semi-circle around him/her. The speaker states a feeling to each member of the group in turn. After each statement, the member who is 'listener' reflects the speaker's feeling as accurately as possible. Members take turns in being the speaker.

Part D
Practise in a relationship

1. Identify a specific relationship in which you could improve your active understanding skills.

2. State as specifically as possible the changes you wish to make in your active understanding skills: for instance, 'Reflecting all his/her main feelings more accurately not only with my words, but with my voice and body messages'.

3. Plan how to implement the change(s) in your active understanding skills, for instance when and in what situations.

4. Indicate the specific consequences for yourself and the other person that you predict will follow from your improved active understanding skills.

5. Implement your plan to show improved active understanding skills.

6. Assess the positive and negative consequences for yourself and the other person of using better active understanding skills. Have your predictions been confirmed or negated? Has this exercise taught you something about how you can strengthen your active understanding skills? If so, what?

EXERCISE 7.3
DEVELOP MY QUESTIONING SKILLS
Instructions

Part A
Different types of questions

Provide an example of each of the following types of questions:

Open-ended question: _____

_____

Specific detail question: _____

_____

Elaboration question: _____

_____

Eliciting personal meaning question: _____

_____

Checking understanding question: _____

_____

Solution-focused question: _____

_____

Part B
Practise in pairs, in a group and in real life

1. *In pairs.* Work with a partner who discusses a problem with you. Help your partner to understand his/her problem more clearly by using the listening skills of paraphrasing, reflecting feelings and questioning. Throughout, pay attention to your verbal, voice and body messages. End by asking your partner to summarize the 'session'. Afterwards, discuss and reverse roles.

2. *In a group.* One person acts as speaker who presents a problem to the group who sit in a semi-circle facing him/her. Each member takes turns in responding to the speaker first by reflecting what he/she has just said and then by asking a question. When finished, the speaker provides feedback on the 'session'. Members take turns as speakers.

3. *In real life.* Monitor your skills of using questions when you listen. Observe the consequences of your questions for others and yourself. Identify specific questioning skills deficits and work to change them.

EXERCISE 7.4
DEVELOP MY CHALLENGING SKILLS
Part A Examples of challenges
Instructions

Provide a tactful challenging response in each of the following areas.

1. *Challenge inconsistencies*

Inconsistency between verbal, voice and body messages

_____

_____

Inconsistency between words and actions

_____

_____

Inconsistency between past and present statements

_____

_____

2. *Challenge possible distortions of reality*
Give two examples

Example 1: _____

_____

Example 2: _____

_____

Part B
Practise in pairs, in a group and in real life

1. *In pairs*. Work with a partner who 'feeds' you inconsistencies on which you can develop your challenging skills. Afterwards, reverse roles.

2. *In a group*. Members of the group take it in turns to provide stimulus statements involving inconsistencies to the whole group. After each statement, each member shares their challenging response.

3. *In real life*. Monitor your skills of challenging when you listen. Observe the consequences of your challenges for others and yourself. Identify specific challenging skills deficits and work to change them.

EXERCISE 7.5
WHAT ARE MY LISTENING BLOCKS?
Part A
Assess my listening blocks
Instructions

Using the scale below, rate each of the following listening blocks according to how much you respond that way in *either* a specific relationship *or* in important relationships for you. First, answer on your own. Then, if appropriate, discuss with another or others.

Always   3
Frequently 2
Sometimes   1
Never   0

Your rating   **Blocks**

_____ Interrupting

_____ Monopolizing

_____ Rehearsing

_____ Switching off

_____ Part-listening

_____ Mind-reading

_____ Being right

_____ Changing the subject

_____ Intimidating

_____ Placating

_____ Reassuring

_____ Advising

_____ Judging

_____ Interrogating

_____ Breaking confidences

Look at the times that you have rated 3, 2 or 1 and assess the consequences in your relationship(s) of each of these ways of responding.

Part B
Practise in pairs and in a group

1. *In pairs*. Each partner identifies what they consider to be their main listening block. The one partner speaks while the 'listener' responds with the speaker's main listening block to let him/her experience what it feels like to be on the receiving end of it. Afterwards, discuss and reverse roles. This exercise can be repeated for other listening blocks.

2. *In a group*. One person sits out front as the speaker and the rest of the group sits in a semi-circle around him/her. The speaker tries to talk to each member in turn who responds with his/her (the group member's) main listening block. After each response, the group tries to identify the listening block. Members take turns at being speakers.

EXERCISE 7.6
GROUP DISCUSSION: SHOWING UNDERSTANDING SKILLS

Instructions

This is intended as a group exercise, though it may be done individually or in pairs. For each part:

1. spend 10–15 minutes answering the question in groups of three or four,

2. each group shares its answers with the whole group,

3. then the whole group ranks the six most important points or skills from the most important to the least important.

Part A
Blocks to rewarding listening

List the six main ways that people block others from talking to them.

Part B
Showing understanding skills

List the six main skills for showing another person that you have clearly understood what they communicate.

ANSWERS TO EXERCISES

Exercise 7.1
Develop My Paraphrasing Skills

Following are suggestions, though other answers might also be appropriate.

Part A   On your own

Question 1
a. 'You feel upset when I don't reply.'
b. 'You're grateful for my assistance.'
c. 'You're going to be lonely when (name of girlfriend) isn't around.'
d. 'You couldn't control your mirth at his mistake.'
e. 'You think I'm making a fool of you.'

Question 2
a. 'You've always been bashful in company.'
  'You've always been timid when socializing.'
  'You've always been anxious with people.'
b. 'I feel excluded by her and can't find the reason.'

'I feel pushed away by her and can't understand it.'
'I feel rejected by her and have no explanation for it.'

Exercise 7.2
Develop My Reflecting Feelings Skills

Part A   Identify and paraphrase feelings words and phrases.

Other paraphrases than those suggested below may also be appropriate.

1. Tony's feelings words and phrases: 'depressing', 'want to get ahead', 'bleak.' Paraphrases of feelings words and phrases: 'a downer', 'wish to be successful', 'unpromising'.

2. Eileen's feelings words and phrases: 'determined', 'exciting', 'successful'. Paraphrases of feelings words and phrases: 'resolved', 'thrilling', 'good.'

Part B   Reflect feelings and reasons

1. 'You feel mad and isolated because you loathe being treated and picked on as though you're different.'

2. 'You feel angry because people think your feelings for Tom are gay.'

EIGHT
Managing Shyness Skills

Venus favours the bold.
Ovid

CHAPTER QUESTIONS

- *What is shyness?*
- *How can shyness be defined in relating skill terms?*
- *How can you develop thinking skills to manage shyness?*
- *What verbal, voice and body messages do you require to introduce yourself effectively?*
- *What skills do you require to start conversations?*
- *What skills do you require to hold conversations?*
- *What skills do you require to end conversations?*
- *What skills do you require to make a dat*

An essential relating skill is the ability to make initial contact with others. Below are two young men, Mick and Rob, who go to the same party, where neither knows anybody else well. Unlike Rob, Mick suffers from shyness.

> Mick, 19, goes to the party having made a big effort to overcome his nerves. Though attractive, he thinks that people do not find him so. On arrival he is given a drink and introduced to a group of people. He listens to them politely, but never contributes to the discussion. He appears tense and lacks warmth and vitality. He

does not move around much and waits for people to talk to him.

Rob, 18, goes to the party excited and determined to do his best to have a good time. He is not afraid to go up to people whom he thinks look interesting and introduce himself. When conversing he appears interested in what others say and participates in a lively and relaxed way. Since he wants to meet new people he moves around. He enjoys himself and helps others to do likewise.

WHAT IS SHYNESS?

Dictionary definitions of shyness emphasize words like bashful and timid. Shyness is a problem for children, adolescents and adults alike. Based on a large-scale shyness survey mainly conducted on American college students, Zimbardo (1977) found that more than 80 per cent reported that they were shy at some points in their lives. Of these, over 40 per cent considered themselves presently shy. Zimbardo's findings focus on people who admit their shyness. In varying degrees, anxiety is always present in social situations, though much of it goes unacknowledged.

Describing shyness

When people feel shy, how do they describe their experience? You can feel, think and act shy. However, some who feel and think shy are very good at covering it up by not acting shy. Such people are privately rather than publicly shy.

• *Feeling shy*. Words that people associate with feeling shy include: timid, anxious, insecure, bashful, lonely, confused, mistrustful, embarrassed, ashamed, afraid, tense, humiliated and vulnerable. Physical reactions that can accompany shy feelings include: blushing, nausea, faintness, perspiring, knotted stomach, pounding heart, shaking, dry mouth and shallow breathing.

• *Thinking shy*. Shy people tend to have negative thoughts about themselves and about what others think of them. Examples of negative thoughts about themselves include: 'I am uninteresting', 'I lack confidence' and 'I lack social skills.' Examples of negative thoughts about what others think include: 'They think less of me because I am shy', 'They are very concerned about my behaviour', 'They may reject me.' For a person who thinks shy, the world is a dangerous place. As John Powell (1969) writes: 'I am afraid to tell you who I am, because, if I tell you who I am, you may not like who I am, and it's all that I have' (p. 12).

• *Acting shy*. Illustrative verbal messages associated with shyness include: staying silent or speaking only when spoken to, disclosing little about yourself and being too ready to agree. Illustrative voice messages include: speaking softly, stammering and, sometimes, loudness masking insecurity. Illustrative body messages include: avoiding situations, averting gaze, smiling too much and a tight body posture. Many shy people handle their social anxieties by wearing masks or acting out defensive roles (Powell, 1969). These roles include: aggression, clowning, conforming, cynicism, inappropriate flirting, monopolizing, self-disparagement and playing the strong, silent type.

Some people are shy with all people in all situations. However, others vary in how shy they feel, think and act depending on whom they are with and in what situations they find themselves. For example, Zimbardo's (1977) shy students were shy with the following categories of people in descending order: strangers, the opposite sex, authorities by virtue of their knowledge, authorities by virtue of their role, relatives, elderly people, friends, children and parents.

There are a range of situations in which people experience shyness. Conversing with strangers, dating, requesting help, going to a party, situations requiring assertiveness (for example, returning something to a shop), going to a dance/disco, showing your body in either non-sexual or sexual situations, starting to go out again after the break-up of a relationship are each situations that may generate shyness.

Defining shyness in relating skills terms

If you are shy, what can you do about it? People differ in the degree to which they are extroverted or introverted. Nevertheless, there is a large learned component in how shyness is both acquired and maintained. Some people who are seriously undercon-fident may need long-term counselling to help rebuild their shattered self-esteem. Most shy people can gain from either individual counselling and/or attending training groups focused on managing shyness. Those who have access to neither need rely on self-help, including reading material such as this chapter

Table 8.1 Some goals for managing shyness and initiating contract

Thinking skills goals	Action skills goals
Develop skills to	Develop verbal, voice and body skills to
Own responsibility for choosing	Introduce myself
Understand the relationship between how I think, feel and act	Start conversations Hold conversations
Use coping self-talk	End conversations
Choose realistic personal rules	Make a date
Choose to perceive accurately	
Explain cause accurately	
Predict realistically	
Set realistic goals	
Use visualizing	

In Table 8.1, I identify many thinking skills deficits and action skills deficits common among shy people. I have chosen to state these deficits in the positive as goals. I do not imply that all the skills deficits are equally present or important for all shy people. You have to work with the deficits that are relevant to sustaining your shyness. Once you have identified your personal deficits, you can then state them in the positive as goals. As the chapter progresses I describe how to overcome each deficit and attain each goal.

When thinking of goals, distinguish between coping and mastery. Coping means managing the situations and people associated with your shyness better. Mastery means not being shy at all. Try to think in terms of progressively coping better. If you focus on mastery, you will put additional pressure on yourself that could be counter-productive. If mastery ends up as a by-product of coping, that's wonderful! If not, you can still be proud of your progress.

DEVELOP THINKING SKILLS FOR MANAGING SHYNESS

If you are shy now, many early learnings contributed to it. These include the examples set by your parents. Zimbardo (1977) observes: 'In general, then, about 70 percent of the time parents and children share the same shyness label; they tend to be shy together' [pp. 62–63]. Also, any negative consequences provided by others when you reached out may have contributed. However, your present problem is how to stop sustaining your shyness if it interferes with attaining relationship goals. One of the main ways in which you sustain your shyness is by thinking shy. I now present nine thinking skills, in each of which you can alter the balance more in the direction of self-support than self-oppression.

Own responsibility for choosing

If you are presently shy and do not like the consequences, you can choose to change. You can empower yourself by assuming responsibility for doing something about your shyness. Admitting that you have a choice whether or not to stay shy is the first step in assuming responsibility for changing. You can choose to develop skills that will help you to feel, think and act more confidently in social situations. With the help of this book, you can identify some of your thinking and act on skills deficits and how to change them. Then, you need to work and practise, work and practise, work and practise until you become much more fluent in the skills. Even then, you will always need to assume responsibility for maintaining and developing your skills.

Understand the relationship between how you think, feel and act

In Chapter 2, I pointed out that thinking, feeling and acting are interrelated. Here I go one stage further to provide you with an STC framework for analysing the relationships between how you think, feel and act (Nelson-Jones, 1996). In this framework,

STC stand for Situation – Thoughts – Consequences, respectively. Consequences fall into three categories: feelings, physical reactions and actions. The idea is that, more often than not, how you feel, physically react and act in specific situations is mediated by your thoughts at T rather than the actual situation. Let's take a before and after example of Janet who becomes shy on first dates with males whom she does not know well.

S1 – *Situation.*

> Janet is eating in a restaurant on her first date with Patrick.

T1 – *Thoughts.*

> Janet's thoughts include 'I must make a good impression', 'I always get tense on first dates', and 'Patrick is evaluating me all the time'.

C1 – *Consequences.*

> Janet's feelings consequences are feeling timid and fearful. Her physical reactions include tension in her face and neck and her mouth going dry. Janet's action consequences include revealing little of herself and smiling nervously.

Now let's imagine that Janet has learned some more effective thinking skills. She may also have learned some more effective action skills that help her to think more confidently on first dates. Following is her revised STC, with the name of her date changed from Patrick to Scott.

S2 – *Situation.*

> Janet is eating in a restaurant on her first date with Scott.

T2 – *Thoughts.*

> Janet thinks 'We're here to enjoy ourselves', 'Some tension is inevitable on first dates and I know I can handle it', and 'This date gives Scott and me the opportunity to know each other better. If we don't hit it off, Scott's not the only fish in the ocean.'

C2 – *Consequences.*

> Janet's feelings consequences are feeling moderately relaxed and confident. She experiences no major physical discomfort. Janet's action consequences include participating actively in the conversation and laughing with amusement.

If you can see the relationships between how you think, feel and act, you are in a better position to identify and develop appropriate skills to manage your shyness. When you detect self-defeating feelings, physical reactions and actions, you can look for thoughts and thinking skills deficits that may contribute to them. As illustrated above, you can combat shy thinking both by directly changing how you think and also by changing how you act which in turn changes how you think. In the final analysis, unless you can act more effectively you are unlikely to maintain your improved thinking skills. To take the above example, Janet requires confirmation, by behaving differently in real life, that her thinking skills benefit her.

Use coping self-talk

Coping self-talk is a very useful thinking skill for managing feelings of shyness (Meichenbaum, 1983, 1985; Meichenbaum & Deffenbacher, 1988). The goals of coping self-talk are to calm your anxieties and to help you deal effectively with the task at hand. Coping self-talk contains three elements: calming self-talk, coaching self-talk and affirming self-talk.

Contrast coping self-talk with negative self-talk. To return to the examples at the beginning of the chapter about Mick and Rob going to the party, their self-talk was as follows.

Mick's negative self-talk

> 'I know that I am going to find this party diffi-cult. Everybody is looking at me. I feel unattrac-tive. I don't want to make a mistake. I'm feeling tense and, when this happens, I know it will only get worse.'

Rob's coping self-talk

> 'I enjoy parties and meeting new people. Though I get a little anxious with strangers I know I can overcome this. I can use my skills of relaxing, selecting interesting people, introduc-ing myself, conversing and, if appropriate, arranging to meet people again. I'll give it my best shot.'

Let's look at calming, coaching and affirming self-statements in turn.

• *Calming.* Simple self-statements include: 'Keep calm', 'Relax' and 'Just take it easy'. In addition, you can instruct yourself to 'Breathe slowly and regularly'.

• *Coaching.* The idea of coaching self-statements is that they guide you in the specific skills you require for competent performance. You could start by telling yourself you can cope: for instance, 'I can handle this situation' or 'My anxiety is a signal for me to use my coping skills.' Then, you can instruct yourself in what you need to do: for instance, 'When I introduce myself I need to smile, say 'Hello', clearly state my name and hold out my hand.'

• *Affirming*. You can remind yourself that you have strengths in social situations. For instance, 'I can listen well', 'Remember, I get on well with many people.'

• *Calming, coaching and affirming*. Often coping self-talk consists of putting calming, coaching and affirming self-statements together: for example, 'Calm down, take turns in listening and speaking, I get on well with many people.'

You can use coping self-talk before, during and after stressful social situations. For instance, before you might say, 'Calm down. Develop a plan to manage the situation.'; during, 'Relax. Smile. Disclose as well as listen.'; and after, 'Each time I use my coping self-talk skills it seems to get easier.'

Another area in which you can use coping self-talk is if you are prone to potentially destructive self-doubt when starting close relationships. For example, if you had a very successful date a couple of evenings ago, but have had no further contact with your date since then, you may handle your insecurity by devaluing yourself and later possibly coming on too strong. Instead, tell yourself to calm down, realistically appraise the feedback you received (much of which may have been very positive) and either initiate contact or wait and see what happens. If you cannot trust yourself to remember the positive feedback, write it down.

Choose realistic personal rules

Your personal rules are the 'dos' and 'don'ts' by which you lead your life. Each of you has an inner rule-book that guides your living and loving. If your rules are self-supporting they can motivate and help you to attain realistic goals. However, if your rules are self-oppressing, they can leave you open to a triple dose of low self-esteem. For example, Phil has a rule that he must be successful on all his first dates. However his first date with Erica does not go well, so this activates his first dose of low self-esteem. His second dose of low self-esteem stems from his thinking that he should not be anxious and depressed about his dating ability. Phil generates his third dose of low self-esteem by moving on to devalue not just his dating ability but his whole worth as a person.

Albert Ellis (1988, 1995) uses the term 'musturbation' to refer to rigid personal rules characterized by 'musts', 'oughts' and 'shoulds'. Ellis regards any emotional and behavioural consequences as determined by your beliefs in relation to the activating event more than by the activating event itself. I prefer the term personal rules to beliefs.

Four important unrealistic personal rules that contribute to people sustaining their shyness are:

1. I *must* be liked and approved of by everyone I meet.
2. I *must* never reveal anything about myself that might be viewed negatively.
3. I *must* never make a mistake in social situations.
4. I *must* never have set-backs in learning to overcome my shyness.

Let's look at an example of an unrealistic personal rule of Janet's regarding first dates.

S1 – *Situation*.

> Janet is eating in a restaurant on her first date with Patrick.

T1 – *Thought*.

> Janet's unrealistic personal rule is 'I must be approved of by everyone I meet.'

C1 – *Consequences*.

> Consequences include timidity and fear, tension in face and neck, and revealing little of herself and smiling nervously.

What skills does Janet require for dealing with her unrealistic personal rule? First, she requires detecting skills; second, disputing or challenging skills; third, restating unrealistic into realistic rules skills.

1. *Detecting skills*. Janet may be helped to detect her unrealistic rule by learning to analyse her thinking in STC terms. When she has unwanted feelings and behaves inappropriately, she checks for any thoughts that may contribute to her distress.

2. *Disputing skills*. Disputing means challenging the false assumptions that you hold about yourself, others and the world. Janet needs to dispute vigorously her unrealistic rule by asking searching questions. Following are questions that Janet might ask to dispute her self-oppressing personal rule that 'I must be approved of by everyone I meet'.

> 'What evidence exists that supports the truth of my personal rule?'
> 'What evidence exists that reveals the falseness of my personal rule?'
> 'What are the worst possible things that might happen to me if I were not to be approved of by someone?'
> 'What exactly, can't I stand about not being approved by Patrick?'
> 'Do I demand the same standards of gaining approval for other people as I apply to myself?'
> 'How exactly might not being approved of by Patrick make me worthless as a person?'
> 'What are the negative consequences to me of my demand that I must be approved of by everyone I meet?'

3. *Restating skills.* Restating involves substituting self-supporting for self-oppressing characteristics in specific personal rules. The main difference is that between demanding and preferential thinking. Unrealistic rules are based on childish demandingness and focused on me, me, me. Realistic rules acknowledge the reality that the world may not always be as you would like, but nevertheless you can cope with it. Furthermore, realistic rules help you evaluate the usefulness of specific characteristics for attaining goals rather than to rate yourself as a whole person.

Following is Janet's STC, incorporating a more realistic personal rule. Again, the subsequent date is with Scott.

S2 – Situation.

> Janet is eating in a restaurant on her first date with Scott.

T2 – Thought.

> 'Though I might prefer to be universally approved, it is unreasonable and unnecessary to demand that this be the case. I can meet my needs for friendship and affection if I only meet some people who like me and whom I like.'

C2 – Consequences.

> Feels moderately relaxed, no major discomfort, participates actively in conversation and so on.

Following are restatements of the second, third and fourth unrealistic rules cited above as common among shy people.

2. 'Nobody's perfect. If I am to have honest and open relationships I need to reveal my vulnerabilities as well as my strengths.'

3. 'To err is human. Though I would prefer not to make mistakes I can use them as learning experiences.'

4. 'Set-backs are part of learning any new skill. They are challenges with which I can cope.'

Many shy people stay shy because of what Ellis (1988) calls low frustration tolerance. Unrealistic expectations about the learning process and smoothness of life can make you vulnerable to set-backs. Also, sometimes your level of performance may be good, but you do not get the outcomes you wish (Bandura, 1986). You can develop skills of supporting yourself and persisting through set-backs rather than giving in to them.

Choose to perceive accurately

Frequently shy people both perceive themselves too negatively and jump to conclusions unfavourable to themselves in specific situations.

Perceive yourself more accurately

For shy people perceiving themselves more accurately is usually a matter of reducing unrealistic negative perceptions and owning realistic strengths (Alden & Wallace, 1995; Rapee, 1993). In a study of vulnerability to depression, British researchers Teasdale and Dent (1987) selected the following self-devaluing adjectives from a list associated with depression: deficient, failure, inadequate, incompetent, inferior, pathetic, stupid, unloved, unwanted, useless, weak and worthless. Arguably, these are many of the same words that shy people use to devalue themselves. In addition, many shy people add to their sense of inferiority by perceiving others as more socially competent, witty and strong than they really are (Alden & Wallace, 1995).

Following are some suggestions for perceiving yourself more positively.

1. *Own your strengths*. List what you, not other people, consider to be your strengths, assets and resources. Modesty is out of place when doing this: probably already you are too skilled at noting your social deficiencies. Add to this list as new ideas come to mind. Then read this list regularly to affirm your strengths. You may also put your strengths on cue cards and read through them regularly or on cassettes and listen to them regularly.

2. *Challenge your negative perceptions*. Use your questioning skills to challenge the accuracy of your negative perceptions. Where is the evidence for them?

3. *Use thought stopping*. When you catch yourself in an unproductive, negative train of thought, silently shout to yourself 'STOP!'. Try to stifle your unrealistic, negative self-perceptions as soon as you become aware of them. The thoughts are likely to return, but just repeat the procedure as needed.

4. *Use thought switching*. When you find yourself ruminating on your social inadequacies, replace them with positive perceptions and an appreciation of positive social experiences. For instance, if you feel lonely and inadequate, switch to thinking of your friends and, possibly, even contact one.

5. *Use visualizing*. Kassorla (1984) advocates mental vacuuming. She gets her clients to imagine a tiny toy vacuum cleaner sweeping across their foreheads and vacuuming up all their negative words and images. Another image is to place all the negative words and images in a balloon that drifts off out of sight.

Perceive situations more accurately

If you are shy, the way you perceive many situations is likely to sustain your discomfort. Each person carries within them some pain and insecurity. Without necessarily knowing it, you can be so influenced by your self-doubts that in specific situations you jump to unwarranted conclusions and then treat these conclusions as facts. Often people are unaware that they may jump to conclusions rather than say to themselves 'Stop...think...what are my choices in how to view this situation?' Psychiatrist Aaron Beck observes that frequently people have underlying automatic thoughts and perceptions that influence their emotions (Beck, 1976; Beck & Weishaar, 1995). Either people are not fully conscious of these thoughts and images or it does not occur to them that they warrant special scrutiny. Beck collaborates with his patients in the scientific or detective work of identifying these self-oppressing perceptions or 'what you tell yourself'.

Here is an example within the STC framework.

> **S** Cameron talks to Fiona at the party and then circulates.
> **T** Fiona perceives: 'Cameron does not like me.'
> **C** Fiona feels depressed and leaves the party early.

However, Fiona might have had many other perceptions at T, including the following.

> 'Cameron is sensible in wanting to circulate at a party.'
> 'Cameron liked me enough to come and talk to me.'
> 'I need to improve my conversational skills if I am going to hold the interest of men like Cameron.'
> 'There are plenty of other men at the party so why keep worrying about Cameron?'
> 'I quite liked Cameron but I didn't find him that fascinating.'

If you are like Fiona and have a tendency to jump to conclusions that are negative for you, you require detecting, disputing and restating skills to combat this.

1. *Detecting skills.* Become aware of the signals that you may be oppressing yourself. These signals include negative feelings about yourself and others, without good cause, and self-defeating behaviour that distances you from others. Also, you can identify the kinds of people and situations associated with devaluing yourself.

2. *Disputing skills.* Monitor your thinking in specific situations and practise making the connections between upsetting feelings and upsetting perceptions. Question your perceptions by logical analysis and search for better explanations. This process involves your engaging in the following kinds of self-talk.

> 'Stop...think...what are my choices in how to perceive this situation?'
> 'Are my perceptions based on fact or inference?'
> 'If they are based on inference are there other ways of perceiving the situation that are more closely related to the factual evidence?'
> 'What further information do I need to collect?'

3. *Restating skills.* If appropriate, you replace your initial perception with the perception that represents the best fit in relation to the factual evidence.

Let's assume that Fiona has some skills in choosing the most realistic perception. She went back in her mind over her contact with Cameron and assessed the evidence for her 'He does not like me' perception. On doing this Fiona discovered that there were no facts to support this conclusion and that it was an inference on her part. She generated alternative perceptions such as the five perceptions listed above. Fiona decided that the most realistic perception was: 'I need to improve my conversational skills if I am going to hold the interest of men like Cameron.' She did not feel devalued by this perception which left her feeling still in control of her life.

Explain cause accurately

How you explain your shyness influences whether you work to overcome it or stay stuck. There are a number of faulty explanations for shyness which can weaken motivation for change. These explanations are often partial truths; the error is to treat them as whole truths. Below are some possibly inaccurate explanations concerning shyness.

• *'It's my genes.'* This is the opinion that you are shy by nature rather than by nurture. Though people possess different biological propensities to anxiety, a considerable part of shyness represents learned behaviour sustained by current thinking and action skills deficits.

• *'It's my unfortunate past.'* Your unfortunate past or 'What others did to you' may have contributed to your acquiring some skills deficits contributing to shyness. However, you sustain your shyness by 'What you do to yourself'. If you have had a very unfortunate past you may require counselling to provide the nurturing and healing you never received from natural or surrogate parents. However, many people, with or without professional help, have learned to overcome skills deficits caused by their unfortunate pasts.

• *'It's up to others.'* Some of you may play a passive rather than an active role when meeting new people. It is as though you wait for events to happen to you rather than take an active part in shaping events. You are letting others assume the responsibility for helping you out of your shell. This may not happen. Sometimes passivity is reinforced by social rules. For instance, though changing, males are still expected to take more risks in initiating contact than females. This double standard may have negative consequences for both sexes: shy females can have insufficiently developed initiating contact skills and shy males can feel excessively pressured to take social initiatives. A major theme of this book is that each person must assume responsibility for making the choices that work best for them. Sitting or standing around waiting for something to happen is frequently not the best choice.

• *'It's all my fault.'* You may consider that everything that goes wrong in social situations is your fault. You may fail to take into account that when two people relate each has a responsibility for the success of the contact, not just you. Your hypersensitivity to feelings of embarrassment and willingness to blame yourself may erode rather than help you gain the confidence to work on your shyness.

The above explanations may describe not only how you became shy but also why you remain shy. Do any of them resonate with the ring of truth for you? If so, work hard at challenging the faulty thinking contained in these explanations. Some research suggests people who explain their social successes and failures to controllable causes experience less shyness and anxiety than those who do not (Bruch & Pearl, 1995). Following are more realistic formulations of each of the above explanations.

> 'Though like many people I'm naturally sensitive, I've mainly learned to be shy.'
> 'Though others undoubtedly contributed to my becoming shy, I currently sustain my shyness through skills deficits that I can work to overcome.'
> 'It is not up to others to make the first move to help me out of my shyness since I am responsible for making the choices in life that work best for me.'
> 'I am only responsible for my own behaviour in social situations rather than needing to accept total responsibility for what happens.'

Predict realistically

You lead your life into the future rather than into the past. Predictions are thoughts and images about the probability of future events. A study of depressed and non-depressed students by psychologists Paula Pietromonaco and Karen Rook (1987) found differences in their decision making style. Depressed students were significantly less likely to assign weight to the potential gains of acting in social situations and significantly more likely to assign weight to the potential risks. Furthermore, for decisions about initiating social contact and establishing intimacy, depressed students expressed a greater reluctance to take the target actions than did the non-depressed students. If you are shy, this does not necessarily mean that you are depressed. However, I have cited the above study because many shy people have a similar pattern of overestimating risk, underestimating gain and hence being less prepared to act.

In my private counselling practice I find that I can help some shy people by building up their skills of generating and evaluating gains.

> Sean, aged 30, had little experience of dating women; his longest experience lasting three dates. In his church group, Sean was on a committee with Suzanne who had been friendly to him and whom he wondered if he should ask

out. Sean questioned 'Why bother to take the risk of seeking the gain?' With his counsellor, Sean generated both the potential risks and gains of taking this initiative. He was already expert at acknowledging risks and needed to learn that: 'It is in my interests to look at gains as well as risks in my decisions'. His list of potential gains for asking Suzanne out included the following;

'I might have a chance of a strong relation-ship'

'I might gain more experience in developing relationships.'

'This might contribute to helping me become happier.'

'I might gain confidence and a more positive self-image.'

'I might develop my ability to express my feel-ings more.'

'I might give myself the opportunity of Suzanne taking some of the initiative too.'

Sean evaluated that the gains of asking Suzanne out outweighed the risks. She later became his first steady girlfriend.

The most conclusive way of gauging the accuracy of your predictions is, like Sean, to put them to the test. Reality testing your previously negative predictions may become easier if you carefully break tasks down, take small steps before larger steps, rehearse what you are going to do and, where appropriate, seek the support of other people.

You may have tried to overcome your shyness before and been unsuccessful. Now, your prediction is: 'I've tried before. What's the use?' However, your past is not necessarily a guide to your future. Unnecessary pessimism may result from predictions that are permanent, 'I have my problem for all time', and pervasive, 'I have my problem in every situation' (Seligman, 1991). You require realistic optimism. For instance, this time you may try harder, understand your shyness better, possess better skills at managing it and be better at enlisting the support of others. The fact that you have tried before does not mean that you cannot now learn new and better skills to help you succeed. Following is a more optimistic prediction than 'I've tried before. What's the use?' that you might tell yourself.

'Though I've tried before, present circumstances are different and I understand better how I maintained my shyness. Now I can develop new and better skills to become more outgoing.'

Set realistic goals

A way that shy people can influence their futures is to set themselves realistic goals. Though the categories overlap, goals can be either for specific situations, say conversing with two new people at a party, or for developing better skills to manage shyness and initiate contact, for instance introducing yourself skills. Well-stated goals can increase your sense of authorship over your life, provide clarity of focus and increase your motivation. Poorly stated goals may represent other people's ideas rather than your own. Also, they may be unrealistically high and place you under unnecessary pressure.

Following are some considerations in setting goals. First, do they reflect your values? Your goals should reflect what you consider worthwhile in life. For instance, you may be happy with just a few close friends rather than with hordes of them. Second, are your goals realistic? Your goals need to adequately acknowledge the constraints of your emotional resources and relating skills. For instance, you need to be realistic about the kinds of people with whom you have something in common. Third, are your goals specific? Ideally you should state them so that you can easily measure your success in attaining them. 'I want to be less shy' is too vague. You need to state specific skills for making yourself a less shy person: for instance, developing specific verbal, voice and body message skills so that you can converse with people effectively. Fourth, do you have a time frame for attaining your goals? Shy people can be experts at avoidance. State whether you wish to attain each goal within a day, week, month, year or some other time frame. For instance, Joe, a 21-year-old college student, set a time frame of 24 hours for his goal of phoning Linda for a date. Joe also set a time frame of a week for telling his father how much he appreciated the financial sacrifices he was making for his college education.

Use visualizing skills

All people think in pictures as well as in words. For some people, using visual images is their main way of interacting with the world (Lazarus, 1984, 1992, 1995). Many shy people have negative visual images of how incompetent they are going to be in social situations and how appalled others will be. Instead, you can focus on the processes and outcomes of competent performance. Say you have an upcoming social situation which you fear you will handle poorly. Before going, you can take the opportunity for visualized rehearsal. Break the tasks down and focus on the skills or processes of competent performance. In addition, identify potential set-backs and develop ways of coping with them. Also, rehearse your coping self-talk skills along with your visualizing skills. Furthermore, visualize some realistic outcomes of skilled performance. For example, you can imagine a specific situation in which other people enjoy your company as you converse with them.

Here is an example of using visualized rehearsal to help overcome shyness in a specific situation.

Rosemary, 43, was married for 19 years to Bill, but they split up about a year ago. Rosemary is just getting her confidence back after the break up and feels very nervous about going out with men again. Last weekend, at her tennis club, Rosemary had a long conversation with Perry, 46, whose own marriage ended six months ago. Perry asked her if she would like to have another chat with him sometime and said he would phone her tonight. Rosemary uses her visualized rehearsal skills to imagine herself behaving competently when Perry phones, for instance both sitting and talking calmly. She also visualizes succeeding in arranging to meet Perry again. A side effect of Rosemary's visualized rehearsal is that she now feels less anxious about relating to Perry.

In the preceding pages I have taken what psychologists call a 'cognitive' or thinking skills approach to managing shyness. If you are shy you may already possess the action skills of making contact in your repertoire. You just need the confidence to use them. Other shy people, along with many who would not consider themselves shy, do not possess adequate action skills in their relating skills repertoire. It is to some of these action skills that I now turn.

DEVELOP ACTION SKILLS FOR CONVERSATIONS

There are different stages in starting relationships. Here the main focus is on helping you to make effective choices when first meeting people. This is the important time in which you make and receive first impressions. During this period you may plant the seeds for relationships to grow later. Alternatively, you may curtail opportunities either by choice or by mistake. When meeting people for the first time try to communicate: (1) a sense of relaxed competence, (2) liking and interest; (3) absence of threat; (4) an initial definition of yourself; and (5) that you are a rewarding person to get to know.

Introducing yourself

I attach great importance to introducing yourself skills. If competent in meeting and greeting people, you get off to a good start. However, the reverse is also true. If you give others a limp handshake and avert your gaze, they may feel uncomfortable. If you crush their hands and seem overbearing, they may instantly dislike you. There are many different contexts in which you meet people – colleges, homes, discos, business venues and so on. Also, you may be meeting one other person or a group of people. Following are some central verbal, voice and body message skills for introducing yourself in a range of situations.

• *Verbal messages.* Give a brief greeting and clearly state who you are: for example, 'Hello. I'm John/Jane Smith.' If others have not introduced themselves already, now they will probably do so without your needing to ask their name. If somebody else is introducing you to a third party, you can say 'Hello' followed by the third party's name. Saying another person's name makes remembering it for future use easier.

- *Voice messages.* Speak at a comfortable volume, clearly and fairly slowly so others can hear you first time. Be careful to avoid being monotonous by using emphasis in appropriate places. Speak with some enthusiasm and do not let your voice trail away at the end.

- *Body messages.* If standing, pull your shoulders back and do not slouch. Adopt an open position to the speaker. Do not get too close. Hold out your hand in a relaxed way and give a moderately firm handshake. Smile and look them in the eye.

How can you develop good skills at introducing yourself? First, you can observe how other people introduce themselves to you and to others. Identify some good role-models and note their verbal, voice and body message skills and the effect they have on others. Second, specify the skills you want to develop. Third, rehearse your skills. You can rehearse at home on your own, for instance in front of the mirror, or with another person. You can also use visualized rehearsal. Fourth, practise your skills in real life, evaluate their impact, and make changes as necessary. When practising your skills in real life, use coping self-talk to calm you down and coach you in what to do. Acknowledge your successes and keep working on your skills so that you maintain and develop rather than lose them.

Starting conversations

Getting started and breaking the ice is easier if you have developed a repertoire of appropriate opening remarks. You can then choose conversational openers and ice-breakers appropriate to the different situations in which you find yourself. Making initial contact is usually done by way of small talk as you 'feel' each other out psychologically to see if you want the contact to continue and on what level. Safe talk is another way of describing small talk. The level of disclosure is usually low in terms of intimacy. You have yet to establish trust and mutual acceptability. However, in situations where you are unlikely to meet again, a 'strangers on the train' phenomenon can occur in which disclosures may be surprisingly intimate (Derlega & Chaikin, 1975).

Often shy people insufficiently acknowledge that the process of starting conversations with new people involves uncertainty on both sides. You can place yourself under unnecessary pressure to be fluent. Some of you may have your favourite opening gambits that have worked well for you in the past. If so, why change? Others of you may wish to build up your repertoire. For instance, you can exchange basic information: 'What brings you here?'; 'Where do you live?' and 'What line of work are you in?' Another suggestion is to pass comments relevant to the occasion, perhaps following them up with a question: 'It's a great party. Do you agree?'; 'I've just arrived. What's happening?' You can also bring up topical events: again perhaps following them up with a question: 'I like this hot weather. Do you?'; 'What do you think of the monarchy?' If you are nervous, sometimes it is best to admit it: for instance, 'I feel nervous because this is the first time I've been here.' Also you can encourage others' attempts to make conversation with small rewards like: 'That's interesting'; 'Really?' and head nods.

Voice messages are very important. Good speech is easy to hear and relaxed. Shy people often need to work on speaking louder. For instance, Adrian is a shy student who talks very softly so as not to draw attention to himself. Sometimes, without being fully aware, you may show your nervousness by speaking very quickly or by slurring your words. Even those without obvious impediments may need to work on the quality of their speech.

Holding conversations

Argyle (1992) lists six types of rewarding verbal utterances that are conducive to developing friendships. First, you can pay compliments: for instance, 'I like your tie'; 'I like your dress.' Second, you can engage in 'pleasure talk'. You stick to cheerful, pleasant topics of conversation. There are a number of obvious ways in which you can keep yourself informed about various topics: reading newspapers and magazines; looking at the TV news; and keeping up to date on the latest developments in your specific areas of interest, for instance by watching your local football team or the latest movies. Third, in the interests of furthering the relationship, you can agree. Fourth, you can use the other person's name and also use 'we' to signal shared activities and group membership. Fifth, you can be helpful, for instance with information, sympathy or practical help. Sixth, you can use humour to break down barriers and increase mutual enjoyment. However, you may need to rehearse your jokes in advance so as not to blow the punch line.

Meeting new people involves searching for common ground. This is partly to find safe talk with which to fill or structure time. In general, people find silences awkward when they do not know each other well. However, this searching for common ground is also part of the exploration of whether you later wish to become friends, lovers or marital partners. You can find out specific information, for instance a shared hobby, a mutual friend and similarity of interests and beliefs. When asking questions, respect another's privacy by not probing too deeply. When talking about yourself, a general rule is you should match or even go slightly beyond the intimacy level of the speaker's disclosures.

A basic conversational sequence involves three steps: speaking-switching-listening. Use your listening, showing active understanding and disclosing skills. When switching, you coordinate who has the floor by sending and receiving voice, body and verbal cues (Argyle, 1991, 1992). When speakers finish they often use a prolonged gaze and stop gesturing with their hands. When not asking questions, the pitch of their voice may fall at the end of sentences. Politeness requires that listeners wait for speakers to finish sentences. When listeners wish to discourage speakers from continuing, they may avert their gaze, stop making 'uh huh' and verbal listening responses and even raise their hands.

Often shy people possess skills deficits in turn-taking. They leave others to do most of the work in bringing up topics and keeping conversations going. Also, shy people often reveal too little about themselves. Low self-disclosure, as well as interfering with the search for common ground, can leave speakers with the feeling that they are the only ones willing to risk sharing themselves. The giving of personal information is too one way.

Ending conversations

All people need to develop exit skills – the skills of ending conversations tactfully. Often, shy people, and even those not so shy, have trouble ending conversations. There are numerous reasons why you may choose to end a conversation. Such reasons range from boredom or heeding a call of nature to having to go when you would really rather stay conversing with someone you find attractive. Breaking eye contact, starting to edge away, making your body orientation less open, holding out your hand are all body messages that you wish to go.

How you end the conversation can have positive or negative consequences for your subsequent relationship. If you wish to meet again, you can show appreciation – for example, 'I very much enjoyed talking with you' said with a smile and with voice messages that indicate you are sincere about it. You could also reinforce this with a comment like 'I hope we meet again.' If your feelings are even more positive you might ask 'I wonder if we could get together again some time?'

If your feelings are negative, your disengaging body messages can become more pronounced, even to the extent of holding out the palm of your hand as a stop signal. You can make closure comments like 'Well, that's about the sum of it' and 'I must be off now' said in a firm voice. Also, you avoid smiling too much. If nothing else works, just leave.

Making a date

Since the position in this book is that of equality between the sexes, both females and males are encouraged to initiate when they want to meet somebody again. Receiving messages from another that they might be interested in dating involves using your decoding skills. Even then you may get it wrong. Males especially may be too ready to read sexual messages into the friendliness of females. Verbal messages that convey interest in dating include: compliments, making it clear that you have noticed the other in the past, reflecting the other's feelings, being helpful and asking the other questions about themselves (Muehlenhard, Koralewski, Andrews, & Burdick, 1986). Body messages include: eye contact, absence of arm and leg barriers, smiling, laughing and light touching – for instance on the hand, arm or upper back. Voice messages include animated speech and variations in emphasis.

Often asking for a date is done on the telephone. Some of the thinking skills discussed earlier are highly relevant to asking someone out. Coping self-talk can help you calm your anxieties as well as stay focused on the task at hand. Possessing realistic personal rules can prevent you from oppressing yourself with exaggerated fears about rejection. Predicting gain as well as risk can assist you in taking the risks that may bring you the gain. Other telephone skills include the following.

• *Clearly identify yourself.* For example 'Hello, this is Jane/John Smith. We met at Frieda and Ronnie's party last week.'

• *Send 'I' messages.* 'I'd like it if we could get together sometime' or 'I was wondering whether you would like to come out with me this weekend?'

• *Offer specific alternatives.* If the answer is favourable, be prepared to offer specific alternatives – for example, different movies or places for coffee. Make suggestions in such a way that the other person feels safe discussing them. Also, you can ask for their suggestions.

• *State your agreement clearly.* At the end it can be useful to summarize your agreement: 'Just to confirm, I'll pick you up at your flat at 8 p.m. to go see the movie at the Palace. I look forward to seeing you then.' A misunderstanding over the first meeting is not the best way to start a relationship.

• *Take refusals politely.* The other person has a perfect right to turn you down. With any luck, the other person will use tact. The other's courage in refusing you merits respect and you should politely end the conversation. If necessary, use appropriate self-talk to cope with the refusal – it certainly is not the end of the world!

CHAPTER HIGHLIGHTS

• Shyness is a very common problem. You can feel, think and act shy.

• Shyness can be defined in relating skills terms by identifying the thinking skills deficits and the action skills deficits that help maintain it. These deficits may be translated into goals for managing shyness.

• You can empower yourself by assuming personal responsibility for doing something about your shyness.

• You can use the STC (situation – thoughts – consequences) framework to identify the interrelationships between how you think, feel and act.

• You can replace negative self-talk with coping self-talk. Coping self-talk has three elements: calming, coaching and affirming self-statements.

• You may possess unrealistic rules, for instance 'I must be liked and approved by everyone I meet', that place you under pressure. Unrealistic rules require detecting, disputing and restating to become more realistic.

• You may need to challenge negative perceptions about yourself and also avoid jumping to inaccurate and self-devaluing conclusions about specific situations.

• Possible inaccurate explanations for the cause of shyness include: 'It's my genes'; 'It's my unfortunate past'; 'It's up to others'; and 'It's all my fault.' You can challenge these explanations and, where necessary, change them.

• Sometimes shy people overemphasize the losses and underemphasize the gains from acting. Also, you may be too pessimistic about the chances of developing better skills to manage shyness. You need to acknowledge gains from acting and be realistically optimistic about becoming less shy.

• You can set realistic goals both for specific social situations and also for developing managing shyness skills.

• You can use visualizing skills to rehearse competent performance and imagine successful outcomes.

• You require good verbal, voice and body message skills for introducing yourself.

• Starting conversation skills include exchanging basic information, making comments relevant to the occasion and bringing up topical events.

• Ways in which you can be a rewarding conversationalist include: paying compliments, being cheerful, agreeing, using another's name, being helpful and using humour. In addition you can search for common ground and engage in self-disclosure, the latter often being an area in which shy people experience difficulty.

• You need verbal, voice and body message exit skills to end conversations tactfully and, where appropriate, signal interest in meeting again.

• Telephone skills for making a date include: clearly identifying yourself, making 'I' message requests, offering specific alternatives and stating agreements clearly.

EXERCISES
EXERCISE 8.1
ASSESS HOW SHY I AM
Instructions

First, do the exercise on your own. Then, if appropriate, discuss with your partner, another or others.

Fill in the worksheet below by assessing your current experience of shyness in each of the dimensions listed. Give specific illustrations where possible. Consult the text if in doubt about the meaning of a dimension.

Dimension	My assessment
Feelings	
Physical reactions	
Thoughts	
Verbal messages	
Voice messages	
Body messages	
People with whom I'm shy	
Situations in which I'm shy	

1. To what extent do you see that any shyness you possess is influenced by considerations relating to your biological sex and to your culture? If so, please explain.

2. Summarize how shy you currently perceive yourself to be. What are the consequences for yourself and for others?

EXERCISE 8.2
DEVELOP MY THINKING SKILLS TO MANAGE SHYNESS
Instructions

First do the exercise on your own. Then, if appropriate, discuss with your partner, another or others.

Work on the thinking skills deficits that you identify as most important to managing your shyness. Consult the text if in doubt about how to complete any part.

Own responsibility for choosing

1. Assess the extent to which you assume personal responsibility for doing something about your shyness.

Understand the relationship between how I think feel and act

1. Put a situation in which you feel shy into the STC framework. Be specific about S1, T1, and C1.

2. Now imagine you think more effectively. Make up a revised STC, being specific about S2, T2, and C2.

Use coping self-talk

1. Identify an upcoming situation in which you expect to feel shy.

2. Identify any negative self-talk that contributes to your shyness.

3. Generate two each of calming, coaching and affirming self-statements. Then, if appropriate, develop self-talk that puts together calming, coaching and affirming self-statements.

4. Put your self-statements on cue cards or on a cassette and rehearse them daily for as long as necessary.

5. Implement your self-talk in real life and assess its consequences.

Choose realistic personal rules

1. Detect any unrealistic personal rules that contribute to maintaining your shyness.

2. Use disputing skills to question the most important unrealistic personal rule that you detected above.

3. Restate the unrealistic personal rule you disputed above into a more realistic rule.

Choose to perceive accurately

Part A Perceive yourself more accurately
If you consider your shyness partly maintained by unnecessarily negative perceptions of yourself:

1. List what you consider to be your strengths.

2. Use questioning skills to challenge your negative perceptions.

3. Use thought stopping.

4. Use thought switching.

5. Use visualizing.

Part B Perceive situations more accurately
1. Detect a particular situation where you may jump to a self-devaluing conclusion.

2. Dispute your self-devaluing conclusion by generating and evaluating different conclusions that you might have drawn.

3. If appropriate, restate your initial perception with the perception that represents the best fit perception in relation to the facts.

Explain cause accurately

1. What do you consider to be the explanations for how you acquired your shyness in the first place?

2. What do you consider to be the explanations for how your shyness is maintained?

3. Challenge any possibly inaccurate explanations for maintaining your shyness now and, if appropriate, either discard them or restate them more accurately.

Predict realistically

1. Think of a particular person with whom you would like either to initiate or to deepen a relationship and yet have felt inhibited from doing so.

2. Make up a worksheet with the following format.

Gains from acting (+s)	Risks from acting (–s)

3. On the worksheet first list your current predictions of gain and risk. These are the ones which, on balance, may inhibit you from acting. Then draw a line under each list.

4. Now generate as many extra predictions of gain and risk as you can and list them in the appropriate columns after your underlines. Pay particular attention to generating gains.

5. Assess your revised list of gains and risks. If appropriate, set yourself goals and alter your behaviour.

Set realistic goals

1. Set goals for managing a specific situation in which you feel shy. Ensure that your goals reflect your values, are realistic, are specific and have a time frame.

Use visualizing skills

1. Think of a specific upcoming situation in which you might feel shy.

2. Think of the verbal, voice and body message skills you need to perform competently in the situation.

3. Visually rehearse yourself acting competently in the situation, including coping with any difficulties and set-backs that occur.

4. Accompany your visual rehearsal with appropriate coping self-talk.

5. Practise your visual rehearsal plus coping self-talk skills daily for as long as you find it helpful.

EXERCISE 8.3
DEVELOP MY CONVERSATION SKILLS
Instructions

Where possible, when doing these exercises work with a partner or in a group. You may find it useful to video-record your rehearsals to obtain feedback.

Part A Introducing yourself skills

1. Assess how good you currently are at introducing yourself. Pay attention to your voice and body as well as to your verbal messages. Also, observe other people's skills at introducing themselves.

2. Specify the introducing yourself skills you want to develop.

3. Rehearse with a partner introducing yourself skills and give each other feedback.

4. If in a group, members can go around practising their introducing themselves skills on each other.

5. Practise your introducing yourself skills in real life, evaluate their impact and make changes as necessary.

Part B Starting conversations skills

1. List comments and topics that you could use when starting conversations.

2. Take turns at demonstrating specific starting conversation comments to your partner, including focusing on voice and body messages. Provide each other with feedback.

3. Rehearse starting a conversation with your partner focusing both on initiating topics and on responding to his/her agendas. Afterwards, hold a feedback session.

4. If in a group, circulate and use your starting conversation skills as you start brief conversations in pairs.

Part C Holding conversations skills

1. List ways that you can be rewarding during conversations.

2. Hold a conversation with your partner in which each of you takes turns in listening–switching–talking and vice versa. Make sure that both of you take responsibility for keeping the conversation going.

3. Now, without interrogating each other, both of you ask questions as you search for common ground. Remember to show active understanding. Where appropriate, respond to a disclosure by your partner with a relevant disclosure of your own. Afterwards, hold a feedback session.

4. If in a group, you can rehearse holding conversations in threes, fours or even more.

Part D Ending conversations skills

1. Assess how good you currently are at ending conversations. Pay attention to your voice and body as well as to your verbal messages. Also, observe other people's skills at ending conversations.

2. Specify the ending conversations skills you want to develop.

3. Rehearse with a partner your ending conversations skills and give each other feedback.

4. If in a group, members can go around practising their ending conversations skills on each other.

5. Practise your introducing yourself, and starting, holding and ending conversation skills in real life, evaluate their impact and make changes as necessary.

EXERCISE 8.4
DEVELOP MY MAKING A DATE SKILLS
Instructions

If possible, do this exercise with a partner or in a group. You may find it useful to audio-record or video-record your rehearsals and play them back.

1. Assess how good you currently are at making dates, either in person or on the phone.

2. Specify the making a date skills that you want to develop.

3. Rehearse your making a date skills with a partner. Role-play both face-to-face requests and telephone requests. Provide each other with feedback.

4. If in a group, members can demonstrate how to make a date. After each demonstration, the other group members provide feedback.

5. Where appropriate, practise your making a date skills in real life, evaluate their impact, and make changes as necessary.

EXERCISE 8.5
GROUP DISCUSSION: MANAGING SHYNESS SKILLS

Instructions

This is intended as a group exercise, though it may be done individually or in pairs. For each part:

1. spend 10–15 minutes answering the question in groups of three or four,

2. each group shares its answers with the whole group,

3. then the whole group ranks the six most important points or skills from the most important to the least important.

Part A
Negative outcomes of shyness

List the six main negative outcomes stemming from being shy.

Part B
Conversational skills

List the six most important skills for holding conversations when first meeting people.

Part C
Making a date skills

List the six most important skills for making a date.

NINE
Choosing a partner skills

*Life is the art of drawing sufficient conclusions
from insufficient premises.*

Samuel Butler

CHAPTER QUESTIONS

- *How do you develop a concept of yourself as a partner?*
- *What are different aspects of love?*
- *What is the connection between relating skills and love?*
- *What are some thinking skills strengths and deficits in selecting a partner?*
- *What are some criteria for choosing a partner?*
- *What are some action skills for dating and courtship?*

On hearing that an egocentric person had fallen in love, Viennese psychiatrist Alfred Adler asked 'Against whom?' The stark fact is that most intimate relationships start in hope and end in pain. This raises the issue of whether many people might choose their partners better. Improved choosing a partner skills might increase their chances of achieving stable, happy and fulfilling relationships. In an Australian study of 500 couples approaching marriage, just over half were highly satisfied and 15 per cent were classified as 'conflicted' (Heath, 1995).

Partners tend to be more demanding of relationships than previously. In 1973 Carl Rogers observed: 'It is becoming increasingly clear that a man–woman relationship will have *permanence* only to the degree to which it satisfies the emotional, psychological, intellectual, and physical needs of the partners' (Rogers, 1973, p. 18). Along with rising expectations about relationships, there is increasing disillusionment. Many young people have observed the marital distress of their parents and want to avoid it in their lives. Also they observe the messy marital breakdowns of public figures, a prime example being Charles and Diana. The higher the expectations, the greater the likelihood of disillusionment. Also, high expectations underline the importance of choosing wisely.

Exploring yourself as a partner

Choosing a partner is a process of discovery in which you explore yourself, other people and the world or relationships. The process can start in early childhood games and then, for some people, become more intense in early adolescence. By late adolescence most people have started seriously thinking about and/or engaging in relationships with the intent of choosing a long-term partner. This choosing process starts with casual dating in which partners are not identified as a couple, progresses to serious dating in which partners are identified as a couple and ends with marriage or *de facto* marriage (Hutson, Surra, Fitzgerald & Cate, 1981).

Another way of looking at the choosing process is that you are trying out and developing a concept of yourself as a partner as contrasted with how you are as a single person. Hopefully, you also are developing some relating skills strengths as a partner too. In choosing whom to date, during casual dating, during serious dating and during any pre-marital cohabitation, you are learning more about yourself, not in isolation, but in relation to a partner. A critical part of this concept of self as a partner consists of the sort of person with whom you are comfortable relating closely. What kind of person can you genuinely love? What characteristics in a partner do you like and dislike? What sort of partner helps you to bring out and develop the parts of yourself that you value? Also, as the divorce statistics show, during marriage the process of learning about yourself and about what you like or dislike in a partner continues. Furthermore, once divorced, many people choose another mate. Thus, even after marriage, you continue developing a concept of yourself as a partner.

As a single person, you are likely to date a number of people whose difference does not fit comfortably with your emerging picture of yourself as a partner. You may only date such people once or a few times. However, you may also engage in and dissolve a number of important love relationships in your quest for a stable long-term partnership (Pistole, 1995). Dissolving any close relationship can be mutually decided, decided by your partner or decided by yourself. Pain is not restricted to ending marital relationships. Ending late adolescent and early adulthood love relationships can be very painful for both partners, leading to feelings of grief, depression, self-pity, betrayal, anger, hurt, rejection, loneliness and low self-esteem. Also, some partners may long for their 'ex' and find it hard to let go emotionally and in practice. However, not all feelings attached to breaking up are negative. For example, many partners are ambivalent: sad at the loss, yet relieved to have ended a relationship that was not working so they can move on. Other partners may be delighted at their new-found freedom.

An important part of finding out about your self-concept as a partner centres on the issues of commitment. The word courtship is often used to describe the process of partners getting to know one another as they move towards commitment to marriage or to stable cohabitation involving financial sharing, property and, possibly, children. During successful courtship both you and your partner consolidate your concept of selves as partners in relation to one another. However, the course of courtship is not always smooth. Hutson *et al.* (1981) distinguish between the following four types of courtship:

Type 1: Accelerated-arrested courtship, with a rapid initial move towards marriage slowing down just before final commitment.

Type 2: Accelerated courtship, a smooth and rapid transition towards marriage.

Type 3: Intermediate courtship, slower than the first two types, but more rapid than the fourth.

Type 4: Prolonged courtship, where relationships 'took a relatively retarded and rocky path toward marriage' (p. 76).

ASPECTS OF LOVE

Nineteenth-century British prime minister, Benjamin Disraeli reportedly advised people never to be so foolish as to marry for love. Nevertheless, nowadays most people in Western cultures select long-term partners whom they love and by whom they feel loved. Beall and Sternberg (1995) see love as consisting of four dimensions: the beloved, the thoughts, the feelings and the actions or relations that accompany love. There are many different aspects of love, some of which I now review.

Romantic love

Dictionary definitions of love emphasize a warm or strong affection or liking for another person. Popular definitions of love emphasize romantic love. Romantic love focuses on the experience of falling in love. In story-book romantic love, you meet a handsome or beautiful stranger and experience strong mutual attraction and sudden intimacy. You explore and experience each other in the best of circumstances and live happily ever after. Everyday romantic love – or 'falling in love' – usually possesses a strong erotic element. Rubin (1970) developed a scale to measure romantic love. He identified three main areas of romantic attachment: needing the other, caring for the other and exclusiveness and absorption.

Romantic love does not last. Frequently, the ending of romantic love is replaced by disappointment. Litvinoff (1992) terms this phase 'the love hangover'. The perceptions of the beloved were so rosy and distorted, that the reality of their imperfections comes as nasty shock. Falling out of love can provide a double dose of disappointment if you lose the myth of perfect relationships as well as that of perfect persons. Some people never learn. Love addicts are serial romantic lovers who, holding on to their illusions, keep searching for perfect partners and relationships. Frequently fear of commitment underlies such behaviour. However, many people pass through a romantic love phase to forge more realistic relationships with either current or future partners.

Passionate and compassionate love

Walster and Walster (1978) distinguished between passionate and compassionate love, with passionate love being similar to romantic love. They state: 'Passionate love is a wildly emotional state, a confusion of feelings; tenderness and sexuality, elation and pain, anxiety and relief, altruism and jealousy. Compassionate love, on the other hand, is a lower-key emotion. It's friendly affection and deep attachment to someone' (p. 2). To some extent, the passionate/compassionate love distinction represents the development of love in a healthy relationship. Whereas passionate love can be immediate, compassionate love takes time to ripen and mature.

Needing and need-free love

Without necessarily using the same words, some writers distinguish between needing and need-free love (Frankl, 1969; Fromm, 1956; Maslow, 1962; Yalom, 1980). The lover's relationship to the beloved can be greedy or generous, getting or giving, selfish or selfless. In reality, people are neither one nor the other, but can be at varying positions on a continuum of egocentricity. Maslow (1962) distinguishes between B-love, love for the Being of another person, and D-love, which is Deficiency-love. He observes of B-love: 'Since it is non-possessive, and is admiring rather than needing, it makes no trouble and is practically always pleasure-giving' (p. 40). Deficiency-love requires gratification from another person to fill what is a deficit or empty hole in the organism. Deficiency-motivated individuals calculate how useful others are to them rather than how they help others unfold their potential.

Underlying the distinction of needing and need-free love is how well individuals relate to themselves. Fromm (1956) notes that the ability to love depends on the people having predominantly obtained a productive character orientation where they have 'overcome dependency, narcissistic omnipotence, and the wish to exploit others or to hoard' (pp. 21–22). To the degree that these negative qualities are present, people are unable to truly love themselves Mature self-love underlies rather than impedes love: it liberates people to affirm themselves through loving others. Fromm defines love as: 'the active concern for the life and growth of that which we love' (p. 22). Love is a positive act in which giving is based on a sense of abundance rather than of depletion. The mature person does not feel impoverished by giving. Selfishness is the opposite of self-love in that selfish people hate rather than love themselves. Also, they are incapable of loving others.

Love as self-transcendence

Need-free love requires the capacity for self-transcendence. Frankl (1963, 1969, 1988) views humans as essentially beings who reach out beyond themselves. They become most human when they transcend the boundaries of themselves by either fulfilling a meaning or by encountering another person lovingly. Love as a form of self-transcendence has various characteristics. It entails relating to another person as a spiritual being. As such, love involves grasping or understanding the inner core of the personality of another person. People are moved to the depths of their being by their partner's spiritual core. Infatuation seldom lasts long. When gratified, the sex drive vanishes promptly. Love, however, has a quality of permanence in that the spiritual core of the other person is unique and irreplaceable. Furthermore, love can outlast death in that the essence of the unique being of the beloved is timeless and imperishable.

Love as a social construction

Two current ways of viewing love are that love is a universal emotion that is defined similarly across all cultures and that love is a universal emotional experience that is defined differently across cultures. A basic assumption of the social constructionist approach is that there is not one particular reality experienced by all people at all periods of time. Instead, humans and cultures are always in a process of actively constructing social information. Beall and Sternberg (1995) propose that love is a social construction that reflects both culture and time period. There are huge variations in how love is defined across the ages and across cultures. For example, in some periods and cultures, love has been viewed as a lofty asexual experience, whereas other cultures and periods have included a sexual component. Also, conceptions of the beloved are shaped by culturally defined patterns of acceptability. In addition, the function of love varies across cultures. Love appears the foundation for marriage in individualistic cultures rather than in collectivist cultures, where kin networks and economic pressures loom larger. Love is not only an idea constructed by cultures, but individuals may also partially create their experiences of love 'through several regulatory mechanisms that encourage or discourage specific feelings' (p. 434).

Love as using relating skills

Relating skills are the component skills of loving another person. Yalom (1980) uses the words 'care' or 'caring' in each of his list of eight characteristics of mature need-free relationships. Caring for another human being is broader than the skills listed in Chapter 11 as caring skills. All the relating skills covered in this book can be used to affirm yourself though loving another. How you listen, disclose, manage anger and solve your relationship problems can each illustrate your capacity to care for each other's growth and, in the process, to grow together.

Love requires actively developing and maintaining your relating skills. Rogers (1973) observes that: 'the dream of a marriage "made in heaven" is totally unrealistic', and that every continuing man–woman relationship must be worked at, built, rebuilt, and continually refreshed by mutual personal growth' (p. 39). I extend Rogers' comments to gay relationships and all intimate friendships. Developing and maintaining your relating skills requires personal responsibility, courage and mental cultivation. You show your love not just by disciplining yourself, but through supporting each other's growth in the interests of your joint relationship. Also, how well you use relating skills can influence the lives of the next generation, for good or ill.

THINKING SKILLS FOR CHOOSING A PARTNER

Choosing an appropriate partner is a fundamental skill in both starting and maintaining successful couple relationships. How can you avoid unnecessarily landing yourself in an unhappy relationship? There are no guarantees. All relationships go through cycles of alienation and affection, with lows as well as highs. You have to steer a course between pollyannaism, 'everything will turn out for the best', and undue pessimism, 'everything will turn out for the worst.' Following are some thinking skills that may increase your chances choosing wisely.

Own responsibility for choosing

Because they leave choosing a partner to chance and romance, many people settle for less happiness in their lives than they might have obtained. You can assume personal responsibility by being proactive, rather than reactive, in seeking and choosing a partner. You cannot wait around for ever for Ms/Mr Right to appear. Also, own responsibility for your emerging concept of yourself as a partner and for how you think, feel and act towards potential partners. This section shows you some of the thinking choices you may make. How you think influences how you feel, so you can exercise some degree of choice in regard to your feelings: for instance, how hurt you feel if someone refuses your invitation for a date. In addition, how you think guides how you act: for instance, if you do not look before you leap, that is your choice. In addition, some people require a heightened sense of existential awareness. You make your life through your choices. Life is finite and cannot be indefinitely postponed (Yalom, 1980).

Get in touch with your feelings

Openness to experience is another way of starting getting in touch with your feelings. If you are open to your experience you are able to perceive incoming information without distorting or denying it. This is highly relevant to selecting a long–term relationship in a number of ways. First, the better your skills at experiencing and exploring your feelings the more you access the core of your personhood. Being in touch with the inner referent of your own valuing process increases the likelihood of your making decisions that will work for you. Second, openness to your feelings may stimulate you to search for a partner. Acknowledge that it is okay to want a partner and give yourself permission to look for one. Below are examples of two young people who deny or dilute wanting a partner.

> Solly, 24, has never had a close relationship and enjoys the creature comforts of living at home with his parents. He likes looking at pictures of attractive women. However, Solly suppresses the strength of his feelings of wanting a partner and a home of his own. When asked, Solly explains that he has never had a girlfriend because he has been too busy concentrating on his studying and his career.

> After a relationship break-up two years ago, Katrina, 27, has buried herself in her work. Currently she still smarts over what happened and mistrusts all men as a result. Katrina

sabotages her happiness by denying her long-
ing for another close relationship and, hence,
failing to take appropriate steps to attain one.

A third reason for being open to your feelings is that you can protect yourself from
prematurely rushing into unsuitable long-term relationships. You may possess an
insufficient sense of your identity and recognize that, at this stage of your life, your
level of security and partner skills are insufficient for long-term relationship satisfaction and success. It is a paradox that most people have to make critical decisions
about choice of partner and career when young and inexperienced. Fourth, your
intuitive feelings can provide much information about how you and others might relate
as partners. Such feelings are not necessarily right, but at least they provide a base for
collecting further information to confirm or negate them. Fifth, if you are rigid,
defensive and not willing to look at your own behaviour this is a critical danger signal
to others to avoid entering a long-term relationship with you. Sixth, even within the
dating and courtship period openness to experience allows you to change and grow, to
be responsive to your changes and growth and to assess your thoughts and feelings in
light of your emerging concept of yourself as a partner.

Choose realistic personal rules

When choosing a relationship, my personification of me chooses my personification of
you. However, I may not really know myself. Instead what I call 'I' or 'me' may be a
clutter of attitudes, rules and values taken over from other people, such as my parents,
as if they were my own. I may perceive you in terms of their values and not mine. You
may do the same to me. The risk of this is that, as either or both of us grow into more
autonomous persons, we get badly out of step with each other. Our relationship,
instead of being built on the rock of stable yet flexible identities, has been built on the
sand of unstable and possibly rigid identities.

Some people may be heavily influenced to get married because they have been
brought up with the rule that marriage is their main role in life. They seek to marry a
role rather than a person. They get married to secure the structure and trappings of
married life without paying sufficient attention to the realities of having a loving
relationship with their spouse. Because of the traditional emphasis on females being
home-makers, women especially may feel pressure to marry and raise a family.
Disparaging remarks like 'old maid' and 'on the shelf' are made about single females
after a certain age. Males also may get married to present a more socially acceptable
image to the world: for instance to advance their careers.

Following are some areas in which potential partners might fruitfully explore the
realism and compatibility of their own and each other's personal rules. Since often
rules are not expressed openly, you may need to be sensitive to hints about their
existence (Beck, 1988).

- *The influence of parental rules.* How do our parents' rules and values influence us
now? To what degree are these rules harmful or helpful? To what extent are we

selecting a partner to please our parents? Both sexes may filter out otherwise suitable partners because of their conscious or unconscious wishes to please and be like their parents. However, some people may rebel rather than conform to parental rules. Such people may be guided in their search for partners by rigid rules about how *unlike* their parents their partners should be. Later on, previously rebellious offspring may revert to parental rules and then be dissatisfied if their partners do not change too.

• *Rules about sex roles.* How should men and women behave? How should husbands and wives behave? How should fathers and mothers behave? To what extent do each of you subscribe to myths about sex roles: for instance 'Males must always be the major breadwinners' and 'A woman must always stand by her man, no matter how badly he behaves'?

• *Rules about relationships.* How should people behave in close relationships? For example, how should they handle issues like anger, conflict, sex, in-laws and friendships? Again, to what extent do each of you subscribe to relationship myths like: 'Frequency of sex must be the main indicator of relationship satisfaction' and 'Conflicts must be avoided rather than resolved'?

Sometimes, given flexibility on both sides, you can negotiate differences in personal rules and reach mutually satisfactory solutions. On other occasions the differences may be more intractable: for instance differences concerning family size and children's education. Where possible find out in advance if either of you feels unable or unwilling to work through a major difference. This may influence your decision about making a long-standing commitment to the relationship.

Choose to perceive accurately

Perceiving yourself and others accurately is difficult at the best of times. Attraction can both clarify and distort perceptions of yourself and of potential partners.

Perceive yourself accurately

There are risks in the dating and partner selection process of both underestimating and overestimating your attractiveness. You may be prone to dwelling on your 'faults' and insufficiently realize your strengths. If you underestimate your attractiveness, you may be afraid to take risks and end up settling for a less attractive partner than you might otherwise have obtained (Argyle & Henderson, 1985). Also, you may be less resilient and willing to persist in overcoming reservations and difficulties with someone for whom you care and who cares for you. In addition, your low self-esteem can contribute to your filtering out positive messages and magnifying negative messages from others. Furthermore, you are more likely to give in to pressure to select a partner against your wishes. Getting into a relationship on the rebound is another risk stemming from self-esteem being low. People who feel vulnerable, incomplete and unable to handle loneliness can select partners for the wrong reasons. Also, beware of oversimplifying the partner finding process by using polarized categories like success or failure and acceptance or rejection. What you perceive as failure or rejection may be based on another's realistic assessment of the differences between you that is in the best interests of you both.

Overestimating your attractiveness has both advantages and disadvantages. Provided your overestimation is not excessive, your added confidence may help you to be relaxed and take realistic risks in the dating and courtship process (Bandura, 1986). However, if people perceive you as conceited and pushy, you lessen their interest in you. Also, if you overestimate your attractiveness, you may lack sufficient insight to detect others' negative reactions to you and their reasons for them.

Perceive potential partners accurately

Following are some ways in which you may perceive potential partners inaccurately.

• *Infatuation.* If you are infatuated with another you are inspired with extravagant and unreasoning passion. Physical attraction is probably the main stimulus for people starting relationships. However, albeit very important, it is only one criteria in selecting a partner. Infatuation is a state of heightened emotionality which burns itself out. Infatuation and lovesickness are part of being alive. However, where possible, protect yourself from making major commitments until you have come down to earth and made a more realistic appraisal. Where there is strong sexual attraction it is all too easy to misperceive each other and to rationalize away potential difficulties in your relationship.

• *Idealization.* A combination of the myth of romantic love, your own insecurities and your date's skills of impression management may lead you to idealize her or him. You see what you want to see. You may inadequately acknowledge messages that contradict your ideal picture. Furthermore, you may insufficiently realize that this wonderful person may not reciprocate the same level of interest.

• *Exaggerating similarity.* Exaggerating similarity is slightly different from idealizing a potential partner. Both involve selectively perceiving the information that you want to perceive. When you exaggerate similarity you overemphasize what you have in common and underemphasize your differences. You fuse yourself with the other and insufficiently perceive your boundaries. Also, you may inadequately note signs of lack of commitment (Colliver, 1992).

• *Transference.* Try to understand the templates or blueprints that you bring from former relationships to current or new ones, especially interactive patterns for giving and receiving emotional pain. In close personal relationships, consciously or unconsciously, you may react in terms of previous relationships: for instance, males to their mothers or former girlfriends; females to their fathers or former boyfriends. Hendrix asserts that when people choose partners they look for someone who has the predominant character traits of their parents and who is 'the ideal candidate to make up for the psychological and emotional damage you experienced in childhood' (1988, p. 12). Hendrix's point is that you go beyond looking for partners to offer what was present in your parental relationships to searching for partners who can provide what was missing. Transference reactions can be positive or negative. Either way they are not a sound base on which to make relationship choices. You need to react to others as they are, not because they remind you of someone else.

• *Falling victim to impression management.* When people date they package themselves to get the other to perceive them favourably. Imagine getting ready for a new date. In varying degrees the girl is 'out to get' the guy and the guy is 'out to get' the girl. Depending on how far out of touch they are with their own valuing processes and identity, the people you date 'sell' themselves as though they are commodities. They emphasize their assets or selling points and strictly control the flow of information about their perceived liabilities. It can be hard to get to know another person well when, both consciously and unconsciously, they put on acts for your consumption. Appearances can be deceptive. For example, conflicts may be smoothed over so as not to interfere with the goal of winning your affection. However later on, in the routine of daily living, these conflicts surface. Some people are very adept at manipulating appearances to conceal their negative points. However, others have hidden assets that become more apparent as you get to know them better.

Explain cause accurately

You need to explain the cause of any strong feelings of attraction accurately. If you are 'swept off your feet', you are choosing to allow this to happen. If you continue seeing someone, again this is your choice rather than saying 'I had no choice but to continue seeing him/her'. Assuming no coercion is involved, the same holds true if you go to bed with a potential partner – having sex is a choice on both your parts.

Also, explain the cause of your negative feelings accurately. You may feel less well disposed towards and narrow your field of potential partners if you explain another's difference from you as her or him being inferior to you. Also, examine closely how you explain your feelings associated with specific situations in the dating and courtship process. For example, misunderstandings in starting up relationships may be due to your hypersensitivity and jealousy rather than to another's negative behaviour – you may be on the look out for signs of unreliability and betrayal. Alternatively, your negative feelings may be due to another's behaviour and yet you find ways of blaming yourself.

Try to be honest in explaining the causes of previous relationship breakdowns with potential or actual partners. You can use this knowledge to develop a clearer concept of yourself as a partner which, in turn, should help you think more clearly about what characteristics you prefer in a future partner. Also, learn from mistakes to improve your relating skills in vulnerable areas in previous relationships. In addition, explain accurately what you did right in previous relationships so you can maintain your confidence and build on your skills strengths.

Predict realistically

The process of selecting a partner involves continually assessing and reassessing the probability of a successful relationship. During this process you gain more information both about your potential partner and your reactions to him or her. If you are not already cohabiting, try predicting what it will be like spending twenty-four hours a day year-in, year-out with a potential partner.

Following are a number of relationship myths. These myths represent unrealistic predictions that have the potential to interfere with the realism with which you select a partner. If you recognize that you possess any of these myths, seriously consider discarding or modifying them.

> 'People who are in love live happily ever after.'
> 'Love overcomes all.'
> 'Love lasts forever.'
> 'Once we're married, I can change him/her.'
> 'My marriage/partnership is not going to run into trouble; it can't happen to me.'
> 'He/she will always be the same.'
> 'The qualities in him/her, I like now I will always like.'

Set realistic goals

Following are three dimensions on which you can choose to set realistic goals. First, there is the overall goal of whether or not you want a partner, including how much priority you attach to attaining this goal. As mentioned earlier, some people are unrealistic in acknowledging the importance of this goal in their lives. On the other hand, you can overestimate the importance of finding a partner: examples being dependent persons who feel incomplete as single persons or those subject to intense family pressures.

Second, there is the outcome goal of what sort of partner you want. Here you need to move beyond fantasy goals to realistic goals that take into account your developing concept of yourself as a partner. Trying relationships can be viewed as a valuable experience in perceiving yourself more accurately and in identifying criteria for suitable partners. Such criteria are personal goals for partner characteristics that suit you as a unique individual – not your parents, your friends nor anyone else. Choosing your own criteria for a partner does not mean that you ignore others' opinions; only that, where possible, you rationally assess their relevance.

Third, there is the process goal of how to go search effectively for a partner. Some people seeking a partner may be lucky enough already to mix with a large range of potential partners. Others may need to take a systematic approach to the task of finding a partner. If so, you can make a search and find a plan that identifies the steps you need to take to develop, access and/or enlarge a 'market' of potential partners. In your plan identify specific sub-goals that might be stepping stones to attaining your overall goal. Also, stipulate a time frame.

Use visualizing skills

Especially if you have a strong imagination, you can use visualizing skills to go backwards and forwards in gaining information about a potential partner (Lazarus,

1984, 1992). Regarding the past, you can look at each other's photograph albums and use these as springboards for getting in touch both verbally and visually with how each of you experienced life before you met. Regarding the future, you can use a skill called time projection. In time projection you visualize how life will be at some point in the future. Following are questions about your future that you might try to answer visually either on your own or with a potential partner.

'How do I see our relationship working out a year from now, five years from now, ten years from now?'
'How do I see myself developing and changing as the years go by?'
'How do I see my partner developing and changing as the years go by?'
'How do I see us dealing with changes in each other and our relationship?'
'What sort of family will we have?'
'What sort of parents will we be?'
'What will we be like when we are old?'

Use systematic decision-making skills

As well as systematically planning your partner search, you can be systematic in assessing potential partners. Even at the best of times, you may be poor at making decisions in a systematic and rational way. You may possess a decision-making style that interferes with your having the mature fusion of 'head space' and 'heart space' necessary for choosing a partner wisely. You may get too anxious and hypervigilent. In this process you may fail either to take into account or to weigh adequately relevant information. Alternatively, you may either make decisions impulsively or be passive and just conform to what others expect of you. Pay attention to both inner and outer information. Good decisions depend not only on collecting sufficient information, but also on your ability to perceive and assess it accurately. In addition, if serious about the relationship, share your thoughts, feelings, hopes and reservations with your potential partner and let her or him do the same. Committing yourself to a long-term relationship is a process of constantly keeping in touch with and exploring your own and one another's viewpoints.

CRITERIA FOR CHOOSING A PARTNER

What are you looking for when searching for and choosing a compatible partner? How realistic are your expectations and goals? Especially if marriage is intended, what you make is a choice for all seasons. What matters to you in the short term may be different from what matters in the long run. Sternberg considers that among the things that increase in importance as relationships grow are willingness to change in response to each other and willingness to tolerate each other's imperfections (Trotter, 1986).

Additionally, the sharing of values, for instance religious values, can become important. Also, a common shift is that from passionate love to compassionate love.

As Aesop observed: 'There can be little liking where there is not likeness.' Couples tend to be similar in many ways. Argyle and Henderson (1985) state: 'They are more similar than by chance in age, social class, religion, height, intelligence, values and beliefs and in some measures of personality' (p. 105). Though complementarity may add spice and interest, most relationships require grounding in a high degree of similarity.

Though the initial saying 'yes' to another human being may be on first sight or meeting, it can take time to gather appropriate evidence to justify your initial choice. Below are a few suggestions to help you set realistic goals for selecting a partner. Trade-offs, compromises and negotiations are inevitable. Each person and each couple will weigh the importance of the following criteria differently. Also their importance for either or both partners is likely to change over time, which can either enhance closeness or draw partners apart.

- *Physical attraction*. Even before the film *10*, many people measured physical attractiveness on a scale from 1, 'not at all attractive', to 10, 'extremely attractive'. Especially for males physical attractiveness may be a very important consideration in starting a relationship. Individuals tend to match themselves on physical attractiveness. People who consider themselves less likely to be accepted may trade down to a less attractive partner. Physical attractiveness is not just a matter of natural attributes. How the individual uses body language, for instance use of gaze and eye contact, also contributes to it.

- *Sexual compatibility*. With premarital sex now so widespread, awareness of sexual compatibility is more important than previously in choosing a partner. Passion as expressed by kissing, hugging, touching and intercourse needs to be satisfactorily given and received. Furthermore, partners need to be able to talk freely about their sexual relationship, including sharing their fantasies. In the first flush of a relationship when sexual relating is often at a high level, you may find it difficult to assess your longer-term sexual compatibility. Since people vary enormously in the importance they place on sexual relating and in the activities they enjoy, a reasonable level of sexual compatibility can be critical for the stability of a relationship. As well as your experience together, further information about sexual compatibility can come from honestly sharing your previous sexual histories.

- *Respect*. How much respect do you and your potential partner have for each other? Respect means concern that, within our interdependence, you see me as I am and allow me to grow as a separate human being. Possessiveness and control are the antithesis of respect. You are secure enough in yourself that you allow me the psychological space to be myself. You are capable of helping me and taking pleasure in my unfolding. You do not need me to constrict myself so that you can sustain a false picture of yourself. I am a person in my own right and not an object for your use. A good test of how well another respects you is how well they listen to you. Poor listeners tend to be too bound up with their own agendas to respect you fully.

• *Trustworthiness and commitment*. All relationships involve contracts of varying degrees of implicitness and explicitness. These contracts or agreements relate to such matters as not engaging in sexual activity with others, not criticizing and standing up for the other person in public, keeping confidences, keeping promises and generally acting in a reliable and dependable way. Another aspect of trust is that of trusting another not to reject or hurt you needlessly. The notion of commitment is closely allied to that of trust. A committed partner does not breach trust. Instead a committed partner keeps trust by staying with the relationship through the hard times which inevitably occur.

• *Emotional responsiveness*. People differ in how important they consider it for themselves and their partner to be emotionally expressive and responsive. A common pattern is that of one partner, more often the woman, wanting to ventilate feelings while the other partner, usually the male, responds by getting into an intellectual problem-solving mode too soon. Genuineness in the expression of feelings is very important. Verbal, voice, body, touch and action messages should speak in the same direction. If you experience someone as either cool and unresponsive or 'blowing hot and cold', warm one moment and pushing you away the next, this at the least merits further exploration.

• *Intimacy*. In his book *The Art of Loving*, Fromm (1956) emphasized the importance of knowledge in loving relationships. Your knowing yourself and willingness to be known can help me relate to you as you are rather than in terms of my inaccurate personification of you. Your openness and ability to reveal yourself as a fallible human being helps me to know you. It also makes it easier for me to drop my social masks and defensive facades. Capacity for intimacy and emotional responsiveness come together in that if you can feel free to disclose not only personal information but also your feelings you share the flow of your being with me. This encourages me to do the same. Our relationship becomes a vibrant process rather than something which is static and dull. We have an open rather than a closed communication system. People differ in how much they value emotional closeness and distance. Consequently, there are risks attached to selecting a partner whose needs for intimacy differ greatly from your own.

• *Sense of humour*. Does the child in the other person appeal to the child in you? Do they have a similar sense of fun and humour? Do you enjoy being silly and playing together? Enjoying each other's sense of humour can both enhance the good times and ease the bad times in your relationship. In a British opinion survey (MORI, 1983), having a good sense of humour was rated above looks in qualities thought desirable in a partner. The capacity to laugh at yourself can be an invaluable asset in close relationships. Partners who are sourpusses or who take themselves too seriously can be crashing bores.

• *Caring*. Caring entails thoughtfulness and having regard for another's feelings. You are sensitive to each other's wishes and, where reasonable, try to meet them; this can involve being positive in finding out the other's wishes as well as reacting to them. Caring plays a very important role in people's judgements of love (Steck, Levitan,

McLane & Kelley, 1982). Caring also involves considerateness. A potential partner can lack considerateness by hurting you unnecessarily.

• *Companionship.* Do you enjoy doing things together and just being together? One of the main approaches to helping depressed individuals is to encourage them to increase the number of pleasant activities in which they are involved (Lewinsohn, Munoz, Youngren & Zeiss, 1986). Similarly, if relationships are to remain happy, you need to engage in a reasonable number of shared pleasant activities. You can still enjoy individual activities as well. You need personal space as well as togetherness. Frequent conversations, both intimate and less intimate, are important ways of keeping in touch with one another both emotionally and practically. Couples vary in the activities they enjoy. Both your and your potential partner's preferences for enjoyable activities are likely to change over the course of your relationship. You may then need to work to keep sharing some pleasant activities.

• *Intellectual compatibility.* To what degree is it important to you to have a partner of your own intellectual capability? Your may perceive as boring conversing on a daily basis with someone you perceive as much less bright than you. Alternatively, you could feel inferior with someone who seems to think much more quickly than you do. Academic intelligence is no guarantee of social intelligence and sensitivity. Nevertheless, many people are likely to feel more comfortable with a partner of roughly the same intellect than where there are wide discrepancies.

• *Compatibility of values.* Values are the underlying principles and priorities on which people base their lives. At any time partners and potential partners have profiles of values, some of which are more important than others. Differences in values are inevitable. However, you need to feel comfortable with each other's major values to sustain a long-term relationship without great strain. In Chapter 4 I listed some values which people can bring to their relationships. Your values are likely to be heavily influenced by cultural and sex-role considerations.

Values are the basis on which you and your partner develop goals for your relationship. You may discover on closer examination that each of you wants and expects different things. This need not be an insuperable obstacle if you can resolve the value conflicts to your mutual satisfaction. However, major unresolved value conflicts are unlikely to go away. Under these circumstances, you should then consider whether it is worth the risk of committing yourself to a long-term relationship.

• *Compatibility of daily activities.* A host of daily living considerations may be important: what sort of TV programmes, music and food each of you likes; your sleeping habits; your attitudes towards tidiness and so on. Can you work through your differences and arrive at mutually satisfactory solutions?

• *Balance of power.* You can assess a potential relationship on the degree of power and influence you are likely to obtain in it. You need to be comfortable with how much power you are likely to have. Glasser (1995) observes: 'love cannot take root in a relationship in which one or both of the partners believe that they have little or no power' (p. 25). Partners can have strong needs for power and still treat each other with respect. Especially if they possess the inner strength to examine their own behaviour, powerful personalities can find ways of working around and solving their relationship problems. However, if you detect that a potential partner is very bossy, controlling and always wanting her or his own way, listen to the alarm bells in your head. Such people are not strong, but weak – in fact, if you enter a long-term relationship with one you risk subjecting yourself to 'the tyranny of the weak'. Also, beware of potential partners who are physical and/or psychological bullies and those who attempt to control you with passive-aggression.

• *Relating skills strengths and deficits.* Though most people do not think of their relationships in skills terms, there is no reason why you should not. Throughout this book various skills for initiating, maintaining and developing relationships are described. You can assess the relating skills of potential partners. How well you get on both now and in future heavily depends on your and your potential partner's relating skills. Teamwork is important. How good are you at working together both to build your strengths and to minimize the negative effects of your deficits? The engagement period is a time of increased commitment when couples can assess each other's relating skills more closely. Cohabitation offers a further opportunity for this.

ACTION SKILLS FOR DATING AND COURTSHIP

In this section I review in some detail skills for searching and finding a potential partner. However, I only briefly discuss disclosing, listening and assertion skills you can use during dating and courtship (Argyle, 1991; Argyle & Henderson, 1985; Hendrick & Hendrick, 1992; Litvinoff, 1993; Powell, 1991). This brevity avoids repetition with lengthier descriptions elsewhere in the book. Often nowadays courtship includes cohabitation. The dividing lines between dating, courtship, cohabitation and marriage are imprecise.

• *Developing search and find skills.* In the section on setting realistic goals, I mentioned that some of you may need to develop systematic search and find plans to locate eligible partners. Here I present some suggestions for locating and making contact with eligible partners. The following brief conversation between a spectator and a famous golfer, who had just played a superb shot from a bunker, highlights how you can make your luck.

> Spectator: 'Gee, you're a lucky golfer.'
>
> Famous golfer: 'You know something. The more and more I practise, the luckier and luckier I get!'

Search skills: How to locate potential partners

1. *Review your existing network.* Take stock of all the people you know who might be potential partners or introduce you to potential partners. Identify those people with whom you might spend more time and those with whom you should spend less time.

2. *Identify gaps in your network.* If you are a woman, you may have many girlfriends whose company you enjoy, but know few, if any, eligible men. If you are a man you may spend much time in sporting, drinking and social activities with your mates, but know few, if any, eligible women. Recognize clearly any significant gaps in your existing network.

3. *Identify ways of meeting eligible partners.* Brainstorm all the different ways that you can meet eligible partners and eligible partners can meet you. Suggestions include meeting potential partners through: friends, relatives and your existing network; your work contacts; sitting next to people in lecture theatres or in cafes; joining clubs; attending social events, like dances, barbecues and church fetes; taking advantage of chance encounters; using introduction agencies, though 'buyer beware'; advertising in magazines; and, even, using the Internet!

4. *Identify ways of not putting off potential partners.* Identify any unintentional signals indicating 'I am not available' or 'I am not interested' that you may send to people whom you might like to know better. Also, identify any significant conversation skills deficits you may possess.

Find skills: How to make contact with potential partners

1. *Activate your network.* Without being crass about it, let appropriate people in your existing network know you are interested in meeting eligible partners. Renew contact with people who might help in your search.

2. *Entertain your friends.* Do not expect all the invitations to go one way. Your friends are more likely to help you, if you are rewarding for them. Take people out for drinks and meals, hold dinner parties, give parties or whatever it takes to show clearly you are in circulation.

3. *Spend less time or no time at all with some people.* Finding a suitable partner is every bit as important as getting a job or buying a car. You cannot afford to squander time on low level activities and acquaintanceships that interfere with attaining your goal.

4. *Join clubs and attend social events.* Be proactive about joining clubs, going on outings and attending social events where you may meet potential partners.

5. *Take advantage of chance encounters.* If you find someone attractive, you can try to catch her or his eye and strike up a conversation: for instance, at a bus stop or in the supermarket. By using good judgement, tact, diplomacy and not pushing your luck, the risks can be minimal.

6. *Accept invitations.* Do not play hard to get. Be prepared to accept invitations to social events and dates graciously, if this will help you achieve your objective. Give moderately eligible potential partners the benefit of the doubt, rather than turn them down too quickly. Some people improve on further acquaintance – when both of you may feel more relaxed.

7. *Give come-ons and turn-offs.* Develop and use a repertoire of verbal, voice and body messages that encourage those whom you want to know better. Politely, and if necessary firmly, discourage the remainder.

8. *Develop your skills of being a rewarding person.* Choosing a potential partner is a two-way process. Other people are much more likely to want to develop friendships and romances with you, if you are warm, attractive and interesting to them. If necessary, seek professional counselling to identify and eliminate obvious and more subtle ways you distance yourself from potential partners.

• *Disclosing skills.* As you and your potential partner get to know one another better, the breadth and depth of your disclosure becomes greater. You express liking and affection. You disclose your daily activities, including sharing news of success. In serious dating, you show distress and anxiety in front of the other. Also, as the relationship develops you give each other feedback and reveal your commitment to the relationship. With an increase in your expression of positive and negative feelings, you increase the chances of both intimacy and conflict. You are also more prepared to ask for personal advice.

Other ways in which you can disclose include: looking each other in the eye during conversation; engaging in intentional touching – for instance hugging, kissing and sexual intercourse; giving birthday cards and presents, including surprise presents; repaying debts and compliments; standing up for the other during his or her absence; refraining from criticizing each other in public; and tolerating each other's friends. In addition, as your relationship deepens, you look after the other when ill.

If and when you start cohabiting, further ways in which you disclose include: sharing the household chores, informing the other about your personal schedule and sharing the costs of the house/flat.

• *Listening and showing understanding skills.* As your relationship develops, you make yourself more physically available to each other. You show trust and unconditional positive regard and do not break confidences. You listen with interest and express increased concern for each other's welfare. Also by disclosing yourselves, you elicit disclosures from each other to which you can listen. Thus, appropriate disclosure is also a listening skill.

• *Assertion skills.* When choosing a partner, there are numerous instances when you may require assertion skills: for example, resisting pressures to have sex or unprotected sex, ending relationships and coping with third parties who disapprove of your choice of girlfriend or boyfriend. As an illustration, when resisting sexual pressures, verbal messages include: 'I know you'd like to keep going, but I won't have intercourse outside a committed relationship', and 'I won't have sex without a condom, because I want to avoid pregnancy and risk of AIDS' (Powell, 1991). Such messages need to be given in a firm voice emphasizing the word 'won't'. Your body messages should include looking the other person in the eye when you speak and, possibly, holding up your hand in a pushing away gesture.

In addition to skills discussed above, as your relationship develops you use numerous other relating skills to deepen and maintain it. Such skills, some of which are described later, include those of managing anger and solving relationship problems. Choosing a partner can include opting out as well as opting in. In such circumstances, you require ending relationships skills and, very probably, starting again skills.

CHAPTER HIGHLIGHTS

• Choosing a partner is a process of exploring and refining your concept of yourself as a partner. This process proceeds from dating, through courtship, to marriage or *de facto* marriage.

• Aspects of love include romantic love, passionate and compassionate love, needing and need-free love, love as self-transcendence, love as a social construction and love as using relating skills.

• Thinking skills for choosing a partner include owning responsibility for being proactive and for how you think, feel and act during the process.

• Get in touch with your feelings about wanting a close relationship and about the suitability of potential partners.

• Rationally assess the influence of parental rules, your rules about marriage, and your rules about relationships.

• When choosing a partner, beware of both underestimating and overestimating your attractiveness.

• Ways in which you may inaccurately perceive a potential partner include infatuation, idealization, exaggerating similarity, transference and falling victim to impression management.

• Explain the causes of both positive and negative feelings towards potential partners accurately. Also, try to be honest about the causes of previous relationship breakdowns.

• Predict realistically and avoid myths about love lasting for ever, perfect relationships, and both partners staying the same.

• Set realistic goals concerning getting a partner, what you want in a partner and the process of finding a partner.

• Use your imagination to visualize what the past has been like for your potential partner and what your future might be like as a couple.

• Use systematic decision-making skills to choose a partner, avoiding deficits like worrying too much. Also, carefully collect and assess pertinent inner and outer information, including holding discussions with potential partners about your compatibility.

• Criteria for choosing a partner include physical attraction, sexual compatibility, respect, trustworthiness and commitment, emotional responsiveness, intimacy, sense of humour, caring, companionship, intellectual compatibility, compatibility of values, compatibility of daily activities, balance of power and relating skills strengths and deficits.

• Search skills for locating potential partners include reviewing your existing network, identifying gaps in your network, identifying ways of meeting eligible partners and identifying ways of not putting off potential partners.

• Find skills for making contact with potential partners include activating your network, entertaining your friends, spending less time or not time at all with some people, joining clubs and attending social events, taking advantage of chance encounters, accepting invitations, giving come-ons and turn-offs and developing your skills of being a rewarding person.

• Further action skills for dating and courtship include disclosing more of yourself, giving feedback, revealing commitment to the relationship, being physically available and expressing increased concern for each other's welfare.

• You may require assertion skills to resist sexual pressure, end relationships, and cope with interference from third parties.

EXERCISES

EXERCISE 9.1
ASSESS MY THINKING SKILLS DEFICITS IN CHOOSING A PARTNER

Instructions

Identify the thinking skills deficits that you possess or might possess when choosing a partner. First assess each thinking skills deficit on your own, before discussing with another or others.

Own responsibility for choosing

1. Are you owning sufficient personal responsibility for being proactive in:
a. searching for a partner,
b. choosing a partner?

2. During the choosing a partner process, how well are you owning responsibility for:
a. your thoughts,
b. your feelings,
c. your actions?

Get in touch with my feelings

1. When choosing a partner, how capable are you of getting in touch with your true feelings?

2. Do you have a sufficient sense of your own identity to choose a partner wisely?

Choose realistic personal rules

1. Identify any parental rules which might influence choosing your partner. Are these rules helpful or harmful?

2. Identify and assess the realism of your rules concerning how men and women should behave, how husbands and wives should behave and how fathers and mothers should behave.

3. Identify and assess the realism of your rules about how people should behave in close relationships.

Choose to perceive accurately

1. When dating and courting, do you overestimate or underestimate your attractiveness? If either, what are the consequences?

2. When choosing a partner, are you at risk of inaccurately perceiving a potential partner in any of the following ways:

infatuation,
idealization,
exaggerating similarity,
transference,
falling victim to impression management?

Explain cause accurately

When choosing a partner, how accurately do you explain cause for:
a. your positive feelings and actions with potential partners,
b. your negative feelings and actions with potential partners, and
c. what went wrong and right in your previous relationships?

Predict realistically

1. Do you possess any false predictive myths about love lasting for ever, perfect relationships and both partners never changing?

Set realistic goals

1. How realistic are your goals for:
a. wanting a partner,
b. the sort of partner you want,
c. the process of finding a partner?

Use visualizing skills

1. Work with your potential partner to develop a visual 'history' of how they were before they met you.

2. Visualize your relationship with a potential partner at various times in the future.

3. Visualize how you see yourself and your potential partner changing as the years go by.

4. Visualize yourself and your potential partner as parents.

Use systematic decision-making skills

1. What patterns have you detected in how you make decisions that might interfere with choosing a partner wisely? For instance, are you too anxious, impulsive or too willing to conform?

2. Are you likely to be reasonably systematic in collecting and assessing information?

3. Are you and your potential partner likely to discuss adequately your own and one another's thoughts, feelings, hopes and reservations about your future possible relationship?

Summary

1. Summarize your main thinking skills strengths and deficits in choosing a partner.

EXERCISE 9.2
WHAT AM I LOOKING FOR IN A PARTNER?
Instructions

Complete Part A on your own and, if appropriate, Part B with a potential partner.

Part A
On your own

Write down how important each of the following criteria is for you in choosing a partner and your main reasons for its importance.

Criteria	Importance and main reasons
Physical attraction	
Sexual compatibility	
Respect	
Trustworthiness and commitment	
Emotional responsiveness	
Capacity for intimacy	
Sense of humour	

Caring	
Companionship	
Intellectual compatibility	
Compatibility of values	
Compatibility of daily activities	
Balance of power	
Relating skills strengths and deficits	
Other criteria not mentioned above	

Summarize your main criteria for choosing a partner.

Part B
Working together

You and your potential partner now share and discuss your answers to Part A. Together, answer the following questions.

1. How well do you think you are matched?

2. Are there any major areas of incompatibility in your potential partnership? If so, please specify.

3. If in question 2 you identified major areas of incompatibility between you:
a. what impact might they have on your future relationship?
b. what, if anything, can you do about them?

EXERCISE 9.3
ASSESS AND IMPLEMENT MY SEARCH AND FIND SKILLS

Instructions

This exercise is in two parts. Complete each part before moving on to the next. If appropriate, discuss your answers with another or others.

Part A
Assessment

1. Assess myself on the following planning skills for locating potential partners
Reviewing my existing network
Identifying gaps in my network
Identifying ways of meeting eligible partners
Identifying ways of not putting off potential partners
Setting goals and sub-goals
Outlining the steps to attaining goals and sub-goals
Stating time frames
Monitoring progress

2. Assess myself on the following action skills for making contact with potential partners
Activating my network
Entertaining my friends
Spending less time or no time at all with some people
Joining clubs and attending social events
Taking advantage of chance encounters
Accepting invitations
Giving come-ons and turn-offs
Developing my skills of being a rewarding person

Part B
Implementation

1. Make a plan

Develop a plan for locating and making contact with potential partners that specifies:
a. my goals and subgoals,
b. the steps I intend taking to attain each goal and sub-goal,
c. a time frame,
d. how I intend to monitor my progress.

2. Implement a plan

Implement my plan to locate and make contact with potential partners by:
a. engaging in goal-oriented activities,

b. monitoring and evaluating my progress,

c. persisting, despite setbacks and difficulties.

Remember: 'The more and more I practise, the luckier and luckier I get!'

EXERCISE 9.4
GROUP DISCUSSION: CHOOSING A PARTNER SKILLS
Instructions

This is intended as a group exercise, though it may be done individually or in pairs. For each part:

1. spend 10–15 minutes answering the question in groups of three or four,

2. each sub-group shares its findings with the whole group,

3. then the whole group ranks the six most important points or skills from the most important to the least important.

Part A
Identifying danger signals

List the six most important characteristics to avoid in a potential long-term partner.

Part B
Identifying strengths

List the six most important strengths that you would like a potential long-term partner to possess.

Part C
Search and find skills

List the six most important skills people require to search for and find a suitable long-term partner

TEN
Trust Skills

*Most people want security
in this world, not liberty.*

H. L. Mencken

CHAPTER QUESTIONS

- *What is trust?*
- *How trusting am I capable of being?*
- *How trusting should I be?*
- *What are some thinking skills for being appropriately trusting?*
- *What are some thinking skills for being trustworthy?*
- *What are some action skills for showing trust?*
- *What are some action skills for clarifying trust?*
- *What are some action skills for being trustworthy?*

The next five chapters on trust, caring, intimacy, companionship and sexual relating focus on relationship-bonding skills. However, paradoxically, the areas in which partners can bond most closely are the same areas in which they can disagree most acrimoniously. The potential for happiness of having important needs and wishes fulfilled in a relationship is matched by the potential for distress and pain if partners perceive these needs and wishes as insufficiently fulfilled.

'Trust me' is a common catchphrase, sometimes said in earnest and sometimes in jest. Issues of trust are at the heart of building, maintaining, repairing and ending relationships. A potential partner can have numerous desirable qualities, but you are unwise to commit yourself to a long-term relationship until you have established his or her trustworthiness. On the other hand, the problem may rest in your inability to be trusting – your suspicion and, possibly, jealousy may break up an otherwise good relationship.

WHAT IS TRUST?

Dictionary definitions of trust focus on a firm belief in the honesty, integrity and reliability of another. Trust implies a perception that another is trustworthy and a confident prediction regarding their future behaviour. The following is a vignette of a person who considers that her trust has been betrayed.

> Jacquie had been married 15 years and had four children, ages 1 to 14. One evening at dinner, her husband Paul, the finance director of a minerals company, announced that he had fallen in love with Jane, whom he had interviewed for a secretarial position. A few weeks later, when they were making love, Paul asked Jacquie if he could call her Jane. Jacquie has now divorced Paul, who has set up house with Jane a few blocks from his former family home. Paul just cannot understand why Jacquie is so against taking up his offer to remain good friends despite the divorce.

Trust is a complex concept some of whose dimensions are explored below.

Trusting and being trustworthy

People can trust themselves, others, and their relationships. Trust of self has various aspects. It can mean that you are secure in your identity and confident in your judgement. Furthermore, you trust your ability to develop your human potential. In addition, trust of self can mean that you have confidence in your own trustworthiness towards others and in your commitment to developing and maintaining any long-standing relationship you enter.

Trust of another can involve the same aspects as trust of self. You can trust another as being secure in their identity and have confidence in their judgement. You can have faith in their ability to develop their human potential. Also, you can have confidence in their trustworthiness towards you and in their commitment to developing and maintaining your relationship.

Two people can also develop trust in the resilience and viability of their relationship. They learn that they can rely on each other's cooperative intentions to work for the good of the relationship, despite its ups and downs. Furthermore, they know that each partner cares for and trusts the potential for growth in the other and wishes to nurture it for their mutual good.

Another way of looking at trust in a relationship is to view it as an interactive pattern or process. Here the degree to which each partner trusts themselves, each other and the relationship influences the other partner's trust. Furthermore, the degree to which each partner is trustworthy influences the other. If one partner either unreasonably mistrusts or acts in an untrustworthy way towards the other, unless checked, this can initiate a downward spiral of trust. Similarly, demonstrating greater trust and trust-worthiness can result in a series of greater increments in trust.

Trust and risk

Deutsch (1973) emphasizes that trust involves risk. Trusting another person can involve risking potential negative consequences that might outweigh potential positive consequences. Deutsch provides many reasons why people may still trust, despite the possibility of harm. Such reasons include: despair, social conformity, innocence, impulsiveness, virtue, masochism, unreasoning faith, risk-taking or gambling and confidence.

Trust involves courage since you can never fully know another human being. However, a distinction exists between appropriate trust and foolhardy trust. The process of appropriate trust entails a reasonable attempt to gain relevant information about another and assess it accurately. With foolhardy trust, for whatever reasons individuals truncate and distort the process of gathering and assessing information. However, you require continuing vigilance even with appropriate trust. There are risks to maintaining as well as building trust. Others may change how they behave either on their own or in response to how you behave. Also, if you are complacent, you risk becoming a less desirable partner. Hence, a degree of mistrust over how attractive you are to your partner can help strengthen and maintain your relationship (Lazarus, 1985).

Areas for trust

Relationships develop trust rules and contracts of varying degrees of explicitness (Argyle & Henderson, 1985; Argyle, 1991). Trust involves sticking to the rules or, if not, renegotiating them in advance. A simple trust rule for virtually all relationships is that of keeping appointments. However, trust rules can differ according to individuals and relationships. Sexual fidelity is a prominent trust rule in most marriages. However, in some marriages affairs are not regarded as a breach of trust as long as they do not threaten partners' primary emotional commitment to each other. Other common marriage rules include caring for each other when sick, financially supporting each other and standing up for each other in public.

People who develop deeply trusting relationships reciprocate the reward of security. One way of looking at trust in personal relations centres around fears of rejection. The question becomes: 'Deep down can I trust this person to accept me and not to hurt me intentionally?' Here the underlying issue is that of acceptance. A second way of looking at trust is in terms of respect. Here relevant questions are: 'Can I trust this person to continue seeing me as a separate individual and not to distort their perception of me to meet their own needs?' and 'Can I trust this person to encourage my growth as a separate individual within the interdependence of our relationship?' A further way of looking at trust is in terms of the duty of care: 'Can I trust this person to guard my best interests?' Yet another way of looking at trust is in terms of commitment, with a relevant question being 'Can I trust this person to honour his or her commitment to developing and maintaining our relationship?'. Here the underlying issues include fear of abandonment and of missed opportunities through misplaced trust.

Mistrust

British author George Eliot wrote: 'What loneliness is more lonely than distrust?' Mistrust or distrust can be realistic or unrealistic. People bring varying degrees of unrealistic mistrust into their relationships. Mistrust can be deep seated – early experiences of trust are very important. Erikson (1963) saw basic trust versus basic mistrust as the main conflict in the first of his eight ages of man. He wrote: 'The firm establishment of enduring patterns for the solution of the nuclear conflict of basic trust versus basic mistrust in mere existence is the first task of the ego, and thus the first task for all maternal care' (p. 249). Trust in personal relations involves the capacity for emotional closeness. Ainsworth, Blehar, Water and Wall (1978) discovered three styles of emotional attachment between mothers and infants: secure, avoidant and anxious/ambivalent. Shaver and Hazan (1988) proposed that adults reproduced Ainsworth *et al.*'s three attachment styles in their love lives. Secure lovers were comfortable with emotional closeness, avoidant lovers became very nervous about it and ambivalent lovers had mixed feelings.

People's level of self-esteem mediates the level of mistrust they experience. Above, I suggested that a modicum of mistrust about one's own and one's partner's trustworthiness may have beneficial consequences for relationships. However, insecurity can lead to foolhardy trust and mistrust. With foolhardy trust, a person may distort the evidence that their partner is cheating on them because they have insufficient trust in themselves to cope with the consequences. With foolhardy mistrust, an individual may become irrationally jealous – for instance, even to the extent of not allowing their partner to glance at the opposite sex, look at pictures of them and watch romantic television programmes. Partners in relationships usually experience degrees of mistrust both about themselves and each other. They identify areas of unreliability and attach subjective weightings to them. Then, they may or may not worry about them.

Trust as a process

Trust and trustworthiness are not static concepts. Rather defining what is trustworthy, trusting and being trustworthy are processes that take place in all relationships, for good or ill. Trust issues are always present in relationships. In order to build a relationship, two people need establish a mutually acceptable level of trust. To maintain the relationship, both partners should ideally adhere to the trust rules explicit and implicit in the relationship. Beck (1988) writes: 'Once developed, the forces for stability – commitment, loyalty, trust – protect the closeness, intimacy and security of the loving bond' (p. 217). Once an important breach of trust occurs, partners have numerous choices. For instance, both individually and cooperatively they can confront and work through the issues surrounding the breach of trust and repair the damage done to the relationship. They can realistically consider that the breach of trust signals the end of their relationship. Alternatively, the breach of trust can activate their skills deficits, for example persistent and angry blaming, that weaken the fabric of the relationship and may contribute to its eventual disintegration.

Trust and forgiveness

Partners in relationships where trust has been seriously breached can choose whether to nurse their resentment and desire to punish their partner. Alternatively, they can attempt to forgive their partner and acknowledge any contribution they may have made to the breach of trust. Martin Luther King (1963) observed that forgiving does not entail ignoring what has happened, but means that you choose not to allow it to remain as an insuperable barrier to your relationship. Forgiveness and acceptance of your partner's and your own human fallibility can be enlightened self-interest that frees you to work on the real problems in your relationship. Clearly, it is easier to forgive a partner who acknowledges a breach of trust and shows a cooperative intent to work the underlying problems than a partner who defensively denies untrustworthy behaviour and repeats it.

You may have been the person who seriously breached the trust of your partner. In such instances, as well as working on issues in your relationship, you may need to confront your guilt and learn to forgive yourself.

THINKING SKILLS FOR DEVELOPING AND MAINTAINING TRUST

Trust and mistrust are not reflex reactions – rather they are mediated by how you think. How can you think in ways that encourage appropriate trust and discourage foolhardy trust? Also, how can you think in ways that encourage your own trustworthiness? In short, how can you enhance appropriate trust in your relationships? Following are some thinking skills you might use.

Own responsibility for choosing

Assuming personal responsibility for your life entails recognizing that you are always a chooser. You can become more aware that you are responsible for your trust choices. You can assess how trusting and trustworthy you are and, if necessary, choose to develop better thinking and action skills. Part of this evaluation consists of assessing the consequences for yourself and others of your trust choices. In addition, you can assume responsibility for developing skills for coping with another's deficits in trusting or being trustworthy. You require much self-discipline to trust appropriately, be trustworthy and deal with others' skills deficits in trusting and being trustworthy.

Get in touch with your feelings

Should you trust your 'gut' feelings about another's trustworthiness? The situation becomes more complicated if you take into account that your 'gut' feelings may reflect what you have been taught to feel rather than what you truly feel. Many people are deceived or deceive themselves into foolhardy trust because they insufficiently listen to their feelings. They may deny or distort their reservations about another and ignore existing evidence that this person is untrustworthy in some important way. In addition, they may fail to gather and assess further evidence to confirm or negate their reservations. The opposite can also happen. Because people insufficiently listen to their deeper feelings, they may exhibit mistrust and jealousy where it is not warranted.

Some people require long-term counselling to overcome their basic mistrust of others. Others may require counselling to help them overcome feelings of insecurity that make them too dependent on and trusting of others. In both instances, effective counselling can provide a healing and learning process centred on experiencing feelings and, where appropriate, trusting others.

You may train yourself to acknowledge and listen to your feelings of trust and mistrust. Clearing a physical space and time can give you the psychological space and time to get in touch with what you truly feel and why. You may get in touch with underlying feelings of anxiety and insecurity that stimulate any tendencies you may possess to trust or mistrust inappropriately.

Choose realistic rules

Trust entails adhering to rules. However, this begs numerous questions, including 'Who sets the rules?', 'How realistic are the rules?' and 'What is the role of conscience?'

• *Who sets the rules?* Each partner brings a set of rules about how they and their partner should behave if they wish to build and maintain their relationship. Furthermore, they bring a set of weightings about the importance of adhering to various rules. For instance, Oliver may have a firm rule that, when dating him, Lucy should not go out with other men. Lucy may have a moderately firm rule that it is all right to see other men so long as she does not have sex with them. Oliver and Lucy's criteria for mistrust already differ. In addition, they may further differ if Oliver has a further firm rule that it is all right for him as a male to sleep with other women while dating Lucy. If Oliver and Lucy are open to each other about their expectations, this could have varying consequences: ending the relationship, agreeing to differ, being less open in future or coming to an agreement about mutually acceptable behaviour. Two advantages of partners jointly setting relationship rules are: the increased likelihood of adhering to rules to which they have agreed and greater clarity about the contract. Alternatively, Oliver and Lucy may not openly discuss their rules. Instead, they may make assumptions about each other's rules and regard violations of their assumptions as breaches of trust.

• *How realistic are the rules?* Partners can make unrealistic demands in their relationships that can serve to generate mistrust. Following are some examples.
   'My partner must always be dependable.'
   'My partner should always be home before me.'
   'My partner should not enjoy the company of other men/women.'
   'We should do everything as a couple.'

'We must not have conflict.'

'We must always agree with each other in public.'

'We must totally trust each other.'

Realistic rules should have realistic consequences. However, partners can also have unrealistic rules about the consequences of perceived breaches of trust. For example: 'If my partner sleeps with another man/woman, we must end the relationship' or 'If my partner displeases me, I must get back at him/her.'

There is no easy answer to the question of 'How realistic are the rules?' Rules can be too lax as well as too rigid. Furthermore, rules that work for some individuals and relationships may not work for others. Skills for challenging unrealistic rules include: identifying them; disputing them; and replacing them with more realistic rules. You can challenge your rules either on your own, jointly, or with professional help.

• *What is the role of conscience?* You may experience guilty feelings that indicate that you have transgressed your conscience. Normal guilt is a call to conscience that sensitizes people to the ethical aspects of their thinking and behaviour. Patricia may feel guilty at continuing to harbour suspicions about Robin's depth of feeling for her when the evidence indicates that he clearly cares. Pamela may feel guilty about having a one-night stand on a business trip. Both Patricia and Pamela's consciences represent rules to which each wants to adhere: Patricia to be more emotionally trusting and Pamela to be more sexually trustworthy. Here guilt has the positive function of reminding both women to live up to their standards.

Conscience can also be unrealistic and punitive. Guilty feelings can be exaggerated or misplaced. Also, partners can play on each other's consciences and manipulate each other's guilty feelings. For instance, Mal may feel excessively guilty about suspecting his wife Ruth of infidelity, despite evidence that this is the case. Perceiving himself as the problem, Mal may do little to confirm or negate his suspicions. For her part, Ruth may deliberately reinforce Mal's guilty feelings – 'How could you think that of me?' – as a means of turning the spotlight off herself. In short, conscience can be for good or ill. You need to listen to your conscience, decide the realism of your underlying rules and then act appropriately.

Choose to perceive accurately

Perceive yourself accurately

You require perceiving skills to trust appropriately and be trustworthy. You may fail to realize that you are too trusting and others may take advantage of this. Alternatively, you may lack insight that you are prone to unreasonable jealousy in which you make another's life a nightmare. You fail to realize that mistrust can set up a vicious cycle in which your aggressive behaviour distances your partner and makes it harder for them to give you the reassurance you crave. You may erroneously see yourself as a victim of your partner's persecution, when in reality your suspiciousness initiated their reaction. When confronted with your jealousy, you may play the victim by taking this feedback as further evidence that your suspicions are justified.

You may also see yourself as more trustworthy than justified. Many people possess a quick eye for other people's inconsistencies and fail to recognize their own. When challenged about their untrustworthy behaviour, they may adopt any of a range of defensive postures – for instance, denial or attack – designed to protect their self-pictures. Such defensive behaviour may involve varying degrees of unconscious self-deception.

Perceive your partner accurately

In the previous chapter, I cited various reasons why people may be too trusting in choosing potential partners. In established relationships people can continue to be too trusting of their partners and face the prospect of disillusionment.

Trust in relationships is based on partners' perceptions of not only how each other acts, but also of how each other thinks and feels. However, frequently partners infer how each other feels and thinks from their actions without checking whether or not such inferences are accurate. Beck (1988) stresses that all the time partners are interpreting each other's behaviour. In distressed relationships, trust can become eroded through continued misinterpretations of the thoughts and feelings behind each other's actions. Beck stresses the role of positive and negative symbolic meanings attached to events. In married life, two major themes of symbolic events trigger excessive reactions: first, caring and not caring, and, second, pride. A bunch of flowers might be a symbol of caring. Coming home late from work may be a symbol of not caring and repeatedly coming home late from work may be a symbol of infidelity. Beck (1988, p. 31) notes that partners can develop a 'negative cognitive set' about each other in which the level of mistrust is so high that they will interpret virtually everything each other does or says in a negative way.

Prevent and counteract inaccurate perceptions

The issue of preventing and counteracting inaccurate perceptions is revisited later in the book. A number of skills are entailed in this process. First, you can develop your awareness of your capacity to misinterpret your own and your partner's thoughts, feelings and actions. Second, in specific situations, you can assess the accuracy of your initial inferences in light of the available facts. You can also gather more information – for instance, by asking your partner what her or his intentions were rather than mind-reading. Third, you can generate alternative ways of viewing either your own or your partner's behaviour or what happened between you. Fourth, you can assess the alternative explanations and then choose the one that best fits the facts. There is no guarantee that, at the end of this process, you will trust your partner more. Collecting more evidence and generating and evaluating alternative explanations may confirm your suspicions. However, hopefully the reverse is the case.

Explain cause accurately

You can explain both mistrust and untrustworthiness with varying degrees of accuracy. Often people need to acknowledge and work on their own problems of being trusting.

For example, instead of acknowledging their problem, a convenient explanation for irrationally jealous people is that their hyper-vigilance is justified by imagined signs of another's potential for infidelity. Anxieties surrounding control and possessiveness often underlie mistrust, with many negative consequences. First, the anxiety is an unpleasant emotion. Second, people who need to control their partners establish additional rules. Independent behaviour or disagreement can be perceived as a breach of trust. Third, the partners of controlling people may feel suffocated, resent the additional rules and possibly rebel against them.

Partners can wrongly explain the causes of both their own and each other's untrustworthiness. For instance, Alec and Rhonda, a married couple in their late 20s blame each other for the breakdown of trust in their relationship due to Rhonda's brief affair with Carl, an older divorced businessman. Rhonda blames Alec for his inability to show affection and poor performance in bed. Alec blames Rhonda for her sexual demandingness, selfishness and devotion to her career. Both partners play the blame game, rather than looking more deeply at their own contribution not only to the breakdown of trust in their relationship, but also to what they might jointly do to repair the relationship, assuming that it is worth repairing. Relationships are interactive processes. Dealing with untrustworthy behaviour necessitates examining how the interactions between partners may be destructive as well as exploring issues of individual responsibility and commitment.

Predict realistically

Trust is about predicting both risk and gain. Also, breaching trust involves calculations of risk and gain. You need to clarify your goals and realistically assess risk and gain in respect of them. Following are four possible thinking skills deficits when predicting.

• *Underestimating risk*. You may underestimate the bad consequences of trusting another. Negative consequences of being too trusting in relationships include: being jilted, getting financially cheated, getting pregnant and getting AIDS. In addition, you may underestimate the negative consequences of being untrustworthy: for instance, guilt feelings and hurting innocent parties such as children.

• *Overestimating risk*. Fear of change, failure and success are powerful motivators that help people overestimate the negative consequences of trusting. Below is a vignette illustrating fear of change.

> Denise is a 30-year old spinster who still lives at home. She struggles with a number of decisions: moving away from home, changing her job and staying in a committed relationship with a man. Over the years Denise has chosen consistently to make the safety rather than the growth choice. She does not trust herself enough to cope with change.

Frequently, unrealistic predictions about failure underlie mistrust. Such fears often consist of two elements: fear of negative consequences and doubts about your ability to cope with them if they occur. You may fail to develop a relationship through unrealistic fears of rejection or of another's untrustworthiness. Also, you can maintain mistrust in your relationships if you overestimate the negative consequences of discussing problems openly. Some people can fear the positive consequences of trusting another – for instance, they may then be forced to handle the consequences of establishing their first long-term relationship.

- *Overestimating gain*. Often, when people start affairs they overestimate the good consequences. They may take for granted the positive aspects of their current relationship and become carried away by the excitement of a new romance. Both the short-term and long-term gains of giving in to temptation may not live up to expectations.

- *Underestimating gain*. Two trends are common in underestimating gain. First, you may be poor at perceiving the potential rewards that stem from trusting and being trustworthy. Second, if you identify the rewards, you may not give them the weight they deserve.

How can you improve your skills of predicting risk and loss concerning trust and trustworthiness? Assessing probability requires reviewing your assumptions about the likelihood of risks and gains occurring. Questions that you might ask yourself in assessing probability fall into two categories: first, 'What rational basis do I have for making a particular prediction?'; and second, 'What irrational considerations might interfere with the accuracy of my predictions?'

Your trust predictions may be based on doubting your skills at coping with particular situations. If so, reassess your coping capacities, including identifying additional sources of support. If your predictive errors lean towards overestimating potential gains and underestimating potential risks, develop skills of generating and evaluating additional risks. However, if you are more likely to overestimate risks, you can develop skills of generating and evaluating additional gains from trusting and being trustworthy.

Use visualizing skills

Especially if you have a strong imagination, you can use visualizing skills to help you trust and be trustworthy. Nancy possesses some insight that she is prone to irrational jealousy involving vivid images of her husband Walter's infidelities. However, Nancy also knows that, if she can catch herself early in the cycle, she can exert some control over her thinking. To become calmer, she visualizes herself lying in a field on a warm sunny day without a care in the world. Then, feeling more relaxed, she reviews the evidence for her jealous thoughts and catastrophic images. As part of this review, Nancy makes out a balance sheet in which she counteracts her jealous images by visualizing the caring and loving things that Walter does for her. In addition, Nancy visualizes herself as a strong and competent woman who does not need to depend on other people all the time. Nancy also visualizes both the gains to their relationship from trusting Walter and the losses if she persists in her jealousy. If Nancy still requires reassurance, she rehearses in her imagination calmly sharing her fears with Walter.

You can also use visualizing skills to counteract foolhardy trust. Some people are too trusting – they require the ability to imagine that their partners actually are engaging in untrustworthy behaviour.

You can use visualizing to help you to stay trustworthy. Temptation is very much in the mind's eye. You can try imagery stopping – shouting to yourself 'STOP' and then switching from the tempting image to another image, for instance imagining something you love about your partner (Kwee & Lazarus, 1986). Also, you can imagine the consequences of breaking trust for yourself, your partner and any others involved. You can have a mental balance sheet in which you counteract temptation by becoming more realistic about the risks of your behaviour.

ACTION SKILLS FOR DEVELOPING AND MAINTAINING TRUST

Following are some illustrative skills, albeit somewhat interrelated, for showing trust, clarifying trust and for being trustworthy.

Showing trust

Disclose yourself

Johnson (1993) emphasizes that trust is built or destroyed through taking risks and then being either affirmed or negated. Let us look at the progressive disclosure of personal information as part of the process of building trust. You show some trust to another by making a disclosure that is a little risky. If the other accepts and is supportive about your disclosure, trust is likely to be enhanced. Trust may be further enhanced if the other risks disclosing at a similar level of intimacy. However, if the other person rejects your initial disclosure, you are unlikely to risk deeper disclosures and may even end the relationship. Where both of you feel relatively safe, you may be prepared to continue testing and building trust by disclosing at a slightly deeper level, and so on. Relationships end up at differing levels of trust. To develop relationships, each partner needs to feel mainly supported and accepted when they disclose important personal information.

Act as if giving the benefit of the doubt

Earlier I mentioned that trust in relationships can be viewed as an interactive process. By not showing trust you may bring about the very consequences you fear. Beck (1988) gives the example of Marjorie who, despite her husband Ken's obvious devotion to her, always held back in her commitment to him. The daughter of a domineering, critical and explosive father, Marjorie would always microscopically examine any of Ken's minor flaws for fear they would turn into a major deficiency reminiscent of her father. Marjorie would not make a full commitment to Ken because she was not sure she could trust him. She would be miserable and think of getting out of the marriage if she found out he was untrustworthy. Beck set up a three month experiment so Marjorie could test the following hypothesis: *'If I totally commit myself to the relationship, look for the positive instead of the negative, I will feel more secure.'* (p. 224). After three months of thinking and acting differently, Marjorie discovered that she was indeed more secure in the relationship. The moral of this story is that you can damage developing and maintaining trust in relationships by holding back in how you act. Sometimes the best insurance is to take the risk.

Clarifying trust

Clarify trust rules

In relationships many trust rules are implicit rather than explicit. However, sometimes partners and potential partners may need to communicate explicitly what their criteria are for trustworthy behaviour. A simple example is that of Joanne and Brett who had been dating for two months when Brett forgot Joanne's birthday. Joanne, who comes from a family in which birthdays were very important, gets very upset and concludes that Brett does not care for her and is untrustworthy in his personal relations. Brett comes from a family where birthdays were not a cause for great celebration. He did not mean to cause offence. In such an instance, Joanne might be wise to share with Brett that birthdays are important to her and, if their relationship continues, she would appreciate him remembering hers. By assertively clarifying her expectation, rather than sulking or getting aggressive, Joanne establishes a trust rule for the relationship.

In many instances, partners need to negotiate trust rules jointly. For instance, Gail and Ernie discuss how much time to spend on their separate interests and how they can keep some quality time for themselves. During this discussion, they get a sense of their common ground and what might be an acceptable compromise. Then they articulate their compromise, which can be viewed as their trust contract. Gail and Ernie agree to review the contract if either anticipates wanting to breach it in any significant way.

Request explanations

People with suspicious natures can ask for too many explanations and put potential partners and partners on the defensive. On the other hand, rather than mind-read another and then nurse mistrust, you can assertively ask for explanations. For instance, Joey and Kevin are a gay couple in their mid-twenties. One evening, quite out of character, Kevin came home three hours later than usual. Joey said he had been worried by Kevin's absence and asked the reason. Kevin explained that he had gone over to his mother's flat and she was very upset over the death of one of her friends. In this instance, there was an innocent and unambiguous explanation for Kevin's absence. However, if Kevin keeps coming home late and explains that he is kept back at the office, Joey has the choice of giving him the benefit of the doubt or confronting him with his suspicions.

Being trustworthy

Send consistent messages

In Chapter 5 I stressed the importance of genuineness in how you disclose yourself. If others are to view you as trustworthy, you need to send honest and consistent messages. In particularly, you appear untrustworthy if your actions do not match your words. You can talk about how much you love someone and how committed you are to them, but the messages that really count are whether your actions speak loud and clear.

Trustworthy behaviour means that you consistently adhere to the trust rules of your relationship. If necessary, you make new rules or clarify existing rules. If you consider a rule unreasonable, you attempt to renegotiate it with your partner rather than break it. This guideline is especially important in sensitive areas for your partner.

Show commitment

For couples, showing commitment to the maintenance of your relationship is a crucial aspect of being trustworthy. To the degree that you are suspicious, uncaring, hostile, selfish and competitive, your partner is unlikely to view you as trustworthy. Furthermore, given the tendency for partners to reciprocate one another's behaviour, you make it more difficult for him or her to be trustworthy to you.

Trustworthy behaviour means working on your relationship in the hard times as well as the good. There is much to be said for a crisis or catastrophe approach to understanding how partners come to be perceived as trustworthy. Misunderstandings, differences, fights and crises occur in virtually all close relationships. Partners can learn how trustworthy each other is depending on how they handle these difficulties. They can find out that their relationship is resilient, that each is prepared to accept the nastier part of the other without quitting, and that each is committed to maintaining the relationship. Difficulties in sound relationships provide opportunities for partners to rise to the challenge of being trustworthy by cooperatively searching for constructive solutions. In weak relationships, either or both partners do not have this commitment. Unresolved conflicts may lead to alienation, which in turn can lead to involvement with third parties and thus to further untrustworthy behaviour.

CHAPTER HIGHLIGHTS

• Trust implies a perception that another is trustworthy and a confident prediction about their future behaviour.

• People can trust or distrust themselves, others and their relationships. In relationships partners influence each other through their trust behaviour.

• Trust involves risk and courage since you can never fully know another human being.

• Themes for trust include acceptance, respect, duty of care and commitment.

• Mistrust can be realistic or unrealistic. Ability to trust is influenced by early childhood experiences.

• When trust is breached, partners have the option of forgiveness and working on the problems in their relationship.

• You need much discipline to assume personal responsibility for trusting appropriately, being trustworthy and dealing with others' skills deficits in trusting and being trustworthy.

• You can train yourself to acknowledge and listen to your feelings of trust and mistrust.

• Trust involves implicit and explicit rules. Rules should be clear and realistic. Conscience can be a call to keeping such rules.

• You need to perceive whether you are too trusting or too suspicious. You can collect evidence and generate alternative explanations which affirm or negate your trust or mistrust.

• Errors in trusting include both overestimating and underestimating risk and gain. You can develop your skills at assessing probability.

• You can use visualizing skills to counteract irrational trust and allow for rational mistrust. Stopping tempting imagery and visualizing negative consequences are skills for remaining trustworthy.

• Skills for showing trust include progressively disclosing yourself and acting as if giving your partner the benefit of the doubt.

• Skills for clarifying trust include setting and negotiating trust rules and requesting explanations for possible untrustworthy behaviour.

• Skills for being trustworthy include sending consistent messages – especially having your actions match your words – and showing commitment to maintaining your relationship when misunderstandings, differences, fights and crises occur in it.

EXERCISES
EXERCISE 10.1
DEVELOPING TRUST AND TRUSTWORTHINESS: MY PREVIOUS EXPERIENCES
Instructions

First do each part of this exercise on your own. Then, if appropriate, discuss with your partner, another or others.

Part A
Developing trust

What are the experiences that have shaped your current ability to trust appropriately in your relationships?

Birth to age 9

Helpful experiences
Harmful experiences

Age 10–19

Helpful experiences
Harmful experiences

Age 20 onwards

Helpful experiences
Harmful experiences

Part B
Developing trustworthiness

What are the experiences that have shaped your current ability to be trustworthy in your relationships?

Birth to age 9

Helpful experiences
Harmful experiences

Age 10 to 19

Helpful experiences
Harmful experiences

Age 20 onwards

Helpful experiences
Harmful experiences

EXERCISE 10. 2
DEVELOP MY THINKING SKILLS FOR TRUST
Instructions

First do each part of this exercise on your own. Then, if appropriate, discuss with your partner, another or others.

Part A
Assessment

Identify the thinking skills deficits you possess or might possess when developing and maintaining trust in a close relationship.

Own responsibility for choosing

1. To what extent do you assume personal responsibility for your choices in trusting appropriately and dealing with another's skills deficits in trusting?

Get in touch with my feelings

1. How good are you at listening to your deeper feelings to avoid foolhardy trust or excessive mistrust?

Choose realistic rules

1. Specify the most important criteria or rules for developing and maintaining trust in a relationship.

2. Where appropriate, work with your partner in formulating and specifying the main trust rules for your relationship?

Choose to perceive accurately

1. Do you perceive yourself as either too suspicious, or too trusting, or appropriately trusting in your relationship(s)? Provide evidence for your view of yourself.

Explain cause accurately

1. If you identify yourself as either unreasonably trusting or suspicious, how do you explain this skills deficit to yourself and to others?

Predict realistically

1. How realistic are you in predicting the trustworthiness of another when either choosing a partner or in a close relationship?

2. If unrealistic in predicting another's trustworthiness, which of the following skills deficits do you exhibit:

- underestimating risk
- overestimating risk

- overestimating gain
- underestimating gain.

Visualizing skills

1. If appropriate, how good are you at using visualizing skills to counteract:
a. irrational jealousy,
b. foolhardy trust?

Part B
Change

1. Summarize your main thinking skills deficits regarding trust?

2. If appropriate, identify one or more of your main deficits and develop a plan to change how you think. In your plan, specify
a. your goals, including a time frame,
b. the steps you intend taking to attain each of your goals, and
c. how you will monitor your progress.

EXERCISE 10.3
DEVELOP MY ACTION SKILLS FOR TRUST
Instructions

First, answer each part of this exercise on your own. Then, if appropriate, discuss with your partner, another or others.

Part A
Assessment

Identify your action skills strengths and deficits for showing trust, clarifying trust, and being trustworthy.

Showing trust

Disclosing myself

strengths
deficits

Acting as if giving the benefit of the doubt

strengths
deficits

Clarifying trust

Clarifying trust rules

strengths
deficits

Requesting explanations

strengths
deficits

Being trustworthy

Sending consistent messages

strengths
deficits

Showing commitment

strengths
deficits

Part B
Change

1. Summarize your main action skills strengths and deficits regarding trust.

2. If appropriate, identify one or more of your main deficits and develop a plan to change how you act. In your plan, specify
a. your goals, including a time frame,
b. the steps you intend taking to attain each of your goals, and
c. how you will monitor your progress.

EXERCISE 10.4
GROUP DISCUSSION: TRUST SKILLS
Instructions

This is intended as a group exercise, though it may be done individually or in pairs. For each part:

1. spend 10–15 minutes answering the question in groups of three of four,

2. each sub-group shares its findings with the whole group,

3. then the whole group ranks the six most important skills from the most important to the least important.

Part A
Developing trust

List the six most important skills people can use to develop trust in a long-term relationship.

Part B
Maintaining and repairing trust

List the six most important skills that people can use to maintain and repair trust in a long-term relationship.

ELEVEN
Caring Skills

*No act of kindness, no matter
how small, is ever wasted.*

Aesop

CHAPTER QUESTIONS

- *What is caring?*

- *What are some dimensions of caring?*

- *What are some feelings and reasons for caring?*

- *What are some thinking skills for caring?*

- *What are some action skills for caring?*

The extent to which partners care for themselves and each other is a central issue in all relationships. Beck writes: 'Caring means letting your mate know that "You are important to me. I am concerned about what happens to you. I will look after you."' (1988, p. 238). Partners show their love and perceive each other's love through their caring behaviours.

A number of analogies highlight the role of caring in relationships. A construction or engineering analogy is that persistent use of caring skills reinforces the foundation of a relationship. Litvinoff (1992) uses a banking analogy. Loving or caring actions when things are going well in a relationship are bank account 'deposits' that partners can draw on in difficult times. Even during bad times, partners may make loving gestures that build up the credit side of their account. A medical analogy is that caring behaviours constitute both preventive medicine and also help to heal sickness. Lastly, a legal analogy is that partners fulfil their contractual duty of care to each other by caring behaviours. Negligence in performing caring behaviours breaches the contract of the relationship and can lead to serious repercussions, including the legal reality of divorce.

Generally, as in the above analogies, caring is thought of as enhancing a relationship. Below are statements indicating positive aspects of caring.

> 'It's been a long struggle, but I'm finally learning to care for myself better.'
> 'He is always there for me when I need him.'
> 'She cares for me enough to allow me to be different.'
> 'We're a team who support each other.'
> 'I really appreciate the way you looked after me when I was ill.'

However, caring, or perceived deficiencies in caring, can also generate negative feelings and outcomes. Below are statements indicating negative aspects of caring.

> 'I feel emotionally exhausted caring for others all the time.'
> 'I feel suffocated with your caring.'
> 'She pushes me away when I try to show affection.'
> 'You ungrateful shit. After all I've done for you.'
> 'You care for nobody, but number one.'

Caring is a complex concept that echoes Oscar Wilde's statement in his play *The Importance of Being Earnest* that 'The truth is rarely pure, and never simple.' Below I discuss some meanings of caring before reviewing feelings, reasons, thinking skills and action skills associated with it.

MEANINGS OF CARING

Defining caring

With dictionary definitions, the verb care consists of two interrelated components: caring for and taking care of. Caring for someone represents the feeling component of caring. If you care for someone, you love or like them and feel concern for and interest in them. Taking care of someone in some way, however large or small, represents the action component of caring. In various ways, you attend to their welfare, look after their interests and provide for them. Caring for another also involves consideration: being thoughtful for others and having regard for their feelings. Consequently, caring can encompass not just positive actions, but avoiding negative actions.

Dimensions of caring

Following are some important dimensions of caring in a relationship.

Self-care

Self-care can be distinguished from selfishness. Caring for yourself means that you prize yourself sufficiently to consider that you are worthy of care. Furthermore, you assume sufficient personal responsibility to see that your legitimate interests are not overwhelmed by your own needs to care for others or others' needs to be cared for by you. You respect your own and your partner's need for autonomy and separateness as well as for connectedness. You are a person in your own right and not just an extension of another, for instance someone else's boyfriend, girlfriend, spouse or parent. Also, you assume responsibility for dealing with your problems. In addition, where appropriate, you encourage others to care for themselves. Below is a vignette that illustrates caring for yourself.

> A month ago Katie's husband Dan was made redundant after 18 years of working for the same accounting firm. Katie wants to offer emotional and practical support to her husband and three children. However, increasingly she becomes aware that she also needs to care for herself. To achieve this end, Katie lists some things she can do to nourish herself, including: going for walks on her own with the dog, eating properly, keeping in touch with understanding friends, taking baths and playing the clarinet.

Self-care means that you acknowledge emotional boundaries and needs for privacy, solitude, space and time alone. When emotionally exhausted, you care less well for others. Often, especially where dependent children are involved, partners find achieving personal space difficult. Probably women are more likely than men to view their role as super-carers. Dorwick (1991) observes that 'men's willingness to be cared for, and women's willingness to collude, is worth consideration.' (p. 107). However, it is possible to overgeneralize – for instance, to feed and educate their families both males and females may persist in jobs they hate. In such instances, people need to find other outlets to care for themselves.

Caring for another

Yalom (1980) writes that: 'To care for another means to care about the being and growth of another.' (p. 373). Most commonly caring is viewed in terms of providing care for another rather than for yourself. For instance, the preceding section on dictionary definitions of caring focused on sending caring messages to others. Some caring messages can be sent daily: for instance, saying 'goodbye' and 'hello' to your partner on going to and returning from work. Other caring messages are more for special occasions: for instance, remembering birthdays and anniversaries. Crises are another opportunity to send caring messages: for instance, after a bereavement. Though not covered in this chapter, you can also show how much you care for another by how you deal with problems in your relationship.

Just as self-care should be based on respecting your own uniqueness and potential, so caring for another involves respecting their difference and potential. A possible distinction exists between ordinary caring and tough caring. In ordinary caring, you send caring messages with the probability that they will please the other. In tough caring, you send messages that may challenge the other's view of themselves. You care for another so much that you are not willing to let them be less than they could be. Hopefully, such caring leads to constructive dialogue and change.

Receiving care

In relationships, partners are both givers and receivers of care. Partners can enhance or damage their relationships by how they receive each other's caring. Below are two vignettes, showing good and bad receiving care skills.

> Jen and Walt have lived together for five years and been married for one year. If necessary, Jen lets Walt know that she wants to receive care by saying 'I really need you to care for me at this moment.' Sometimes Jen also gently tells Walt what she needs him to do and say.

> Nikki and Steve, both in their early twenties, are going through a rough patch in their relationship. When Steve affectionately puts his arms round her shoulders, Nikki snaps 'I can't bear you touching me.'

There are numerous issues and skills surrounding receiving care. Jen used skills of requesting care and then shaping it to suit her needs. Nikki, however, failed to use skills of declining Steve's caring without causing him unnecessary hurt. Such behaviour does not help Nikki and Steve to address the underlying problems in their relationship. Expressing appreciation is another receiving care skill on which many partners can fruitfully work.

Interactive patterns of caring

As with trust, the way two people care in a relationship can be viewed as an interactive pattern or process in which partners' experiences of giving and receiving care influence each other. In any close relationship, there is a tension between autonomy and dependence. The ideal relationship is one where interdependence is mixed with autonomy. Here both partners exist as separate selves and there is a fluid state between individualism and sharing dependencies. Partners manage an appropriate balance between caring for themselves and caring for and receiving care from each other.

Prominent among the less stable caring interactive patterns is that reflecting a discrepancy between the partners' wishes for emotional closeness and emotional distance. Such interactive patterns can take various forms. For instance, the more one partner exhibits caring behaviour, the more the other may withdraw. Alternatively, the more one partner demands to receive care, the more the other partner may avoid providing it. A third variation is for one partner both to exhibit much caring behaviour and demand care in return, only to find little, if any, care coming back.

Another potentially unstable caring pattern in today's world is that between the care-taking female and the cared-for male. A variation of this pattern is that between the protecting male and the dependent female. The rise of feminism has challenged such patterns. The repercussions of the changing power relationships between the sexes are still being worked out. Not only are men gradually sharing more of the female caring functions – for instance, child-rearing, but women are sharing more of the male caring functions – for instance, bread-winning.

Yet a further potentially unstable caring pattern is where partners take an accounting approach and operate rigidly on the basis of reciprocity – 'You scratch my back, and I'll scratch yours'. Such relationships fare badly when either or both partners perceive themselves as receiving less care than they give. Since perceptions of care are subjective rather than objective, rigid reciprocity of care patterns provide much opportunity for relationship distress and breakdown.

FEELINGS AND REASONS FOR CARING

People's feelings about and reasons for caring are rarely pure and simple. Below I suggest positive and negative feelings and reasons for caring. In addition, feelings and reasons for caring can vary in such dimensions as strength, persistence, complexity and ambivalence.

Self-care

Positive feelings and reasons

Ideally, people are able to care for themselves on the basis of self-love and a secure sense of their identity. Recapitulating the discussion in chapter 9 on needing and need-free love, mature self-love underlies rather than impedes love of others. Partners with satisfactory experiences of being cared for when growing up and who observed their parents demonstrating effective self-caring skills are likely to have both confidence and skills to care for themselves. They have sufficient strength to have a nurturing relationship both with and for themselves (Dorwick, 1991). Caring for themselves enables them to care properly for others, including their partner.

Negative feelings and reasons

Harmful reasons for caring for yourself manifest deficiencies in self-esteem and self-love. Your self-centredness reflects a sense of depletion and emptiness. You become selfishly focused on yourself since you do not have sufficient care to give to others. You may hide your self-preoccupation under a mask of cynicism. Insufficiently caring for yourself can stem from and contribute to negative feelings. Such feelings include: emotional exhaustion, insecurity, anxiety, depression, anger, bitterness and self-pity.

Caring for another

Positive feelings and reasons

Altruism means unselfish concern for the welfare of others. Humans are capable of higher and not just baser motivations (Argyle, 1991; Batson, 1990; Maslow, 1962, 1970). You can altruistically care for the being and growth of another. Altruism reflects mature, need-free love. You can transcend your existential isolation and find meaning in caring for another. Care is also motivated by affection and liking. Affectionate partners receive joy and fulfilment in giving and sharing. They identify or empathize with the inner world of the other. By projecting themselves into this inner world, they can go some way toward anticipating and meeting the other's needs. When you truly love someone you ask: 'How can I relate lovingly to this special person in the interests of their happiness and development?' rather than 'What's in it for me?' Frequently, care in relationships entails giving encouragement, hope, confidence and support to your partner. By bringing your partner more alive, you feel more alive yourself. Also, an element of anxiety about pleasing another person and maintaining their interest in you can help partners avoid taking each other for granted.

Care for another can stem from compassion or a feeling of deep sympathy and pity for their plight. Also, care can be motivated by considerateness or regard for another's thoughts and feelings. Other positive reasons for providing care include: joy in giving, protectiveness, tenderness, courage, commitment, a sense of duty, enlightened self-interest and forgiveness. In addition, you can feel rewarded by another's expression of appreciation for what you have done.

Negative feelings and reasons

Caring may spring from less than positive feelings and reasons. You can be sexually attracted to a person without wishing to exploit them. However, either intentionally or sometimes unintentionally, people can demonstrate caring as a manipulative tool in sexual conquests. They show caring in ways that treat the other person as an object to be 'bedded'. When sex is over, they may withdraw caring or even become hostile. With or without sexual attraction, many people try to project a 'good girl/guy' image as a way of stage-managing others' impressions of them.

People can also show caring to manage their anxieties. Possessiveness can be a central feature of anxiety-motivated caring. Instead of respecting another as a separate person, you seek to control them for your own ends. The provision of care becomes conditional – 'I care for you so long as you do what I want' rather than unconditional – 'I care for you as a separate and unique individual.' Possessive caring can also demand recognition – 'You must acknowledge my generosity.' Consequently, such caring can be doubly damaging – 'First, you should do what I want and then, second, you should thank me for it' – rather than liberating. Taking under the guise of giving is another way of viewing possessive caring.

Showing caring to manage anxiety can also reflect power imbalances in relationships. The less powerful person may demonstrate caring as a way of 'buttering up' or appeasing the more powerful person. Often such demonstrations of caring mask anger. Spouses who feel dominated by their partners may care more out of fear than love. Partners who feel insecure may show caring to hold on to relationships rather than confront the problems in them.

Often people with low self-esteem, who have been inadequately cared for themselves, fill the gap by giving excessive amounts of care to others. Their levels of self-love and self-care are insufficiently high to allow them insight into their own neediness.

Receiving care

Positive feelings and reasons

You can feel affirmed when you receive care. You can feel wanted, loved, contented, understood and worthy of care. Joy and happiness come from receiving as well as from giving. You can feel affection and appreciation for the giver of care. You can enjoy the pleasure your happiness provides to the carer. Also, you may feel motivated to reciprocate the care in some way, either now or later. In addition, you may feel safer to take the risks of trying new behaviours, revealing more of yourself and being more fully alive in the relationship.

On occasion, you may take time to appreciate the care offered to you. For instance, initially you may feel unworthy to receive another's care. However, if the care is genuinely provided, your feelings of unworthiness may turn into feelings of enhanced self-esteem. Also, you may feel anxious if your partner demonstrates caring by challenging some aspect of your behaviour: for example, your lack of commitment to your studies or career. However, if you move beyond your discomfort to look more closely at your behaviour, you may appreciate your partner's display of tough rather than tender caring. Underneath, he or she may be saying: 'I care for you enough not to allow you to be less than you might truly be'.

Negative feelings and reasons

You can play various roles that manipulate your partner to provide you with care. Such roles include playing helpless, playing sick, playing poor, playing the victim, playing the martyr, playing angry and playing the sex object. You may demand to receive care regardless of the other's feelings and physical state. Alternatively, you may control a carer through flattery, for instance by continually complimenting them on their generosity.

You can feel negatively when you receive too much or the wrong kind of care. Such negative emotions include feeling controlled, dependent, overwhelmed, invaded, misunderstood, manipulated, belittled and under unwelcome obligations. You probably resent clumsy and unwanted attempts to care for you. Such attempts can cause an uncomfortable conflict between politeness and telling the truth.

Interactive patterns of caring

Positive feelings and reasons

You can reciprocate caring in such a way that each of you is enhanced by the processes and outcomes of your caring. Each of you is fully present in important caring encounters and do not relate as though part of you is elsewhere. Together, at least momentarily, you are able to transcend your existential isolation to give and receive each other's caring. Also, partners with effective interactive caring patterns understand that developing each other's human potential is important for each of you as individuals and for the health of your relationship.

Negative feelings and reasons

You can feel negative emotions if you perceive there is an imbalance in the give-and-take of care in your relationship. You may resent that your partner is not pulling his or her weight, even to the point of ending the relationship if the imbalance persists. In such instances, your negative emotions could have positive consequences for your future happiness. Change in an interactive pattern of caring can also precipitate negative emotions – for instance, when either the protector gets fed up with the clinging behaviour of the protected or the protected partner grows in independence.

SOME THINKING SKILLS FOR CARING

Acting in a caring way is easier if you can also think in a caring way. This section explores thinking skills that can enhance self-care, caring for another, receiving care and working with a partner to forge an effective interactive pattern of caring.

Own responsibility for choosing

If you are to care for yourself, you need to own responsibility for doing so. You cannot assume that someone else will provide answers to your existential challenge to nurture yourself and deal with your problems. Similarly, if you are to care for others, it is your responsibility to recognize the costs and benefits of doing so and to make appropriate choices. To a large extent you can choose how you think, act and feel as a carer. You can also acknowledge that you are always a chooser when you receive care. How you think, act and feel is largely under your control and not the care-giver's. The responsibility is also yours, though not yours alone, for being sensitive to the nature of the caring pattern you establish with your partner and, where necessary, changing your behaviour.

Get in touch with your feelings

How can you access and strengthen altruistic and caring feelings? You can acknowledge rather than repress your altruistic feelings. Maslow (1962, 1970) stressed that humans repress their higher as well as their lower potentials. You can also acknowledge the pleasure you give and receive when you act on such feelings effectively. In addition, you can train yourself in inner focusing. First, find the psychological and physical space to be truly alone. Then, rather than react to what is going on outside, listen to and explore what is going on inside you. You can also strengthen your altruistic feelings by developing your capacity for empathy for another's internal world and outer circumstances. Sometimes this may require a conscious effort to switch off your self-pre-occupation and switch into imagining how life is for them – or you can even ask them.

Though often caring is pleasurable, on other occasions it requires inner strength. There may be times in a relationship, for instance sickness, where the balance of caring becomes very uneven. Also, in times of stress and conflict, caring becomes difficult. Skills for strengthening your will to care are similar to those for accessing caring feelings: for instance, inner focusing and developing empathy. Additional skills include nurturing yourself and managing feelings – like anger and self-pity – that block caring. People who received little care when growing up may require counselling to strengthen their ability to care for themselves and others.

Use coping self-talk

You can influence how you care by how you talk to yourself. Statements that might make it easier to care for yourself include: 'I am worthy of care', 'I deserve some care', 'I am more effective when I care for myself as well as for others' and 'Let's develop a plan for how I can care for myself.'

Sometimes providing care is associated with anxiety about whether it will be accepted or rejected. In fact, partners can inhibit caring gestures for fear of rejection. Calming and coaching self-statements are two important elements of coping self-talk. Calming self-talk statements include: 'Calm down', 'Relax', 'Breathe slowly and regularly' and 'Take it easy'. Coaching statements tell you how to perform a task skilfully: for example, 'I will wait to give my present until he/she is relaxed.'

Receiving care, especially when unwanted, can also trigger anxiety. Again, you can use both calming and coaching self-statements to help you cope with both current and future situations.

Choose realistic rules

You may possess unrealistic rules that restrict your freedom of choice and engender negative emotions. Your unrealistic rules can have some truth in them, but they are too rigid. Below are some illustrations.

Self-care

> 'I must always put other people's needs above my own.'
> 'Women must always look after men.'
> 'Men must always provide for women.'

Caring for another

> 'I must always get it right.'
> 'I must always be appreciated.'
> 'I must not ask people what they want.'

Receiving care

> 'I must never refuse care.'
> 'Others must know what I want.'
> 'I must never ask for care.'

Interactive patterns of caring

> 'We must give and take the same amount.'
> 'We must have the same needs for giving care.'
> 'We must have the same needs for receiving care.'

What can you do about unrealistic rules? First, identify them and acknowledge their negative consequences for yourself and others. Second, dispute or challenge the logic of unrealistic rules by asking questions like: 'Why must I never refuse care?' and 'Do I think less of others who set boundaries on the amount of care they receive?' Third, change your unrealistic rule into something less rigid: for example 'While I would prefer that people give me the amount of care I want, in some instances I may need to set limits on the amount of care I accept.'

Choose to perceive accurately

Perceive yourself accurately

Inaccurate perceptions can interfere with your taking adequate care of yourself. For instance, especially if female, you may act as super-carer and not fully perceive how drained you feel. Whatever your sex, you may perceive yourself as unworthy either to care for yourself, for another or to receive care. On the other hand, you may possess a self-serving bias in which you perceive yourself as better at giving and receiving care than you really are. An example is that of Lily, age 24, who fails to see how she controls with caring, her partner, Alicia, age 25. Alicia increasingly feels suffocated with Lily's demands for approval for everything she does: for example, she expects praise whenever she cooks. Lily is insufficiently sensitive to Alicia's messages that she is too possessive and demanding.

Both as a giver and receiver of care, you can place unnecessarily negative labels on yourself. Negative self-labels attached to providing care include: 'weak', 'unmanly' and 'sucking up'. Negative self-labels attached to receiving care include: 'vulnerable', 'dependent' and 'unable to stand on my own two feet.'

Perceive another accurately

You can perceive inaccurately by mind-reading how your partner wants to receive care. For instance, you may inadequately acknowledge differences and project your own wishes for caring on to them. An example is giving presents that you like rather than finding out what another wants. You may compound your initial perceiving error by then not noticing their discomfort. People whose anxieties motivate them to be very controlling insufficiently perceive the separateness and uniqueness of their partners.

You may also err on the side of giving too much or too little care because you fail to perceive what your partner wants. In some instances, partners do not communicate clearly their wants for care. In other instances, clear messages about how they want to receive care are not heeded.

You can perceive inaccurately because you expect your partner to mind-read your needs for care. Here, rather than perceive your partner as insufficiently caring, you may more accurately perceive yourself as not sending sufficiently clear requests for care.

Explain cause accurately

Skills deficits in caring for yourself, caring for another, receiving care and in your caring interactive pattern with your partner can be sustained by explaining cause inaccurately. For example, people poor at caring for themselves may explain this by their upbringing, religious teaching, biological sex or their partner's lack of concern for them. Often missing is an adequate acknowledgment of their own contribution to sustaining their insufficient self-care. Upbringing, religious teaching, biological sex and other people's behaviours may each influence you. However, you depower yourself by explaining all the cause of your problem to external factors. By assuming responsibility for your self-care problem, you take back the power to change what you can to improve your situation.

You can inaccurately explain your reasons for caring both to yourself and to your partner. Earlier in this chapter, I reviewed positive and negative reasons for caring. If you are honest to yourself in explaining your reasons for providing care, you are better placed to guard against negative reasons, for instance, possessiveness, which might adversely affect your relationship. Also, you are less likely to project yourself either too positively or negatively to your partner. Be careful not to be a saint or a martyr. Also, beware of pretending not to care, if you really do care.

How accurate are you in explaining the cause of your partner's care? Another's reasons can be explained too positively or too negatively. For example, you may protect yourself against the implications of your partner's lack of care by explaining that 'underneath he/she really does care for me'. It may be preferable to raise the issue with your partner to find out whether or not what is underneath is the same lack of caring you perceive on the surface. As relationships deteriorate, partners tend to become prone to Beck's (1988) 'negative cognitive set'. By systematically biasing their perceptions and explanations, they place their partners in the psychological 'dog house' where they can do nothing right, not even care. Partners are unprepared to assess the evidence for their perceptions and explanations. Also, they fail to give one another the benefit of the doubt for having positive caring intentions. Each explains that they are victims of the other's persecution.

Partners can inaccurately explain their interactive patterns of caring. For example, if engaged in an emotional closeness–emotional withdrawal pattern, probably you and your partner possess insufficient insight into how you sustain one another's behaviour by your own.

Predict realistically

You may be poor at predicting the consequences of how you care for yourself, for others and how your receive care. For example, partners need skills of predicting the consequences of caring for themselves too little or too selfishly.

There are numerous risks and gains attached to caring for another. You may unnecessarily inhibit your caring behaviour because of unrealistic fears about rejection or making mistakes. Also, you may fail to see the gains to yourself, your partner and your relationship if you show caring in appropriate ways. In addition, you may fail to predict the consequences of not maintaining your caring behaviour: for instance, your partner may feel hostile and think you take him/her for granted.

You also require realism in predicting the consequences of how you receive care. For instance, if poor at showing appreciation, the likely consequences are that another will be less ready to care for you. However, if you show appreciation when you do not mean it, you may continue to receive the care you do not want.

Caring patterns, in which partners reciprocally influence one another's behaviour, have predictability built into them. Nevertheless, you require realism in predicting the consequences for good or ill of maintaining your particular caring pattern. Partners can inaccurately predict the durability of their caring patterns. For instance, males who expect their wives to be the predominant home-makers and females who expect their husbands to be the predominant bread-winners are each vulnerable if their partner wants to modify or change roles in the pattern. If either or both of you wants to change the balance of your pattern of caring, you need to assess the risks and gains of so doing.

Set realistic goals

You may need to develop skills of setting realistic goals in the areas both of self-care and caring for others. Following are questions that you may ask yourself.

> 'What is an appropriate balance between self-care and caring for others?'
> 'In what specific ways can I be more (or less) caring?'

'How realistic are each of these ways of caring?'
'How committed am I to implementing these caring goals?'
'What is the time-frame for achieving my caring goals?'
'How will I monitor and evaluate whether or not I have achieved my caring goals?'

When setting caring goals, consider whether and how to involve others. For instance, check with your partner whether your goals for caring for them match their wishes for being cared for by you. Also, as a couple you may wish to set joint caring goals. Such goals can encompass how each can care for themselves as well as how you can care for one another.

Use visualizing skills

You can use visualizing skills to help you care for yourself more effectively. You can draw up a balance sheet in which you imagine both positive and negative consequences of caring for yourself. In addition, you may be more likely to engage in self-care activities if you imagine the pleasures of participating in them.

Visualizing skills can also assist you to care for others more effectively. For example, you can use visual images to imagine what might make others happy. Also, you can use visualizing to plan and rehearse how to give and receive care competently. In addition, if you are prone to unnecessarily negative images about the consequences of caring, you can generate more positive images to replace the negative ones.

SOME ACTION SKILLS FOR CARING

Following are some action skills for caring. Here I mainly emphasize sending positive caring messages. However, you can also show caring in how you deal with your own and your partner's anger and how you solve problems in your relationship. Such skills are covered in later chapters.

SELF-CARE

Since the main focus in this chapter is on caring for one another in a couple relationship, I deal briefly with some skills of self-care.

• *Request space and privacy*. Instead of assuming that others will know your self-care needs, you can request physical and psychological space.

• *Set limits*. You can either negotiate or, if necessary, unilaterally set limits on the amount of care you offer others. You require assertion skills to do this, the topic of a later chapter.

- *Help others to care for themselves.* Without intending it, you may be encouraging dependency in others. For instance, a woman may be very protective about her kitchen and so prevent her partner developing culinary skills. You may need to help others to develop self-care skills: for instance, laundry, ironing, cooking, gardening, maintaining the car, looking after finances. Also, you may require better skills at sharing tasks with your partner.

- *Be self-reliant.* You may require better skills of coping with your own problems. Some people easily slip into the trap of dependency rather than caring for themselves. Before you seek help from another, think whether you might be better off looking after yourself.

- *Identify and engage in pleasant events.* Since a major purpose of self-care is to nourish yourself, you need to identify ways of doing this. Earlier in this chapter, I gave the example of Katie who, shortly after her husband Dan was made redundant, made a list of ways she could care for herself. Katie then needs to implement at least some of the items on her list.

CARING FOR ANOTHER
Show caring

Paraphrasing Shakespeare's statement 'They do not love that do not show their love', 'They do not care that do not show their care.' If you think caring thoughts but do not show them, as far as your partner is concerned you may as well forget them.

Send caring messages

Caring messages contain the themes that another is important to you, emotional support, concern for their welfare, desire to give happiness and to avoid hurt, and respect for the other's difference and potential for growth. You can demonstrate caring through sending sincere verbal, voice, body, touch and action messages.

- *Verbal messages.* Verbal messages of caring include statements such as 'I love you', 'I care for you' and 'I want to help you'. You can also show caring through the quality of your listening responses.

- *Voice messages.* Voice messages are extremely important in expressing caring. Frequently voice messages for caring express tenderness: for instance, a soft yet easily audible voice, clear articulation, an emphasis on words like care and love and a comfortable speech rate. Your voice should convey kindness and concern rather than harshness and disinterest.

- *Body messages.* Your body messages can support or negate verbal caring messages. Your gaze, eye contact, body orientation and facial expression should all demonstrate your interest and concern for the other. Similarly, when others share problems, you need to show good attending and listening skills.

• *Touch messages*. Support and caring can be expressed by a hug, a half-embrace, an arm over the shoulder, or a hand on top of or holding a hand, among other ways. As with all touch messages, you are in another's close intimate zone and consequently require sensitivity about their willingness to be touched. Nevertheless, touch can be a wonderful way to express caring.

• *Action messages*. Action messages indicating caring include looking after your partner when ill and giving birthday cards and presents. Numerous action messages are mentioned in the following review of caring behaviours.

Some caring behaviours

When preparing this book I asked 41 Relate (marriage guidance) counsellors in Britain and 15 Australian postgraduate counselling psychology students to list ways that either they show caring to their partner (or a hypothetical partner) and how their partner (or a hypothetical partner) shows caring to them. Below are some illustrative suggestions derived from their responses.

• *Physical affection*
Massaging shoulders when tired
Giving cuddles
Kissing when coming and going
Offering his/her hand when sitting watching TV
Looking at me with loving eyes
Physical closeness
Holding me

• *Positive feedback*
Paying compliments
Looking pleased at seeing me, e.g. smiling
Saying 'I love you'
Saying 'I care'
Telling me I look nice
Enjoying my company
Welcoming me home
Leaving notes with messages of caring
Expressing pleasure at what I do for him/her
Offering congratulations for achievements

• *Giving gifts*
Sending cards on important occasions
Bringing me flowers
Bringing small, special presents
Little surprises and treats
Finding books or plays I may find interesting
Remembering birthdays and anniversaries
Sending photographs of 'our' memories

- *Showing interest*

Asking about feelings/mood
Asking how my day has been
Showing concern that my travel is safe
Concern for my health
Remembering to ask how a particular event went
Telephoning before a special/difficult event
Ringing when he/she is away
Taking time to learn about the things I enjoy doing
Trying to fit his/her time schedule with mine

- *Offering support and understanding*

Always being ready to listen to my worries
Offering emotional support and reassurance
Responding to what I say or leave unsaid
Laughing with me
Crying with me
Recognizing when I may be stressed
Being there for crises and growth points
Challenging me

- *Practical help at home*

Making cuppas – for instance, morning tea
Cooking meals, including special meals
Bringing breakfast in bed
Making the home cosy
Washing up
Caring for children
Paying bills and checking insurance
Opening the garage door before I come home
Taking care of me when I'm ill

- *Spending time together*

Sharing everyday tasks
Spending ordinary time together
Arranging time to walk the dog together
Sharing fun as well as pressures
Sexual relating and physical closeness
Organizing 'relaxing times'
Time for conversation and support
Sharing decision-making
Arranging and booking holidays
Doing the crossword with him/her
Planning for our future together

- *Respect for difference*

Accepting me in all (most) emotional forms

Accepting me in all (most) physical forms
Letting me be me and not her/his image of me
Absorbing my panics and anxieties without recrimination
Giving me time to explore what's going on in my life separate from her/him
Respecting my need for psychological space
Allowing and anticipating my time for personal space

Check what care another prefers

Before, during and after you can check whether and how to show caring to another. You can ask your partner how they like to be cared for, what you do that they like or dislike or what you are not doing that they would like. Such checking does not oblige you to show caring in ways that you do not want. However, it enables you to know more about your partner's preferences and wishes.

During and after specific caring behaviours, you can assist your partner to feel safe about providing feedback concerning the direction, quantity and quality of your care. If you genuinely want to please your partner, you do not want her or him putting on false shows of appreciation. You require listening and showing understanding skills to establish an emotional climate conducive to honest feedback.

RECEIVING CARE

Express appreciation

People are more likely to continue giving care to those who show appreciation. If you do not acknowledge your partner's caring behaviours, you lower the chances of these behaviours being repeated. Without necessarily meaning it, you may give them the impression you take for granted what they do. Thus your neutral message of not acknowledging their care can easily turn into a negative message.

You can express appreciation by verbal, voice, body, touch and action messages. You can choose which messages are appropriate for each situation. Simple verbal messages are 'Thank you' and 'I appreciate that.' Your voice messages can emphasize words like thank and appreciate. Your body messages might include a smile and good eye contact. Your touch messages could be a hug or a kiss. Your action messages could be doing a favour for the care-giver in return.

Provide honest feedback

Expressing appreciation is a form of feedback. However, even when pleased with how another cares, you may still wish to let them know how to please you even more. Here emphasize the positive rather than accentuate the negative.

If you are dissatisfied with some aspect of another's care, for instance with a present that you do not like, you can provide the giver with some tactful, but honest feedback. Providing such feedback can be difficult since you do not wish to cause hurt or offence. Nevertheless, in the interests of the integrity of your relationship, you may be wise to do so. You can send an 'I' message that acknowledges the other's effort, but then gently let them know how you feel. If people persist in caring for you in inappropriate ways, use stronger verbal, voice and body messages.

Request care

Some people get angry when they do not receive the care they want. Preferable is to assume responsibility for obtaining it. So long as you are not too demanding, one way to get the care you want is to request it. Earlier I gave the example of Jen telling Walt when she needed care and, if necessary, how to give it. Partners in effective relationships want to please one another and to see one another as caring persons. Requests for care symbolize commitment to the continuing health of the relationship. Not requesting care can create undercurrents of dissatisfaction that may later surface as open hostility.

DEVELOPING YOUR INTERACTIVE PATTERN OF CARING

Cooperate to exchange caring behaviours

You and your partner can work as a team to increase your exchange of caring behaviours. Behaviour exchange (Babcock & Jacobson, 1993) and reciprocal reinforcement (McKay, Fanning & Paleg, 1994) are other terms to describe such cooperation, which is often recommended as part of marital counselling. However, you can also use this cooperative approach to prevent conflicts. Together you work to increase the balance in your relationship bank account to help tide over difficult times. In Chapter 17 on solving relationship problems, I describe a six-step approach to how you can increase your exchange of caring behaviours.

CHAPTER HIGHLIGHTS

• Dictionary definitions of caring emphasize caring for, the feeling component, and taking care of, the action component.

• Dimensions of caring include self-care, caring for another, receiving care, and interactive patterns of caring.

• People can have positive and negative reasons for caring. Ideally caring for yourself and others is based on a secure sense of your worth. People with low self-esteem can care for themselves too much or too little.

• Caring for another involves respecting their difference. Possessiveness is a central feature of anxiety-motivated caring.

• Receivers of care can feel affirmed and wanted. However, some people manipulate their partners to provide care. You can feel negated if provided with too much or the wrong kind of care.

• In effective interactive patterns of caring, partners reciprocate caring so that each is enhanced by the processes and outcomes of their caring.

• Acting in a caring way is easier if you can also think in a caring way. Choose to own responsibility for caring and to get in touch with altruistic feelings.

• Use coping self-talk to encourage appropriate self-care and to handle anxieties associated with caring for another.

• You may possess rigid rules that interfere with each dimension of caring. Identify, dispute and change your unrealistic rules to more realistic ones.

• You can perceive your caring, or your partner's caring either too positively or too negatively. Also, you can inaccurately explain your own and your partner's reasons for caring. In both instances search for evidence that counteracts your misinterpretations.

• You can be unrealistic about predicting the consequences of how you care for yourself and others, how you receive care, and about the durability of your caring pattern.

• Set realistic goals for self-care and caring.

• Use visualizing skills both to imagine your goals and how you can act competently to attain them.

• Action skills for self-care include: request space and privacy, set limits, help others to care for themselves, be self-reliant, and identify and engage in pleasant events.

• You show caring through sending verbal, voice, body, touch and action messages.

• Categories of caring behaviours include: physical affection, positive feedback, giving gifts, showing interest, offering support and understanding, practical help at home, spending time together and respect for difference.

• Skills for receiving care include: expressing appreciation, providing honest feedback and requesting care.

• You and your partner can develop your interactive pattern of caring by cooperating to exchange caring behaviours.

EXERCISES

EXERCISE 11.1
MY FEELINGS AND REASONS FOR CARING
Instructions

For each part of this exercise, first assess your feelings and reasons on your own. Then, if appropriate, discuss with your partner, another or others.

Part A
Self-care

1. Positive feelings and reasons.

2. Negative feelings and reasons.

3. Summary of my feelings and reasons.

4. Areas for change, if any.

Part B
Caring for another

You may focus either on a specific other or on others in general.
1. Positive feelings and reasons.

2. Negative feelings and reasons.

3. Summary of my feelings and reasons.

4. Areas for change, if any.

Part C
Receiving care

1. Positive feelings and reasons.

2. Negative feelings and reasons.

3. Summary of my feelings and reasons.

4. Areas for change, if any.

Part D
Interactive pattern of caring

Answer in regard to a specific relationship.
1. Your and your partner's positive feelings and reasons.

2. Your and your partner's negative feelings and reasons.

3. Summary of your feelings and reasons.

4. Areas for change, if any.

EXERCISE 11.2
DEVELOP MY THINKING SKILLS FOR CARING

Instructions

First do each part of this exercise on your own. Then, if appropriate, discuss your answers with your partner, another or others.

Thinking skills

Following are nine thinking skills:
Own responsibility for choosing
Get in touch with my feelings
Use coping self-talk
Choose realistic rules
Choose to perceive accurately
Explain cause accurately
Predict realistically
Set realistic goals
Use visualizing skills

Part A
Self-care

1. Assess your thinking skills deficits.

2. Identify your main deficit or deficits and specify the steps you intend taking to change it/them.

Part B
Caring for another

1. Assess your thinking skills deficits.

2. Identify your main deficit or deficits and specify the steps you intend taking to change it/them.

Part C
Receiving care

1. Assess your thinking skills deficits.

2. Identify your main deficit or deficits and specify the steps you intend taking to change it/them.

Part D
Interactive pattern of caring

Focus on a specific relationship.

1. Assess yours and your partner's thinking skills deficits.

2. Identify your main deficit or deficits and specify the steps you intend taking to change it/them.

EXERCISE 11.3
DEVELOP MY ACTION SKILLS FOR CARING
Instructions

First, do each part of this exercise on your own. Then, if appropriate, discuss your answers with your partner, another or others.

Part A
Assessment

Identify your action skills strengths and deficits for self-care, caring for another and receiving care.

Self-care

Request space and privacy

strengths
deficits

Set limits

strengths
deficits

Help others care for themselves

strengths
deficits

Be self-reliant

strengths
deficits

Identify and engage in pleasant events

strengths
deficits

Caring for another

Show caring

Physical affection
strengths
deficits

Positive feedback
strengths
deficits

Giving gifts
strengths
deficits

Showing interest
strengths
deficits

Offering support and understanding
strengths
deficits

Practical help at home
strengths
deficits

Spending time together
strengths
deficits

Respect for difference
strengths
deficits

Check what care another prefers
strengths
deficits

Receiving care

Express appreciation
strengths
deficits

Provide honest feedback
strengths
deficits

Request care
strengths
deficits

Part B
Change

1. Summarize your main action skills strengths and deficits for:
1.1. self-care
1.2. caring for another
1.3. receiving care

2. If appropriate, identify one or more of your deficits and develop a plan to change how you act. In your plan, specify:
a. your goals, including a time frame,
b. the steps you intend taking to attain each of your goals, and
c. how you will monitor your progress.

EXERCISE 11.4
GROUP DISCUSSION: CARING SKILLS
Instructions

This is intended as a group exercise, though it may be done individually or in pairs. For each part:

1. spend 10–15 minutes answering the question in groups of three or four,

2. each sub-group shares its findings with the whole group,

3. then the whole group ranks the six most important skills from the most important to the least important.

Part A
Self-care

List the six most important skills people can use to care for themselves.

Part B
Caring for another

List the six most important skills people can use to care for another person.

Part C
Receiving care

List the six most important skills people can use to receive care.

Part D
Interactive pattern of caring.

List the six most important skills partners can use in establishing an effective pattern of caring with one another.

TWELVE
Intimacy Skills

*All of us, without exception, have difficulty with
intimacy, and over time, we will either move
forward or drift backward in this dimension.*

Harriet Goldhor Lerner

CHAPTER QUESTIONS

- *What is intimacy?*

- *Why is intimacy with the self important?*

- *What are some limitations of intimacy?*

- *What are positive and negative feelings and motivations associated with intimacy?*

- *What are some thinking skills for intimacy?*

- *What are some action skills for intimacy?*

Everyone craves the reward of intimacy in their close relationships. Winnicott calls these rewards 'the magic of intimacy'. He observes that: 'each person has a polite or socialised self, and also a personal private self that is not available except in intimacy' (Winnicott, 1986, p. 66). However desirable, intimacy is a process that eludes some partnerships all of the time, many partnerships much of the time, and all partnerships some of the time. Intimacy does not always come with the territory in relationships that possess the outward form of closeness, for instance marriage. Rather partners struggle to attain, maintain and develop differing degrees of intimacy in their relationships. Furthermore, at any time partners can withdraw and regulate the degree of intimacy they offer each other (Argyle & Henderson, 1985). Such holding back is more likely to be ongoing when relationships deteriorate.

MEANINGS OF INTIMACY

Defining intimacy

Adjectives associated with the noun intimacy include private, personal, close and familiar. Frequently, in everyday usage, intimacy means either expressing personal feelings or sexual closeness. Beck (1988) observes: 'Intimacy can range from discussing everyday details of your life, to confiding the most private feeling that you would not share with anybody else, to your sexual relationship' (p. 242).

The Latin word *intus*, meaning within, is the basis of the word intimacy. Non-sexual intimacy entails partners getting in touch with their internal worlds and sharing them with each other. A person's internal world comprises his or her personal biography, feelings, thoughts, fantasies, goals, hopes, fears and disappointments in different areas. Areas of your internal world can include: spiritual, sexual, intellectual, occupational, recreational and social. In intimate relationships not only do partners share their internal worlds, they are sufficiently open to each other's experiencing to allow their own internal worlds to be changed by it. Dorwick (1991) writes of intimacy as *'one person willing to engage with the reality of someone else – and to risk being changed by that experience'* (p. 296). This willingness to take risks and change may occur in different areas of intimacy with different people.

Dimensions of intimacy

Following are some important dimensions of intimacy that resemble the dimensions of caring discussed in Chapter 11. Simply stated, intimacy with yourself is knowing your internal world; reaching out is sharing your internal world; receiving intimacy is sharing another's internal world; and your interactive pattern of intimacy is how you and your partner coordinate the sharing of your internal worlds.

Intimacy with yourself

Intimacy with yourself provides the foundation for intimacy with others. Winnicott states that: 'the healthy person's inner world is related to the outer or actual world and yet is personal and capable of an aliveness of its own' (p. 31). A number of writers (Dorwick, 1991, 1993; Lerner, 1989; Rogers, 1973; Winnicott, 1986) observe that the process of intimacy is best served by partners developing a secure sense of themselves as separate persons. Rogers regards it as a paradox that in a 'process partnership', 'when each partner is making progress toward becoming his or her own self, the partnership becomes more enriching' (p. 212). Lerner (1989) observes: 'Popular notions of "selfhood" do not easily translate into clear guidelines for genuine intimacy and solid connectedness with others' (p. 201). The goal is to have a relationship 'where the separate "I-ness" of both parties can be appreciated and enhanced' (p. 201).

Intimacy with yourself involves knowing and exploring your internal world. You possess sufficient emotional literacy to experience, identify and accurately label your feelings and thoughts. Your significant feelings are either present or readily accessible to your awareness. You are able to listen to the flow of your emotions without needing to deny or distort them. You possess a basic acceptance of yourself as a person that allows you to be open to your contrasting emotions. You can experience happiness, joy and strength as well as sadness, psychological pain and vulnerability. Where appropriate, you can explore your feelings further and, as a result, either accept, strengthen, refine or discard them.

Another way of viewing intimacy with yourself is that you are capable of solitude (Dorwick, 1991, 1993). You have sufficient comfort with yourself that, if necessary, you can live without a relationship. You can choose whether or not to be alone or with other people. You do not need to compulsively enter relationships to escape from the pain of loneliness.

Intimacy is a process that takes place both within partners and between them. The degree of intimacy that partners can offer to each other is likely to be limited by the degree of intimacy they are able to provide for themselves. If you are out of touch with your own feelings, you are unlikely to experience others' feelings accurately. If you think defensively and rigidly, you will be restricted in how you respond to others' thoughts and feelings. However, if you possess a secure sense of your identity and a genuine acceptance of yourself as an independent, yet fallible, human being, you are more likely to experience the full of humanness of another.

Partners enter relationships with a capacity for intimacy with themselves that is partly genetic and partly learned from interactions with significant others. Once in a relationship, they can influence each other's development as separate selves, for good or ill. Intimacy with yourself is not to be confused with selfish individualism. Rather your level of inner strength and insight is such that you can reach out and experience others without needing to distort or manipulate them for your own ends. In fact, a sense of self-intimacy enhances rather than detracts from your intimacy with others.

Reaching out

Intimacy with another involves reaching out and sharing your internal world with them. Authenticity, genuineness, honesty and realness are nouns that describe the process of reaching out intimately. If your relationship develops, you increasingly drop your social masks, facades and defences. You are willing to be known and to share vulnerable and childlike parts of yourself as well as your strengths. Eric Berne, the founder of Transactional Analysis, regarded intimacy as 'a candid game free relationship, with mutual free giving and receiving and without exploitation' (1972, p. 25).

Frequently, the notion of encounter is used to describe special moments of intimacy. Partners experience and communicate their thoughts and feelings in a way that transcends the boundaries of their existential isolation and is deeply enriching. They encounter each other in an 'I–Thou' relationship (Buber, 1970). Powell (1969) distinguishes between five levels of conversation: level 5, cliche; 4, reporting the facts about others; 3, my ideas and judgements; 2, my feelings (emotions) 'Gut Level'; and 1, peak communication. In peak communication, partners or close friends attain a complete emotional and personal communion. They encounter each other in 'an almost perfect and mutual empathy...like two musical instruments playing exactly the same note, filled with and giving forth precisely the same sound' (p. 62).

Receiving intimacy

Receiving intimacy entails allowing yourself to become open to the internal world of another and to be influenced by it. Openness to your partner's internal world requires you to accept and respect them as different. You strive to create an emotional climate whereby they feel safe to risk revealing themselves to you authentically. You listen to them empathically and assist them to explore and experience their thoughts and feelings. Where appropriate, you share your own experiencing, ask questions, provide feedback or challenge them. You gently, or otherwise, allow your partner to be vulnerable, happy, sad or whatever they may feel at the time.

Receiving intimacy means that you are concerned enough about your partner to want to know them fully. Such knowledge includes their thoughts and feelings about their childhood, their subsequent background, their present lives and their relationship with you. Fromm (1956) writes of knowledge of another being not just at the periphery, but penetrating their core. You sense the underlying meanings and nuances that their surface behaviour masks: for instance, angry behaviour masking hurt and worry. In effective relationships, partners also acquire more information about each other in terms of breadth of topics as well as depth, or revealing more risky information (Altman & Taylor, 1965; Altman and Taylor, 1970).

Interactive patterns of intimacy

What are some patterns of partners influencing each other with their intimacy behaviour? One of the most consistent findings of the self-disclosure research is that people tend to reciprocate the intimacy level of each other's disclosures (Cozby, 1973; Derlega & Chaikin, 1975; Berg & Derlega, 1987). Following is a vignette illustrating reciprocity of disclosure.

> Nobby and Sally have been dating for three months. At first, Sally thought that Nobby was the strong, silent type. As Nobby disclosed more of himself, Sally was surprised to find out how sensitive and emotional he was, how much he valued close friendships and how willing he was to listen to her talk about her goals in life. Nobby, on the other hand, was learning that Sally was a very determined person who wanted to combine having her own business with raising a family. He admired her openness and willingness to share her doubts about her femininity. Sally's openness made it easier for Nobby to share his doubts about not being the typical male and his feelings of hurt at the ridicule he had received because of this. Both Sally and Nobby were also able to share what they liked and disliked about their bodies.

In choosing whether to deepen the intimacy level of a relationship, one of the main ways you psychologically feel each other out is by making progressively more intimate disclosures. Simply stated, the process of deepening a relationship involves matching the intimacy level of another's disclosures prior to disclosing at a still more intimate level. If you both wish to develop your relationship, you are likely to coordinate the deepening of the intimacy level of your disclosures. More often than not, relationships do not make a smooth progression to more intimate disclosures, but instead trace a jagged line in that direction.

The progressive matching of the intimacy level of disclosures deepens relationships for a number of reasons. One explanation is that your disclosure is a reward to another, indicating liking. The disclosure is to be matched if the relationship is to remain in balance. Another explanation emphasizes how disclosures are received. If your disclosure is met with acceptance by another, this acceptance not only established the other as less threatening and more like you, but also gives the other permission to make a similar disclosure. Consequently, by accepting disclosures as well as by disclosing, you develop trust in your relationships.

Dysfunctional patterns of intimacy can be too distant, too enmeshed or in imbalance. Reciprocating a shallow level of disclosure exemplifies too distant an intimacy pattern. Possibly both partners fear intimacy and, hence, relinquish some of their capacity to reap its rewards.

The word enmeshment means entangled as in the meshes of a net. Either or both partners lose some of their individual sense of self if they become too fused. When enmeshment occurs both partners settle for a less than genuine intimacy by developing an emotionally constricting 'we-self' at the expense of their individual selves. Often in enmeshed relationships, one partner's viewpoint is more dominant than the other's. This is a 'lose-lose' situation with the dominant partner deprived of some of the individuality of the less dominant partner. In turn, the less dominant partner is both deselfing and also assisted in this process by her or his more dominant partner. Furthermore, partners deprive one another of the potential for growth in intimacy resulting from the interaction of two separate people secure in their identities, yet with flexible boundaries of self.

Relationships can also become enmeshed if partners spend all their time with each other. To be intimate with your partner does not mean that all the time you need be with her or him.

An example of an unbalanced intimacy pattern is that of one partner, frequently the female, striving for greater emotional closeness, with the other partner, usually the male, preferring to keep emotionally distant. Sometimes a pursuer–distancer pattern develops in which the harder the partner requiring closeness pushes, the more the other partner withdraws. Following is a vignette illustrating this pattern.

> Troy and Hilary are a couple in their late 20s who have been married for three years. When they were courting and in the first year of marriage, Hilary used to admire Troy's calm and collected attitude to life. She saw this as a sign

of quiet strength. Over the past year or so, Hilary has increasingly perceived Troy's calmness as evidence of lack of real caring for her. The more she resents his behaviour and shouts at Troy to show more love, the more he withdraws. Hilary has insufficiently acknowledged that Troy was brought up in a family where his father showed little emotion and was physically absent much of the time, while his mother overwhelmed him with the amount and intensity of her feelings, including her hatred for his father. Troy grew up with no role-model of a male showing feelings. Hilary's behaviour reactivates anxieties associated with Troy's childhood feelings of powerlessness at the strength of his mother's feelings.

Another unbalanced intimacy pattern is where one partner plays more the parent role and the other partner more the dependent child role. Children have a habit of growing up!

Limitations on intimacy

Before examining some thinking skills and action skills for developing and maintaining intimacy, I draw your attention to some limitations on intimacy.

Existential isolation

Humans enter and leave the world alone. As the saying goes: 'You cannot die another person's death for them.' Throughout their lives humans exist in their separate skins. Yalom (1980) states that one of the important facts that patients in existential counselling need to discover is that, no matter how close they get to other people, they must still face life alone. Patients have to learn the limits of intimacy as well as its rewards. In relationships, no matter how much partners care and share, ultimately they exist separately. Partners cannot avoid the mandate to assume personal responsibility for their individual lives.

Individual differences

Partners are different. The ways in which they wish to give and receive intimacy vary. Their wishes for emotional privacy vary. Imagine each partner as a large house. Independent of any intimacy skills strengths or deficits they possess, each partner may want the other partner to enter most rooms in their house, but not necessarily all rooms all of the time. Also, each partner may have more interest in entering some rooms than others. To expect a perfect situation of total openness and total interest is unrealistic. Partners can respect each other's wishes for privacy, though as relationships develop these private areas are likely to become fewer. Also, partners need acknowledge that they cannot always expect to give and receive total interest.

Sex-role learning

Frequently, women are thought to have better intimacy skills than males (Dorwick, 1991; Jourard, 1971; Lerner 1989). Derlega and Chaikin (1975) write of the 'inexpressive male'. They note that wives are more interested in communicating personal feelings than their husbands. More often than females, males are brought up to hide their feelings. Males are more likely to deny and distort feelings and, consequently, to seem distant from them. However, as the work on sex-roles of Bem (1974, 1982) indicates, males and females are encouraged to value and express different feelings: for instance, females, sensitivity, and males, ambition. Furthermore, males and females tend to have different ways of reacting to disclosures of feelings: females being more inclined to listen and empathize and males more inclined to problem-solve. The above are generalizations and differences exist within the sexes. Nevertheless, the learning of sex roles can present barriers to, if not limitations on, sharing intimacy.

Realistic negative consequences

A Hungarian proverb warns 'Tell the truth and you get your head bashed in'. Should partners 'let it all hang out' in disclosing about themselves and giving feedback to their partners? Total honesty may not always be the best policy. You have to consider the consequences of what and how you disclose your inner world. Lerner (1989) gives the example of Jo-Anne who cancelled her subscription to *Ms* magazine because her husband believed she was less flexible to his demands. She asks whether the reader would judge Jo-Anne differently if they knew that she was a middle-aged woman, with no formal education, no marketable skills, three dependent children and a husband who would leave her if she stood up to him too much. Another example of the limitations of total honesty is that of Marvin who criticized his wife so frequently and brutally that she divorced him (Lazarus, Lazarus, & Fay, 1993). Possibly, if Marvin had been more honest about his own limitations as well as his wife's, he would have been more tactful and diplomatic.

Practical considerations

A host of practical considerations can limit intimacy. Such considerations include: cramped living space, noise, shortage of money, fatigue, dependent children, caring for in-laws, work pressures, health problems and so on. If possible, in the interests of themselves and their relationship, partners need find ways of addressing or circumventing such practical limitations.

FEELINGS AND REASONS FOR INTIMACY

Below I suggest positive and negative feelings and reasons associated with intimacy. However, the positive-negative distinction is too simple – ambivalence features prominently in intimate relations.

Intimacy with yourself

Positive feelings and reasons

The capacity to be intimate with yourself requires self-acceptance. This is a fundamental acceptance of your value as a person. However, you can still evaluate separate parts of yourself as being helpful or harmful to your current functioning and future development. You are able to acknowledge your emotions without significant repression, suppression or inhibition. You do not require a range of defensive security operations to protect your picture of yourself. You possess the inner strength to confront the existential ultimate concerns of death, isolation, freedom and meaninglessness without being overcome by anxiety.

Negative feelings and reasons

Powell (1969) observes that it is almost a universal law that the extent of egocentricity in people is proportionate to the amount of psychological pain in them. In varying degrees people possess debilitating anxieties that limit their access to their internal worlds. They have assimilated standards for behaviour taken from their parents and significant others as their own and react to their experiencing in terms of these rather than their own standards. They can be distant from their feelings, easily threatened, and possess many 'no-go' areas that preclude self-understanding. The fear of looking too closely inwards can lead to treating experiences superficially. People can substitute self-preoccupation for genuine intimacy with themselves.

Reaching out

Positive feelings and reasons

Positive reasons for wishing to reach out and share your internal world include wishing to be known as you truly are and to know yourself better. Reaching out has two components: reaching out *from* and reaching out *to*. The rewards for reaching out from yourself include lessening your existential isolation, the relief of living an open rather than a secret life, being spontaneous and knowing yourself better. The rewards of reaching out to another include defining yourself, being affirmed by their reactions, and showing them that you like and trust them. You reach out of your separateness to enhance the possibility of connectedness and, in special moments, may deeply encounter your partner.

Negative feelings and reasons

Debilitating anxiety can motivate people to reach out too much or too little. Anxiety-motivated intimacy is a form of pseudo-intimacy. Rather than genuine disclosure, people disclose to manage others' impressions of them. Reasons for such disclosure include possessiveness, self-promotion and manipulation to achieve ulterior motives, for instance gratitude. Pseudo-intimacy involves concealing under the guise of revealing. In addition, people can play various roles that act as decoys or camouflages for what they truly feel: for instance, acting the clown, acting angry, acting cynical, acting fragile, acting strong and being dominating (Powell, 1969).

Anxiety can also motivate people not to risk disclosure. A common conflict is that between wanting intimacy and viewing closeness as dangerous – wishing to be known, yet fearing it. Dorwick (1991) cites that the perceived dangers of intimacy include: loss of self; loss of the other; becoming too vulnerable; giving another intolerable power to make you unhappy; and curtailment of your freedom. A degree of intimacy can give rise to fears about greater intimacy and thus prevent further reaching out. Colliver (1992) observes that whenever deep intimacy threatens men who fear commitment they describe their experience in such terms as: 'losing my independence', 'being tied down', 'constantly being accountable' and 'being in prison'. In addition, they describe their feelings as 'claustrophobia', 'suffocating' and 'being smothered' (p. 45). Women can also fear commitment for the same reasons. In addition, people of both sexes who have experienced relationship break-ups can become very wary of again opening up their internal worlds to another partner.

Receiving intimacy

Positive feelings and reasons

Receiving intimacy can be broken down into allowing another person to reach out to you and allowing yourself to be affected by their disclosures. You can show your loving concern for a partner by creating the emotional climate of trust and acceptance in which they feel it safe to share their internal world with you, including their shadow side. You can get the reward of their appreciation of your willingness to listen and understand. Your life can feel enhanced by their realness to you. You can experience the specialness of genuinely warm and game-free communication. In addition, you can share another's relief at being listened to non-judgementally when they share risky areas. Furthermore, you can take pleasure in supporting their self-understanding and personal development.

As you receive another's internal world, you are not distant and detached. What your partner shares matters to you. You allow yourself to experience their emotions and to be influenced by them. One way of being influenced by another is to share their feelings, be they laughter or tears. Another way is to allow your knowledge of them to increase your love and caring for them. In addition, their disclosures can reduce your feelings of existential isolation by identifying common ground and shared humanity. Also, you may gain the excitement of broadening your horizons by participating in another's life.

Negative feelings and reasons

You may not wish to receive another's intimacies, or at least not so much of them. You may feel pressured for sympathy, support or agreement when you do not wish to give it. You may feel overwhelmed by the intensity of their feelings and their demand that you react to them. On occasions, you may feel bored, confused and uncertain how to respond. Also, instead of building common ground, further revelations may highlight the differences between you. In fact, you may find some disclosures repellent. In addition, you may feel threatened by what another says: for instance, revealing an affair.

You may possess ulterior motivations in receiving another's intimacies. By faking willingness to listen to personal disclosures, you may gain various rewards: for instance, flattery, gifts and a peaceful home. By gaining another's confidence, you may increase their dependency on you and hence your control over them. In addition, the more your know about another, the more power you have to hurt them when you fight.

Interactive patterns of intimacy

Positive feelings and reasons

A tension between separateness and connectedness is at the heart of intimacy. Lerner (1989) observes: 'It is only in long-term relationships that we are called upon to navigate that delicate balance between separateness and connectedness and that we confront the challenge of sustaining both – without losing either when the going gets rough' (p. 5). Partners can affirm and enhance both themselves and each other if they can develop, maintain and, if necessary, repair a flexibly reciprocal sharing of intimacies. Out of love, friendship, altruism and mutual self-interest, each partner supports and affirms the other. They possess sufficient commitment to themselves and each other to realize they are more fulfilled if they develop as separate selves that they willingly share. They accept themselves and each other as persons of integrity and goodwill and, where appropriate, negotiate differences. They are open to changes in themselves and each other and attempt to use such changes constructively to strengthen rather than weaken their relationship.

Negative feelings and reasons

In an ideal relationship both people feel free to share their internal worlds and to have such sharing understood and reciprocated by their partners. However, intimacy patterns built on reciprocity can face problems. One problem is that the relationship plateaus at a relatively superficial level. Another problem is that partners can reciprocate withdrawal of intimacy, with neither willing to make the first move in halting this process. Anxiety about genuine intimacy is a major contributing factor to dysfunctional patterns of intimacy that are too distant, enmeshed or unbalanced. Other feelings associated with dysfunctional intimacy patterns include selfishness, dependence, dislike, disinterest, disloyalty, disengagement, insecurity and fear of change.

SOME THINKING SKILLS FOR INTIMACY

This section explores some skills you can use to increase your chances of achieving intimacy.

Own responsibility for choosing

You can acknowledge that you are always a chooser in how you develop, maintain, repair and, if necessary, end intimacy. Intimacy with yourself and others requires assuming responsibility for your thoughts, feelings and actions. Throughout life you engage in a process of defining yourself. To a large extent you can choose the thoughts and feelings that comprise your internal world. You also need to assume responsibility for making effective choices regarding how much of your internal world you present to the external world and for deciding where you place boundaries between your internal world and the external world. If you are to become more open, acknowledge responsibility for the ways in which, up until now, you have chosen to maintain unnecessary distance when sending and receiving communications.

Understand the relationship between how you think, feel and act

People do not just react to events in their lives without thinking about them. Intimacy with yourself and others requires you to understand how people's thoughts influence how they feel and act. In Chapter 8 I presented the STC framework which provides a tool for understanding and working with your own and other people's internal worlds.

> **S** – Situation
> **T** – Thoughts
> **C** – Consequences

The S stands for any specific situation which you, your partner or both of you may face. The C stands for consequences which fall into three categories: feelings, physical reactions and actions. The T stands for any thoughts that you or another may have, including visual images. Let's take an example of two ways of thinking about the same situation and their different consequences.

> **S** – Cliff is sitting in the living room and Dorothy comes home and is silent.
> **T(1)** – Cliff thinks 'Dorothy is angry and doesn't want to talk to me.'
> **C(1)** – Cliff feels hurt, physically tenses up, and angrily says to Dorothy, 'Why are you withdrawing from me again?'

> **S** – Cliff is sitting in the living room and Dorothy comes home and is silent.
> **T(2)** – Cliff thinks 'Dorothy has had a hard day at work and needs time to unwind.'
> **C(2)** – Cliff feels sympathy, is physically relaxed, smiles warmly at Dorothy and says 'You look worn out.'

You can develop the skill of not just reacting to situations (S), but of checking how you think at T to see if you can make different choices which will beneficially influence how you feel, physically react, and act at C. Intimacy that accurately takes into account Ts as well as Ss and Cs is three dimensional rather than two dimensional.

Get in touch with your feelings

Intimacy with yourself requires you to be responsive to what you feel, based on your own valuing process, rather than what you have been taught to feel, based on other people's valuing. Similarly intimacy with others requires each of you to be in touch with and share your true feelings as contrasted with feelings that are 'hand-me-downs' from your parents, past relationships and other sources – the 'shoulds' in the world of emotions. The more you are in touch with the flow of your emotions, the greater is the likelihood that you can share and receive intimacy.

In varying degrees people emotionally react to specific situations in unauthentic ways rather than acknowledge their true feelings. Some people deny or dilute their needs for human intimacy by becoming too independent. They become anxious at the thought of allowing another to become close. Others exaggerate their needs for intimacy by becoming too dependent and clinging.

How can you become more emotionally literate? First, you can acknowledge the legitimacy and importance of your own and other's feelings. Second, you can develop the skill of inner focusing – finding the physical and psychological space to tune in to what you really feel. Third, you can use some of the thinking skills described in this section to clear away blocks to acknowledging your underlying feelings. Fourth, you can learn more about what you feel by sharing your feelings and allowing others to react to them. Fifth, you can avoid becoming too dependent on one person for your sources of intimate nourishment. Sixth, for those still excessively anxious over obtaining or losing intimacy, you can seek professional counselling.

Use coping self-talk

You may perceive that there are risks attached to disclosing specific aspects of your internal world, be they positive or negatively evaluated by you. Assuming that you decide to make a specific disclosure, you can use coping self-talk to help yourself do it in an appropriate way. Coping self-talk can assist you to feel better and act more effectively. To reiterate, coaching self-talk consists of calming, coaching and affirming self-statements.

Let's take the example of Kirsty who decides to reveal to her partner Gary that, as a child, she was sexually abused by an uncle. Kirsty has never told anyone this before. Kirsty's calming self-statements include: 'Calm down' and 'Breathe slowly and regularly.' Kirsty's coaching self-statements include: 'Tell Gary that I have something important about my past that I want to share with him' and 'Be honest about the details of what happened and how I now feel.' Kirsty's affirming self-statements include: 'I'm a valuable person in my own right' and 'I have good skills at sharing sensitive information and handling other people's reactions to it.'

Often partners require coping self-talk when receiving disclosures. For example, if Gary starts feeling anxious when hearing Kirsty's disclosures, he can tell himself to calm down and use his listening skills.

Choose realistic rules

You may possess unrealistic rules concerning intimacy. You may turn your preferences into demands that restrict your freedom to think and act rationally in relation to yourself, others and your relationships. Following are examples of intimacy rules that may be unrealistically rigid.

Intimacy with yourself

'Males must not focus on their feelings.'
'I must not have negative feelings about others.'
'I must not have positive feelings about myself.'

Reaching out

'I must always keep my distance.'
'I must always be in an intimate relationship.'
'I must have immediate and total affection.'

Receiving intimacy

'I must always be polite.'
'I must always actively help him/her solve his/her problem.'
'Others must always treat my feelings with great respect.'

Interactive patterns of intimacy

'We must have the same needs for emotional closeness.'
'We must not share intimacies outside our relationship.'
'We must put career and other daily activities ahead of creating time to talk to each other about our relationship.'

To reiterate, dealing with unrealistic rules requires three steps. First, identify any unrealistic rules and their negative consequences. You can use the STC framework to help you analyse specific situations in which you possess one or more unrealistic rules. Second, dispute or challenge the logic of unrealistic rules by asking questions like: 'Where is the evidence that I must have immediate and total affection?', 'Could I stand it if I did not receive immediate and total affection?', 'Does not having immediate and total affection make me a rotten person?' and 'Do I expect to give immediate and total affection to others?' Third, restate the unrealistic rule into something less rigid: for example, 'In the context of a supportive relationship, I prefer my partner and I to be honest about our feelings for each other.'

Choose to perceive accurately

Perceive yourself accurately

You may fail to perceive yourself accurately. To maintain your self-picture you may edit out significant personal information, both positive and negative. For instance, you can exaggerate either your strengths or deficits or a mixture of the two. You may consider yourself so unlovable that you cannot accept another's affectionate interest. You may engage in various defensive processes to contain your anxiety and maintain your current way of viewing yourself. Following are some defensive processes that can block intimacy – frequently people remain unawares that they use them (Freud, 1949; McKay, Fanning, & Paleg, 1994; Yalom, 1980).

• *Avoiding*. You may avoid people and situations that you find threatening: for example, situations where you may be asked to share your internal world or allow another to open up deeply to you.

• *Withdrawing*. When situations become emotionally charged, you may lower the temperature by either psychologically or physically withdrawing or both. You may play various roles and psychological games that create distance in your relationships (Berne, 1964; Powell, 1969).

• *Compulsive activity*. You may always be too busy to engage emotionally with another person. You may take refuge in your work, hobbies or outside friendships.

• *Compulsive relating*. You may enter relationships not because you genuinely find another person attractive, but because you cannot stand the pain of loneliness or the social stigma of not being in a relationship. Because you have entered a relationship under false pretences, it may be difficult for you to attain intimacy.

• *Serial relating*. You do not allow yourself to develop a deep relationship with anyone. When genuine intimacy threatens, you end the relationship and move on to the next.

• *Compulsive sexuality*. You may avoid intimacy with anyone by focusing on them as bodies to be used for sexual pleasure rather than as persons with whom to develop relationships.

• *Dependency*. You may allow yourself to become dependent on another person rather than acknowledge and develop your own strengths.

• *Denial*. You may repress significant aspects of yourself: for instance, anger, concerns about death, or altruistic feelings. You may also deny certain aspects of the feedback you receive from others: for instance, their love for you.

• *Distortion*. You may filter incoming information by magnifying or minimizing it: for example, not acknowledging the full extent of a compliment or criticism. Also, you may fail to acknowledge sufficiently the effect of your upbringing on how you think and feel.

• *Projection*. Rather than acknowledge aspects of yourself that you do not like, you may become very conscious of these qualities in others: for instance, *their* need to control and *their* manipulativeness.

- *Rationalization.* Excuses, excuses, excuses. You may be adept at finding reasons for your less acceptable thoughts, feelings and behaviours.

- *Competing.* You may need to see yourself superior to your partner and to others with whom you relate. You exaggerate your virtues and their faults.

- *Attacking.* You avoid acknowledging your own hurt and inadequacies by inwardly attacking your partner. Outwardly, you may criticize, ridicule, nag and blame them. Verbal abuse may be accompanied by physical abuse.

- *Identification with the aggressor.* You may start making excuses for another's aggressive behaviour and secretly admire their strength at the same time as denying how furious you are with them.

- *Sex-role stereotyping.* You may resist seeing qualities in yourself that do not accord with the traditional stereotype of your sex. You think in rigid terms – 'Women are...' and 'Men are...'

Since you may not be aware of it in the first place, letting go of defensive thinking can be difficult. Anything you do that increases your self-esteem is likely to lower your need to defend yourself. In addition, if you become aware that you are using a defence, review the negative consequences to yourself and your relationships of maintaining it. Also review the possible gains of relinquishing it. Then, either on your own or with the help of your partner, you can strive to see yourself more accurately.

Perceive another accurately

The corrosive effects on intimacy of each partners' defensive thinking can scarcely be overemphasized. Partners expand their defensive thinking because, in order to protect their own distorted self-pictures, they need to distort their pictures of one another. Thus intimacy becomes doubly difficult. However, by striving to overcome your own defensive thinking, you can perceive others more accurately.

Partners can also perceive each other inaccurately through insufficient information. Here they may attain greater intimacy by continuing to collect information about each other – their pasts, presents and hopes for the future. Taking the trouble to know your partner well can also protect you against insufficiently acknowledging how they differ from you. In addition, partners can perceive each other inaccurately through jumping to conclusions about each other's thoughts, feelings, motivations and actions. People tend to perceive in others only the thoughts and emotions they are capable of in themselves. You can protect yourself against misinterpreting your partner if you listen to them carefully and, if necessary, ask them to explain themselves.

Explain cause accurately

You can offer all sorts of reasons why you are less than successful in developing and maintaining intimacy in your relationships. Illustrative explanations for insufficiently reaching out to another person include: 'It's my nature', 'It's my upbringing', 'It's my culture', 'It's my sex-role conditioning' and 'I've tried to get through in the past, so it's no use trying again.' Illustrative explanations for not receiving another's intimacy include: 'He/she is manipulating me', 'He/she is trying to gain power over me', 'He/she never listens to me', 'I don't really care about him/her (when underneath I really do care)' and 'It's up to him/her to make the first move to improve communication in our relationship.'

If any of the above explanations are ways in which you block intimacy, challenge their accuracy. Often what happens is that people convert partial truths into whole truths. For instance, you may have been brought up in a family of under-disclosers. However, that is no reason why you cannot now assume responsibility for developing your intimacy skills.

In addition, you can challenge the accuracy of your explanations for not receiving another's disclosures. For instance, you can challenge the explanation 'He/she never listens to me' by asking yourself questions like: 'How well do I disclose and listen to him/her?' and 'Can I think of any occasions where he/she has listened to me?' and 'Why should I let my thinking and behaviour be controlled by his/her thinking and behaviour?'

Predict realistically

You can be poor at predicting the risks and gains of intimacy with yourself, reaching out, receiving another's intimacy and developing and maintaining your and your partner's pattern of intimacy. Fears attached to knowing yourself better include acknowledging existential anxiety, guilt, vulnerablities, your shadow side and ways in which you have fallen short both of parental teaching and of your potential. Fears attached to intimacy with others include losing yourself in the relationship, having your disclosures used against you, breaches of confidentiality, getting badly hurt and losing your partner when the relationship ends. Fears attached to changing interactive intimacy patterns include being taken advantage of and facing the unwillingness or inability of your partner to change.

You require the ability to be realistic about assessing the gains of seeking greater intimacy as well as the risks. You can ask yourself such questions as: 'What is the up-side as well as the down-side of risking greater intimacy?', 'Where is the evidence to support or negate my predictions?', 'What is the level of trust in the relationship?', 'What are my strengths and where are my support factors if my efforts at increasing intimacy get rejected?', 'If my initial efforts at greater intimacy get rejected, what are the pros and cons of trying again?' and 'What action skills do I need to deepen or repair the intimacy level of the relationship?'

Set realistic goals

Intimacy is not something that automatically happens and continues. You may need to develop skills of setting realistic intimacy goals. You may set yourself overall goals for a relationship: for instance, the level of intimacy that you seek in it. In addition, you may set yourself more specific goals: to reveal a personal secret, to share a particular feeling or to arrange a time to talk about your relationship.

When setting intimacy goals you require realism about your partner's wishes for emotional closeness or distance. Together you may need to negotiate intimacy goals that work for your relationship. Such goals may involve partners in changing: for example, sharing more of themselves, being less demanding for intimacy or requesting intimacy more tactfully. Whether setting intimacy goals on your own or with a partner, you need to consider the time frame and how you are going to monitor and evaluate whether you have achieved your intimacy goals.

Use visualizing skills

You can use visualizing skills to increase intimacy. For example, by using your imagination, you can develop a better understanding of another's life experience, both past and present. In addition, you can visually rehearse how best to reach out to another. Such imaginal rehearsal can have the twin goals of calming your anxiety and increasing your chances of behaving competently.

You can use visual images to remember your partner when you are parted, be it for a working day or for longer periods. Such visual remembrance may stimulate you to contact them and ask how they are going. Also, you can use visualizing skills to strengthen your motivation for positive displays of intimacy by imagining another's pleasure in receiving what you say and do. In addition, you can inhibit actions that impede intimacy by imagining their negative consequences: for example, criticizing your partner in public.

Together you and your partner can develop intimacy by sharing your dreams and fantasies. Also, you can develop visual pictures of life you want to lead, both now and in future.

SOME ACTION SKILLS FOR INTIMACY

Following are some suggestions for skills of sharing your internal world, allowing another to be open with you, and maintaining an effective interactive pattern of intimacy.

Reaching out

Express feelings

Expressing your feelings involves revealing to the external world the emotions of your internal world. Thus expressing feelings entails a translation of your inner sensations into outer expressions. Sometimes the process of translation is immediate – for instance your startled reactions to a loud noise. On most occasions, expressing feelings involves conscious choices regarding both how you label feelings and also whether and how you reveal them.

Identifying and labelling your feelings accurately requires intimacy with yourself. For instance, Bob asks his partner Lois if she will go out to dinner with him that evening, and she politely but firmly refuses. Bob might have a range of possible feelings including hurt, anger, anxiety, relief, resignation, cheerfulness and concern. If Bob thinks about his feelings or wants to talk about them to Lois, he needs to put them into words. Some slippage may occur between Bob's feelings and their verbal description. For instance, he may find it difficult to admit that he is hurt, finding it more comfortable to label his feeling as anger. Bob's other deficits include insufficiently acknowledging his ambivalence and the nuances in the intensity of his feelings. In addition, Bob may lack the vocabulary to identify and express his feelings adequately. To send good feelings messages, it is useful to build up a repertoire of words to describe and to catch the nuances of your own and others' feelings. Earlier, in Table 2.1, I listed some feelings words you might use.

Apart from identifying and labelling your feelings accurately, other skills for expressing feelings include: sending 'I' messages and sending consistent verbal, voice and body messages. With feelings you find difficult to express, you can think through and rehearse how best to communicate them prior to taking the risk of doing so.

Let yourself be known

Intimacy requires letting yourself be known. You need to reveal personal information as well as your feelings. Following are some action skills for letting yourself be known.

• *Take the initiative*. Instead of waiting to be asked questions about yourself, you can take the initiative in talking about yourself. You can help your partner gain knowledge of your past, present and future.

• *Request disclosure time*. You can develop skills of letting your partner know that you want their attention. If you want to share a sensitive disclosure, you can either choose or arrange a time when you can talk the matter through. You can signal the importance of such a discussion to you.

• *Assert yourself*. You may need to use assertion skills to ensure that your partner listens to you. For instance, if they switch the focus back to themselves, you can let it be known that you wish to continue. They can have their turn to talk about themselves either later or another time.

• *Take calculated risks*. Revealing negative aspects of yourself can deepen relationships. You can attempt to attain greater intimacy by taking calculated risks. If you have never tried, you have not collected the evidence that you will worsen rather than improve your relationship by risking specific disclosures. You need not 'let it all hang out'.

• *Reciprocate intimacy*. If your partner reveals something more intimate about themselves, you can match their intimacy level by self-disclosing in the same or another area.

• *Tune into your partner's reactions*. You cannot only notice but be responsive to how your partner reacts to your disclosures. If you have revealed something which changes their picture of you, they may require your help in dealing with this change. You also need to learn what interests your partner about you and how not to bore them.

• *Be worth knowing*. You need to develop as a person by keeping actively engaged in life. If you allow your internal world to become impoverished and have few external interests, you will have little of interest to disclose.

Receiving intimacy

This section focuses in particular on assisting your partner to share very private information. Each of us has imperfections that we fear to reveal to others. Words and phrases to describe such information include: negative or risky self-disclosure, unacceptable parts of ourselves, secrets, skeletons in the cupboard or stigmas (Goffman, 1963; Jourard, 1964; Rogers, 1973). Following are some skills of assisting your partner to share negative aspects of her or his internal world.

● *Show unconditional acceptance.* Unconditional acceptance means accepting another unconditionally as a valuable person independent of their specific behaviours. If your partner struggles to tell you something of which they are ashamed, be careful not to be judgemental about them and it. The fact that your partner fears telling you means that they already judge the information negatively, but trust you sufficiently not to make matters worse.

● *Encourage the experiencing and exploring of feelings.* Use active listening and showing understanding skills to help your partner experience the feelings attached to the disclosure, for instance, anxiety, relief or tears. Assist them to reveal as much of the story as they are comfortable with at this stage. Give your partner space to explore their thoughts and feelings about what they are telling you. Where appropriate, ask questions that encourage them to continue and elaborate their story.

● *Show involvement.* You can show that you care for your partner not only by listening, but by actively showing your support. If your partner appears hesitant, you can tell them of your concern and willingness to be there for them. Also, you can respond to specific parts of their story with comments like 'That must have been awful for you'. In addition, you can express appreciation for their trust in you as well as admiration for their courage.

● *Use effective voice messages.* You can show that you understand the intensity of their feelings by varying the emphasis of your voice. Also, you can show your compassion by speaking gently.

● *Use effective body and touch messages.* Use body messages such as interested and responsive facial expressions and good use of gaze and eye contact. Also, consider using touch messages: for instance, either placing your hand on theirs or your arm round their shoulders.

● *Choose whether or not to reciprocate.* What your partner says may trigger something that you would like to reveal about yourself. Be sensitive that this may not be the best time to switch the agenda from your partner's concerns. Nevertheless, on some occasions, sharing something shameful about yourself may ease your partner's burden of self-devaluation as well as yours.

Above, I have focused on skills of helping another to reveal negative information. However, intimacy also entails sharing and receiving positive information. You may help your partner to feel more positively about themselves by accepting aspects of themselves that they find unacceptable. In addition, you may need to use good receiving intimacy skills to assist your partner to reveal what they like about themselves. Many people require loving assistance in owning and revealing their strengths.

Maintaining your interactive pattern of intimacy

Following is a vignette of a couple who allowed their pattern of intimacy to run down and then took steps to repair it.

> Bert and Jillie, a couple in their late 30s, had been married for 15 years and had two girls, aged 12 and ten. Until recently Bert had been a company lawyer who worked long hours, including taking work home evenings and weekends. Jillie was a school teacher. Not seeing much of Bert, she adjusted her schedule to include numerous committees and outside activities. When Bert's company was unexpectedly taken over, he lost his job. As part of his soul-searching on being made redundant, Bert decided to seek a less demanding job so he could spend more time with wife and family. This prompted a series of discussions with Jillie about how they wished to relate in future. Jillie was sceptical if Bert would change his ways. Nevertheless, they agreed to set aside an evening a fortnight to have a social evening together, to do the shopping together on Saturday mornings and have coffee out afterwards. They also agreed to go camping more. To Jillie's delight, Bert turned down some job offers that would have left them little time to have a relaxed intimate relationship. Eventually he took a job where he could restrict his work. Jillie relinquished some of her outside activities to spend more time at home. Bert and Jillie discussed early warning signals for their relationship becoming distant again, for instance Bert's irritability, Jillie experiencing difficulty getting through to him and Jillie looking for satisfaction outside the home. They agreed in future to confront the problem of distance in their relationship early on.

Talk about how you relate

An important skill in maintaining an effective relationship is to talk to each other about how you relate. Egan calls this skills immediacy, or 'you-me' talk. He distinguishes between relationship immediacy ('Let's talk about how we've been relating to each other recently') and here-and-now immediacy ('Let's talk about what's going on between you and me right now as we're talking to each other') (Egan, 1977, p. 235). Thus Egan's 'you-me' talk can either have a recent past or a present focus. Another focus for 'you-me' talk sessions is how partners want their relationship to develop in future. For instance, in the above vignette, Bert became dissatisfied that he was a status-seeking and money-making machine rather than a person. Then he and Jillie engaged in some 'you-me' talk to establish different goals for their relationship. Bert would have found it harder to maintain his change if Jillie maintained her high level of outside activity.

When talking about your how you relate, partners require skills of giving and receiving feedback. Partners can share positive and negative feelings about how each other relates. Other areas for feedback include: how committed we are to the relationship, what issues we have avoided in the past, what issues we are not bringing up at this moment, what we want from our relationship, what are the strengths in our relationship, what is missing in our relationship, the influence of one another on how we give and receive intimacy, how we might improve our relationship, and the impact of other relationships on our relationship. Skills for 'you-me' talk sessions include: getting in touch with what you think and feel, sending 'I' messages, being specific and inviting rather than cutting off discussion of the points you make. In addition, tact and diplomacy can help soften painful communication.

Allocate time to maintain your relationship

As the statistics for divorce and separation show, relationships can easily deteriorate into serious conflict. Stresses of work, family and outside activities interfere with couples spending quality time together. There is no magic wand to wave for maintaining intimacy in your relationship. Like Bert and Jillie, you and your partner can deliberately allocate time for enjoying each other's company and conversing. Then, at least, you give maintaining intimacy a chance. Also, become aware when you start spending less time together and repair your intimacy pattern before it is too late.

CHAPTER HIGHLIGHTS

• Intimacy entails people getting in touch with their internal worlds and sharing them with each other.

• Intimacy with yourself involves knowing and exploring your internal world. Your capacity for intimacy with yourself influences how intimate you can become with others.

• Intimacy with others involves both reaching out to them and receiving their disclosures.

• Interactive patterns of intimacy relate to how well people coordinate their exchange of intimacy. Dysfunctional intimacy patterns can be too distant, too connected or unbalanced.

• Limitations on intimacy include: existential isolation, individual differences, sex-role learning, realistic negative consequences and practical considerations, such as cramped living space.

• Intimacy with yourself can reflect either self-acceptance or egocentricity or a mixture of both.

• You can reach out to enhance yourself and another person. However, anxiety can motivate people to reach out either too much, too little or for the wrong reasons.

• Receiving intimacy can be broken down into allowing another person to reach out to you and allowing yourself to be affected by their disclosures. You can receive another's disclosures either to assist them or for ulterior motives.

• In effective intimacy patterns, partners feel free to share their internal worlds and to have such sharing understood and reciprocated.

• You are always a chooser in how you develop, maintain, repair and, if necessary, end intimacy.

• The STC (situation–thoughts–consequences) framework provides a useful tool for understanding the connections between how you think, feel and act.

• Intimacy with yourself requires you to be responsive to feelings based on your own valuing process.

• Use coping self talk – using calming, coaching and affirming statements – to help you manage the anxiety attached to certain disclosures.

• Challenge and replace your unrealistic rules concerning intimacy with yourself, reaching out, receiving intimacy and your interactive pattern of intimacy.

• Review the ways in which you block accurate perception of yourself and others by means of defensive processes. You perceive more accurately if you have sufficient information about your partner and do not jump to conclusions about them.

• Review and change any unrealistic explanations you may have that interfere with sharing and receiving intimacy.

• Be realistic about predicting the gains of greater intimacy as well as the risks.

• Set realistic goals for the level of intimacy you seek in a relationship and for making specific disclosures.

• Use visualizing skills to understand your partner better, remember them, strengthen your positive feelings for them, and jointly set goals for your future.

• A useful action skill for reaching out is the ability to identify, label and then express your feelings.

• Skills for letting yourself be known include: taking the initiative, requesting disclosure time, asserting yourself, taking calculated risks, reciprocating intimacy, tuning into our partner's reactions and being worth knowing.

• Skills for assisting your partner to share very private information include: showing unconditional acceptance; encouraging them to experience and explore feelings; showing involvement; using effective voice, body and touch messages; and choosing whether or not to reciprocate.

• Skills for maintaining an effective interactive pattern of intimacy include 'you-me' talk about how you relate and also allocating time for enjoying each other's company and conversing.

EXERCISES
EXERCISE 12.1
DEVELOP MY THINKING SKILLS FOR INTIMACY

Instructions

First do each part of this exercise on your own. Then, if appropriate, discuss with your partner, another or others.

Thinking skills

Following are ten thinking skills.
Own responsibility for choosing
Understand the relationship between how I think, feel and act
Get in touch with my feelings
Use coping self-talk
Choose realistic rules
Choose to perceive accurately
Explain cause accurately
Predict realistically
Set realistic goals
Use visualizing skills

Part A
Intimacy with myself

1. Assess your thinking skills deficits.

2. Identify your main deficit or deficits and specify the steps you intend taking to change it/them.

Part B
Reaching out

1. Assess your thinking skills deficits.

2. Identify your main deficit or deficits and specify the steps you intend taking to change it/them.

Part C
Receiving intimacy

1. Assess your thinking skills deficits.

2. Identify your main deficit or deficits and specify the steps you intend taking to change it/them.

Part D
Interactive pattern of intimacy

Focus on a specific relationship.

1. Assess your and your partner's thinking skills deficits.

2. Identify your main deficit or deficits and specify the steps you intend taking to change it/them.

EXERCISE 12.2
DEVELOP MY EXPRESSING FEELINGS SKILLS
Instructions

First do each part of this exercise on your own. Then, if appropriate, discuss with your partner, another or others.

Part A
Identifying and labelling my feelings

Complete the following sentences regarding your feelings in relationships. Focus on how you actually feel rather than on your thoughts. Indicate the intensity of your feelings. If you have conflicting feelings, state what these are.

When someone ignores me I feel _____

When someone cries I feel _____

When someone praises me I feel _____

When someone talks about themselves all the time I feel _____

_____

When someone gets angry with me I feel _____

When someone acts superior to me I feel _____

When someone attracts me I feel _____

When someone breaks a confidence I feel _____

When someone is very late for an appointment I feel _____

_____

When I am in a group of strangers I feel _____

When someone deeply understands me I feel _____

_____

How good are you at identifying and labelling your feelings in your relationships?

Part B
Feelings I find easy and difficult to express

1. Take a piece of paper. At the top write 'Feelings I find easy and difficult to express'. On the next line, at the top of the left column write 'easy', and at the top of the right column write 'difficult'.

2. In each column write feelings you find easy and difficult to express. You may do this with regard either to a specific relationship or to people in general. Table 2.1 may give you some ideas about different feelings.

3. Do you detect any theme(s) in the feelings you have listed as either easy or difficult to express? If so, please specify the theme(s).

Part C
Sending feelings messages

1. For each of the following feelings write down (a) verbal messages; (b) voice messages; and (c) body messages that you could use to express the feeling appropriately either in a specific relationship or to people in general.

Love _____   Anger _____

_____   _____

_____   _____

Fear _____   Sadness _____

_____   _____

_____   _____

Happiness _____   Boredom _____

_____   _____

_____   _____

_____   _____

2. Look at the feelings you listed as difficult to express in Part B of this exercise. For each of these feelings write down (a) verbal messages; (b) voice messages; and (c) body messages that you could use to express the feeling appropriately. Rehearse and practise expressing these feelings.

EXERCISE 12.3
DEVELOP MY DISCLOSING AND RECEIVING
PERSONAL INFORMATION SKILLS

Instructions

Complete each part of the exercise on your own. Then, if appropriate, discuss with your partner, another or others.

Part A
Disclosing personal information

1. Assess your strengths and deficits in each of the following skills of revealing personal information.

Taking the initiative

Requesting disclosure time

Asserting myself

Taking calculated risks

Reciprocating intimacy

Tuning into my partner's reactions

Being worth knowing

2. If appropriate, identify one or more of your disclosing personal information skills deficits and develop a plan to change how you act. In your plan, specify:

a. your goals, including a time frame,

b. the steps you intend taking to attain each of your goals, and

c. how you will monitor your progress.

Part B
Receiving personal information

1. Assess your strengths and deficits in each of the following skills of receiving personal information.

Showing unconditional acceptance

Encouraging the experiencing and exploring of feelings

Showing involvement

Using effective voice messages

Using effective body and touch messages

Choosing whether or not to reciprocate

2. If appropriate, identify one or more of your receiving personal information skills deficits and develop a plan to change how you act. In your plan, specify:

a. your goals, including a time frame,

b. the steps you intend taking to attain each of your goals, and

c. how you will monitor your progress.

EXERCISE 12.4
DEVELOP OUR 'YOU-ME' TALK SKILLS
Instructions

If in a relationship, complete the first part of this exercise on your own and ask your partner to do the same. Then, if appropriate, do the second part of the exercise together.

Part A
Assessment

1. What positive feelings and thoughts about how your partner relates to you have you left unsaid?

2. What negative feelings and thoughts about how your partner relates to you have you left unsaid?

3. How committed are you and your partner to your relationship?

4. What issues have you and your partner avoided talking about in the past?

5. To what extent do you and your partner avoid talking about what is going on in your relationship in the 'here-and-now'?

6. What are the strengths of your relationship?

7. What is missing in your relationship?

8. How do you and your partner influence one another in how you give and receive intimacy?

9. Are there any other relationships that significantly impact, for good or ill, on your relationship? If so, how?

10. How might you and your partner work together to improve your relationship?

Part B
Action: Hold a 'you-me' talk session

1. Set aside a time to hold a 'you-me' talk session with your partner about your relationship.

2. Decide with your partner which of the above questions you wish to address in this session.

3. Conduct a 'you-me' talk session. Remember to send 'I' messages, be specific, invite rather than cut off discussion and use tact and diplomacy.

4. Evaluate with your partner the benefits, if any, of holding 'you-me' talk sessions about your relationship.

5. Hold further 'you-me' talk sessions as you both see fit.

EXERCISE 12.5
GROUP DISCUSSION: INTIMACY SKILLS
Instructions

This is intended as a group exercise, though it may be done individually or in pairs. For each part:

1. spend 10–15 minutes answering the question in groups of three or four,

2. each sub-group shares its findings with the whole group, and

3. then the whole group ranks the six most important skills from the most important to the least important.

Part A
Reaching out

List the six most important skills partners can use to reach out to one another.

Part B
Receiving intimacy

List the six most important skills partners can use to receive intimacy from one another.

Part C
Maintaining intimacy

List the six most important skills partners can use to maintain intimacy in their relationship with each other.

THIRTEEN
Companionship Skills

*We do not mind our not arriving anywhere
nearly so much as not having any company
on the way.*

Frank Moore Colby

CHAPTER QUESTIONS

- *What is companionship?*
- *What is personal space?*
- *Why are both togetherness and personal space important?*
- *What are some activities for companionship?*
- *What are some thinking skills for companionship?*
- *What are some action skills for companionship?*

An important relating skill is being a good companion with whom to share activities. Glasser (1995) observes: 'The key to friendship is sharing and expanding common interests and, at the risk of being repetitious, friendship is the key to a good marriage' (p. 34). Montgomery and Evans (1983) call doing good things together as a couple, 'coupling'. Your relationship is more likely to stay fresh and be fun if you are creative about how you spend time together. There is a limit to the amount of intimate conversations you can have before these conversations become repetitive and 'navel-gazing'. Following are some vignettes that illustrate aspects of companionship.

> Mel and Meryl have been married for over ten years. Every evening when they come home from work they spend at least an hour having a drink and talking over the main events,

thoughts, and feelings of their days. On fine days they sit in their garden to do this.

Max and Christine met as part of a group of secondary school friends who went bowling. Max and Christine, now both in their early 20s, have been living together for 18 months. They still enjoy going bowling together. Sometimes other couples come along too.

Sandy and Rhonda have been happily married for nearly 20 years and have three children. Each family member plays a musical instrument. Often the family makes music and sings together. Sandy also plays the guitar in a rock band that does gigs in the local area. Rhonda is not threatened by this. She sees it as a chance for Sandy to have space away from the family and a complete break from his factory work.

Diane is an ambitious young dress-shop owner very wrapped up in running her business. Her boyfriend Jamie is getting fed up because she consistently puts her business far above spending time with him.

Super (1980) takes a life-span life-space approach to occupation when he identifies nine major areas (child, student, 'leisurite', citizen, worker, spouse, home maker, parent and pensioner). People in relationships perform many different roles both individually and together. A simple distinction is that, apart from paid employment, a couple's activities can be broken down into domestic and leisure.

Partners spend a large proportion of their lives in leisure activities. Argyle (1992) provides the following breakdown of average daily time spent on non-work activities. These figures come from the British General Household Survey, which interviews about 20,000 households each year.

Domestic work (including child care)	3 hours 42 minutes
Personal care (including sleeping, eating)	10 hours 38 minutes
Leisure outside home	1 hour 39 minutes
Leisure at home	4 hours 3 minutes

Survey findings indicate that British men and women enjoy different quantities of leisure time: men, 380 minutes, and women, 307 minutes. Of their total leisure time, men spent 110 minutes outside the home and 270 minutes inside. The corresponding figures for women were 89 and 218 minutes (Argyle, 1992).

Leisure activities can fulfil many psychological needs. Researchers Tinsley and Eldredge (1995) proposed ten psychological benefits of leisure participation: novelty, belongingness, service, sensual enjoyment, cognitive stimulation, self-expression, creativity, competition, vicarious competition and relaxation.

Togetherness

How can doing things together strengthen and deepen your relationship? First, you find out more about one another's likes and dislikes and whether you are still compatible. Also, you discover whether each is committed to spending time with the other. Second, your companionship helps both you and your partner avoid loneliness. Third, many domestic activities become less wearisome if jointly performed. Fourth, leisure activities enable you to play, have fun and enjoy each other's company. Arguably, partners who play together, stay together. When dating, couples engage in many rewarding leisure activities, for instance going out to dinner and going to movies. In long-term relationships you still require amusement and diversion from the daily grind. Also, you continue needing opportunities to smile, laugh and be humorous. Fifth, doing things together provides a vehicle for your ongoing relationship conversation. Shared activities have an emotional as well as a functional purpose. Sixth, you can avoid boredom and find meaning in leisure. Seventh, sharing activities can be a source of strength during rough times in your relationship. Such activities may help you keep in contact despite feelings of hurt, pain and anger.

Personal space

In the context of this chapter, personal space means the freedom to pursue your own activities, interests and friendships independent of your partner. Each of you comes to a relationship with a history of previously developed activities. Many of these activities you can share with your partner, but for others your interests differ. In addition, as time goes by each of you may develop new and different pursuits.

In good relationships, the distinction between personal and shared activities becomes blurred. For example, partners can be sitting in the same room, one reading the paper and the other knitting, and both enjoying each other's company. Also, partners can be doing different things in different parts of the house or flat and still provide each other with a sense of companionship.

Partners can take pleasure in the stimulation each other derives from their separate interests. The relationship is strengthened by the fact that it is not based on the 'joined-at-the-hip' or 'ball-and-chain' principles – each partner feels free to develop separately as well as together. Furthermore, separate interests can add spice and stimulation to relationships. Also, sometimes it is a good idea if you can witness your partner being valued by other people for part of themselves not shown in your relationship.

Talking to a carbon copy of yourself is intensely dull. Also, people living in close contact can see too much of each other. Separate leisure pursuits can prevent relationships from becoming unhealthily intense and suffocating. Allowing each other personal space can foster rather than militate against enjoying shared activities.

Interactive patterns of companionship

Following are three main interactive patterns of companionship.

• *Total togetherness*. Lazarus (1985) remarks about total togetherness that 'This represents the romantic ideal where two people merge so completely that they become as one. In practice, where this is possible, it would probably result in emotional suffocation' (p. 31). Enmeshment is another term for total togetherness. Lazarus considers that most married people have transferred responsibility from their parents to their spouses, often unnecessarily saying 'I'll have to ask my wife/husband' when asked to do something they know their partner hates, but they like. He advocates due consideration for your partner, especially on major decisions, at the same time as some latitude to make unilateral decisions. Total togetherness is more likely to be a problem in English-speaking Western cultures, with their emphasis on possessive individualism – 'my spouse is my property' – and the nuclear family, than in Eastern cultures, where more value is placed on group harmony and the extended family.

• *Much distance*. Partners mainly go their separate ways. For instance, Linda's main recreational interest is Scrabble and Colin's is boating. In fact, Linda has come to hate boating and Colin has never been keen on Scrabble. Overall, there is much distance and very little common ground in how they spend their leisure time. Furthermore, Linda and Colin take little interest in hearing about each other's Scrabble or boating.

• *Mainly togetherness, but some personal space*. Partners engage in many recreational activities together, but respect each other's difference and wish to develop as separate persons. Enjoying personal leisure activities strengthens them individually and as a couple. Lazarus (1985) suggests 75–80 per cent togetherness represents an excellent marriage. Many couples settle for less than this, for instance 60–70 per cent, yet still enjoy strong relationships. Some emotionally close couples may spend still fewer hours together, but enjoy their quality. Shared activities in themselves do not guarantee satisfaction. Habituation can lead to boredom. Togetherness may be enhanced by partners sharing stimulating or exciting activities (Reissman, Aron & Bergen, 1993).

The above are balanced or symmetrical companionship patterns where each partner either wants the same as the other or, willingly or unwillingly, has adjusted to the other's wishes. Companionship patterns may also be unbalanced, with one partner seeking more recreational investment than the other is prepared to give. The total togetherness and much distance companionship patterns are especially vulnerable if either or both partners change in incompatible ways. Sometimes outside factors cause one partner to have more leisure time than the other, for example either differences in job demands or if one partner becomes unemployed.

COMPANIONSHIP ACTIVITIES

What activities can partners jointly engage in to bring them the rewards of companionship? Much of your relationship centres around routine activities. Some of these activities are domestic chores, some of which you do together. Other activities may be more enjoyable parts of your daily routine, like having meals together, being in bed, watching television or listening to music. Still others may be special events – for instance, eating out or going to a concert.

MacPhillamy and Lewinsohn developed a *Pleasant Events Schedule* of 320 items (Lewinsohn, Munoz, Youngren & Zeiss, 1986). They ask respondents to rate each item according to how often each event happened in the past month and how enjoyable or rewarding it was in this period. As in the *Pleasant Events Schedule*, the frequency and the degree of pleasure each of you derives from different joint activities are two major considerations when assessing the amount and quality of companionship in your relationship. For instance, frequently watching large amounts of TV may provide only moderate pleasure and a limited quality of companionship.

Companionship at home

The home-based activities discussed here relate more to leisure than to domestic work. Watching TV is the main leisure activity at home. In Britain, women spend on average four and a quarter hours and men three and three-quarter hours a day watching it (Argyle, 1992). TV watching can both promote and impede companionship. Couples can share their interest and enjoyment in the same programs. On the other hand, too much TV watching may interfere with couples conversing and engaging in more active rewarding activities. In 1986 a large-scale *Social Trends* survey in Britain found the following participation rates in home-based leisure activities: watching TV, 99 per cent; visiting/entertaining friends or relatives, 95 per cent; listening to radio, 88 per cent; listening to records/tapes, 73 per cent; reading books, 60 per cent; gardening, 46 per cent; DIY, 43 per cent; and dressmaking/needlework/knitting, 27 per cent (Argyle, 1992). Nowadays playing with computers is an increasingly popular home-based activity.

What can you do together at home to enjoy each other's company. Table 13.1 provides some suggestions.

Table 13.1 Illustrative home-based companionship activities

art activities	having coffee/tea	playing with pets
conversing in bed	having sex	praying together
cooking	listening to CDs/cassettes	reading together
craft work	listening to the radio	singing
DIY	massaging/back rubbing	sitting outdoors
eating snacks	meditating/doing yoga	sleeping
entertaining friends	petting/necking	sunbathing
entertaining relatives	planning holidays	talking about people
gardening	playing indoor games	telling jokes
having a bath/shower	playing music	watching TV
having a drink	playing with computers	

Companionship outside the home

Couples spend much less leisure time outside than inside the home. Activities that get couples out of the house are important. They provide variety and stimulus to your relationship. Also, they can prevent otherwise enjoyable home based activities from becoming monotonous.

Many outside activities are extensions of home-based activities: for example, giving and receiving entertainment with friends and relatives. There are limits to which you can pursue many activities in the home, for instance fitness activities and playing music. Other activities are impossible to do at home, for instance horse-riding. Table 13.2 provides suggestions for outside the home companionship activities.

Table 13.2 **Illustrative outside the home companionship activities**

amateur drama	enjoying nature	shopping
amateur music	evening classes	skiing
art activities	field trips/nature walks	snooker/billiards/pool
athletics	fishing	squash
attending concert/ opera/ballet	folk dancing	surfing
badminton	gambling	swimming
barbecuing	golf	table tennis
basketball	health clubs/saunas	tennis
bingo	helping someone	visiting the city/town centre
bird-watching	hiking/rambling	visiting the countryside
boating	holidaying	visiting friends
bowling	horse-riding	visiting galleries/ museums
camping	going to parties	
card-playing	going to pubs	visiting historic buildings
choral societies/choirs	going to restaurants	visiting libraries
church activities	going to talks/lectures	visiting parks
cinema	going to the theatre	visiting relatives
computer games	jogging	visiting the seaside
community service	leisure classes	voluntary work
craft activities	looking at stars/moon	walking
cricket	motor-cycling	walking the dog
cycling	night-clubbing	watching sporting events
dancing	overseas travel	
darts	photography	yoga/meditation classes
discos	picnicking	
driving	pop concerts	
	rock climbing	

SOME THINKING SKILLS FOR COMPANIONSHIP

Following are some thinking skills that can influence how well people offer and receive companionship.

Own responsibility for choosing

Life is finite. Some partners use their anxiety about death, isolation and meaning-lessness to engage in a compulsive round of empty activities. Others are able to assume responsibility for choosing activities that have genuine significance for them. Partners need to assume responsibility for making the most of their non-work existences. People are meaning-getting rather than have meanings given to them (Frankl. 1988; Yalom, 1980). You can actively search for ways of finding meaning in activities with your partner rather than passively wait for something to happen. If you are mainly bored together, you can choose to see this as a challenge to enrich your relationship through shared activities rather than blame each other. If you feel suffocated by each other, you can choose this as a challenge to develop personal as well as joint activities. The kinds of questions you and your partner can ask as you develop your unique relationship include: 'What is the underlying purpose of our lives?', 'What values might guide our choice of shared activities?' and 'How can we find and create real meaning in our lives?'

Get in touch with your feelings

Individuals in relationships may need to get in touch with many different feelings so they can enjoy activities and companionship. For example, each needs to discern what activities are likely to be meaningful to them and which are not. Discerning meaning entails the ability to listen to your feelings. In addition to finding meaning, each partner needs to discover what they enjoy. Partners require spontaneity, fun and play. Also, both singly and together, they need be creative about what they do.

Partners also require skills of getting in touch with their stress levels. Both individ-ually and jointly they can use relaxing non-work activities to cope with stress. Also, many people, when thinking of taking up or restarting activities, require skills of confronting and working through fears and anxieties about participating.

Partners can acknowledge the warm and positive feelings they can get from compan-ionship. Some may need to review their lifestyles to see if they are missing these feelings. Others may need to listen to their consciences to see if their behaviour makes it difficult for their partner to engage in sufficient rewarding activities, either with or without them.

Use coping self-talk

Often people feel anxious about changing their pattern of activities. Take the example of Doreen and Trevor who want to become more socially active and decide to give a dinner party. As the event comes nearer, both become increasingly anxious about its success. Doreen worries about her culinary skills and Trevor about his conversational skills. However, using coping self-talk should help them contain their anxiety and stay task-oriented. As mentioned earlier, coping self-talk consists of making calming, coaching and affirming self-statements. Both Doreen and Trevor can tell themselves the following calming self-statements: 'Stay calm' and 'Breathe slowly and regularly'. Sample coaching self-statements for Doreen include: 'Prepare as much as possible in advance' and 'Make a list of things I need to do when the guests arrive, so I don't forget.' Sample coaching self-statements for Trevor include: 'Prepare in advance a number of topics that I can talk about' and 'Make sure to use active listening skills.' In addition, Doreen and Trevor can each affirm themselves with self-statements reminding them about their strengths and about occasions in the past where they have used good culinary or conversational skills.

Choose realistic rules

You and your partner, both individually and as a couple, may possess unrealistic rules concerning companionship and personal space. Often an unrealistic rule that you have for yourself, you expect to hold good for your partner as well. Following are examples of companionship rules that may be unnecessarily rigid.

Personal rules

I must never do anything without my partner.
I must always be approved for the companionship I give my partner.
I must never be lazy.
I must always do everything very well indeed.
He/she must like what I like.
Work must come before leisure (or vice versa).
I must never be bored.
I must never be alone.

Relationship rules

We must do everything together.
We must mean everything to each other.
We must not differ in what we want to do.
All leisure decisions must be jointly made.
We must never intrude on each other's personal space.
Good husbands do household repairs/good wives do the laundry (Lazarus, 1985).
We must never be bored.
We must be the life and soul of the party.

As with any other unrealistic rules, dealing with unrealistic companionship rules requires identifying them, challenging their logic and restating them in a more realistic format. For instance, Paula and Kenny, both aged 18, have been in a relationship for three months and are starting to feel suffocated by thinking they must do everything together. Rather than blame each other and then break up, they decide to question how rational is their rule: 'We must do everything together.' Following are some questions that they can ask themselves.

'Where is the evidence that we must do everything together?'
'What will be the consequences if we continue doing everything together?'
'Do we expect other couples to do everything together?'
'Is there room for any acknowledgment of difference in our relationship?'
'What is the role of personal space in our relationship?'

By challenging their relationship rule 'We must do everything together', Paula and Kenny decide that they want to replace it with something more realistic. They agree on the following restatement: 'We care for each other very much and are committed to our relationship. We want to spend most of our free time together. However, we support each other in pursuing individual interests as well. We can jointly decide the balance we want between togetherness and personal space.'

Choose to perceive accurately

Perceive yourself accurately

How accurately do you perceive your attitude toward recreation? For instance, you may talk about having fun, but underneath consider that recreation is a waste of time (Lazarus, Lazarus & Fay, 1993). As a result, you and your partner may fail to enjoy the amount and range of shared activities that could make your relationship more mutually satisfying. Also, you may notice the signs of stress in others, but fail to notice them in yourself. Instead of being fun to be with, you are tense and irritable. Alternatively, you may be so focused on your own recreation that you fail to perceive the effect this has on others: for instance, drinking or gambling away the family finances and/or expecting your partner to act as your domestic help.

How good a companion are you and how do you know? As relationships move out of their 'honeymoon' period, you may become a less good companion (Beck, 1988; Montgomery & Evans, 1983). You can become wrapped up in your career and interests and take your partner's companionship for granted. Together you may progressively invest less of yourselves in your relationship. Watch out for signs that personal space is turning into interpersonal distance before this process becomes irrevocable.

Anxiety can cause you to be a less good companion than you otherwise might be. For example, at two extremes you may either avoid social activities or compulsively engage in them. Also, you may have tendencies toward controlling what your partner does and says rather than supporting him or her. In addition, you may inappropriately compete with your partner in activities that are intended to be relaxing.

Perceive your partner accurately

How accurately do you perceive your partner in the area of companionship? You may inaccurately perceive your partner's wishes for companionship and personal space.

Also, you may inaccurately perceive your partner's perception of what kind of companionship and personal space you want. Asking them what companionship they want is one way of collecting evidence and reality-testing your perceptions. Also, you can tactfully tell them what sort of companionship you like. In addition, you require sensitivity to their reactions to the quantity and quality of companionship you provide. For instance, you may be quick to sense their pleasure and poor at sensing their displeasure and resentment. Alternatively, you may be hypersensitive to signs that what you do is never good enough.

Fourth, especially during periods of strain in your relationship, you need beware of negatively labelling your partner as 'selfish', 'insensitive' and '*always* wanting his or her way' and '*never* taking your feelings into account'. If anything, there may be a bias toward perceiving a partner's companionship too positively at the start of a relationship and too negatively as the relationship develops (Beck, 1988). At times you may need to search for positive evidence and give each other the benefit of the doubt in ambiguous situations.

Explain cause accurately

Partners differ in the explanations they offer for the quantity and quality of companionship in their relationship. Following are some explanations for offering little companionship in the relationship.

- *'It's my nature.'* One or both partners consider themselves 'loners' or unsociable by nature.

- *'It's my upbringing.'* Life has taught me to place a high value on personal space relative to togetherness.

- *'It's my sex.'* Either or both partners are only prepared to engage in activities characteristic of their sexes: for instance, she will not go to football matches and he refuses to take tea with her female friends.

- *'It's my career.'* My career is so important and demanding that I have neither the time, interest or energy to offer and receive much companionship.

- *'It's my health.'* I am under so much stress/ill health that I wish to avoid further demands on my energy.

- *'It's my parents/children.'* The perceived demands of looking after parents and children take precedence over maintaining companionship with a partner.

Below are some explanations for not trying to change an unsatisfactory level of companionship.

- *'My partner is too possessive.'* Either or both partners perceive it is safer to keep their distance from the controlling tendencies in the other than to engage in much companionship.

- *'We've nothing in common.'* Partners perceive their differences to be so wide that either or both does not wish to surmount them.

- *'We've tried before.'* Partners may have made previous unsuccessful half-hearted and whole-hearted attempts to rekindle the companionship in their relationship.

- *'My partner is not prepared to change his/her ways.'* Here one partner casts himself or herself as the victim of a rigid partner, hence conveniently avoiding all responsibility for the couple's companionship problems.

- *'He/she is having an affair.'* One partner, rightly or wrongly, perceives the other partner's withdrawal of companionship as due to an affair.

Partners can challenge the adequacy of their explanations to assess how much truth they contain. For instance, the explanation 'We have nothing in common' can be challenged by looking for things the couple has had in common from the start of their relationship up until now. Even, the explanation 'He/she is having an affair' can be challenged. First, the affair may not exist. Second, even if it does exist, it may result from and not be the cause of lack of companionship. Third, if the couple address their relationship problems they may still achieve a tolerable level of companionship.

Predict realistically

For various reasons, partners inaccurately predict the risks of maintaining their companionship behaviour. For example, Jock, 28, inaccurately predicts that his partner, Tony, 27, will stay in their relationship if he continues his workaholic behaviour. Bruce, 42, inaccurately predicts that his wife Sharon, 35, will happily continue supplying the food and playing second fiddle to him on social occasions. Sharon is going to a feminist assertiveness group and Bruce's days of ruling the roost are numbered. Both Jock and Bruce require greater sensitivity to their partners as persons so that they can assess risk properly.

Partners can also inaccurately predict the gains from changing their companionship behaviour. In the above examples, Jock may have been afraid of jeopardizing his career by spending more time with Tony. However, had he and Tony worked out a mutually acceptable compromise, Jock might have been happier at home and at work. Similarly, Bruce and Sharon could possibly find a mutually acceptable formula whereby each feels valued. In short, Jock and Bruce require better skills of assessing both risk and gain. Also, they require skills of negotiating differences.

Frequently partners are anxious about trying out new companionship activities inside or outside the home. Earlier I gave the example of Doreen and Trevor who, for different reasons, worried about holding a successful dinner party at their home. Many partners fear taking up outside the home activities, such as swimming, dancing, golf or going to evening classes. Again focusing on the gains of trying something different and not just on the risks can help you feel more confident. Also, possessing some of the thinking skills mentioned above – for instance choosing realistic rules and using coping self-talk – can contribute to optimism about your level of performance and about attaining desired outcomes (Bandura, 1986; Seligman, 1991).

Set realistic goals

Many couples are reasonably satisfied with the level of companionship in their relationship, but numerous others are not. You and your partner may wonder whether you could obtain more satisfaction from what you do together. One way to go about setting goals is to review together the lists in Tables 13.1 and 13.2 of home-based and outside the home companionship activities and to discuss which activities you want to do more or less of. Another more systematic way is, either jointly or independently, to rate each of the activities on both lists according to the following scale: 0, no good as a companionship activity; 1, I do or would enjoy this as a companionship activity; and 2, I do or would very much enjoy this as a companionship activity. Then go through the list again and delete those activities which are not realistic for you as a couple. The remaining activities provide a pool of enjoyable activities in which you either currently engage or might engage. You can then discuss with each other which activities to drop and which to start or develop. Resulting from this discussion, set companionship activities goals that are mutually enjoyable, realistic, specific and have a time frame. Then develop a clear plan for the coming week or month about how you intend attaining each of your goals. As part of your plan, you need to address factors that might interfere with attaining your goals: for instance, creating more time to spend together.

Sometimes the process of setting companionship goals highlights differences between partners. In chapter 17 I review managing conflict and solving relationship problems skills.

Use visualizing skills

Visualizing skills can help you increase your participation in and enjoyment of companionship activities. For example, visualizing can help you choose what you want to do by imagining what it would be like doing it. Also, you can increase motivation for specific shared activities by picturing the rewards of doing them. Alternatively, you can lessen your motivation with negative images.

Sometimes due to anxiety people get negative images about activities they might otherwise enjoy. Mental relaxation and mental rehearsal are two visualizing skills you can use, either singly or sequentially, to manage your anxiety when thinking about or shortly before engaging in an activity. One mental relaxation technique is to close your eyes and visualize a restful scene like lying on a beach on a warm sunny day without a care in the world. You hold this image until you feel more relaxed. With mental rehearsal, you visually rehearse performing the anxiety-generating activity competently. Often mental rehearsal is best performed in conjunction with coping self-talk, consisting of calming, coping and affirming self-statements.

SOME ACTION SKILLS FOR COMPANIONSHIP

Following are some action skills that you can use to increase the quantity and quality of companionship in your relationship. Many of the thinking skills discussed in the previous section influence how effectively you can act.

Manage time effectively

Both individually and as a couple you may be poor at managing time. Following are two examples of poor time management skills.

> Donna, age 19, is disorganized in her work as a student. She never feels on top of her studying and complains about lack of time to spend with her boyfriend Rich, 20.

> Pauline, 33, is a dentist and her husband Kent, 30, is a computer programmer. Both have busy schedules that allow for some spare time. However, Pauline and Kent are poor at letting each other know their schedules and coordinating them so that they can spend recreation time together.

You may, like Donna, think that your insufficient work organization interferes with your personal life. If so, you can try and gain more control over your work by listing what you have to do, setting priorities, and time-tabling when you will do them. In addition to your time-tabling skills, you may require other skills like getting started on assignments skills and saying 'no' to requests that help you avoid work. Some individuals are very organized in their work. However, they place such high value on work that they need to time-table more recreation and organize their work accordingly.

Couples like Pauline and Kent need to coordinate how they manage time. A starting point might be for each partner to monitor how they currently spend time by filling out for the next seven days a time-table broken down by hours. Then, partners can compare time-tables and discuss how best to spend more time together.

Schedule activities and abide by contracts

Apart from scheduling work time, partners require skills at scheduling domestic chores, time together and personal space. Much of this scheduling can be achieved by informal discussion. However, some couples require a more systematic approach to scheduling joint activities. For instance, couples trying to repair a relationship by increasing the amount of shared pleasant activities should agree not only on which activities to share, but also on when and how frequently to do them. Then consider time-tabling agreed companionship activities for the next week, few weeks or a month.

Each partner's agreement to participating in the activity at a given time constitutes a form of contract with one another. Especially, when relationships are fragile, realize that keeping or breaking such contracts increases or decreases trust. Consequently, renegotiate agreements rather than break them unilaterally. Misunderstandings may be avoided if you write agreements down. This may just be a simple matter of writing agreed activities in your diaries. A more formal approach is writing out agreements in contract form, with or without signing them. Then you can post such contracts prominently.

Gather information

Often partners can gain enrichment in life by gathering more information about available activities. People vary greatly in how good they are at this. Possibly more attention is paid to teaching people job search information skills than leisure search information skills. Once you have identified activities you are interested in, you may then require information as to what they involve, how difficult or easy it is to learn them, and what facilities there are in your locality for participating in them.

> Lynette and Wayne, a couple in their late 20s, think they might enjoy playing tennis. Neither has played much tennis in the past. They decide to gather information systematically about the following: where are the private and public courts in the area and how good they are; the charges and reputations of the tennis clubs that have good courts; and who are the good coaches in the area and how much they charge. Sources of information about where and how good the local tennis courts are include: the classified section of the telephone directory, phoning the council, getting in touch with national or local tennis associations, looking at maps of the area, asking friends and acquaintances and going along and seeing the different facilities. Lynette and Wayne apply the same systematic information gathering skills to finding out about tennis clubs and coaches.

Develop skills for specific activities

Some joint activities, like walking, you can do without assistance. However, there are many other activities that are more enjoyable both functionally and socially if you possess a certain level of skill. Examples abound of shared activities that require a commitment to attaining a certain level of performance to gain full enjoyment from them: for instance, bridge, craft activities and most out-door sports. Continuing the above example, Lynette and Wayne decided that they would find tennis more enjoyable if they took some tennis lessons together. To do this, they joined a tennis club that had a combination of reasonable fees, good courts and a strongly recommended coach. They were reasonably confident that, once their tennis improved, they possessed the socializing skills to integrate into the club. Like Lynette and Wayne, you and your partner may need to put in the time and effort to develop the skills of specific activities. In addition, each of you needs to maintain a minimum level of skills for your mutual enjoyment.

Partners can help each other develop skills for shared activities. When learning a new skill you can offer support to and practise with each other. Sometimes, one of you already has an existing interest, for example folk dancing, in which you can help your partner. Where there are obvious imbalances in domestic duties, by pulling more of his or her weight the less domestically active partner can free up the other partner's time and energy to develop specific skills.

Develop socializing as a couple skills

Some couples find that, for various reasons, their social life becomes increasingly restricted. Sometimes this restriction reflects either or both partners possessing deficits in their time management and activity scheduling skills. Partners may also restrict their social life when there are serious difficulties in their relationship. However, on other occasions, a restricted social life may be due to such factors as moving house or country, language difficulties, parenting responsibilities and shortage of money.

Partners enter relationships with previous friendships and commitments. You may decide to socialize together with some of these people, socialize separately with others, and see much less of the remainder. In addition, partners require skills of networking and making new friends. While retaining your individuality, partners need to socialize as a couple. For example, you require the skills of preparing and serving food and drink. Also, partners require conversational skills that support and enhance one another, for example bringing the other into the conversation, knowing when to keep quiet and retrieving mistakes. In most social relationships, be careful about seeming to criticize one another and making intimate disclosures (Argyle & Henderson, 1985). However, partners who develop genuinely close relationships with other individuals or couples may feel safe in talking more openly about their relationship.

Be rewarding to each other

Partners are more likely to continue being companions if each finds what you do together to be rewarding. You can reward each other by making many shared activities fun. For instance, you can use humour to see the funny side of situations, tell jokes and stories and clown about. You can show enjoyment at each other's pleasure and achievements. Also, you can express appreciation for each other's companionship. In addition, you can be a receptive audience as you share thoughts and feelings about what you do.

Some partners may need to develop some of the above skills. All partners need to maintain them. Also, when relationships run into trouble, partners can go some way to repairing your relationship by relearning how to have fun together again. One approach is to try to recapture some of the magic from fun things you did when courting.

Assertively request and decline companionship

Do not expect your partner to be an expert mind-reader of how much and what sort of companionship you want. Ineffective ways of requesting companionship include silence, whingeing, nagging and becoming aggressive. It is preferable to specifically, tactfully and, if appropriate, firmly and persistently request what you want. In addition, you can provide your partner with feedback that improves the kind of companionship he or she already offers: for instance, what kind of affection you like receiving in public.

Partners can also assertively set limits on the amount of companionship they are willing to provide. When Kylie's husband Kim retired, she became frustrated with his always wanting her to be available to do things with and for him. She saw herself as being placed in an unwanted mothering role to a dependent child. Accordingly, she set limits on what she was prepared to do. In addition, Kylie encouraged Kim to develop some interests of his own and share more of the domestic chores.

Sometimes, you may need to decline requests to attend events or participate in specific activities that you do not enjoy. Lazarus (1985) gives the example of Fred and Kay, whom he was seeing for marital therapy. A problem in their relationship centred around attendance at cocktail parties, which Kay loved and Fred hated. Fred had no objection to Kay going to cocktail parties on her own. Once, Kay addressed her anxiety about how she could explain Fred's absence by her side, both she and Fred found a new found freedom that spread to other areas of their relationship. Compromise, whereby you limit the number of football matches or cocktail parties you go to, is another way of assertively setting limits on companionship. Alternatively, you may trade presence or absence of companionship at football matches for presence or absence of companionship at cocktail parties (McKay, Fanning, & Paleg, 1994).

Develop your own and support your partner's personal space activities

Many of the action skills discussed above – for instance, managing time and gathering information – are relevant to developing your own personal space activities. Partners can also support each other in gaining and maintaining enrichment from personal activities. For instance, you can be a sounding board for your partner's ideas about engaging in new activities; support them in taking the first steps to learn new activities, either on their own or with others; do domestic chores to free up their time for personal interests, for instance preparing a meal when your partner has an evening class; be an audience for their achievements, such as attending their amateur dramatics presentations; and share their enjoyment and frustrations. You can also respect your partner's wishes to set some limits on talking about what they are doing. Showing support and interest differs from being nosy. Your partner may request some emotional privacy along with space for personal activities.

CHAPTER HIGHLIGHTS

- Partners can be good leisure companions to each other both inside and outside the home. There is some evidence that men enjoy more leisure time than women.

- Both togetherness, doing things together, and personal space, doing things on your own, are important. Partners' companionship patterns can become too fused or too distant.

- Partners may improve the quality of their relationship by engaging in more shared pleasant activities. Suggestions are made for home-based and outside the home companionship activities.

• Partners individually and jointly need to own responsibility for finding meaning in their companionship activities.

• You may need to become more in touch with feelings relevant to companionship: for instance, wanting fun, feeling stressed and enjoying being together.

• Use coping self-talk consisting of calming, coaching and affirming self-statements to help you engage in companionship activities.

• You may have rigid personal and relationship rules that interfere with companionship. Identify, dispute and restate such rules so that they become more realistic.

• You require accuracy in how you perceive yourself as a companion and how you perceive your partner's companionship preferences and attempts to provide companionship for you.

• You can offer inaccurate explanations for providing too little or insufficiently good companionship. In addition, you can offer inadequate explanations for not trying to change an unsatisfactory level of companionship.

• You may need to become more realistic in predicting the losses from maintaining your present companionship behaviour and the gains from changing it.

• Couples who are dissatisfied with the level of companionship in their relationship can review possible companionship activities and set realistic goals for participating in chosen activities.

• Visualizing skills for companionship activities include: imagining different possibilities, mental relaxation and mental rehearsal.

• Partners may need to manage their work time more effectively to free up and coordinate time for companionship.

• Partners require skills of scheduling domestic chores, shared pleasant activities and personal space.

• When starting and developing a shared activity, you may require skills of systematically gathering information. Also, often you need to develop and maintain skills for specific activities.

• Some couples can improve their socializing as a couple skills: for instance, making joint friends, preparing food and drink and supporting and enhancing one another.

• Partners can bring humour and fun into their time together. Also, they can express appreciation for one another's companionship.

• As well as assertively requesting companionship, you may need to assertively decline companionship. Reasons for declining companionship include activities you do not enjoy and assisting your partner to avoid dependency on you.

• As well as developing your joint activities, you require skills of developing your own personal activities and supporting your partner in developing his or hers.

EXERCISES
EXERCISE 13.1
IDENTIFY AND CHOOSE COMPANIONSHIP AND PERSONAL SPACE ACTIVITIES
Instructions

This exercise assumes you are in a relationship. Complete Part A on your own and Part B with your partner.

Part A
Identify activities

Companionship activities

1. Using the following rating scale:

0 no good as a companionship activity
1 I do or would enjoy this as a companionship activity
2 I do or would very much enjoy this as a companionship activity

a. rate each item in Table 13.1 Illustrative home-based companionship activities, and
b. rate each item in Table 13.2 Illustrative outside the home companionship activities.

2. For each activity you rated 1 or 2, estimate how many times you engaged in it in the past week.

3. How satisfied are you with your current pattern and frequency of companionship activities?

Personal space activities

1. Using the following rating scale:

0 no good as a personal space activity
1 I do or would enjoy this as a personal space activity
2 I do or would very much enjoy this as a personal space activity

a. rate each home-based item in Table 13.1 that you would prefer to do on your own, at least sometimes, and
b. rate each outside the home item in Table 13.2 that you would prefer to do on your own, at least sometimes.

2. For each activity in Tables 13.1 and 13.2 you rated 1 or 2, estimate how many times you engaged in it in the past week.

3. How satisfied are you with your current pattern and frequency of personal space activities?

Part B
Choose activities

1. Share and discuss your answers to both sections of Part A of this exercise.

2. Share and discuss your views on the balance of togetherness and personal space in your relationship.

3. Share and discuss your views on the balance of home-based and outside the home companionship and personal space activities in your relationship.

4. Discuss how, if at all, you might increase the satisfaction each of you can obtain from existing or new companionship activities. If appropriate, choose new companionship activities and drop or lessen some current activities.

5. Discuss how, if at all, you might increase the satisfaction each of you can obtain from existing or new personal space activities. If appropriate, choose new personal space activities and drop or lessen some current activities.

6. Together develop a step-by-step plan to initiate and/or develop during the next week or month one companionship activity.

7. Either individually or together, develop a plan to initiate and/or develop during the next week or month one personal space activity each.

EXERCISE 13.2
DEVELOP THINKING SKILLS FOR COMPANIONSHIP
Instructions

This exercise assumes you are in a relationship. Complete Part A on your own and Part B with your partner.

Part A
My thinking skills

Thinking skills

Following are nine thinking skills.
Own responsibility for choosing
Get in touch with my feelings
Use coping self-talk
Choose realistic rules
Choose to perceive accurately
Explain cause accurately
Predict realistically
Set realistic goals
Use visualizing skills

Offering companionship

1. Assess your thinking skills deficits.

2. Identify your main deficit or deficits and specify the steps you intend taking to change it/them.

Receiving companionship

1. Assess your thinking skills deficits.

2. Identify your main deficit or deficits and specify the steps you intend taking to change it/them.

Developing personal space activities

1. Assess your thinking skills deficits.

2. Identify your main deficit or deficits and specify the steps you intend taking to change it/them.

Part B
Working together

1. Share and discuss your answers to Part A.

2. Focus on your interactive pattern of companionship and examine how you influence one another through your feelings, thoughts and actions.

3. Identify your main thinking skills deficits, if any, in developing and maintaining an effective companionship pattern and specify the steps you intend taking to change it/them.

EXERCISE 13.3
DEVELOP ACTION SKILLS FOR COMPANIONSHIP
Instructions

This exercise assumes you are in a relationship. Do Part A on your own and Part B with your partner.

Part A
My action skills for companionship

1. Assess your strengths and deficits in each of the following action skills for companionship.
Managing time effectively
Scheduling activities and abiding by contracts
Gathering information
Developing skills for specific activities
Socializing as a couple skills
Being rewarding to each other

Assertively requesting and declining companionship
Developing your own and supporting your partner's personal space activities

2. If appropriate, identify one or more of your companionship skills deficits and develop a plan to change how you act. In your plan specify:

a. your goals, including a time frame,

b. the steps you intend taking to attain each of your goals, and

c. how you will monitor your progress.

Part B
Working together

1. Share and discuss your answers to Part A of this exercise.

2. If appropriate, identify one or more of your companionship skills deficits and develop a plan to work together to change how you act. In your plan, specify:

a. your joint goals, including a time frame,

b. the steps you as a couple intend taking to attain each of your joint goals, and

c. how you will jointly monitor your progress.

EXERCISE 13.4
GROUP DISCUSSION: COMPANIONSHIP SKILLS
Instructions

This is intended as a group exercise, though it may be done individually or in pairs. For each part:

1. spend 10–15 minutes answering the question in groups of three or four,

2. each sub-group shares its findings with the whole group,

3. then the whole group ranks the six most important skills from the most important to the least important.

Part A
Offering companionship

List the six most important skills people can use in offering companionship to a partner.

Part B
Receiving companionship

List the six most important skills people can use in receiving companionship from a partner.

Part C
Personal space activities

List the six most important skills that partners can use in developing personal space activities in their relationship.

FOURTEEN
Sexual Relating Skills

Nature knows no indecencies:
man invents them.

Mark Twain

CHAPTER QUESTIONS

- *How can sexual relating be defined?*

- *What are some functions of sex in close relationships?*

- *What does being a sexual person mean?*

- *What is sexual equality?*

- *What is the sexual response cycle?*

- *What are some helpful and harmful feelings associated with sexual relating?*

- *What are some thinking skills for sexual relating?*

- *What are some positions for heterosexual intercourse?*

- *What are some other sexual activities?*

- *What are some conditions surrounding most sexual activity?*

- *What are some communication skills for sexual relating?*

- *What are sexual problems and dysfunctions?*

- *What is sex therapy?*

All people are sexual from birth. Every person possesses the capacity for sexual feelings, fantasies, thoughts and behaviours. However, for humans sex involves more than 'doin' what comes natur'lly'. When growing up you learned sexual relating skills strengths and deficits. Furthermore, you can maintain your deficits at your own and others' expense. Noted sex researchers William Masters and Virginia Johnson observe that: 'Half of all American marriages are troubled by some form of sexual distress ranging from disinterest and boredom to outright sexual dysfunction' (Masters, Johnson & Kolodny, 1986, p. 440). Probably, in the mid 1990s, Australasian and British levels of sexual dissatisfaction approximate the above American figure. Sexual relating is fraught with pleasures and difficulties: for instance, each of you may have different sexual appetites and tastes. In addition, sexual relating takes place in the context of your overall relationship in which numerous other skills are important: for instance, trust, caring, intimacy and companionship skills.

Defining sexual relating

In its most basic form sexual relating is a physical activity involving mutual genital contact for the purpose of procreating the species. Other terms for this activity are sexual intercourse, copulation, having sex and a four-letter word for intercourse ending in the letter k – if you think it is 'talk', then you are wrong! However, sexual intercourse is far from the only kind of sex act: others include kissing, finger tipping and masturbating. Also, numerous behaviours are sexual, but do not constitute specific sex acts: for instance, flirting, dating and having romantic dinners. Furthermore, the whole of your body can be viewed as an erogenous zone, not just your genitals (Kassorla, 1980).

Sensual relating is a broader way than specifically sexual relating to view how you can integrate sex and physical contact into your relationship. Sensuality refers to the bodily senses as distinguished from the intellect. In sensual relating, you relate to each other as physical persons through your five senses of sight, sound, smell, touch and taste. Ideally, you feel comfortable with your body and with sharing its physical and psychological warmth with your partner. You do not relegate touching to erotic situations. Instead, daily you express your need for physical contact and tenderness by affectionate kissing, hugging, stroking, touching, hand holding and lying in each other's arms. Sexual relating is likely to be stronger if you can develop it in the context of a good sensual relationship. Glasser (1995) makes a similar point when he writes: 'I am convinced that lovemaking is a twenty-four-hour-a-day activity. It is expressed throughout the day by loving touches; warm caring looks; little kindnesses; intimate conversations; and cuddling' (p. 95).

Functions of sexual relating

In heterosexual relationships, sexual relating has procreational, relational and recreational functions (Masters, Johnson & Kolodny, 1986). The procreational function is that of conceiving children. The relational function has many dimensions. For instance, effective sexual relating can promote family stability and lessen the likelihood of infidelity. With or without children, sex can bring partners closer together through the pleasure bond (Masters & Johnson, 1970). Good sex affirms partners physically, psychologically and, some would say, spiritually. Effective sexual relating represents a deep and continuing expression of trust, caring, intimacy and companionship. Furthermore, it demonstrates partners' cooperation to produce mutually rewarding experiences (Argyle, 1991).

Sexual relating is also recreational. Sex can be a means whereby partners get away from the daily cares and concerns of work and domestic lives. Comfort (1993) observes that 'sex is the most important form of adult play' (p. 130). Sex can be fun and games. You can be spontaneous, creative and cut through social facades. You can laugh and be merry as you release and enjoy your own and each other's 'erotic child' (Kassorla, 1980).

Being a sexual person

Just as you are unable to form a good intimate relationship with another unless you can form a good intimate relationship with yourself, unless you are comfortable with yourself as a sexual person, you are unlikely to have a good sexual relationship with another. Comfort with your own sexuality allows you to explore your own and your partner's sensuality without the constraints of what is 'acceptable' for the different sexes. What feels good for both of you is what you do, not what society tells you to do.

The most fundamental level of being a sexual person is the so called animal level. You accept your bodily functioning and impulses without unnecessary inhibitions. You are comfortable with your body and with allowing another person to have intimate knowledge of it. Your sexuality is part of a sensual approach to life and is not compartmentalized only for use in the bedroom. You possess a positive body image regarding your overall shape, form and size (Slade, 1994). Also, you accept and feel positively about the shape, form and size of your genitals, breasts and other sexual characteristics.

You are responsive to the flow of sexual experiencing, arousal, tenderness and affection within you. However, you can choose whether and when to act on these feelings and achieve release 'through masturbation, intercourse, or any mutually acceptable caress that couples exchange' (Masters & Johnson, 1970, p. 279). You are aware of your sexual fantasies. You can choose whether or not to ruminate over your fantasies, share them or act on them. You possess sexual attitudes and beliefs that are appropriately conducive to the procreational, relational and recreational dimensions of sex. You are capable of emotional commitment and of transcending yourself as you fuse love for another with sexual activity (Maslow, 1970). You are knowledgeable about engaging in mutually satisfying sex and capable of acting on this knowledge with a suitable partner.

The above is an idealized statement of what being a sexual person entails. The aim of this chapter is to help you further develop skills for affirming yourself and your partner through your sexuality.

Sexual equality

Though with obvious differences, anatomically males and female bodies are very alike. In terms of their sexual functioning, men and women are also 'incredibly and consistently similar' (Masters & Johnson, 1970, p. 38). However, women's capacity to respond to sexual stimulation is far greater than that of men and men are far more fertile than women. Emotionally females and males are also very similar. Both are highly sexual. For example, in an American study of the early years of marriage, sexual satisfaction was at least as important to wives as to husbands (Henderson-King & Veroff, 1994). The idea of the passive female who lies on her back with the male on top of her aggressively thrusting is a gross stereotype of the range of feelings of which each sex is capable.

In all cultures, males and females are subject to sex-role conditioning. Sexual knowledge (or lack of it) and attitudes towards sensual and sexual pleasure are two key areas where males and females can receive different sexual socialization. For example, males more than females may be socialized to be sexual rather than sensual (Watters, Askwith, Cohen, & Lamont, 1985). In Australia, Britain and North America sex-role conditioning has led to many women feeling that they are second-class citizens. Often in the past, women's potential for sexual arousal and pleasure was viewed by both sexes as less than that of males. Also, women's wishes in regard to sex were sometimes viewed as less important. Alberti and Emmons (1990) list the following among characteristics of sexually non-assertive females: passivity, misguided compassion, silence and suffering, giving in, doing your duty and manipulation.

However, males too have not escaped unscathed from their sex-role conditioning. Jokingly, young males have been observed to need four items to measure their sexual prowess: a ruler, for the length of their penis; a piece of string, for its thickness; a clock, for how long they can delay ejaculating; and a counter, for how many times they get 'it'. Many males accept too much responsibility for the success of sexual encounters. Also, frequently male socialization generates counter-productive expectations and anxieties about sexual performance. Furthermore, many males have experienced difficulty in expressing vulnerability, affection and tenderness. Alberti and Emmons (1990) list the following among characteristics of sexually non-assertive and/or aggressive males: silence, lack of emotion, insulation, control, machismo, inflexibility, exploitation and score keeping.

Increasingly, there is a trend towards sexual equality (Masters, Johnson & Kolodny, 1986). Sex is recognized as something that partners do *with* each other for their mutual gratification rather than something that is done *to* or *for* the other partner. Both males and females need to develop as sexual persons and to accept responsibility for the success of their sexual encounters. Each sex requires sensitivity to their own and their partner's unique erotic capabilities and preferences. Both sexes require openness, honesty, patience, concern, compassion, confidence, playfulness, gentleness, strength and also one another's help. Sexual equality entails each sex in acknowledging their right to be treated with respect and sensitivity and their responsibility to treat their partner the same way. In short, sexual equality challenges you to build a cooperative partnership for your mutual pleasure.

A few words regarding those of you in homosexual relationships. The comments on relational and recreational sex apply to you as does the section on developing yourselves as sexual persons. Because you are in same sex relationships, some of the comments on sexual equality problems in heterosexual relationships have less relevance. However, all the above comments about desirable aspects of sexual equality apply to homosexual as well as to heterosexual relationships.

THE SEXUAL RESPONSE CYCLE

The following reviews of the sexual response cycle assume basic knowledge of sexual anatomy. Readers wishing more information about sexual anatomy are referred to books by Masters, Johnson & Kolodny (1986), Kaplan (1987), Comfort (1993) and Litvinoff (1992).

Masters and Johnson's version

Masters and Johnson studied by means of direct laboratory observation over 10,000 episodes of sexual activity in 382 women and 312 men. They found that human sexual response was a cycle with four phases: excitement, plateau, orgasm and resolution (Masters, Johnson & Kolodny, 1986). The phases are not always discrete and can vary considerably between people and with one person at different times. The physiology of sexual response is the same for males and females, be they heterosexual or homosexual. Two basic physiological reactions occur during the sexual response cycle. The first is vasocongestion, in which the amount of blood concentrated in the body tissues of both sexes' genitals and the female breasts increases. The second is increased neuromuscular tension or myotonia, in which there is a build up of energy in the nerves and muscles throughout the body.

Excitement phase

Humans get aroused through touching and feeling, sexy thoughts and fantasies, hearing romantic music and smelling body odours. Vaginal lubrication is the main sign of sexual excitation in the female. The walls of her vagina secrete moisture. As lubrication increases the fluid sometimes flows out of her vagina moistening her vaginal opening. Women vary in the quantity, consistency and odour of their vaginal lubrication. The amount of vaginal lubrication does not necessarily indicate level of sexual arousal and readiness for intercourse. Other female excitement responses include: enlargement of the diameter of the vagina's inner lips, increased size of the clitoris and, for most women, erect nipples.

Erection of the penis is the main sign of physical erection in the male. The penis becomes harder, thicker and points outwards or upwards. Other male excitement responses include: the smoothing out of the scrotum, the testes being partly drawn towards the body, and, for some men, erect nipples.

For both males and females, the build up of excitement can vary in time and intensity with the occasion. Also, excitement can be dampened or reversed through distractions, for instance, a door knock or a tactless remark. Alternatively, either or both partners may choose to reverse the excitement phase with or without then choosing to return to it.

Plateau phase

In the plateau phase high levels of sexual excitement are maintained and set the stage for orgasm. The word plateau is somewhat inaccurate since for both sexes neruromuscular tension generally increases, particularly in the buttocks and thighs. In addition, hearts beat more rapidly, blood pressure heightens and breathing quickens.

During the plateau phase in women, vasocongestion causes the opening of the vagina to narrow by 30 per cent or more. This narrowing of the outer vagina or orgasmic platform provides for a tighter grip of the penis. The clitoris pulls back against the pubic bone and this change, combined with the vasocongestion occurring in the vaginal lips, causes the clitoris to retreat under its hood. The vagina's inner lips enlarge greatly, doubling or even tripling in thickness. The breast size of women who have not nursed a child increases markedly. However, for women who have breast fed a child, increase in breast size is either less pronounced or non-existent. In about half to three quarters of women and about a quarter of men, a sex flush starts late in the excitement stage or early in the plateau stage. This spotty skin colour change generally begins just below the breastbone and then spreads rapidly over the breasts and front of the chest.

For males, during the plateau phase, their testes continue to elevate, though for men over fifty full elevation may not be attained. With some males, small amounts of clear fluid or 'pre-cum' come from the tip of the penis.

Unwanted distractions may deter both males and females from maintaining the plateau phase. Alternatively, as part of relaxed and gourmet love-making, partners may choose to reverse and then rekindle this phase.

Orgasm phase

Climax and coming are other words for orgasm. Orgasms last for a few seconds and consist of rhythmic muscular contractions followed by rapid relaxation. Psychologically orgasm is usually a time of intense pleasure. However, the intensity of and degree of satisfaction derived from orgasms varies between people and across different occasions for the same person.

For females, orgasm is characterized by simultaneous rhythmic contractions of the uterus, the outer vagina (orgasmic platform), and anal sphincter. Mild orgasms may have three to five contractions and intense orgasms ten to fifteen. As orgasm continues the contractions diminish in force and frequency. Most women do not ejaculate during orgasm. Unlike males, if restimulated, females are capable of further orgasms within seconds or minutes of each other. Kassorla (1980) observes that 'a healthy woman can enjoy repeated orgasms for as long as she wants to' (p. 215). However, it is the exceptional woman who is multiorgasmic during most of her sexual activity. Some women never experience multiple orgasms and others rarely (Masters, Johnson & Kolodny, 1986).

Unlike with females, male orgasm consists of two stages. In the first stage, a series of contractions force semen into the bulb of the urethra and the man experiences a sense of ejaculatory inevitability. At this point he cannot voluntarily stop ejaculation. In the second stage, the male experiences contractions throughout his penis that cause ejaculation involving the spurting of semen or 'cum' from the tip of his penis. Initially rhythmic contractions occur at 0.8 seconds. However, after the first three or four contractions, intensity and frequency taper off. In general, men's orgasms are more uniform than women's. Usually, men take much longer than women to become orgasmic again. However, the refractory period for potent young males may be minutes rather than hours.

Resolution phase

In the resolution phase females and males return to the unaroused state. Heavy breathing and fast heart rate may continue just after orgasm, but gradually go back to normal. In addition, the sex flush disappears.

In females, during the resolution phase, the narrowing of the vaginal lips reverses, the vagina contracts in both length and diameter, the clitoris returns to its normal size and position, breasts cease being enlarged and nipples lose their tautness. During this phase, women may experience discomfort if their clitoris, vagina or nipples are stimulated.

In the resolution phase, the male erection diminishes in two stages. First, there is partial loss of erection as the orgasmic contractions cause blood to be pumped out of the penis. Second, there is a slower stage in which the penis returns to its smaller and softer normal state. During this stage, the testes decrease in size and move back into the scrotum.

American Psychiatric Association's version

Another version of the sexual response cycle is provided by the American Psychiatric Association. Here the four phases of the sexual response cycle are desire, excitement, orgasm and resolution. The desire phase 'consists of fantasies about sexual activity and the desire to have sexual activity' (American Psychiatric Association, 1994, p. 493). The APA excitement phase combines the excitement and plateau stages of the Masters and Johnson version. In both sexual response cycle versions, the orgasm and resolution phases are essentially the same.

FEELINGS ASSOCIATED WITH SEXUAL RELATING

Sexual relating is both simple and complex. Pleasure and pain can each be associated with various sex acts. However, here I focus more on helpful and harmful feelings attached to the emotional rather than to the physical side of sexual relating.

Helpful feelings

Sexual relating is a process of discovery about your own and your partner's sexuality. Ideally, both partners have sufficient confidence to be open to the challenges and changes that may arise from this process. As mentioned earlier, specific sex acts are best grounded in a sensual relationship in which you feel free to express your need for physical contact with your partner in non-sexual as well as sexual situations. Sexual relating starts with at least a flicker of sexual arousal in either or both partners. Consequently, responsiveness to your sexual impulses and wishes is helpful along with the capacity to experience another's arousal and interest in you.

Sexual relating in close relationships is based on genuine respect and love for yourself which frees you to be concerned about the growth, happiness and pleasure of your partner. You are confident and accepting about your animal nature and your body. You are strong enough to express your caring, tenderness and affection for your partner through your sexuality. Other feelings conducive to effective sexual relating include relaxation, spontaneity, playfulness, creativity, commitment to your relationship, trust of your partner, cooperative intentions, willingness to risk being vulnerable and sensitivity and compassion towards your partner's vulnerability. Also, if you and your partner are happy outside your sexual relationship, this provides a good emotional context for fulfilment inside it.

Harmful feelings

Numerous negative feelings can interfere with sexual satisfaction. For the most part, such feelings manifest debilitating aspects of anxiety. For example, you can inhibit, repress or suppress your sexual feelings when it might be more healthy for you to acknowledge and express them. Another problem is that some people's anxieties inhibit them from experimenting with new activities and talking openly to their partner about what they like. Also, you may feel inhibited by guilt feelings over imagined or real transgressions. Instead of healthy involvement you can exhibit unhealthy detachment and, possibly, fear of commitment (Colliver, 1992).

Many people's sexual relating is beset by fears concerning their emotional worth and physical attractiveness. You may allow yourself to become unnecessarily dependent on fulfilling your partner's wishes because of your self-doubts. In addition, anxieties about performance can lower rather than enhance sexual performance. Instead of relaxing and 'doin' what comes natur'lly', you can tense up and either perform too mechanically or not perform at all.

Your lack of genuine self-love may show itself in insufficient respect for your partner. For example, both males and females can use their sexuality to dominate, control and manipulate their partners. You may collude in behaviours that damage both yourself and your partner: for instance, sex acts that you find distasteful or allowing your partner to make sex conditional on your providing them with presents or other services. In addition, partners can show disrespect through undue pressure, clumsiness, unprotected sex, faking involvement, infidelity, spitefulness, aggressiveness and sexual violence. Furthermore, some people's lack of self-respect leads them to become sex addicts and compulsively treat others as objects for their gratification rather than as persons.

Negative feelings generated in other parts of your relationship can interfere with sexual relating. Masters and Johnson advise *'Don't carry anger into your bedroom'* (Masters, Johnson & Kolodny, 1986, p. 457). For some, sex becomes part of the power struggle in their relationship, with sex being withheld, demanded or conducted without sufficient tenderness. However, sometimes cooperating to have a good sexual experience helps couples feel less angry (Lazarus, 1985).

SOME THINKING SKILLS FOR SEXUAL RELATING

How humans think influences how well they perform sexually. Masters and Johnson (Masters, Johnson & Kolodny, 1986) illustrate this point by stating that inhibitions and guilt, performance anxiety, erotic boredom and blind acceptance of sexual misinformation and myths account for about 80 per cent of the sexual dissatisfaction in American society. Following are some thinking skills relevant to sexual relating.

Own responsibility for choosing

Each person is responsible for their sexual relating choices. Sexual responsibility has many components. You can choose to develop your knowledge and skills about how to relate sexually. You select with whom you have sex. Each of you can take responsibility for your own and each other's sexual satisfaction. You can choose to be faithful to your partner in a close relationship. You and your partner can choose to help one another with your sexual problems and vulnerabilities. Also, each of you can choose to take responsibility for contraception and for avoiding sexually transmitted diseases.

You are responsible for your choices regarding how you think, feel and act in sexual situations. You can choose how you think about sexual relating and the degree to which you stay sexually ignorant – this section on thinking skills highlights many common errors. While your sexual feelings and physiological reactions represent your animal nature, you can choose to develop your skills at acknowledging, expressing and managing these feelings. Also, you can choose the verbal, voice, body, touch and action messages that you send in sexual situations.

Get in touch with your feelings

How can you feel positively about sex and how can you identify your erotic likes and dislikes? People who are skilled in bed are relaxed and comfortable with their sexuality. You may have been brought up by parents either or both of whom did not demonstrate relaxed comfort with their own sexuality. In addition, many other factors contribute to feeling inhibited, for instance, religious injunctions or misinterpretations of them. Your sexual feelings are a central part of your whole being and as such require treasuring rather than repressing, inhibiting or disparaging. You may need to give yourself permission to acknowledge and value yourself as a sexual person, including the strength of your feelings. In addition, you may need to use your skills of inner listening to clear a physical and psychological space to get in touch with what you truly feel about being a sexual person rather than how others have told you to feel. Furthermore, you can use many of the other thinking skills described in this chapter to challenge negative perceptions of being a sexual person. Also you can discuss your sexuality with people who have an open and accepting attitude towards theirs. The more relaxed you are about your sexuality, the less you are likely to suffer from debilitating performance anxieties.

Masturbation is an important way that most young people explore their sexuality. Especially, if in a safe relationship, you can explore the erotic potential of your body through touch. Also, reading appropriate books on sex can guide you and your partner as you explore and experiment to get in touch with your erotic potential and preferences (Comfort, 1993; Kaplan, 1987; Litvinoff, 1992; Masters, Johnson & Kolodny, 1986).

Use coping self-talk

You can use coping self-talk to help you to act more effectively in specific sexual relating situations. For example, Glenys would like her partner Roger to spend more time stroking her clitoris and to do it more gently. Glenys currently inhibits herself by negative self-talk: for instance, 'I'm only being silly wanting more caressing down there from him', 'Roger is going to get annoyed' and 'I'm too nervous to even think of telling him.' Glenys can replace her negative self-talk with coping self-talk in which she uses calming, coaching and affirming self-statements. Sample calming self-statements include: 'Calm down', 'Relax', and 'Breathe slowly and deeply.' With coaching self-statements Glenys reminds herself how to act effectively: for example, 'Use tact and diplomacy. Tell Roger how much pleasure he gives me when he strokes my clitoris and ask him to keep doing it, but more gently.' Affirming self-statements Glenys might use include: 'I have a right to sexual fulfilment', 'Roger really wants to please me', and 'I'm capable of making my points when I need to.' Males can also use coping self-talk to help them act effectively with their partners: for instance, they may feel threatened about asking their partner to try a new position, admitting vulnerability or revealing ignorance.

Choose realistic personal rules

You and your partner may individually possess unrealistic rules that interfere with your sexual happiness. In addition, you may jointly share unrealistic rules that work against rather than for your sexual relationship. The term Ellis uses to characterize unrealistic rules and beliefs is 'musturbation' (Ellis, 1995). Others use the term 'myths' (Lazarus, 1985; Litvinoff, 1992; Montgomery & Evans, 1983). Following are some illustrative unrealistic rules, musturbations or myths. The sting of these rules is in the tail – they possess the potential to harm sexual relating.

Body image

My/my partner's body must be thin
My/my partner's breasts must be large.
My/my partner's penis must be long and thick.

Sex-roles

Men must take the initiative in sex.
Women must please men.
Women must be more faithful than men.

Sexual feelings

Men must not show tenderness.
Women must not show sexual abandonment.
I must not have negative feelings about my partner's sexual performance.

Sex acts

Women must not engage in cunnilingus (mouth–genital contact).
People must never engage in homosexual acts.
Intercourse must always be the main sexual activity.

Sexual performance

Men must be two feet long, hard as a steel and able to go all night (Zilbergeld, 1978).
Women must show pleasure whatever their partner does.
Partners must always have mutual orgasms.

Approval

I must have my partner's approval.
I must let my friends know how successful in bed I am.
I must not reveal sexual abuse in childhood.

Power and control

Women must always do what men want.
Women must never be dominant.
One partner must always be in control.

Change

My partner and I must work at sex.
Change must come quickly.
We must never discuss our sex lives with other people.

How can you overcome your unrealistic rules in regard to sex? First, you can become aware that they exist. For instance, words like 'should', 'ought' and 'must' may signal that you possess unrealistic rules. Also, negative feelings like inhibition and performance anxiety may be cues for underlying unrealistic rules. Acting in negative and self-defeating ways can also indicate rigid rules. Second you can dispute or challenge how rational the rules are. Either on your own or with your partner you can ask yourself for evidence that supports or negates the rule: for example, 'Where is the evidence that we must always have intercourse when we have sex?' and 'What might be the consequences if sometimes we have sex without having intercourse?' Third, you can restate the unrealistic rule into a more realistic version: for example, 'While we enjoy having intercourse most times we make love, we also enjoy other forms of sexual contact like stimulating each other's genitals and masturbation and do not wish to force ourselves to have intercourse every time we have sex.'

Choose to perceive accurately

Perceive sex accurately

Some people perceive sex negatively. Woody Allen jokingly says: 'Is sex dirty? Only if it's done right.' The idea that sex is evil or dirty can contribute to sexual problems and dysfunctions. Masters and Johnson (Masters, Johnson & Kolodny, 1986) observe that such attitudes are forced upon children in certain rigidly religious families. However, they stress that the religious beliefs themselves are not troublesome. An Australian study discovered that, for both males and female subjects, parents' negative attitudes in early childhood both to sex with each other and also towards their children's sexual development was associated with later sexual dysfunction (McCabe, 1994).

Females, especially may find it difficult to value their sexuality. The double standard whereby it is okay for males, but less okay for females to be open about their sexuality lingers on. In addition, partners may unthinkingly perceive specific sexual acts negatively rather than as part of the range of natural sexual activities. Furthermore, people may be intolerant of homosexual feelings, thoughts and behaviours in themselves and others. Sometimes religious beliefs can contribute to homosexual oppression and self-oppression. Despite an increasingly scientific and less moralistic approach to homosexuality, homophobia is still fairly widespread in Australasia and Britain. Often homophobic people exaggerate the importance of sex in homosexual relationships instead of perceiving its role as similar to that in heterosexual relationships, with the exception of procreation.

Perceive yourself accurately

You may be prone to negative perceptions about your body: 'Parts of my body are not attractive enough' or 'My body is not sexy enough' (Beck, 1988, p. 360). Alternatively, you may be narcissistic about your physical attractiveness perceiving yourself as god's gift to men or women. You may have an inadequate perception of yourself as a sexual person and of your unique sexual wishes and preferences. In addition, you may possess considerable misinformation about what effective sexual relating entails and not realize this. Your sexual relating skills deficits may include being demanding and critical of your partner and being excessively interested in your own pleasure. You may possess little insight into your own feelings of vulnerability and needs to prove yourself. People engage in sex with varying degrees of sexual selfishness. For example, Gary, aged 19, spends little time in stimulating his partner Kylie, 19, and thinks that love-making stops when he has had his orgasm. For her part, Kylie strives to please Gary, but inadequately acknowledges the importance of her own sexual pleasure.

For various reasons, you may be poor at owning your strengths. You may be quite skilled at love-making, but riddled with doubts about your ability to satisfy your partner. You may expend too much effort in wondering what your partner is thinking and whether or not you will let him or her down. Your 'spectatoring' of how you perform sexually interferes with spontaneity.

Perceive your partner accurately

At worst, either or both partners can perceive the other as objects for their sexual gratification rather than as persons worthy of respect. You may possess an incomplete or inaccurate picture of how to pleasure your partner. For example, you may perceive that what pleasures you is what pleasures her or him. You may inaccurately mind-read what your partner wants. You may mistakenly believe that 'sex should be good without you needing to talk about it' (Litvinoff, 1991, p. 217). Also, you may fail to take into account that your partner, not you, is the final arbiter of his or her sexual feelings and wishes. In addition, you may insufficiently attend to your partner's feelings of sexual vulnerability and preferences about the frequency, timing and location of sex.

It is possible to perceive your partner's sexual knowledge and love-making skills in too positive a light. By seeing him or her too rosily, you may disparage yourself and insufficiently acknowledge the extent to which your partner fails to fulfil your sexual needs. Some people are good at projecting an image that they are better in bed than they really are – beware of colluding in their self-deceptions.

In addition, partners can misinterpret one another's sexual behaviour. For example, if your partner masturbates or looks at erotic literature, this does not automatically mean that she or he is no longer sexually interested in you. However, if you misinterpret your partner's behaviour, you may feel inferior and find excuses for not having sex. Another example is that of partners who wrongly interpret as rejection or anger one another's not wanting sex on particular occasions.

How can you counteract inaccurate perceptions about sex, yourself and your partner? First, you can gather more sexual information through reading, talking to people and, if appropriate, attending courses and workshops. Second, you can reality-test the accuracy of your perceptions by challenging them and searching for evidence that confirms or negates them: for example, in your own mind you can test the hypothesis that you know what your partner's sexual wishes are. Third, you and your partner can increase the accuracy with which you perceive yourselves and each other by improving your sexual communication. For example, if you want your nipples caressed better, you can communicate this both verbally and by taking your partner's hand and showing him or her how to maximize your pleasure. Fourth, if your negative perceptions are resistant to change, you and your partner can seek counselling.

Explain cause accurately

You require accuracy in how you explain the cause of the adequacy of your sex life. Following are some illustrative explanations that may cause and maintain sexual problems.

• *'Sex is natural.'* You may limit your sexual performance if you rely on the explanation that good sex comes just naturally rather from knowledge and practice as well.

• *'Our relationship is not the cause.'* Sexual problems can result from difficulties and resentments in your non-sexual relationship. Partners differ in the degree to which they can compartmentalize sex from the rest of their relationship. A rule of thumb is 'The better the communication outside the bedroom, the better the sex inside it.'

• *'It's your fault.'* Each partner is responsible for their sexual fulfilment in the relationship. Frequently, blaming a partner just increases the difficulties. Overcoming sexual difficulties requires cooperation. Each partner needs to examine and, where necessary, develop their sexual relating skills.

• *'It's my fault'*. You can assume too much responsibility for your partner's sexual pleasure and orgasms. Also, you can assume too much responsibility for your own insufficient sexual fulfilment. As mentioned above, good sex is a cooperative activity in which both partners are responsible for successful outcomes.

• *'Improving our sex life is impossible.'* 'Partners may provide various reasons why improving their sex lives is impossible including: 'He/she is only interested in his/her own pleasure'; 'He/she never listens'; 'I'm naturally frigid'; 'My upbringing was too strict'; and 'It's against my religious principles.'

When you become aware that you and your partner have become stuck in a less than satisfactory sexual relationship, identify the explanations each of you offers for this state of affairs. Then challenge the explanations by searching for evidence about how true they are. For example, if you think: 'Improving our sex life is impossible because my partner is only interested in his/her own pleasure', search for specific evidence of where your partner has shown interest in promoting your sexual pleasure and not just his or her own. Also, since partners often reciprocate each other's actions, look for evidence indicating that you have shown insufficient interest in your partner's pleasure. Furthermore, ask yourself whether you have given your partner adequate feedback of your dissatisfaction with his/her behaviour. Identify specific instances where you gave such feedback and how he or she reacted. You could also ask your partner whether he or she is satisfied with your sexual relationship and is willing to try to improve it. At the end of this process, you may find that your initial explanation for the permanence of your sexual dissatisfaction no longer holds true.

Predict realistically

In many areas, partners can lessen their sexual fulfilment by inaccurately predicting the consequences of their actions. Predictions of incompetence and rejection can inhibit people from dating, courting and making marriage proposals. Also, frequently after the initial excitement of courtship and cohabitation partners decrease the amount of non-sexual sensual contact they share. Such behaviour carries two risks that partners may insufficiently acknowledge: first, making their daily relationship less rewarding and, second, providing a less affectionate emotional climate for their sexual relationship. As well as ignoring risks, such partners insufficiently acknowledge the gains from maintaining their sensual relationship.

Relaxed sex requires partners to be confident in their ability to attain a satisfactory level of performance. Predictions of unsatisfactory performance or failure are major factors in inhibitions and performance anxieties. For people with low sexual confidence, sexual relating is associated with danger and not just with pleasure. Unfortunately, predictions of sexual incompetence and failure can turn into self-fulfilling prophesies.

Sharing sexual information and secrets is another area in which a partner's erroneous predictions can interfere with sexual fulfilment. Fears about asking for what you want can mean that you never get what you want. Also, harbouring secrets about significant sexual experiences – for instance, sexual abuse, rape, homosexual experience or an affair – can intrude upon the emotional trust and openness desirable for genuine sexual intimacy.

Avoiding unwanted pregnancies and sexually transmitted diseases is an important area where sexual partners need accurately predict consequences. Often this is a matter of predicting the consequences of antecedent behaviours, such as consuming alcohol, that create vulnerability to lapses in sexual judgement.

Partners can systematically assess the realism of their predictions. Such an assessment entails looking at gains as well as at risks or losses. For example, you could ask yourself: 'What are the gains of telling my partner what I want sexually?' as well as 'What are the risks of telling him or her?' If you are prone to catastrophic predictions, you can assess your recovery skills when faced with worst-case scenarios. You may be a stronger person than you initially think. Often, the best way to assess a prediction is to act and then assess the consequences: for example, telling your partner what you want sexually and then seeing how he or she reacts. On many occasions, you may need to develop specific skills – for instance how to pleasure yourself and another person – so that you can feel sexually confident.

Set realistic goals

What are realistic goals for sexual relating? Each couple has to negotiate its own unique sex life and decide what goals work best for them. Frequency of sexual relating is one area in which partners' goals may be unrealistic – their targets may be uncomfortably high. Frequency of sex can guarantee neither sexual satisfaction nor relationship satisfaction.

Following are some findings on frequency of sex that take age into account. Masters and Johnson observed that, in their 20s and 30s, the average American married couple had intercourse two or three times a week, after which frequency slowly declined until, past age 50, frequency of intercourse was once a week or less (Masters, Johnson & Kolodny, 1986).

In a British national survey of nearly 20,000 respondents aged 16–59, sex was defined as vaginal intercourse, oral sex or anal sex (Wellings, Field, Johnson & Wadsworth, 1994). For both males and females, the median of the distribution never exceeded five acts of heterosexual sex in the last four weeks (the median divides a set of values, in this case heterosexual sex acts, into two groups of equal size – half of the values are larger and half are smaller than the median). An indication of how frequency of sex acts varied is shown in the 95th centile (95 per cent reporting less frequency) being 20 for males and 25 for females. Frequency of sex varied substantially with age for both males and females, ranging from a median of five acts per month for women aged 20–29 and for men aged 30–34, thereafter declining to a median of two for men aged 55–59, with more than 50 per cent of women in this age group reporting no sex acts in the last four weeks.

Partners may also set unrealistic goals for quality as well as quantity of sex. They may expect each sex act to be sheer ecstasy in the context of romantic bliss. The goal of mutual orgasms every love-making session is a clear example of unrealistic expectations setting partners up for disappointment. Even if very skilled at sexual relating, sometimes you will be more in the mood, better able to excite your partner, and more fulfilled than others.

Use visualizing skills

Sexual fantasies are an important part of being a sexual person. Women and men 'are more similar than different in their sexual fantasy patterns' (Masters, Johnson & Kolodny, 1986, p. 280). Frequently, sexual images are extremely X-rated (Britain) or R-rated (Australia) and incorporate ideas that would seem unusual in everyday discourse. If shared or enacted, the content of your fantasies might land you in gaol, get you fired or lead to your face being slapped. The range of content of sexual fantasies is almost limitless. The imagery can differ in vividness and the action can be explicit or vague. The time can be the past, present or future. Common themes in sexual fantasies include: experimentation with different sexual acts and experiences; seduction and conquest; having sex with different partners; participating in group sex; watching others have sex; being a rape victim or victimizer; idyllic encounters; and sadomasochism.

Sexual fantasies can have many positive functions (Comfort, 1993; Kassorla, 1980; Litvinoff, 1992; Masters, Johnson & Kolodny, 1986). Your sexual fantasies can show you what turns you on. You can try out different sexual activities in your mind to see how arousing they are. Also, before you initiate sexual contact, you can arouse your sexual appetite by tuning into existing fantasies or creating new ones. During sex, you can use fantasy to enhance arousal, increase the attractiveness of your partner and relieve boredom (Tokatlidis & Over, 1995). Also, you can imagine what it would be like to experiment with different activities here-and-now. Such fantasies may lead to more creativity, variety, spontaneity and fun. In addition, some people find it arousing if they share and listen to their partner sharing sexual fantasies external to their relationship, including fantasies about having sex with other people (Friday, 1973). Comfort (1993) writes: 'Infantile, symbolic, fetishistic and generally wild fantasies are part of love, and only a problem if they take up too much time and start spoiling the reciprocity of sex' (p. 141). However, when considering sharing or actually sharing your fantasies, take your partner's feelings and sensitivities into account.

You can use visualizing to help you perform more competently. Lazarus (1984) offers the following basic rule: '*If you wish to accomplish something in reality, first picture yourself achieving it in imagination.*' (p. 73). He states that when impotent males and non-orgasmic women imagine themselves engaging in enjoyable and passionate sex, a transfer to real love-making soon follows. You can also use visualizing to rehearse and practise engaging in new sexual activities: for example, fellatio or cunnilingus. Other uses of sexual fantasies include: aiding masturbation, especially if on your own; acting as a safety valve for non-socially sanctioned impulses; and providing what in many instances is a harmless and pleasant way of passing the time.

Sexual fantasies have the potential for harm as well as good. For instance, you can exist in a Walter Mitty world of sexual fantasy, without assuming the risk of real relationships. Also, even during intercourse, you can imagine having sex with people other than your partner as a way of distancing yourself from working on problems in your relationship. In addition, it is an invasion of your partner's privacy to force her or him to listen to your sexual fantasies unwillingly. An even more serious abuse of fantasy is as a prelude to being sexually violent towards your partner.

SEXUAL ACTIVITIES

This is the game of twenty toes
It's played all over town.
Some play it with their toes turned up
Others with their toes turned down.

Anonymous

In close relationships, partners' sexual activity forms part of their broader emotional and sensual relationship. When relating sexually, ideally partners are responsive to the flow of their own and one another's feelings. They think about how best to give pleasure as well as how to receive it. In addition, their actions enhance and affirm their own and their partner's pleasure and well-being.

Sexual intercourse

Heterosexual intercourse involves the male penetrating the female's vagina with his erect penis and thrusting back and forth. There are numerous positions for 'making love' – lying down, sitting, standing up and so on. I now mention five of the more usual positions. Partners can use more than one position during a single love-making session.

• *Man lying on top, face to face.* This 'missionary position' is probably the most commonly used position in Australasia and Britain. The woman lies on her back with her legs spread somewhat apart. She can also bend her knees or wrap her legs around her partner. Also, she can caress him. An advantage of this position is that partners can look at each other and kiss. For couples wanting children, another advantage is that this position gives the best chance of conception. Disadvantages include the difficulty of manually stimulating the clitoris and the man's weight sometimes being too heavy.

• *Woman lying on top, face to face.* Here the woman possesses more control over the timing and depth of her partner's thrusting. However, the man may find it less easy to thrust. Partners can look into each other's eyes and kiss. Since the man does not need to support himself, his hands are free for stroking the woman's breasts, genitals or other parts of her body.

• *Woman sitting on top, face to face.* Here the woman has even more control of the tempo and penetration of the man's thrusting than when lying on top. Partners can see more of each other and play with one another's chests or breasts. In addition, either partner can manually stimulate the clitoris. Mouth to mouth kissing is still possible, if wanted. This position can be used in the later stages of pregnancy.

• *Lying side to side, face to face.* The side by side position gives partners much opportunity to caress and hug one another. Neither partner carries the other's weight. Disadvantages include insufficient leverage for active penile thrusting and the greater likelihood of the penis coming out of the vagina than in other positions.

• *Rear entry, woman kneeling or lying down*. With rear entry 'doggy style', the man inserts his penis from behind into the woman's vagina as she kneels. The woman may have her back horizontal or sloping downwards. Some people object to the sheer animality of this position, but others find it exciting. Alternatively, rear entry may take place with the partners lying on their sides, the so called 'spoon position'. During pregnancy some women find the spoon position especially satisfactory. In rear entry positions, eye contact and mouth to mouth kissing are difficult. However, usually the man can manually stimulate his partner's clitoris or breasts.

In addition to penile–vaginal intercourse, partners may engage in anal sex. Stimulation of either sex's anus can be done manually, by using one or more fingers, or orally. Penile–anal intercourse is far from being restricted to male homosexuals (Masters, Johnson & Kolodny, 1986). However, some heterosexuals look upon this activity negatively. In addition, penile–anal intercourse can be physically painful for the receiving partner. If vaginal penetration is to follow anal penetration, always wash the penis thoroughly to avoid transmitting germs into the vagina.

Touching

Touching has many functions before, during and after sexual activity. Already, I have stressed the importance of maintaining a sensual relationship independent of sex. Before sexual activity, touch can be a 'turn-on' message about your willingness to engage in sex. During sexual activity, touch can both affirm your love and tenderness for one another as well as stimulate and excite. In addition, partners can use touch to communicate how they like to receive pleasure. After sexual activity, you can enjoy the warmth and closeness of one another's bodies.

There are many dimensions of touch. The intention of touch can be passionate or companionate. You and your partner may actively touch each other simultaneously or in turns. Your touches can be exploratory, focused or somewhere in between. Touch can be gentle or strong – here it is important to take your partner's wishes into consideration. The target of touch can be different parts of the body and not just the genitals: for example, nipples, hair and ear lobes. You can regard all of the body as an erogenous zone. Apart from lying together, cuddling or hugging your partner with your arms, legs or both, the main ways of touching one another are with your mouth and hands (Litvinoff, 1992).

• *Touching with your mouth*. Methods of touching that involve the mouth include kissing one another's lips, kissing with open mouth, kissing and exploring one another's mouth with your tongues, licking, sucking, nibbling, biting and blowing.

• *Touching with your hands*. Methods of touching that involve the hands include caressing with your finger tips, stroking, rubbing, scratching, holding, squeezing, patting, smacking, kneading, massaging and tickling.

Partners can touch each other in oral–genital sex. The term 'cunnilingus' is used for oral stimulation of the female genitals. The term 'fellatio' is used for oral stimulation of the man's genitals. The term 'soixante neuf', French for 69, is used for partners simultaneously engaging in oral–genital stimulation.

Masturbation

Masturbation is variously described as genital self-stimulation, producing an orgasm by genital self-stimulation and any act of sexual self-stimulation regardless of whether it involves the genitals and orgasm. Other parts of the body used for self-pleasuring include the nipples, breasts, inner thighs and anus.

The most common form of female masturbation is lying on her back and manually stroking her clitoris, mons or vaginal lips. However, other women prefer to masturbate when lying on their stomachs. Some women rub their genitals against objects such as pillows. Few women masturbate by inserting something into their vaginas. An increasing number of women use hand-held vibrators to enhance their pleasure. The most common form of male masturbation is rubbing one hand up and down the shaft of his penis with increasingly rapid movements until ejaculation.

Attitudes towards masturbation have changed radically over the past century. Thomas Szasz observes: 'Masturbation, the primary sexual activity of mankind. In the nineteenth century, it was a disease; in the twentieth century, it's a cure' (Szasz, 1973, p. 10). Masturbation is an important way that young people can explore and experience themselves as sexual persons. Also, as suggested above by Szasz, masturbation is used as part of sex therapy for helping people become more relaxed with their sexuality.

In close relationships, sometimes partners masturbate, either solo or simultaneously, as part of their love making. Such masturbation may turn one another on. Alternatively, though not a strict use of the term, partners can masturbate one another. In addition, there may be occasions when partners masturbate alone without harming their relationship. Examples are when one of the partners is absent or ill or where great differences exist in partners' sexual appetites. In one American survey, 72 per cent of young married husbands masturbated with an average frequency of about 24 times a year, and 68 per cent of young wives masturbated, averaging ten times per year (Masters, Johnson & Kolodny, 1986).

Masturbation has dangers as well as advantages. Some people use masturbation as a way of avoiding the risks of entering genuine relationships. Also, partners in close relationships may masturbate instead of trying to improve their sex lives together. In addition, sometimes people accompany masturbation with depraved and degrading fantasies which they later enact in real life.

Conditions for sexual activity

Numerous variations exist in the conditions for sexual activity. Partners' preferences may be similar or different. Variety is also important. Sometimes an analogy is made with eating: sexual appetite can be satisfied in various ways and eating the same food all the time becomes monotonous (Comfort, 1993; Litvinoff, 1992; Masters, Johnson & Kolodny, 1986).

- *In the mood.* For sex to occur, at least one partner must start somewhat in the mood.

If the other partner is not initially in the mood, they may like the process of being aroused. However, this may not always be the case. Partners require sensitivity concerning one another's feelings and moods about both having and not having sex. Some partners feel more randy after being out in the fresh air or exercising physically. Getting in the mood is best achieved in the context of a tender and sensual relationship outside the bedroom.

• *Turn-ons and turn-offs.* Partners build up a repertoire of signals that give and receive messages about when they are in the mood for sex. Good lovers become keenly attuned to what turns one another on: for instance, certain forms of eye contact, touching, breathing, clothing, conversation and so on. Partners can also turn each other off sex: for instance, by bad breath, poor hygiene, dirty knickers or underpants, coarse language and being too pushy. Also, beware of tactless criticism. Glasser (1995) writes: 'Criticism directed at a partner's sexual performance is the ultimate sexual turnoff' (p. 47).

• *Surroundings.* Sex need not always take place in the bedroom at home. Some partners may enjoy making love in front of a blazing fireplace, in the bath, on the stairs, in hotels and motels or outdoors – for instance, in a field or on a beach. However, to protect your own and other people's sensitivities, privacy is important. If there is a possibility of being interrupted at home, lock the door and take the phone off the hook. The lighting of the surroundings for sex may be bright, dim or non-existent. There may be music in the background or silence.

• *Timing and duration.* Partners can choose to have sex at any time – not just between 11 p.m. and midnight on Saturday evenings! For instance, you may enjoy a lunch time 'nooner' or a leisurely afternoon of love-making. The duration of your lovemaking may range from a 'quickie' to as long as you can maintain your interest and energy.

Preventing conception and sexually transmitted diseases

Both partners engaging in sexual activity need to assume responsibility for contraception and for preventing sexually transmitted diseases (STDs). Approaches to these two main preventive concerns have commonalities as well as differences. In both instances, a distinction exists between the theoretical effectiveness and actual effectiveness of the method (Masters, Johnson & Kolodny, 1986). For instance, if a woman forgets to take the pill and then becomes pregnant, this most likely represents user rather than method failure. Also, using condoms that are poor quality or past their use-by date increases the risk of conception and of transmitting STDs – here, user failure and method failure can interact.

Contraception

Partners seeking to control birth are well advised to consult with doctors and family planning clinic advisers to select the method or methods that best combines prevention, health and comfort. Contraceptive methods focused on the female include: birth control pills that prevent female ovulation; the IUD or interuterine device that most likely prevents conception by interfering with implanting the fertilized egg in the lining of the uturus; the diaphragm, a round, shallow dome of thin rubber inserted inside the vagina to block the mouth of the cervix so that sperm cannot enter; and the cervical cap that fits snugly over the cervix and keeps in position by suction; spermicides or vaginal chemical products that kill sperm and contain an ingredient that blocks the entrance to the cervix; and the contraceptive sponge, permeated with the common spermicide nonoxynol-9, which is inserted into the vagina. In addition, couples may use the rhythm method which depends on not having intercourse during the period of the menstrual cycle when the woman is most fertile.

The condom or rubber sheath that fits over the man's erect penis and blocks sperm from entering the vagina is the main form of contraception focused on the male. Withdrawal, whereby the male withdraws his penis from the vagina, is another method of contraception, though it has a failure rate of 20 to 25 per cent (Masters, Johnson & Kolodny, 1986).

Preventing sexually transmitted diseases

Sexually transmitted diseases range from gonorrhoea, which is potentially treatable, to AIDS, which is always fatal. In a committed relationship, sexual fidelity is the main method of preventing sexually transmitted diseases. Outside of a committed relationship, celibacy is the only sure way of not catching STDs. Use of a condom significantly lowers the risk of obtaining or transmitting STDs. Knowledge of STDs can increase your caution as well as help you to notice symptoms of STDs in yourself or a partner. Sexual honesty is desirable so that your partner can protect himself or herself. If necessary, assertively ask direct questions about your partner's sexual health and ensure that a condom is used. If you think you have an STD, the more promptly you are tested and treated, the greater the chances of your preventing or managing well any serious complications arising from the disease.

COMMUNICATION SKILLS FOR SEXUAL RELATING

Behold me! I am worthy
of thy loving, for I love thee!
Elizabeth Barrett Browning

Partners can communicate about sex both in and out of bed. Often partners can best talk in detail about sexual problems and difficulties out of bed, thus keeping the bed associated with pleasure and warmth. Each of you may find it difficult to communicate clearly at the best of times. When it comes to talking about sex you may be embarrassed, inhibited, beat around the bush or do your best to avoid the subject altogether. In addition, other unfinished business in your relationship may become intrusive. Following are some skills for communicating about sex.

Express tenderness and affection

In close relationships the emotional side of sex is very important. Some partners may never have developed good skills of expressing tenderness and affection in or out of bed. Others may possess good skills, but fail to demonstrate them after courtship and the early stages of marriage or cohabitation. Partners like to feel valued not just for their bodies, but for themselves. In the chapter on caring skills, I mentioned many ways in which you can show affection and appreciation for your partner. Sometimes, people really love their partners but fail to say so. If you fall into that category, try finding a time to say 'I love you' to your partner in a way that reflects your true feelings for him or her. Also, be prepared to develop your skills of affectionate hugging and tender caressing.

Develop a comfortable language for sex talk

There is a joke about a bloke in outback Australia who walks into a pub and, seeing three women sitting at the bar, says to them: 'Do any of you sheilahs want a fuck?'. After a pause one of women replies: 'Well it wasn't on my mind, but…aw…strewth…you've talked me into it…you sweet talking bastard.' People vary in what language they find acceptable when talking about sex. For instance, some might find the language of the above joke offensive and many others would not bat an eyelid. In addition to the above four-letter word, there are many other terms that describe intercourse: among them, 'bonking', 'banging', 'rooting', 'rogering', 'shagging', 'screwing', 'getting laid', 'having sex', 'having nookie', 'having a poke' and 'having it off'. Many different words can be used to describe other sexual acts, for example fellatio can become 'blow job' and masturbation, 'wanking'. Furthermore, slang terms exist for erogenous parts of both the female and male bodies: for instance, breasts can become 'boobs', 'tits', 'mammaries', 'head lights' and 'fun bags' and a penis can be called a 'cock', 'dick', 'prick', 'tool' or 'bed flute'. No law of nature decrees that some of these terms are right or wrong. Each couple has to develop a language in which they can comfortably discuss sex without the constant fear of giving or receiving offence.

Tune into your partner's sexuality

Being skilled in bed requires you to be responsive to the flow of feelings and sexual sensations in your partner. You and your partner can create a safe emotional climate for talking about and experiencing your sexuality by using the listening skills described earlier in this book. Be sensitive to his or her feelings of vulnerability in talking about sex either in general or in relation to specific aspects. However, much of the information you receive is not verbal, but comes from other sounds and from seeing and touching your partner. For instance your partner's voice messages, such as their sighs and heavy breathing, can indicate the location and degree of their pleasure. In addition, by observing and physically feeling your partner's reactions, you get numerous messages about how he or she experiences various aspects of your love-making. Furthermore, if you allow it, your partner may guide you in how to provide more pleasure. Much of this communication may be nonverbal – for instance, placing your hand on a certain part of his or her body and applying the right amount of pressure or friction.

Disclose your sexuality

You can talk about yourself as a sexual person. Your disclosures may make it easier for your partner to reciprocate. For instance, you can share various aspects of your sexual history so that both you and your partner understand more about the origins of your current attitudes and behaviour. You can let your partner know what you like in bed. Sometimes, you can do this by positive feedback: 'That feels great' or 'Keep doing that, I love it.' On other occasions you may wish to improve or modify an otherwise enjoyable behaviour: for instance, 'I like it when you play with my testicles, but please do it lower down and more gently.' On still other occasions, you may wish to stop a behaviour: for instance, 'Please stop biting my neck. It hurts.' In addition, you can request sex acts, for instance: 'Please lick my cunt', though be sensitive to language and to your partner's reactions. Also, you can share your sexual fantasies, though again carefully monitor how your partner responds.

You can disclose yourself with appropriate voice messages that frame the verbal messages you send. However, on other occasions your voice messages will be sufficient in themselves. If you find yourself holding back on expressing pleasure through sighs and heavy breathing, you may gain more pleasure and sexual freedom by being more open. Also, you provide your partner with added feedback and excitement.

Much of the time you disclose yourself as a sexual person through your touch behaviour – how you hug, kiss and use your hands. You can be playful, sensitive and creative in how you touch your partner. In addition, you can use touch to guide your partner in how to pleasure you.

Be assertive

With sexual equality, each of you has a right to express sexual likes and dislikes (Alberti & Emmons, 1990; Butler, 1992). Sometimes you may need assertion skills to resist sexual pressure (Patton & Mannison, 1995; Powell, 1991). For instance, early in a relationship you might respond to a request for sex with: 'I find you attractive, but I want to get to know you better first.' You may need to be firm about ensuring use of condoms, stopping sex talk you find distasteful and curtailing physical activities you dislike or find painful. Since the next chapter of this book reviews how to use assertion skills in response to another's negative behaviour, I only mention the topic briefly here.

Have fun

Woody Allen quips about sex: 'It was the most fun I ever had without laughing.' Sex is adult play (Comfort, 1993). As such, it should not be taken with deadly seriousness. However, one person's fun can be another person's idea of stupidity or crassness. There are numerous ways that you can have relaxed fun – couples need to choose what works best for them. You can use humour to joke about sex both inside and outside the bedroom. You can be playful and frolic as you make love. In addition, you may choose to act out harmless fantasies. Regarding adult play time, Comfort (1993) writes: 'The rules are only those of childplay – if it gets nasty or spiteful or unhappy, stop the game:

while it stays wild and exciting, it has a climax children's games lack; that is the privilege of play when you are an adult' (p. 131).

Discuss issues

As well as each of you revealing your sexual likes and dislikes, undoubtedly together you will need to discuss and negotiate many issues connected with your sex life. Sometimes you will have common goals: for instance, how to obtain more privacy for sex or get fun out of it. However, there may be times when you and your partner differ on what, where and when you like to have sex. In such instances, goodwill, willingness to understand one another's positions, negotiation and compromise are useful attributes and skills. On occasion, you and your partner will need to discuss, in a climate of trust and mutual support, sexual doubts, fears and feelings of vulnerability. In addition, you can protect your sex life by, where necessary, making time both to have sex and also to talk about it. Lastly, many issues connected with your relationship and lives outside the bedroom may intrude into your sex life. Relating skills that you can use to address such issues include those of managing anger and solving relationship problems, the topics of later chapters in this book.

SEXUAL PROBLEMS AND DYSFUNCTIONS
Sexual problems

From time to time, every sexual relationship experiences problems. Sexual problems include 'dissatisfaction with sexual frequency, sexual boredom, incompatibility with respect to sexual activities and lack of sexual fulfilment' (Goldsmith, 1988, p. 31). Sexual problems can also encompass inhibitions and performance anxieties.

Partners differ in when they feel in the mood, get tired, become sick, go through ups and downs in their external relationship, and they are subject to stresses – for instance, money worries, job pressures, the needs of children and demanding relatives. In attempting to understand any sexual problem, there are at least four relevant contextual questions to ask: (1) 'Do important problems exist in our overall relationship?'; (2) 'Are either or both of us having an affair?'; (3) 'Are there stresses, possibly external, that interfere with either or both of our energy levels and feelings of well-being?'; and (4) 'Are there medical considerations that contribute to the sexual problem?' If you answer any or all of the above questions in the affirmative, your efforts at managing the sexual problem need to address them. For instance, each of these factors could contribute to the common problem of partial loss of desire.

Loss of desire can also be due to erotic boredom. Here, lack of knowledge and poor thinking skills can inhibit trying out and enjoying different sexual activities. Also, you can think effectively, but act incompetently. If so, you may need to rehearse and practise becoming more skilled in particular sex acts. Partners enter sexual relationships with different experiences and skill levels. You can share your experiences and help one another to become more skilled. Also, you can use effective thinking skills to overcome your inhibitions, guilt and performance anxieties. Needless to say, this is best done in the context of a mutually supportive emotional relationship.

Another way of looking at sexual problems is from the standpoint of improving what already may be a reasonably satisfactory sex life. The problem is how to make something good even better, without placing unrealistic pressures on either of you. You can cooperate to develop a plan for improving your sexual knowledge, thinking skills, capacity for sexual responsiveness, competence in different sexual activities and communication skills.

Extramarital sex

Regarding affairs, in the large-scale British survey of sexual behaviour only one in fifty respondents believed that extramarital sex 'to be not at all wrong, and some four out of five people (78.7 per cent of men and 84.3 per cent of women) are of the opinion that it is always or mostly wrong' (Wellings *et. al.*, 1994, p. 249). However, what people say and do can differ. In a Dutch study of 125 couples – 79 per cent married and 21 per cent cohabiting – 26 per cent of the men and 18 per cent of the women reported having had sex outside their primary relationship in the past year (Buunk, 1995). Also, 22 per cent of the women and 19 per cent of the men indicated that they had a partner who had been involved in such behaviour during that period. Though caution is required in generalizing from Dutch findings, the incidence of sexual affairs in Australasia and Britain may be much higher than that indicated by the British attitudes to extramarital sex reported by Wellings and her colleagues.

Sexual dysfunctions

The American Psychiatric Association's diagnostic manual states: 'The *Sexual Dysfunctions* are characterized by disturbance in sexual desire and in the psychophysiological changes that characterise the sexual response cycle and cause marked distress and interpersonal difficulty' (American Psychiatric Association, 1994, p. 493). Though the terms overlap, sexual dysfunctions can be regarded as more severe and less common than sexual problems. Numerous physiological, psychosocial and cultural factors can contribute to sexual dysfunctions.

Following are brief descriptions the main sexual dysfunctions (American Psychiatric Association, 1994). Additional American Psychiatric Association categories are: sexual dysfunction due to a general medical condition, substance-induced sexual dysfunction and sexual dysfunction not otherwise specified.

- *Sexual desire disorders*. The sexual desire disorders are hypoactive sexual desire disorder, where there is a deficiency or absence of sexual fantasies and desire for sexual activity, and sexual aversion disorder, where there is aversion to and active avoidance of genital sexual contact with a sexual partner.

- *Sexual arousal disorders*. The main characteristic of female sexual arousal disorder is a persistent or recurrent inability to attain, or to maintain until completion of sexual activity, an adequate lubrication-swelling response of sexual excitement. The main characteristic of male erectile disorder is a persistent or recurrent inability to attain, or to maintain until completion of the sexual activity, an adequate erection.

- *Orgasmic disorders.* The main feature of both female and male orgasmic disorders is a persistent or recurrent delay in, or absence of, orgasm following a normal sexual excitement phase. Premature ejaculation is the reverse of male orgasmic disorder in that its main feature is the persistent or recurrent onset of orgasm and ejaculation with minimal sexual stimulation before, on or shortly after penetration and before the person wishes it.

- *Sexual pain disorders.* The sexual pain disorders are dyspareunia, which is not due to a medical condition, and vaginismus. The main feature of dyspareunia is sexual pain associated with intercourse – usually during, but sometimes before or after. Dyspareunia can affect both sexes. The main feature of vaginismus is the recurrent or persistent involuntary contraction of the perineal muscles surrounding the outer third of the vagina when vaginal penetration with penis, finger, tampon or speculum is attempted.

Sex therapy

Sex therapy is the term used to describe the professional treatment of sexual dysfunctions and problems. There are many different approaches to sex therapy. The Masters and Johnson approach involves an intensive two-week program in which couples work with a male–female co-therapy team (Masters, Johnson & Kolodny, 1986). During this period couples are asked to free themselves from their everyday worries. The program commences with psychological and physical assessment of the sexual and non-sexual problems that the couple faces. On the third day partners are given their first exercise, called sensate focus, in which in the privacy of their hotel room or bedroom they take turns in non-genital pleasuring of each other. Over the next few days body touching in sensate focus is expanded to include the breasts and genitals. Throughout partners are instructed to increase their awareness of physical sensations and not focus on sexual performance. Accompanying the exercises are therapy sessions focused on broader relationship issues as well as on sexual functioning. Masters and Johnson supplement the above general features with specific approaches tailored to the different sexual dysfunctions. At the end of 1994, Masters closed his St Louis sex laboratory and clinic. Johnson had retired a few years previously.

In Kaplan's approach (Kaplan, 1974; 1987), couples are seen once or twice weekly, usually by a single therapist, and continue to live at home. Kaplan stresses that couples' underlying inner conflicts and relationship problems can give rise to resistances to the rapid behaviour modification of sexual dysfunctions. She observes: 'The symptomatic patient may resist sexual improvement if the treatment process taps into old, unresolved sexual conflicts. Even more frequently it is the partner who unconsciously sabotages treatment because he or she finds her partner's rapidly growing sexual adequacy threatening' (Kaplan, 1987, p. xv). Her approach combines the sex therapy approaches developed by Masters and Johnson with psychodynamically oriented therapy sessions. Kaplan uses masturbation in the early stages of treating female and male orgasmic disorders.

Couples, where either or both partners show symptoms of a sexual dysfunction, should seriously consider seeking treatment from suitably qualified and experienced sex therapists. The most common form of sex therapy is once weekly for a period of three to twelve months, depending upon the dysfunction. Dysfunctions may largely stem from one partner's problems or from relationship issues. If either partner experiences a sexual dysfunction, inevitably your relationship becomes affected. At least at some stages of therapy, sex therapists prefer to treat both partners together to gain cooperation in resolving both sexual and relationship issues. Apart from medical practitioners, sources for referral to qualified sex therapists include your local branch of Relationships Australia or Relate (Britain).

CHAPTER HIGHLIGHTS

• In its most basic form sexual relating is a physical activity involving mutual genital contact for the purpose of procreating the species.

• Besides procreation, other functions of sexual relating include building and maintaining relationships and recreation.

• All humans are sexual from birth. However, many have difficulty experiencing and expressing themselves as sexual persons.

• Sexual equality means that each sex has the same rights and responsibilities regarding the expression of their sexuality.

• The Masters and Johnson version of human sexual response cycle has four phases: excitement, plateau, orgasm and resolution. The American Psychiatric Association's version also has four phases: desire, excitement, orgasm and resolution.

• Helpful feelings associated with sex include acknowledgement of sensuality, love and respect for your partner, and a wish to give as well as to receive pleasure.

• Harmful feelings connected with sex include inhibitions, performance anxieties and wanting to manipulate and control your partner.

• Each person needs to assume responsibility for their sexual satisfaction and for their choices regarding how they think, feel and act in sexual situations.

• You may need to give yourself permission and opportunity to acknowledge and value yourself as a sexual person, including the strength of your feelings.

• You can use coping self-talk – consisting of calming, coaching and affirming self-statements – to help you act more effectively in specific sexual relating situations.

• You and your partner may individually and jointly possess unrealistic rules or 'musturbations' that limit your sexual satisfaction. You can challenge such rules and restate them so that they are more realistic.

• Challenge and alter inaccurate negative perceptions about sex, your sexuality and your partner's sexuality. Sometimes you may need to challenge unrealistic positive perceptions too.

• Dispute and change inaccurate explanations of cause about the adequacy of your sex life and the possibility of change.

• Effective sexual relating requires realistic confidence about your level of performance and about disclosing sexual wishes and secrets. In addition, you need to predict accurately the consequences of your birth control and preventing STDs behaviours.

• Each couple requires realistic goals and expectations concerning the quantity and quality of their sex life.

• Sexual fantasies can have many positive functions: for instance, turn-ons, sources of ideas for variety and fun and a means of rehearsing competent performance. Negative functions of sexual fantasies include avoiding either relationships or working on sexual relating problems.

• In close relationships, partners' sexual activity forms part of their broader emotional and sensual relationship.

• Positions for heterosexual intercourse include: man or woman lying on top, face to face; woman sitting on top, face to face; lying side to side, face to face; and rear entry, woman kneeling or lying down.

• Partners can engage in penile–anal intercourse as well as stimulate the anus manually or orally.

• Touching has many functions before, during and after sexual activity. Apart from hugging, the main methods of touch are with your mouth and hands.

• Most commonly females masturbate by lying on their backs and manually stroking their clitoris, mons or vaginal lips.

• Most commonly, males masturbate by rubbing one hand up and down the shaft of the penis with increasingly rapid movements until ejaculation.

• Numerous variations exist in the conditions for sexual activity including: mood, turn-ons and turn-offs, surroundings and timing and duration.

• Partners engaging in sexual activity need to assume responsibility for contraception and for preventing sexually transmitted diseases.

• Partners can communicate about sex both in and out of bed. Communication skills include: expressing tenderness and affection; developing a comfortable language for sex talk; tuning into one another's sexuality; disclosing your sexuality; being assertive; having fun; and discussing issues.

• From time to time every sexual relationship experiences problems, for instance partial loss of desire by either or both partners.

• Medical considerations, relationship problems and external stresses may contribute to sexual problems. Partners can develop their thinking and action skills to improve their levels of sexual satisfaction.

• Sexual dysfunctions are characterized by disturbances in the normal sexual response cycle that cause marked distress and relationship difficulties.

• Sexual dysfunctions are grouped into four main disorders: sexual desire disorders, sexual arousal disorders, orgasmic disorders and sexual pain disorders.

• Sex therapy for couples focuses on relationship issues as well as on specific techniques for overcoming each sexual dysfunction.

EXERCISES
EXERCISE 14.1
DEVELOP THINKING SKILLS FOR SEXUAL RELATING

Instructions

This exercise assumes you are in a sexual relationship. Complete Part A on your own and Part B with your partner.

Part A
My thinking skills

Either in relation to a specific sexual problem or to your overall sexual relating, assess yourself on each of the following thinking skills.

Owning responsibility for choosing

a. My strengths
b. My deficits

Getting in touch with my feelings

a. My strengths
b. My deficits

Using coping self-talk

a. My strengths
b. My deficits

Choosing realistic personal rules

a. My strengths
b. My deficits

Choosing to perceive accurately

a. My strengths
b. My deficits

Explaining cause accurately

a. My strengths
b. My deficits

Predicting realistically

a. My strengths
b. My deficits

Setting realistic goals

a. My strengths
b. My deficits

Using visualizing skills

a. My strengths
b. My deficits

Part B
Working together

1. Share and discuss your answers to Part A.

2. Focus on your sexual relating and examine how each of you is influenced by one another's thoughts and actions.

3. Identify the main thinking skills deficits, if any, that limit your sexual satisfaction as a couple and specify the steps you intend taking to change it/them.

EXERCISE 14.2
DEGREE OF COMFORT WITH SEXUAL ACTIVITIES
Instructions

This exercise assumes you are in a relationship. Complete Part A on your own and Part B with your partner.

Part A
My comfort zones

Assess how psychologically comfortable you feel about engaging in each of the following sexual activities.

Sexual intercourse

Man lying on top, face to face
Woman lying on top, face to face
Woman sitting on top, face to face
Lying side to side, face to face
Rear entry, woman kneeling or lying down
Other positions (specify)

Anal sex

Penile–anal intercourse
Other methods (specify)

Oral–genital sex

Fellatio
Cunnilingus

Manually stimulating partner's genitals

Masturbation

Partner present
On your own

Part B
Discuss with partner

1. Each partner shares their comfort zones and discusses the reasons for them.

2. If necessary, identify ways in which you can introduce more variety into your love-making.

EXERCISE 14.3
DEVELOP A COMFORTABLE LANGUAGE FOR TALKING ABOUT SEX
Instructions

Do this exercise with your partner. For each of the following parts of the body, items of clothing, sexual responses or sexual activities that are relevant to your sexual relating:

1. generate as many ways of calling it/them as you can, and

2. agree on the words that you are both comfortable using.

Parts of the body and items of clothing

Penis
Testicles
Nipples
Anus
Breasts
Vagina
Clitoris
Underwear (male)
Underwear (female)

Sexual responses and activities

Desire
Arousal

Undressing
Orgasm
Intercourse
Fellatio (mouth–genital contact on man)
Cunnilingus (mouth–genital contact on woman)
Masturbation
Contraception

EXERCISE 14.4
DEVELOP COMMUNICATION SKILLS FOR SEXUAL RELATING
Instructions

This exercise assumes that you are in a relationship. Do Part A on your own and Part B with your partner.

Part A
My communication skills for sexual relating

1. Assess your strengths and deficits in each of the following communication skills for sexual relating.
Expressing tenderness and affection
Tuning into my partner's sexuality
Disclosing my sexuality
Being assertive
Having fun
Discussing issues

2. If appropriate identify one or more of your communication skills deficits and develop a plan to change how you act. In your plan, specify:
a. your goals, including a time frame,
b. the steps you intend taking to attain each of your goals, and
c. how you will monitor your progress.

Part B
Working together

1. Share and discuss your answers to Part A of this exercise.

2. If appropriate identify one or more of your joint communication deficits and develop a plan to work together to change how you act. In your plan, specify:
a. your joint goals, including a time frame,
b. the steps you as a couple intend taking to attain each of your joint goals, and
c. how you will jointly monitor progress.

EXERCISE 14.5
GROUP DISCUSSION: SEXUAL RELATING SKILLS
Instructions

This is intended as a group exercise, though it may be done individually or in pairs. For each part:

1. spend 10–15 minutes answering the question in groups of three or four,

2. each sub-group shares its answers with the whole group,

3. then the whole group ranks the six most important skills from the most important to the least important.

Part A
Sexual equality

List the six most important skills individuals can use in becoming sexually equal to one another.

Part B
Sexual activity skills

List the six most important physical skills partners can use in sexual relating.

Part C
Sexual communication skills

List the six most important non-physical communication skills partners can use in sexual relating.

FIFTEEN
Assertion Skills

Nothing is so strong as gentleness and
nothing is so gentle as real strength.
Ralph W. Stockman

CHAPTER QUESTIONS

- *What is assertion?*

- *What are rights and responsibilities connected with assertion?*

- *What are some advantages of assertion?*

- *How does assertion compare with nonassertion and aggression?*

- *What are some thinking skills for assertion?*

- *What are some dimensions of acting assertively?*

- *What are some action skills for assertion?*

Broadly speaking, assertion may be thought of as any positive statement you make that affirms your existence. As such, trust, caring, intimacy, companionship and sexual relating skills each entail assertion. A distinction exists between oppositional assertion, expressing negative feelings, and affectionate assertion, expressing positive feelings (Butler, 1992; Wolpe, & Wolpe, 1988). Oppositional assertion entails coping with others' negative behaviour whereas affectionate assertion means behaving positively toward others. Because positive assertion is so important in relationships, in preceding chapters I covered skills like caring and intimacy. In this chapter, I address how to cope assertively with behaviour you perceive negatively. The subsequent two chapters, reviewing skills of managing anger and solving relationship problems, also address coping with negative behaviour.

Rights and responsibilities

Many books on assertion focus on how to attain your rights (Alberti & Emmons, 1990; Dickson 1982; Kotzman, 1989). These books assume that people in relationships have the same human rights, regardless of biological sex, roles or title. Such rights include: being treated with respect as an intelligent human being; stating your priorities, feelings, opinions and values; saying 'yes', 'no' or 'maybe' and being heard; saying 'I don't know', changing your mind or making mistakes; declining responsibility for others' problems; and dealing with others without being dependent on them for approval.

There are risks as well as benefits to focusing on rights in close relationships. For example, a focus on rights can be at the expense of acknowledging that your partner has the same rights too. Also, you can insufficiently acknowledge that your rights are accompanied by responsibilities toward your partner and your relationship. Furthermore, there may be no absolute standards for what constitutes your or your partner's rights: for example, your right to play loud music may conflict with your partner's right not to listen to it. In such instances, your partner may perceive your pursuit of rights as irresponsible. Some rights, such as the right to absence from physical violence are transparent, others are more matters of perception. Also, the dividing line between assertively and aggressively standing up for your rights is sometimes thin.

Advantages of assertion

What are some of the advantages of using assertion skills when faced with negative behaviour in a close relationship? First, you increase your partner's awareness not only of their behaviour, but of your reactions to it. For example, until he told her, Cheryl did not realize how much joking about her partner Fred in public upset him. Up to now Fred had gone along with the joke and colluded in his misery. Second, if your partner accepts the feedback, you have provided him or her with the opportunity to change. Such change can be good for both of you. You gain from the absence of the unwelcome behaviour and your partner gains from not upsetting you unnecessarily. Third, if your partner does not entirely accept your feedback, you can discuss your respective viewpoints and try to negotiate a solution. Fourth, your openness can forestall resentment and hidden agendas that might increasingly poison your relationship. Fifth, your use of assertion skills may increase your self-esteem: you can feel better for raising issues. Also, you can still have a *process* success, knowing you have used good skills, without necessarily having an *outcome* success, getting what you wanted. Sixth, if both partners use good assertion skills, they establish an open communication system in their relationship. An open communication system, unlike a closed system, is conducive to constructive feedback and change (Satir, 1972).

DEFINING ASSERTION

In many situations you can make positive statements about yourself by how you cope with another's negative behaviour. For example, you can disagree with what another says or does. You can say 'no' and set limits. You can request a change in behaviour. Furthermore, you can handle another's defensiveness and unwillingness to hear you. In addition, you can stop others from defining you on their terms at your expense.

Nonassertive, aggressive and assertive behaviour

In most situations, you may feel, think and act in three main ways: nonassertive, aggressive or assertive (Alberti & Emmons, 1990). You can also receive another's behaviour nonassertively, aggressively or assertively. In reality, people react to single situations and across different situations with various mixtures of nonassertion, aggression and assertion. Nobody is completely assertive.

Nonassertive

Nonassertive behaviour is passive, compliant, submissive and inhibited. Dickson (1982) uses a character called 'Dulcie the doormat' to illustrate being nonassertive. You do not like what is happening to you, but collude in allowing it to continue. You buy peace at the expense of denying your rights. Sometimes, realistically, nonassertive behaviour may be the best option: for instance, for a limited period Anna chooses to put up with her partner Larry's irritability because she realizes that, after a back operation, he is still weak and in pain. On other occasions though, nonassertive behaviour is 'wimping out'.

Aggressive

Aggressive behaviour is self-enhancing at the expense of another. You are unfriendly, quarrelsome and unnecessarily hostile. You behave as though you 'have a chip on your shoulder'. You try to get your way through dominating and overpowering rather than by influencing another. Your behaviour is unnecessarily threatening, even to the point of physical violence. In colloquial terms, you behave 'like a shit'. Passive aggression is a variation on aggressive behaviour. Here you hurt your partner by withdrawing from meeting his or her needs in some way and playing the victim. Both aggressive and submissive behaviour reflect feelings of low self-esteem. Submissive behaviour depowers yourself and aggressive behaviour attempts to depower others.

Assertive

Assertive behaviour reflects confidence and respect for both yourself and others. It entails responding flexibly and appropriately strongly to different situations. You are in control of yourself and behave in ways that enhance both you and the other. Where possible, you use gentle strength. Colloquially, you 'have your act together'. Alberti and Emmons (1990) offer the following working definition of assertion:

> *Assertive behavior promotes equality in human relationships, enabling us to act in our own best interests, to stand up for ourselves without undue anxiety, to express honest feelings com-*

fortably, to exercise personal rights without denying the rights of others (p. 7).

Following are some examples of acting nonassertively, aggressively or assertively.

• You have cooked a special dinner for your partner who arrives an hour late without contacting you.
Nonassertive: 'It's all right. Good to see you.'
Aggressive: 'Damn you. Now the dinner is spoiled.'
Assertive: 'I'm concerned at your being so late without contacting me. Was there a reason for this?'

• You live with somebody who rarely pulls their weight in cleaning the flat.
Nonassertive: You say nothing, but resent it deeply.
Aggressive: 'You lazy idiot. Do you think I like acting as your servant all the time.'
Assertive: 'I'm annoyed because you almost always leave the cleaning to me. I want us to work out an arrangement so that we share the chores more evenly.'

You may also express positive thoughts and feelings in nonassertive, aggressive and assertive ways to maintain changes in behaviour.

• You have been wanting your partner to cut the lawn for some time and he/she finally keeps his or her word and does it.
Nonassertive: Be pleased, but say nothing.
Aggressive: 'That's great. It's about time you kept your word.'
Assertive: 'The lawn looks lovely. Thank you.'

The above examples focus nonassertive, aggressive and assertive verbal messages. However, your voice and body messages are also very important. Furthermore, to act assertively you also need to feel and think assertively. It is to these thinking skills that I now turn.

SOME THINKING SKILLS FOR ASSERTION

Alberti and Emmons (1990) observe : 'Right *thinking* about assertiveness is crucial. Thoughts, beliefs, attitudes and feelings set the stage for behavior' (p. 79). A number of key thinking skills can release you to behave more assertively. These thinking skills overlap with those for combating shyness. Currently, many of your thoughts may hold you back. Learn to rid yourself of such counterproductive thinking.

Own responsibility for choosing

A theme of this book is that you are always a chooser. You can choose how you define your rights and responsibilities. You can choose whether or not to assert yourself. If you do not say 'no', set limits and request behaviour changes, when you could do so, you choose to suffer the consequences for your lack of assertion. If your assertive behaviour succeeds, you still have numerous choices: how to think and feel about your success, and how to maintain your own and the other person's changed behaviour. If your assertive behaviour is unsuccessful, your choices include: how to think and feel about not succeeding, whether and how to try again and what to think about the other person.

Get in touch with your feelings

Assertive people respect themselves and feel that they are worthy of respect. A distinction can be made between false assertiveness, based on the uncritical internalization of others' thoughts and values, and genuine assertiveness, based on openness to your own experiencing and values. At times, you may become aware that your decision whether or not to assert yourself involves working through past learnings and agendas to identify what you truly feel. For example, your parents may have brought you up to be self-denying. Consequently, respecting yourself enough to be assertive means 'going against the grain' of parental injunctions. In addition, when you assert yourself with your partner, beware of just replaying old videotapes of what your parents considered appropriate behaviour.

Many people deny or minimize feelings that can initiate and strengthen acting assertively. For instance, you can be out of touch with your wants and wishes. You can deny, inhibit or suppress angry feelings. Also, you can suppress feelings of care for your partner and commitment to your relationship that might encourage you to be assertive in the interests of both of you. Sometimes the problem may be less experiencing a feeling but needing to clarify it so that you can assess its significance. For instance, you may first experience a vague sense of unease that 'something is wrong'; then notice you feel somewhat depressed; then become angry at a specific behaviour of your partner; and then become resolved to request assertively that he or she change the behaviour. Skills for experiencing and clarifying your feelings include: acknowledging the importance of feelings; finding the physical and psychological space to listen to them; learning to label them accurately; and looking for causes for feelings in how you and others think and act. In addition, you can develop feelings of self-esteem and inner strength by acting assertively.

Use coping self-talk

Many people interfere with their effectiveness in asserting themselves by negative self-talk. Illustrative negative self-talk statements include: 'I'm no good', 'I'm a failure', 'I'm going to stuff it up.' 'I'll only make matters worse', 'Why bother?', 'What's the use?' and 'He/she never takes any notice of me'. If you engage in negative self-talk, you can counteract it with coping self-talk. As mentioned already, coping self-talk consists of calming, coaching and affirming self-statements.

Let's take the earlier example of having cooked a special dinner for your partner who arrives an hour late without contacting you. Your negative self-talk statements might be: 'He/she doesn't love me', 'He/she never considers my feelings' and 'After all the trouble I've been to, then he/she does this to me.' You identify your negative self-talk as inaccurate or at least decide to give your partner the benefit of the doubt. You counteract your negative self-talk with coping self-talk. Your calming self-statements include: 'Relax' and 'Take it easy.' Your coaching self-statements include: 'Smile and seem pleased to see him/her' and 'Give him/her the opportunity to explain why he/she is late.' Your affirming self-statements include: 'I can handle this' and 'I know he/she cares for me.'

Above I have illustrated using coping self-talk in relation to specific situations requiring assertion. You can also use self-talk to develop a more general capacity to be assertive. For example, you can rehearse and practise the following self-statements that encourage and legitimize assertion: 'I have a right to say/do that', 'I have a responsibility to stand up for myself', 'I believe in equality in my relationships', 'My opinions count' and 'I am important'.

Choose realistic personal and relationship rules

When growing up, you may have been subject to many pressures not to be assertive. Also, you may have lived with parents who demonstrated nonassertion or aggression. There are many sources from which, rightly or wrongly, you may have internalized faulty assertion rules. Below I mention some sources for learning to become nonassertive. Also I illustrate unrealistic rules that can interfere with open communication.

- *Your family.* 'You must avoid conflict and commenting on unusual behaviour.' 'You must not openly talk about sex.'

- *Your religion.* 'You should care for others rather than look after your needs.' 'You should always be gentle and self-effacing.'

- *Your gender.* 'Women should not be strong and independent.' 'Men should cover up their feelings.'

- *Your culture.* (Asian) 'You must be very conscious of saving people's face.' (Anglo-Saxon) 'You should not express emotions too openly.'

- *Your race.* 'Whites are better than blacks.' 'Whites are less smart than Asians.'

- *Your peer group.* 'You must conform to group norms.' 'You must be popular.'

- *Your age.* 'Children should be seen and not heard.' 'Parents know better than children.'

- *Your schooling.* 'Teachers know better than pupils.' 'Older children know better than younger children.'

Probably everyone possesses some unrealistic personal rules that interfere with assertion. These reflect musturbatory demands on yourself and your partner. Following are some personal rules that either are or possess the potential to be unrealistic.

> I/my partner must be nice.
> I/my partner must avoid conflict.
> I/my partner must be liked.
> I/my partner must be feminine.
> I/my partner must be masculine.
> I/my partner must not wear the pants.
> I/my partner must not have wishes of my own.
> I/my partner must never hurt each other.
> I/my partner must not seem vulnerable.
> I/my partner must now show anger.
> I/my partner must not make a mistake.
> I/my partner must not admit a mistake.

The first step in overcoming unrealistic personal rules that hinder assertion is to become aware that you possess them. Next you can logically analyse how realistic they are and what their positive and negative consequences are for you. Then, you can restate them into flexible rules that work better for you. Below is an example.

> *Unrealistic rule*: 'I/my partner must never hurt each other.'

> *Realistic rule*: 'While I prefer not to hurt my partner, I think it is important to our relationship to confront significant issues between us, even though sometimes this may cause pain.'

It is important that you and your partner develop and adhere to assertion rules that support your relationship. For instance, assuming both partners agree, the above personal rule regarding hurt could be extended to become the following relationship rule: 'While we prefer not to hurt each other, we think it is important to our relationship to confront significant issues between us, even though sometimes this may cause pain.' Below I suggest some additional relationship rules regarding assertion.

> It is important to let each other know where we are emotionally.
> Each of us cares sufficiently about the other to want to know their thoughts and feelings.
> Each of us wants to meet the legitimate preferences of the other.
> Each of us cares enough about the other to be considerate in the way we assert ourselves and to allow time and attention to process together the implications of our assertions.

Choose to perceive accurately

Perceive yourself accurately

Assertion requires you to perceive that you have rights and responsibilities. Furthermore, assertion requires giving yourself permission to pursue your rights: for example, 'It's okay to say no to activities that do not reflect my intrinsic feelings at the moment' (Butler, 1981, p. 93). You may inhibit your assertion by negatively labelling yourself: for instance, as 'selfish', 'domineering' and 'bossy'. In addition, others may encourage you to perceive your assertion negatively. Among adjectives attached to assertion by women are 'unfeminine', 'bitchy' and 'castrating' (Butler, 1981, 1992).

Alternatively, you may label your behaviour too positively. You may perceive yourself as assertive when your actions are either nonassertive or aggressive. If you are nonassertive, the perception of being assertive and doing all you can may be a convenient defence against actually being assertive and facing its consequences. If you are aggressive, the perception of assertion provides an acceptable mask for your hostility.

When considering assertion, you also need to perceive your options rather than do the first thing that comes into your mind. Sometimes you may do nothing. Montgomery and Evans (1983) call this editing: 'getting your petty complaints into perspective and editing out the unimportant ones' (p. 104). If you decide to proceed, you can generate a range of assertive options and then choose the one most likely to attain your goals.

Perceive your partner accurately

Assertion requires you to perceive your partner accurately. You may underreact or overreact because you perceive him or her as more vulnerable or stronger than in reality. Also, you may wrongly transfer feelings and thoughts from previous relationships – for instance, with your parents or a previous lover – on to him or her and then act accordingly. Furthermore, you may exaggerate the symbolic meaning of your partner's actions. For instance, Beck (1988) gives the example of Ken's statement 'I've decided that we need a new boiler' possessing the symbolic meaning 'You underestimate me' to his wife Marjorie. Marjorie thinks 'Why didn't he consult me first before he decided?' (p. 30). Because of her hypersensitivity to indications of lack of respect, Marjorie will now find it difficult to behave assertively.

In addition, you may fail to perceive the impact of your assertive behaviour on your partner. You may have come on too strong or too weak. If you came on too strong, you can attempt to repair the damage. If you came on too weak, you can be firmer next time. If you inaccurately perceive your partner's reactions, you lose flexibility in knowing how best to continue your assertion.

What skills can you use to perceive more accurately? You question the evidence for your perceptions: for instance, 'Where is the evidence that, if I stand up for my rights, I am castrating?', 'Where is the evidence that my partner underestimates me?' or 'Where is the evidence concerning the effectiveness of my assertion?' As part of this process, you can generate and consider alternative perceptions. You can then choose the perception that best fits the available facts.

Explain cause accurately

If you are nonassertive in many situations, there are many explanations of varying degrees of accuracy. Some explanations focus on yourself: for instance, you are submissive and lacking in confidence because of your nature or upbringing. You may see yourself as the helpless victim of circumstances. You may also think that your partner should know what bothers you without being told. In addition, you may have tried unsuccessfully to assert yourself in the past and concluded that it is no use trying again. You may consider your partner's behaviour is so deeply ingrained that it is no use trying to change him or her.

You might like your partner to become more assertive, but think that he or she should be able to do this without your help. Furthermore, if your partner reacts negatively to your attempts at assertion, you may automatically blame him or her for being defensive or bloody-minded rather than search for alternative explanations.

The danger of all these potentially faulty explanations for how you and your partner behave is that they are dead ends. You need to become aware both of your faulty explanations and of their consequences for you and your relationship. You can then distinguish between fact and inference and form explanations that are more conducive to acting assertively. Such explanations make two assumptions: first, that each of you is responsible for your own thoughts, feelings and actions; and second, that you are jointly responsible for constructively developing your relationship.

Predict realistically

Sometimes assertion in close relationships seems much more risky than in relationships with less to lose. You may find that you are testing the limits of your partner's commitment to your relationship. You may catastrophize the consequences of assertion and greatly overestimate the probability of negative outcomes. Furthermore, you may minimize your resources for coping with negative consequences.

However, you may fail to be assertive because you underestimate the positive consequences of assertion. Minimization of the potential for reward rather than maximization of the potential for loss holds you back. Because you inadequately perceive the gain side of the loss/gain ledger balance, you are unwilling to take risks that might have a high chance of bringing genuine gains to your relationship.

Awareness of any tendency you may have to either overestimate the negative or underestimate the positive consequences of assertion is the starting point for working on these thinking skills deficits. Then challenge your existing thinking by realistically appraising both potential gains and losses. If you tend to underestimate the gains you can work hard to generate and assess the realistic benefits of assertion, both in general and in specific situations. You can also become more aware of your strengths and of any support factors, for instance your partner or friends, that can help you become more assertive.

Set realistic goals

To change yourself, you need to know where you are, where you want to go, and then develop a plan to get from *here* to *there* (Alberti and Emmons, 1990). You may decide that you would like to become more assertive in your relationship. However, such a wish requires you to elaborate what you mean by becoming more assertive. For example, do you want to become more assertive across a range of situations or in regard to one or two specific situations?

Wanting to become more assertive can bring you face-to-face with your avoidance behaviour. You can increase your chances of being assertive if you set goals that are realistic, specific and have a time frame. Realistic assertion goals have two components. First, they seek realistic outcomes. In close relationships, consider both specific outcomes and the broader consequences for your relationship. Second, realistic goals allow a reasonable chance of enacting the level of performance to attain desired outcomes. You can have considerable control over your level of performance but only influence its outcome: your partner or others may have different ideas.

When specifying goals, make them as measurable as possible. For instance, using more assertive voice messages is a vague goal. More specific is the goal of speaking louder and more firmly when you ask your partner to stop criticizing you in public. Your goals also require a time frame. These may be long-term, medium-term or short-term goals. A short-term goal is, within seven days, to request that your partner stop criticizing you in public. Medium-term goals may possess anything from three months to a year time-frames and long-term goals anything beyond that. Frequently, when building confidence and skills, it helps to take a step-by step approach in which you set yourself progressively more difficult sub-goals (Bandura, 1986).

Use visualizing skills

You can use many visualizing skills to enhance your assertiveness. First, you can use imagery to help select assertion goals. Second, you can stop imagining the dire consequences of being assertive. When you catch yourself indulging in negative images, you can imagine a large neon sign flashing 'STOP' off and on. You can also vigorously shout 'STOP' to yourself at the same time as visualizing the image. Then, switch to more positive or congenial images (Kwee & Lazarus, 1986; Lazarus, 1989).

Third, you can use mental rehearsal to focus on your enacting competent verbal, voice and body messages in a specific situation. Start by getting a real picture of the scene in your imagination as if in a photograph and then turn it into a moving picture that contains your assertive behaviour (Lewinsohn *et al.*, 1986). You can enhance your motivation by imagining the positive outcomes for yourself and others of your assertion. You may also imagine ways of coping with different responses from your partner to your assertion. Before, during and after your mental rehearsals you can use calming, coaching and affirming self-talk, as appropriate. Many people do not rehearse scenes thoroughly enough and then find themselves at a loss for words in real situations (Lazarus, 1984). Fourth, you can use mental relaxation, in which you picture yourself in a restful scene, to calm you down before and possibly after your assertion.

DIMENSIONS OF ACTING ASSERTIVELY

Acting assertively follows from acknowledging significant feelings and thinking assertively. Table 15.1 is a grid for looking at the choices involved in acting nonassertively, aggressively or assertively. In assertive behaviour your thinking is disciplined, realistic and goal-oriented; your basic feeling is that of adequacy and you keep in check any self-defeating feelings; your verbal message is clear; your voice and body messages back up your verbal message with an appropriate degree of strength; and, if necessary, so do your actions. Nonassertive and aggressive behaviour is deficient, to a greater or lesser degree, in each of these dimensions.

Table 15.1 A grid for looking at the choices involved in nonassertive, aggressive and assertive behaviour

	Your thoughts	Your feelings	Your verbal messages	Your voice messages	Your body messages	Your actions
Nonassertive behaviour						
Aggressive behaviour						
Assertive behaviour						

When being assertive, your voice and body messages can greatly add or detract from your verbal message. For instance, a firm tone of voice may communicate to others that your verbal assertion is to be taken seriously, while a weak tone dilutes it. Assertion is not only a matter of presence or desirable verbal, voice and body messages, but also involves absence of undesirable messages. Be careful not to give messages that put others down.

Following are some verbal, voice and body messages relevant to most instances of assertion.

- **Verbal messages**

- *Send 'I' messages.* Send 'I' messages that accept responsibility for your thoughts, feelings and actions rather than 'You' messages. For instance, 'I would like you to cooperate in this way (specify)' is preferable to 'You are uncooperative'.

- *Communicate clearly.* Say what you really mean. Give specific feedback. Do not 'beat around the bush', make something else the issue, change the subject or hold forth (Litvinoff, 1992).

• **Voice messages.** Voice messages likely to support an assertive verbal message include the following.

Volume. Speak reasonably loudly. Do not put on a 'little girl' or 'little boy' voice.

Articulation. Clearly articulate your words, even if it means speaking slowly.

Pitch. Avoid being shrill.

Emphasis. Emphasize the words that back up your assertive message: for example, 'Please do not phone me again' with an emphasis on the 'do not'.

Rate. Speak at a measured pace. Do not rush your words. Avoid withdrawing into silence.

• **Body messages.** Body messages likely to support an assertive verbal message include the following.

Gaze and eye contact. Look another directly in the eye when delivering your assertive message. Maintain a good gaze when your partner responds.

Facial expression. Be genuine, for instance not smiling when you are serious.

Posture. Stand or sit erect with your chest out and shoulders slightly back. Avoid slouching.

Gesture. Use deliberate and non-threatening hand and arm movements to help express yourself in a constructive fashion. For instance, when you are telling someone that they have gone far enough, you can hold up your hand with palm facing outwards.

Proximity. Do not physically avoid your partner. Avoid 'hitting and running', making an assertive statement and leaving before your partner has time to respond.

Absence of threatening messages. Beware of head shaking, door slamming, fist shaking and finger pointing.

Absence of distracting messages. Try to eliminate messages indicating anxiety, such as tugging at your hair, fiddling with your fingers or shuffling your feet.

Example

Phil wants to stop his former girlfriend, Alison, from keeping coming around to his flat to try to rekindle their relationship. He decides to use the following assertion skills when she next comes to the door.

> *Verbal messages* Alison, we've *talked enough* already. I *don't* want you to come around again. Please *go now.*

> *Voice messages* Firm, reasonably loud, measured pace, emphasis on italicized words.

> *Body messages* Stand erect with chest out, her body facing his, strong eye contact.

If Alison does not go, Phil can repeat his assertive message; if she still does not go he can slowly but firmly shut the door.

Muscle

How forceful to be so that another 'gets the message' is a consideration relevant to all assertion situations. Muscle refers to the degree of strength of your assertion (Butler, 1992). As a rule of thumb, assertive messages should be at the minimum level of muscle to achieve their objectives. Where possible, assume good intentions, be friendly, use tact and diplomacy and be gentle. Your partner's goodwill is precious to maintaining your relationship, so avoid using a cricket bat where a feather would do. It is better for your partner to feel that they change willingly rather than under duress. The more muscle you use, the greater the risk of eliciting resistances and anger and also of leaving a residue of resentment that can surface later.

Butler provides the following example of different degrees of muscle that she could use with a friend who is frequently late in meeting her to go to the ballet. Level one is a polite request 'Arden, I would appreciate you being at my house by seven. I don't like arriving late.' If Arden did not respond, level two would be: 'Arden, as I mentioned before, it's really important that we arrive at the ballet on time. I would really like you to get here by seven.' If Arden continued to be late, she would move to the third level of muscle: 'Arden, I'm going to leave for the ballet at seven. If you're not able to be here by that time, I'll meet you at the theatre.' Here she communicates the consequences of failing to comply with her request. At level four, she carries out the consequence by leaving for the theatre alone (Butler, 1992, pp. 110–111).

In the above example, Butler used progressively stronger verbal messages that, if necessary, she was prepared to back up with an action message, driving to the theatre without Arden. She could also support her verbal messages with progressively stronger voice and body messages. You may need to use differing degrees of muscle to get your partner to maintain a behaviour change. Again, use the minimum force necessary.

Timing

Timing refers to when you deliver assertion messages. Sometimes you have virtually no choice, for instance if someone makes an unwanted sexual advance. On other occasions, you require assertion skills to counter remarks you cannot anticipate. Frequently, however, you can choose when and where to be assertive. It may be easier for you to deliver assertion messages when your feelings are back under control, your energy level is good, you have sufficient time to do it properly, and you have thought through what to say and how to say it. Also, consider when your partner might be most receptive to your assertion messages. Though not always possible, try to avoid times when he or she is in a bad mood or concentrating on doing something.

Become aware of your avoidance behaviour. Frequently, you do better to confront another's negative behaviour early on. Keeping putting it off can allow the behaviour to continue, if not worsen. However, on other occasions, adopt a wait-and-see approach to avoid delivering premature assertion messages.

A six-step framework for acting assertively

The following is a six step framework for acting assertively in specific situations in your relationship.

1. *Be aware.* Become aware of where you may be acting either submissively or aggressively. Listen to feedback from your partner as well as to your own thoughts and feelings.

2. *Specify goals.* You may fail to be assertive through lack of clarity concerning your goals. Be specific as to what you want and assess whether it is in the best interests of your relationship. During this process you may generate and evaluate many goals prior to deciding which is best.

3. *Develop a plan.* Develop a plan to attain your goals. Your plan is likely to focus on how to change your thinking as well as your behaviour. Take into account appropriate verbal, voice, body and action messages.

4. *Rehearse and practise.* Practice may not make perfect, but it can increase competence. Especially if you anticipate finding your assertion difficult, rehearse and practise it in advance. You may role play with another how you want to behave. Alternatively you can use visualized rehearsal and practice. Remember to anticipate set-backs and difficulties in your practice.

5. *Implement your assertion.* Pick an appropriate time to give your assertive message and go ahead and do it.

6. *Evaluate.* Evaluate how well you used assertion skills and their positive and negative consequences for yourself, your partner and your relationship. Learn from both successes and mistakes. Be prepared to persist in building skills.

When developing assertion skills, you can work on easier problems before moving on to more difficult ones. Success in being assertive in the 'shallow end' can provide confidence to move on to the 'deep end'.

SOME ACTION SKILLS FOR ASSERTION

Following are some action skills for assertion. For each skills area, you need to consider the appropriate verbal, voice and body messages, degree of muscle and timing. Also, take into account the extent to which your relationship is conducted on 'a level playing field'. For instance, males often have greater control over financial resources than women. Also, males tend to be physically stronger. Other areas of possible inequality in relationships include physical attraction, race, culture, language and verbal ability. Consequently, you require realism about the consequences of acting more assertively.

Disagree

In equal relationships, each partner feels free to disagree. You do not think that you have to be in total harmony with each other all the time. You can add spice to your relationship and broaden your horizons through difference as well as through agreement. However, you can disagree without being unnecessarily disagreeable. Disagreements can range from minor differences of opinion to major upheavals. Skills of assertively disagreeing can help you prevent the former turning into the latter.

When conversing, one approach to disagreeing is to counter another's idea by directly stating your opinion: for example, you counter 'I want us to go and play tennis' with 'I want us to go to the movies'. You can soften this by reflecting the other's opinion to show that you have clearly heard them, before stating your own : for example 'You want us to go and play tennis, but I want us to go to the movies.' In addition to 'I want to …', following are words that show you disagree without first signalling disagreement.

'I'd prefer to …'
'I'd like to …'
'I think that …'
'I feel …'

Another approach to disagreeing is first to state your disagreement and then make an 'I' statement about your position: for instance, 'I disagree. I want us to go to the movies.' In addition to 'I disagree', following are words you can use to start such statements.

'I beg to differ.'
'I see things differently.'
'I'm not comfortable with that.'
'I'd prefer that we didn't.'

When disagreeing, support your verbal messages with appropriate voice and body messages. In addition, listen carefully to your partner's reactions. Furthermore, you can prevent your relationship from becoming unnecessarily negative if you also show your partner when you agree with all or part of what they say or do.

Say 'no'

You may need to learn to say 'no' assertively. Part of this is learning not to feel afraid or guilty about saying 'no'. Another part of this is actually saying 'no' backed up by voice, body and, if necessary, action messages that show you mean what you say. Below are two examples of people saying 'no' and not fully meaning it.

> Monica, 42, keeps asking her boyfriend Jack, 47, for money so that she can go to the casino and gamble. Jack usually starts by saying 'no' and then ends up giving her some money.

> Sue, 23, wanted to end her relationship with Rick. She told him she did not want him coming around to her flat anymore. However, when he came, she would talk to him at the entry door for a while, and then let him in and give him a coffee. Sometimes they would also have sex.

In the above examples, both Monica and Rick know that Jack and Sue do not mean what they say. Jack and Sue's words say 'no', but their actions say 'yes' and reward exactly the kind of behaviour they want to discourage. Preferable is firmly to say 'no' and, if necessary, calmly to reinforce this message with appropriate actions. In Jack's case an appropriate action might be never to give Monica gambling money. In Sue's case, appropriate actions include: not talking at the entry door and shutting the door, if Rick did not go away.

Set limits

In this book, saying 'no' means refusing another's behaviour altogether whereas setting limits means placing restrictions on its amount. In setting limits, you require clarity regarding your goals. For example, Sue and Christian, a couple in their late 20s have a mutual friend called Eva who lives in a nearby town and keeps phoning them up two or three times a week to talk about her problems. Sue and Christian like Eva and want to help her. However, they also value their privacy and increasingly resent Eva's intrusions on it. Reviewing their own behaviour, Sue and Christian realize that they have been rewarding Eva's dependency on them by taking all her calls and allowing her to go on at length. Together, Sue and Christian establish a goal of allowing Eva to phone them once a week at a mutually convenient time. Having established their goal, Sue and Christian, decide to let Eva know next time she calls that they value her friendship, are interested in her and happy to talk, but would prefer just one good conversation a week. Sue and Christian decide that, if Eva asks for a reason, they will state that they both lead busy lives and need more space for themselves. If Eva persists in phoning them twice or thrice weekly, they can remind her of their request and ask her to think about it. If Eva still does not get the message, Sue and Christian can consider saying 'no more phone calls'.

Often, as in the above example, setting limits involves not colluding in another's dependency on you. If your partner has a tendency to off-load responsibility for their problems and decisions to you, following are some verbal messages that can help you hand back responsibility to him or her.

'What are your choices?'
'How is your current behaviour helping you?'
'What are your goals in the situation?'
'How can you handle the situation better?'
'What are your options?'
'It's your choice.'
'What skills do you require?'

Request changes in behaviour

People in relationships build up patterns of behaviour. When you request a change in your partner's behaviour you may have one of three goals: getting him or her (1) to do something that they are not already doing; (2) to do something that they are already doing either more and/or better; and (3) lessening or stopping an unwanted behaviour. You may be nonassertive, aggressive or assertive in each of these three areas. Below are some examples.

• **Requesting a new behaviour.** Doris wants Tim to bring her flowers on birthdays and anniversaries.
Nonassertive: Keep commenting on how other people bring their partners flowers on birthdays and anniversaries.
Aggressive: 'You've got no imagination. Don't you know that a woman likes flowers on birthdays and anniversaries?'
Assertive: 'When you don't bring me flowers on birthdays and anniversaries, I feel sad. I'd really appreciate it if you could do so.'

• **Requesting more of an existing behaviour.** George wishes that Wanda would show more interest in his job.
Nonassertive: Say nothing, but feel bad.
Aggressive: 'You only seem interested in your own job. Why don't you take more interest in mine?'
Assertive: 'When sometimes you don't appear interested in my work, I feel hurt. I value your opinions and want to be able to talk with you about my job.'

• **Requesting less or the stopping of an existing behaviour.** You study for an exam tomorrow and your partner plays a CD very loud.
Nonassertive: You thump the table and curse to yourself.
Aggressive: 'Turn that bloody CD player down. Don't you realize that I have work to do.'
Assertive: 'When you're playing a compact disc so loud, I can't concentrate on revising for my exam tomorrow. Please turn the volume down.'

You can follow the FFR (feedback, feeling, request) format when requesting a behaviour change, though not slavishly in that order. The first F provides your partner with a specific feedback about the behaviour that bothers you by its presence, absence or insufficiency. The second F is how you feel about the current situation. R is your request for change. In each of the above examples, the assertive request uses the FFR format.

When requesting a behaviour change, consider giving honest positive feedback as well. It is very easy to initiate a negative cycle. You may soften your requests if you comment on the positive as well as on the negative aspects of your partner's behaviour (Kassorla, 1984). Also, where possible, emphasize the positive by stating what you want rather than what you do not want. A simple example is to rephrase, 'You look awful when you wear curlers at breakfast' to 'I like seeing your beautiful hair without curlers at breakfast.' In addition, remember your partner is more likely to maintain a behaviour change if you show appreciation to him or her for doing so.

Handle defensiveness

Bolton (1986) comments on the human tendency to be defensive and how, as part of sending an assertive message, you may need to handle the 'push-push back phenomenon' (p. 158). There are internal and external agendas when faced with another's defensiveness. The internal agenda concerns how you handle your own thoughts and feelings. Defensiveness is a common initial reaction to assertive messages. It does not necessarily indicate either that you have asserted yourself poorly or that you may not ultimately be successful. Even if unsuccessful, you can only be responsible for your own behaviour. The expectation that your partner will always do what you want is unrealistic and can only contribute to your denigrating yourself when he or she does not.

The external agenda concerns how you behave toward your partner. Beware of reacting defensively to another's defensiveness. You risk getting sucked into an upward spiral of defensiveness in which the real topic of your assertion message may become lost in accusation and counter-accusation.

Assuming you decide to persist in the assertion you have a number of options. First, you may pause after the negative response and then calmly yet firmly repeat your behaviour change request. Second, you may reflect your partner's feelings before repeating your request.

> *Partner A:* 'When you play a compact disc so loud, I can't concentrate on revising for my exam tomorrow. Please turn the volume down.'
>
> *Partner B:* 'Why the hell are you complaining?'
>
> *Partner A:* 'I realize you are angry at my request, but I badly need to concentrate on my revision and would be grateful if you could turn the CD player down.'
>
> *Partner B:* (still not too pleased) 'OK'.

A third option is to use more muscle. For instance, you may both use a firmer voice and also strengthen your verbal message by saying 'I'm serious, please turn the CD player down'. A fourth option is to try to negotiate a mutually acceptable solution – for instance, negotiating times when your partner can play the CD player loud and times when you can revise without it. The skills of solving relationship problems are covered later in the book.

Deal with power plays

Power plays are attempts by others to get you to do what they want rather than what you want (Berne, 1964; Steiner, 1981). An important way another can power play you is to define situations on their terms. Anxious people can become very skilled at manipulating others. In close relationships, this can become the tyranny of the weak in that the more vulnerable partner controls the more adequate partner by playing on guilt feelings, wishes for a peaceful life, and tendencies to collude. Ern uses anger to get what he wants. Mike obscures the issue to avoid dealing with his partner directly. Vera finds that tears are very effective in getting her partner to bend to her wishes. Joan withdraws affection if her partner does not give her the feedback she wants. In all the above instances people use power plays – anger, mystification, tears and withdrawal of affection – to get what they want at their partner's expense. Sometimes a whole relationship has underlying assumptions that place one of the partners at a disadvantage. This may be the case where, on the basis of traditional sex-role assumptions, males discourage females from pursuing careers.

Becoming aware of others' attempts to operate on your self-definition and to manipulate you is the first step in being able to handle their power plays. You then have a number of options. First, being nonassertive and at least tacitly acquiescing in their false definitions and manipulations. Second, being aggressive and perhaps escalating the tension and emotional temperature by counterattacking. Third, being assertive by quickly yet firmly persisting in your definition of yourself and the situation. This option may also include working on your own tendencies to either acquiescence or escalation. In addition, you may confront your partner with how they behave and invite discussion of it. Fourth, if you are relating to a highly manipulative person, you can get out of the relationship. Ending a relationship can also be an assertive option.

Encourage one another's assertion

In a close relationship based on assumptions of teamwork and equality, you feel responsible for the happiness and fulfilment of one another and not constantly absorbed with securing your own rights. Assertion for 'us', rather than just either for 'me' or for 'you', is motivated by your positive feelings for each other. This can involve both of you demonstrating daily quiet strength, caring and vigilance. Following are some of the many ways you can encourage one another's assertion for the sake of your relationship.

• *Possess realistic relationship goals and rules.* You can openly discuss the goals of your relationship: for example a commitment to honest and open communication on the basis of equality. You can also try to clarify the relationship rules most likely to attain them: for example: 'Each of us cares enough about the other to be considerate in the way we assert ourselves and to allow time and attention to process together the implications of our assertions.' In short, you give each other permission to be assertive.

• *Provide rewarding consequences.* The consequences you provide for one another's assertions can either encourage or discourage them. You can provide rewards for assertive messages by treating them with respect and concern. You can show respect and concern by the quality of your listening and understanding. At times, you can even praise each other for having the courage to be assertive in difficult areas.

• *Demonstrate thinking and acting assertively.* Thinking and acting assertively can be contagious. If you are open and honest, it generally makes it easier for your partner to be the same way. Your joint openness protects your relationship against destructive cycles of mutual inhibition or aggression.

• *Provide openers and confront.* You can show that you care for each other's views by asking about them. If you think that your partner holds back and requires encouragement to be assertive, offer that encouragement. If necessary, you can confront your partner with the need to be assertive.

• *Show understanding*. If either of you thinks that you have a problem with assertion, the other can be there to offer assistance and support as you explore how to become more assertive. Sometimes this assistance and support involves help in working through painful past experiences contributing to present difficulties.

• *Encourage outside assertion*. If each of you adopts assertion as a way of life outside your relationship, this may make it easier to be assertive within it. You can support each other in your attempts to be assertive in your outside contacts.

Assertion for 'us' requires constant vigilance. It is easy to settle for less than your relationship's full potential for happiness and fulfilment. Working together as a team you are more likely to attain the potential than if each of you is always bound up with your own assertion agendas.

CHAPTER HIGHLIGHTS

• Assertion is any positive statement that affirms your existence.

• An important area of assertion is that of standing up for your rights and coping with another's negative behaviour.

• In most situations, you may act in three main ways: nonassertive, aggressive or assertive.

• You can own responsibility for choosing whether or not and how to assert yourself.

• Assertive people respect themselves and do not deny and minimize feelings that can initiate and strengthen assertive actions.

• Use coping self-talk – consisting of calming, coaching and affirming self-statements – to support your assertion.

• Choose realistic personal rules that give you the flexibility to be assertive. In addition you and your partner can develop and adhere to assertion rules that support your relationship.

• You can perceive your rights, responsibilities and your own and others' assertive actions with varying degrees of accuracy. Test the reality of your perceptions against the available evidence.

• You can explain the causes of your own or your partner's insufficient assertion with varying degrees of accuracy. Again, look for supporting evidence.

• Develop skills of realistically appraising the gains and losses of assertion, both in general and in specific situations.

• Set short-term, medium-term and long-term assertion goals that are realistic and specific.

• Use visualizing skills to stop imagining the dire consequences of assertion. Instead, picture and rehearse asserting yourself competently.

• Assertive verbal messages require the support of good voice and body messages. If necessary, your actions should back up what you say and how you say it.

• Muscle refers to the strength of your assertive messages. Deliver assertive messages with the minimum force necessary for achieving your objectives.

• Where possible, time the delivery of your assertive messages when there is a probability that you will do so competently and your partner will listen.

• Six steps in acting assertively are: be aware, specify goals, develop a plan, rehearse and practise, implement your assertion and evaluate it.

• Develop skills of disagreeing without being unnecessarily disagreeable by stating a position with or without first signalling disagreement.

• Develop skills of saying 'no' and showing you mean it by matching your actions to your words.

• Develop skills of setting limits on another's behaviour. Also, you can encourage others to depend on themselves rather than on you.

• You can assertively request another to change their behaviour by means of the FFR (feedback, feeling, request) format.

• Skills for handling defensiveness elicited by your assertive messages include repeating the message, reflecting the defensive feeling and then repeating the message, and using more muscle.

• When others attempt to define you negatively, you can deal with their power-playing by persisting in your definition of yourself and the situation.

• Skills you can use to encourage one another's assertion include: rewarding it, demonstrating thinking and acting assertively yourself and, if necessary, confronting one another with the need to be assertive.

EXERCISES

EXERCISE 15.1
ASSESS MY ASSERTION SKILLS
Instructions

This exercise is in two parts. Complete each part on your own. Then, where appropriate, discuss with your partner, another or others.

Part A
Assess how assertive I am

For each of the items below, indicate with the appropriate code which of the following three options best describes how you either do or might respond.

NA – nonassertively
AG – aggressively
AS – assertively

You respond	Items
1. _____	The person with whom you live is not doing a fair share of the household chores.
2. _____	You disagree with something your partner says in public.
3. _____	Someone is overdue in paying back money to you.
4. _____	A trades person (e.g. plumber, painter) has not done a proper job.
5. _____	You are being pressured to take a drink that you do not want.
6. _____	You do not wish to do a favour for someone.
7. _____	You think your partner has done something to you which is unfair.
8. _____	You want to clarify what someone has said.
9. _____	You are talking with a group of people and want to leave.
10. _____	You want your partner to tidy up the bathroom after he or she uses it.
11. _____	You want your partner to phone you if he or she is going to be late getting home.

12. _____ You want to turn down a social invitation.

13. _____ Your neighbour's dog keeps barking at night.

14. _____ You wait a long time in a restaurant for someone to serve you.

15. _____ You wish to return defective merchandise to a shop.

16. _____ You want to take an unpopular stand on a controversial issue.

17. _____ Someone interrupts when you are talking about something important to you.

18. _____ You think that you have been overcharged for something.

19. _____ You want your partner to spend more time with you.

20. _____ You think that you have been criticised unjustly.

1. Count up the number of times you answered in each category.

2. To what extent do you consider you are assertive, nonassertive, aggressive or a mixture of each and why?

Part B
Identify specific problem situations

Fill in the personal problem list, by identifying specific situations in which you would like to be more assertive.

Personal problem list

1. _____

2. _____

3. _____

4. _____

5. _____

6. _____

7. _____

8. _____

9. _____

10. _____

EXERCISE 15.2
DEVELOP MY THINKING SKILLS FOR ASSERTION
Instructions

Answer the following questions on your own. Then, if appropriate, discuss with your partner, another or others.

1. In relation to one of the situations in which you would like to be more assertive on your personal problem list in Exercise 15.1, assess your strengths and deficits in each of the following thinking skills.
Own responsibility for choosing
Get in touch with my feelings
Use coping self-talk
Choose realistic personal and relationship rules
Choose to perceive accurately
Explain cause accurately
Predict realistically
Set realistic goals
Use visualizing skills

2. Specify how your current thinking skills interfere with your acting assertively?

3. Identify one or more of your main thinking skills deficits and develop a plan to change how you think. In your plan specify:
a. your goals, including a time frame,
b. the steps you intend taking to attain each of your goals, and
c. how you will monitor your progress.

EXERCISE 15.3
DEVELOP MY ACTION SKILLS FOR ASSERTION
Instructions

First do Part A on your own, before discussing with your partner, another or others. Do Part B with your partner or someone else.

Part A
Assessment

Take a relationship that is important to you and assess the strengths and deficits of how you act in each of the following assertion areas.
Disagreeing
Saying 'no'
Setting limits
Requesting a new behaviour
Requesting more of an existing behaviour
Requesting less of or the stopping of an existing behaviour

Handling defensiveness
Dealing with power-plays
Encouraging your partner's assertion

Part B
Action

Either for the personal problem situation on which you developed your thinking skills in Exercise 15.2 or for another situation:

1. specify your action skills goals,

2. develop a plan to attain your goals, taking into account appropriate verbal, voice, body and action messages,

3. rehearse and practise, both with a partner and using visualized rehearsal,

4. implement your assertion skills, and

5. evaluate how well you used your assertion skills and their positive and negative consequences for yourself and others.

EXERCISE 15.4
GROUP DISCUSSION: ASSERTION SKILLS
Instructions

This is intended as a group exercise, though it may be done individually or in pairs. For each part:

1. spend 10–15 minutes answering the question in groups of three or four,

2. each sub-group shares its findings with the whole group,

3. then the whole group ranks the six most important skills from the most important to the least important.

Part A
Sending assertive messages

List the six most important skills people can use in sending assertive messages to a partner.

Part B
Receiving assertive messages

List the six most important skills people can use in receiving assertive messages from a partner.

Part C
Encouraging one another's assertion

List the six most important skills partners can use to encourage one another's assertion.

SIXTEEN
Managing Anger Skills

If you are patient in one moment of anger,
you will escape a hundred days of sorrow.

Chinese proverb

CHAPTER QUESTIONS

- *What is anger?*

- *What are some positive functions of anger?*

- *Are there sex differences in anger?*

- *What is acceptance, tolerance and forgiveness?*

- *What are some positive and negative feelings associated with anger?*

- *What are some thinking skills for managing anger?*

- *What are some action skills for managing anger?*

- *How can partners help one another to manage anger?*

Laura is working late in the evening preparing for her nursing exams the next day. She asks her boyfriend Darren to make her a coffee. Darren replies: 'Make it yourself'.

Alex and Shirley have been married for 15 years. Every time they get home after going out as a couple, Shirley criticizes Alex for something he said or did when they were out.

Kevin is under a lot of stress at work. He is also very irritable at home. When his wife Joanna draws his irritability to his attention and asks him what is wrong, Kevin gets even angrier and tells her that she does not understand what he is going through.

Linda resents her partner Brian spending so much time talking to his mother, Eva, on the phone. Linda angrily tells Brian that: 'I'm pissed off with the way you let yourself be controlled by that demanding bitch.'

As in the above examples, anger features prominently in most close relationships. This chapter focuses more on how you can manage your own anger, whereas the next chapter reviews joint approaches to solving relationship problems.

Defining anger

Anger represents a hostile feeling of displeasure. Tavris (1989) observes that ultimately anger is an emphatic message: *'Pay attention to me. I don't like what you're doing. Restore my pride. You're in my way. Danger. Give me justice'* (p. 47). Angry feelings can vary in intensity from mild irritation to rage and fury. Anger can also turn into hatred where partners develop a strong and persistent dislike for one another. Both anger and hatred can be fuelled by resentments at perceived and real harms, insults and injuries sustained in the past (Dalrymple, 1995).

Angry feelings can be demonstrated by verbal, voice, body, touch and action messages. Verbal messages can vary from assertive expressions of anger to aggressive put-downs such as: 'You stupid bitch/bastard', 'Fool', 'You clumsy oaf', 'You worthless fraud', 'You've got it all wrong again' and 'You always screw up'. Voice messages range from shouting and emphasizing attacking comments to giving your partner the silent treatment. Body messages include: scowling, glaring, fist clenching, finger stabbing and stomping out of the room. Touch messages include anything from a mild push to murder. Action messages include withdrawal of desirable actions, for instance not giving a birthday gift and sending blunt messages, such as angry letters or a legal writ. In addition, your body may experience anger through physiological reactions such as heightened blood pressure, hypertension, ulcers and insomnia.

Anger and violence

Anger often causes partners to attack each other psychologically. You and your partner know the chinks in one another's armour. Consequently, you can be skilled at causing pain. However, in hurting your partner you can also be hurting yourself. Anger is an unpleasant physical sensation. Also, angry thoughts are scarcely happy thoughts. In addition, your anger may lead your partner to retaliate and even escalate the level of anger.

Anger can also lead to physical violence. In one American study of domestic violence, a domestically violent husband had in the past year to have: '(a) pushed, grabbed, shoved, slapped, or tried to hit his wife six or more times...; (b) kicked, bit, or hit her with a fist at least twice...; or (c) beat her up, threatened her with a knife or gun, or used a knife or gun on her at least once...' (Jacobson *et al.*, 1994).

Female and male anger

It is a stereotype that, as a result of their upbringing, males express their anger and females suppress it. Very few American studies into the experiencing and expression of anger have shown sex differences (Tavris, 1989; Sharkin, 1993). Both sexes have trouble, experiencing, expressing and managing anger. Speilberger's (1988) State/Trait Anger Expression Inventory was administered to a large number of American adults. Males had higher scores on anger-in (pouting and sulking, harbouring grudges, feeling secretly critical of others, keeping things in, feeling 'angrier than I'm willing to admit'). However, no sex differences were found for anger-out (readiness to express anger, strike out, make sarcastic remarks and so on) (Tavris, 1989).

It is also a stereotype that being physically violent is exclusively a male problem. In a study of over 2000 American families, either or both of the spouses had used physical violence in 12 per cent of the families. In half the violent families, both spouses attacked each other with equal frequency; in one quarter, only the wife was violent; in the other quarter only the husband was violent (Tavris, 1989). However, the outcomes of male violence were more severe due to their relatively greater strength and tendency to use guns and knives. It has been suggested that the function of violence differs between males and females, with men tending to use violence as a method of control and women using it for self-defence or retaliative purposes (Jacobson *et al.*, 1994). However, Tavris (1989) considers that women are not 'naturally' less aggressive than men when they feel angry. The finding that the wife only was physically violent in a quarter of violent families supports her point. Caution needs to be exercised in generalizing American findings to other cultures. Even in America, the criminal statistics are heavily weighted towards male violence.

Frequently expression of anger does not take place on 'a level playing field' between the sexes. As mentioned in Chapter 15, males tend to be stronger and control more resources. The Australian National Committee on Violence Against Women defined violence against women as: 'behaviour adopted by the man to control his victim which results in physical, sexual and/or psychological damage, forced social isolation, or economic deprivation, or behaviour which leaves a woman living in fear' (National Committee on Violence Against Women, 1991). Eastel (1994) argues that violence against women is well entrenched in Australian society. She sees many women and children as hostages in their homes and asserts that domestic violence is under-reported because many women subscribe to the following three rules: 'Don't talk', 'Don't trust' and 'Don't feel'. Probably, in Australasian and British cultures, the overall incidence of and severity of physical violence – including threatening it – by men against women is higher, if not considerably higher, than the reverse. Physical violence by either partner against the other sex, or in gay relationships against the same sex, is unacceptable. Psychological violence always accompanies physical violence. Psychological violence used on its own by partners of both sexes with poor managing anger skills is far too common in close relationships.

Positive uses of anger

Anger can also have positive outcomes in relationships. Angry feelings do not in themselves destroy relationships, but handling them poorly may do so. Anger can be a *guide* to a clearer definition of yourself. Lerner (1985) sees some women as afraid to acknowledge their anger because to do so *'would expose our differences, make the other person feel uncomfortable, and leave us standing alone'* (p. 93). However, both sexes can use anger to become more expert at knowing who they are and what they want. In addition, anger can be a *signal* for yourself and your partner that something is wrong in your relationship and requires attention. This should be a cue to examine your own thoughts, feelings and actions and not just those of your partner. Also, anger can be a *motivator* leading to more honest communication, assertive requests for behaviour change and to confronting festering issues.

In some situations anger displays may serve positive functions, especially if the displays are assertive rather than aggressive. For example, anger can serve as a *call for attention*, if your partner is not receiving milder messages. Also, anger displays can be used to *curb or control* unwanted behaviours, though it is clearly preferable that partners do this willingly.

A controversial issue is the use of anger as a *purge* so that afterwards you and your partner calm down and become more rational. An improved emotional climate does not always follow angry outbursts. 'Letting it all hang out' and ventilating anger can make matters worse rather than better (Tavris, 1989). Usually as your level of arousal increases, your capacity to be reasonable decreases. Furthermore, your partner may close his or her ears to what you say and retaliate. Lazarus and his colleagues consider that 'blowing off steam' is self-defeating and that it is better to express emotions assertively (Lazarus, Lazarus & Fay, 1993). Nevertheless, in close relationships partners can establish rules and develop skills that allow anger to be ventilated and then used constructively rather than for tearing each other apart.

Acceptance, tolerance and forgiveness

The concepts of acceptance and tolerance touch on anger in many ways. For instance, the degree to which you accept yourself is likely to influence how accepting you are of your partner (Gordon, 1970). You can fully accept yourself as a person, even though you may possess an emotion such as anger that you wish to change (Ellis, 1977). Acceptance is related to tolerance or the ability to accept variations in the standards you apply yourself and to other people. You are less likely to be angry with your partner the more you can tolerate his or her separateness and difference. Also, if self-accepting, you are more likely to avoid what Ellis (1977; 1987) terms low frustration tolerance (LFT). Low frustration tolerance contributes to anger when your partner fails to meet your standards, be your standards tolerant or otherwise.

In addition, acceptance is related to letting go. For instance, you may become less angry if you relinquish some of your struggle to change your partner. The German poet Schiller wrote: 'Happy is he who learns to bear what he cannot change!' In addition, forgiving is another way in which you can become less angry.

FEELINGS ASSOCIATED WITH ANGER

Anger is almost invariably preceded, accompanied and followed by other feelings as well. Though the distinction between positive and negative feelings is a simplification, it may serve to illustrate some aspects of anger.

Positive feelings associated with anger

Inasmuch as anger represents a constructive life force to be a person in one's own right and to be taken notice of, it has a positive base. As with infants' anger, adults' anger can be in the service of genuine self-affirmation. Feelings of anger can indicate high as well as low self-worth. Your anger can indicate that you value and respect yourself enough to have your wishes taken into account. Also, your anger can indicate you value and care for somebody else sufficiently to become angry with them. Many people would much prefer that their partner be angry with them rather than indifferent. Furthermore, your angry feelings may be associated with confidence that you can do something about them in the interests of yourself and your relationship. In addition, you may be angry because you wish to protect your partner's interests and perceive them as being violated by others. However, if angry feelings become disproportionate in intensity and duration to provocations, then they can become destructive to self and others.

Negative feelings associated with anger

Usually anger indicates that you are in some form of psychological pain. Anger is a way you have learned to exhibit or mask that pain. Ideally anger represents a proportionate state of arousal to an anger-evoking event. The intensity of appropriate anger may range from mild irritation to controlled fury. However, some people experience too little anger through repressing, inhibiting and suppressing it whereas others spiral into uncontrollable rages.

Anger in relationships can be anxiety-motivated and interact with other feelings like the need to possess and control your partner. In addition, you cannot only have angry feelings, but also have feelings about your angry feelings: for instance, first getting angry with your partner and then becoming angry with yourself or depressed about your anger (Ellis, 1977). Table 16.1 shows some common negative feelings associated with anger.

Persistent anger is like a psychological toothache. You can become so self-absorbed with your anger and resentment that you can scarcely think of anything else. As such, anger can be the mortal enemy of love. Powell (1967) quotes the following statement from a psychiatrist friend of his: 'This is a pain-filled world, and so, a loveless world that we live in. Most human beings are so turned-in by their own pains that they cannot get enough out of themselves to love to any great extent' (p.   short, destructive anger reflects either temporary or persistent self-loathing rather than genuine self-affirmation.

Table 16.1 Some negative feelings associated with anger

anxiety	persecution
competitiveness	powerlessness
depression	resentment
disappointment	revenge
fear	self-pity
frustration	spite
hurt pride	stress
jealousy	tiredness
low self-esteem	vulnerability

SOME THINKING SKILLS FOR MANAGING ANGER

A one-word amendment to Shakespeare's saying 'Love's best habit is a soothing tongue' is to substitute mind for tongue. A soothing *mind* is the precondition for a soothing *tongue*. There are many occasions when you can exhibit love and caring for your partner by disciplining your thinking so that you either prevent, or do not express, or dilute your expression of anger. Mental cultivation to manage your anger is essential for effective relating. On the one hand you can choose to think yourself into hatred, aggressive blaming, nursing resentments, wanting to cause psychological pain and acting violently. On the other hand you can choose to think yourself into a calmer, more rational and more problem-solving frame of mind.

Own responsibility for choosing

The first step in assuming responsibility for managing your anger is to realize the extent to which you choose to anger yourself. William Glasser, the founder of Reality Therapy, uses active verbs that imply personal agency to describe feelings: for instance, 'depress-ing', 'anxiety-ing' and 'anger-ing' (Glasser, 1984: Glasser & Wubbolding, 1995). Glasser regards angering as the most common of all the behaviours partners choose when things are not the way she or he wants them to be (Glasser, 1995). To a large extent you choose the thoughts, feelings and physical reactions that you describe as anger. You also have a choice regarding whether or not and how you enact anger.

Another reason why people get angry is that they have an exaggerated sense of their permanence and importance in the universe (Roscoe, 1994). A deep awareness of death, impermanence, the vastness of the universe and human frailty can enhance people's perceptions of the futility of angering themselves unnecessarily. However, strike a balance between detachment and involvement.

Understand the relationship between how you think, feel and act

In Chapter 12, I introduced the STC (Situation – Thoughts – Consequences) framework for understanding how your thoughts influence how you feel and act. When you feel or act angrily, you can examine your thoughts to see if they are contributing to your becoming disproportionately angry. For example, if your partner teases you, you are more likely to take it in good spirit if you think the teasing motivated by fun rather than by spite. However, if you wrongly thought the teasing was motivated by spite, this thought would fuel your anger.

A more sophisticated version of STC is to substitute Thinking Skills for Thoughts at T (Nelson-Jones, 1996). The STC framework now becomes Situation – Thinking Skills – Consequences. Each of the other thinking skills described in this section may influence how angry you feel and act. You can learn to identify and address the thinking skills deficits that characterize your anger: for example, you may possess unnecessarily rigid rules or have a tendency to perceive others disparagingly. Knowing your characteristic thinking skills deficits speeds the process of identifying anger-engendering thoughts in specific situations.

Get in touch with your feelings

Develop skills of getting in touch with your angry feelings and labelling them accurately. For various reasons, your may deny or distort your experiencing of anger. Explore your anger trail to discover the other feelings that are associated with or underlie your anger. Many such feelings are listed in Table 16.1. In addition, you can get in touch with feelings from past relationships that feed forward and have the potential to damage current relationships: for instance, anger arising from childhood hurts or rejections by previous lovers. Another set of feelings to experience more fully are those that might prevent or soften your anger: for instance, love and caring for your partner. Also, get in touch with positive feelings about yourself that give you the inner strength to experience, express and control your anger.

You can develop skills of tracking your level of anger arousal (Alberti & Emmons, 1990; Montgomery & Evans, 1983). For instance, becoming aware of your angry feelings when you are 20 per cent angry may make it easier for you to be rational than when 50 per cent angry. At some stage your level of arousal may become so high – say 90 to 100 per cent – that it is impossible for you to be rational until you calm down. Identify and heed early warning signals for anger. Early warnings may come from: your feelings, such as hurt; what you say, for instance making sarcastic comments; your body messages, such as clenched fists; your voice messages, for instance becoming louder; your physical reactions, such as tightness around the neck; and your thoughts, for instance thinking of your partner negatively.

If, during fights, you acknowledge how angry you are, you have some chance of either restraining your anger or withdrawing until calmer. Also, if aware that after fights you ruminate and nurse resentments, you can attempt to reduce the mental and physical costs of doing so.

Use coping self-talk

If you tend to be impulsive when angry and 'shoot' your mouth, consider using coping self-talk. Anger-evoking situations may be viewed as challenging you to respond in task-oriented rather than in impulsive and self-defeating ways. Simple self-instructions like 'calm down', 'cool it', 'count to ten' and 'take it easy' can often give you the time and space to get your feelings more under control (Goldstein & Keller, 1987). Once this takes place you have considerably more choice concerning both whether or not and how to express your anger.

> Beth is angry with Barry because he said he could collect her from work and has kept her waiting for half an hour. When he finally arrives looking tired and rushed she tells herself: 'Take it easy. Count to ten. He is obviously tired and this is no time for either of us to have a row.' Barry apologizes and says that he was delayed by having to change a flat tyre.

In many relationships provocations are relatively predictable. You know that your partner may tease you, leave their clothes around, not do a domestic chore or some other thing that you dislike. Here you can use coping self-talk to help achieve your goal of managing a specific provocation better. This entails making choices that increase your sense of competence and lessen the likelihood of your anger being both unpleasant for yourself and counter-productive in your relationship (Meichenbaum, 1983; Novaco, 1977). Remember, using coping self-talk involves: calming self-statements, for instance 'stay calm'; coaching self-statements, about how you can best perform the task at hand; and affirming self-statements that enhance your confidence.

Following are examples of coping self-talk statements you can use before, during and after provocations and fights.

Before

'Keep calm and remember what I want to achieve in this situation.'
'Remember, stick to the issues and avoid put-downs.'
'I can handle this situation if I don't let my stupid pride get in the way.'

During

'Stay cool. I'm not going to let him/her have the satisfaction of getting to me.'
'Relax. My anger is a signal telling me to calm down and keep by goal in mind.'
'Just because he/she is being competitive, there is no reason for me to get sucked in.'

After

'I'm learning to cope better without being aggressive.'
'Even though the situation is unresolved, I'm glad I didn't come on strong.'
'Using my coping self-talk prevents me from feeling powerless and overwhelmed.'

Choose realistic personal rules

Ellis considers that the main cause of anger is that people are unwilling to relinquish childish demandingness (1977). An important way you can control anger is to dispute and replace unrealistic rules, based on absolutistic and demanding thinking, with more realistic rules, based on rational and preferential thinking (Ellis, 1995). Often, in close relationships, people make unrealistic role-related claims on one another: for instance, 'You're my wife and I expect you to act that way' (Butler, 1981, p. 141). Also, in long-term relationships submerged unrealistic rules have time later on to emerge.

You can create your anger by possessing unrealistic musturbatory rules about how you, your partner, your relationship and life should be. Following are illustrations of potentially anger-engendering rules.

About yourself

I must never make mistakes.
I must always be right.
I must control my partner.
I must be rational and consistent all the time.
I must never be vulnerable.
I must always be hard on myself.
I must never show anger.
I must justify myself.
I must punish my partner for wrongdoings.
I must never forgive and forget.
I must never apologize.

About your partner

A wife/husband must always ...
My partner must approve of me all the time.
My partner must never make me angry.
My partner must never disagree with me.
My partner must never criticize me.
My partner must always let me be right.
My partner must always let me have my way.
My partner must always be able to read my mind.
My partner must not in any way attempt to restrict my freedom.
My partner must always be feminine/masculine.
My partner must meet 100 per cent of my needs.
My partner must never be allowed to get away with it.
Where cultural differences exist, my partner must always adjust to my culture.

About our relationship

Our relationship must never have conflict in it.
Our relationship must seem conflict free to outsiders.
We must never discuss our relationship with third parties.

We must compete rather than cooperate with each other.
We must have definite rules for our relationship.

About life

Life must be fair.
Life must be free of hassles.

When you find yourself getting angry, it helps if you do not act impulsively. Instead stop and think whether any of your unrealistic rules contribute to it. You can develop the skill of backtracking from your angry feelings or actions to the thoughts that generate and sustain them. Then you evaluate how realistic are your rules. You can dispute your rules by asking questions like: 'Where is the evidence to confirm or negate their realism?'; 'Do I expect the same of other people's relationships?' and 'What are the positive and negative consequences of maintaining my rule(s)?' Often you will find that your rules are partially true, but you have made them too rigid: for instance, a rule might be 70 per cent realistic and 30 per cent unrealistic.

A final step is to restate your unrealistic anger-evoking rules into more realistic rules. Following are some guidelines for stating realistic rules: (a) express preferences rather than demands; (b) emphasize coping rather than perfectionism; (c) base them on your own valuing process; (d) allow flexibility so they are amenable to change in light of new information; and (e) word them so that they lead to a functional rating of specific characteristics and not to a global self-rating of your or your partner's personhood. Following are some examples of restating anger-evoking rules into more realistic rules.

Unrealistic rule: 'I must always get my revenge.'

Realistic rule: 'My interests are not best served by thinking in terms of revenge. I can work out more appropriate strategies for gaining my preferences and keeping our relationship intact.'

Unrealistic rule: 'My partner must never criticize me.'

Realistic rule: 'Feedback is important in our relationship. However, I would prefer that my partner uses tact and diplomacy when giving feedback.'

Choose to perceive accurately

*How strange it is to see with how much passion
People see things only in their own fashion.*

Molière

An important skill for partners wishing to avoid the slide from fusion to fission is that of, wherever possible, perceiving one another through kind rather than unkind eyes.

Beck (1988) observes that marital conflict 'fosters and exaggerates egocentric perspectives' (p. 61). Partners systematically bias their perceptions by 'framing' one another negatively: for instance, 'He likes to see me suffer' and 'She is so manipulative.' Once this framing process starts, partners misinterpret positive or neutral acts as negative and perceive negative acts even more negatively. Clearly such negative framing fans and sustains anger.

Identify tricks of the mind

Beck observes that distressed couples can fall prey to a number of cognitive distortions or tricks of the mind that interfere with perceiving themselves and their partner accurately. If you can identify your characteristic ways of misinterpreting, you are in a stronger position to correct them. Following are some common tricks of the mind (Beck, 1988; Beck & Weishaar, 1995).

- *Tunnel vision.* Partners focus only on that part of the overall picture that they want to see: for example, continually finding fault with one another.

- *Arbitrary inference.* Drawing a specific conclusion about yourself or your partner without supporting evidence. For example, you wrongly perceive your partner's silence as anger.

- *Mindreading.* Ascribing thoughts and intentions to your partner either without checking with him or her or, if you've checked, thinking you know better. For instance, you can erroneously mindread that your partner wishes to hurt you.

- *Overgeneralization.* Using imprecise language that is far too global: for example, 'He/she *never* does anything round the house.' or 'He/she *always* keeps me waiting.'

- *Magnification.* Making your partner and events out to be worse than they really are. Exaggerating negative consequences.

- *Negative labelling.* Placing negative labels on your partner and then reacting to them as though they were the whole truth: for instance, 'He/she's impossible', 'He/she doesn't give a damn', 'She's a castrating bitch', and 'He's a narcissistic bully.'

- *Polarized thinking.* Thinking in black-and-white terms: for instance, 'He/she either loves me or he/she doesn't' or 'Either we get on really well or we don't get on at all.'

Reality test your perceptions

This section focuses on not being unnecessarily hard in the way you judge other's behaviour. This also can be a way of not being too hard on yourself.

> Jimmy and Peggy had been going out for two months. Every time Peggy said that she found another man attractive, Jimmy felt jealous, put down and angry with her.
>
> Cindy and Pete were newly weds. When Pete started coming home from the office a little

later than usual, Cindy concluded that he was becoming bored with her. She resented this.

Libby and Andy had been living together for six months. Libby was becoming extremely uptight because Andy was not more openly affectionate. She concluded that he did not love her any more.

You can jump to conclusions that trigger anger (Fiendler, Marriott & Iwata, 1984). Let us assume that the interpretations of their partner's behaviour that Jimmy, Cindy and Libby chose to give themselves were erroneous. This may have been partly due to their own insecurities and partly because they have insufficiently developed skills of propositional thinking. Propositional thinking means treating your thoughts as hypotheses and then using the process of scientific enquiry to generate and review evidence that confirms or negates your hypotheses (Beck, 1988; Beck & Weishaar, 1995). The outcome of each of Jimmy's, Cindy's and Libby's misinterpretations was that they felt angry with their partner.

An obvious but often overlooked skill of trying to interpret your partner's behaviour is to ask them about it. You check out their reasons before jumping to conclusions. Another skill is to generate alternative interpretations and then choose the one that best fits the factual evidence. Here are some examples.

1. Alternative interpretations that Jimmy might have for Peggy's behaviour.

- 'I tell her how I find other women attractive so why shouldn't she tell me the same about men.'

- 'Peggy would not make such comments to me if she did not feel safe with me.'

- 'Our relationship is deteriorating and she does not try to be tactful any more.'

2. Alternative interpretations that Cindy might have for Pete's behaviour.

- 'He told me that they have a big job on at work. It's my own insecurity talking when I feel he is bored with me.'

- 'Pete has a girlfriend at the office and our marriage is already on the rocks. He is being unfaithful.'

- 'Pete is working extra hard to ensure that we are on a sound financial footing.'

3. Alternative interpretations that Libby might have for Andy's behaviour.

- 'He never has been openly affectionate, but he has always been there for me when I want him.'

- 'Andy is good at showing affection. It's just that I am very demanding.'

- 'Andy came from a family where neither parent was openly affectionate and he needs help in becoming more expressive.'

If you become aware that you have a tendency to become unnecessarily aggressive, a useful skill for curbing your 'knee-jerk' reactions to perceived provocations is to search for alternative and better ways of interpreting them. As part of reality testing your perceptions, you can ask the following questions.

'Stop...think...am I jumping to conclusions?'
'Are my perceptions based on fact or inference?'
'Am I distorting the evidence through one or
more tricks of the mind?'
'If based on inference, are there alternative
interpretations more closely related to the
facts?'
'If necessary, what further information do I
need to collect?'
'What is the interpretation I choose because it
best fits the facts?'

Stopping and switching perceptions

Frequently partners need to discipline themselves to possess kinder and more innocent perceptions about one another. Brainwash yourself if you possess dirty brains! When you find yourself ruminating about your partner's negative qualities for no good purpose, thought stopping and thought switching are skills you can use. You can inwardly shout to yourself to 'STOP' and repeat this admonition a number of times. Then you can switch either to more positive thoughts about your partner or to other distracting thoughts.

Perceive assertion accurately

The emphasis in contemporary psychology on partners learning to be more assertive brings with it a real danger to relationships – partners may perceive assertion inaccurately. You can consciously label aggression as assertion if you insufficiently understand the concept, including how to deliver assertive verbal, voice and body messages. In addition, you can deceive yourself about being assertive when you are being aggressive. With emotions aroused, standing up for yourself can become standing either over or on top of your partner.

Perceive your own and one another's anger accurately

Partners require insight into their own and one another's anger. For instance, if you possess an awareness of how 'over the top' you have reacted, you can then try and repair your relationship. However, if you combine fury with defensiveness, you lose your flexibility. In addition, you create a double or triple problem for your partner: first, your anger; second, your trying to define him or her negatively; and third, your negative reactions if he or she reacts to your anger and defensiveness. In short, anger plus defensiveness can be a much bigger problem in relationships than anger on its own. Partners get to know whether one another's anger is a passing phenomenon or likely to be sustained by defensiveness.

Explain cause accurately

Blaming is probably the most common way that you can anger yourself by explaining cause wrongly. Lazarus and his colleagues write: 'Blaming, accusing, condemning, chiding or reproaching others or yourself is destructive. In fact, these actions hinder constructive, creative solutions to conflicts' (Lazarus, Lazarus & Fay, 1993, p. 69). Though you can blame yourself, most commonly in close relationships blaming involves externalizing the cause of your problems and anger outside of yourself. Blaming is a thinking skills deficit for many reasons. First, you fail to acknowledge your own contribution to problems. Almost invariably, the causes of relationship problems are neither black or white. Also, usually when you blame you explain cause defensively. Either unintentionally or intentionally you tell yourself stories intended to make you seem totally right and the other person seem totally wrong. Second, when you blame you may make your partner not only responsible for the problem but for your angry reactions as well: for instance, by thinking and possibly saying, 'It's all your fault. Look how angry you've made me.' Third, blaming can have unwanted negative consequences: for instance, your partner reacts defensively and counterattacks. Fourth, blaming mainly addresses the past rather than the future. You can stay stuck because, first, you blame your partner for creating a problem and then you blame him or her for not solving it. Fifth, blaming contributes to feelings of powerlessness. For instance, Adam explains to his counsellor that he keeps bashing his wife Hannah because her nagging makes him so furious. Rather than collude, the counsellor replies: 'Well, you're not going to let her keep controlling you like that are you?'

How can you explain the cause of your anger more accurately? You can become more mindful of the risks of blaming. Also, you can monitor the frequency, duration and intensity of your blaming thoughts. Whenever you catch yourself blaming, ask yourself the following questions: (1) 'How have I contributed to the creation of the problem?'; (2) 'How am I contributing to the maintenance of the problem?'; (3) 'What is the outcome I would really like for myself and for our relationship?'; and (4) 'What can I do to achieve that outcome?'

Predict realistically

Consequential thinking involves thinking through the consequences for yourself and others of your thoughts, feelings and actions. Frequently, anger blinds people from accurately predicting the consequences of their actions. You can sow the seeds of anger in relationships if you underestimate the gains from showing caring and kindness to your partner. Also, you can underestimate the gains from assertive expressions of anger that provide specific feedback and invite discussion. In addition, you may underestimate your ability to show anger effectively: for instance, your fears of getting out of control may be groundless. Also, if you have become more in control of your anger, you risk backsliding when you start underestimating the gains from maintaining self-control.

> Rob was a married man with three children, who came for counselling having hit his 16-year-old daughter, Ruth, when she came home from a date two hours later than agreed. Rob's wife, Betty, was fed up with his angry outbursts and their marriage was heading for the rocks. After a couple of months of counselling in which Rob acquired and used anger management skills, he thought he had lost some influence in the family by adopting a more reasonable approach to provocations. Using a whiteboard, Rob's counsellor, Sue Clark, developed with him a balance sheet of the positive and negative consequences of using his skills. As a result, Rob saw the balance was heavily in favour of continuing to use his anger-management skills.

Perhaps most often partners underestimate the losses from anger displays and, consequently, fail to exert sufficient self-discipline. You can insufficiently take into account the pain your behaviour causes and how it may create, sustain and escalate problems. You can come on too strong and too frequently. You can fail to give your partner the benefit of the doubt by predicting that, if you give an inch, he or she will take a mile (Lazarus, Lazarus & Fay, 1993). In addition, you may underestimate the losses from staying the same. For instance, you may think 'Once a victim, always a victim'. As a result, you continue your painful martyrdom.

Set realistic goals

You can set unrealistic goals for yourself, your partner and your relationship that leave you vulnerable to unnecessary anger. Such goals can stem from your unrealistic rules. For example, you may strive for perfection in yourself, your partner and your relationship. Also, you may have unrealistically high goals for your career or leisure pursuits that are stressful in themselves and also import stress into your relationship. In addition, your expectations of the level of satisfaction you can derive from your relationship can be far too high. Furthermore, you can possess unrealistic goals about changing your partner. The reverse can also be true – your goals may be too low. You might be less angry, happier and more fulfilled if possessing the courage to set higher goals for yourself, your partner and your relationship.

Ellis (1977; 1995) distinguishes between inelegant and elegant goals. An inelegant goal might be learning to upset yourself less with anger in relation to a specific situation. However, Ellis urges you to consider striving for the more elegant goal of 'surrendering your anger for a more forgiving, less damning attitude toward the world and the people in it' (p. 245). Ellis's is the same message as that of religious leaders, such as Jesus Christ and Buddha. By adopting a more accepting philosophy of life, you may learn to be forgiving of yourself as well as of others.

Use visualizing skills

You can use visualizing, or consciously changing the images in your mind, to help you manage anger better. Ways that you can use visualizing include the following.

• *Visualized rehearsal.* When preparing how to handle anger-evoking provocations you can visually go through the various steps in how you want to behave. Once you have worked this out you can repeatedly imagine yourself handling the provocation competently. You can accompany these 'movies in your mind' with a soundtrack of coping self-talk.

• *Visualized relaxation.* Visualization is best achieved by sitting or lying in a quiet and comfortable place, shutting your eyes and having no distractions. Here I describe two skills of visualized relaxation: visualizing the tension leaving your body and visualizing a restful scene.

Visualizing the tension leave your body

Following is some self-talk you can use for visualizing the tension leave your body. Talk to yourself in a soft, dreamy voice.

> I'm going to count to ten in groups of two, and after each group of two relax a different muscle grouping. It's as though I'm going to be turning out the different lights in a house at night. One, two ... focus on the tension leaving my legs and feet ... the upper part of my legs, my knees, the lower part of my legs, my feet and my toes. I'm enjoying the peaceful calm sensations of relaxation as the tension leaves my legs and feet. Three, four ... focus on the tension leaving the trunk of my body ... the upper part of my back, the lower part of my back, my sides, my chest/breasts, my stomach, my buttocks. My relaxation is getting deeper and deeper and deeper. Five, six ... focus on the tension leaving my arms and hands ... the upper part of my arms, my biceps, my elbows, the lower part of my arms, my hands and my fingers. My arms and hands feel warm and relaxed, warm and relaxed, warm and relaxed. Seven, eight ... focus on the tension leaving my head and face ... my forehead, the area around my eyes, my nose, my cheeks, my mouth, my jaw, my neck, my ears, the back of my head and the top of my

> head. My head feels drowsier and drowsier and drowsier. Nine, ten ... focus on the tension leaving the whole of my body ... my head and face, my arms and hands, the trunk of my body and my legs and feet. I enjoy the sensations of peace and calm, peace and calm, peace and calm as the tension flows from the whole of my body and my relaxation becomes deeper and deeper and deeper.

Visualizing a restful scene

You may visualize restful scenes not only as a prelude to other forms of visualization, for example visualized rehearsal, but also as a way of calming yourself down when angry. Visualizing a restful scene may follow either visualizing the tension leaving your muscles or progressive muscular relaxation, which is described later in this chapter. Each of you probably has one or more special scenes where you feel relaxed, for instance looking at a valley with lush green meadows or sitting in a favourite chair at home. The following is an example of a visual relaxation scene.

> I'm lying on an uncrowded beach on a sunny day enjoying the pleasant sensations of warmth on my body. I feel the caressing of a gentle breeze. I can hear the peaceful noise of the sea lapping against the shore nearby. I'm enjoying the soft touch of my towel and the sand. Also, I'm enjoying the salty smell of the sea and the fresh air. I haven't a care in the world. I experience feelings of peace and calm, peace and calm, peace and calm as my sensations of relaxation and well-being get deeper and deeper and deeper.

• *Visualizing the opposite.* When in the grip of anger, hatred and resentment, you can use visualizing to help access kinder feelings about the person with whom you are angry. At their cancer clinic in Dallas, Texas, the Simontons have used a imagery process to help patients let go of resentments and forgive people who have hurt them Patients are asked to get a clear picture in their minds of the person to whom they feel resentment. They are then instructed to: 'Picture good things happening to that person. See him or her receive love or attention or money, whatever you believe that person would see as a good thing' (Simonton, Matthews-Simonton, & Creighton, 1978, p. 152). The Simontons report that as patients continue to use the process of visualizing good things happening they gain a different perspective on the persons resented. Consequently, they begin to feel more relaxed, less resentful and more forgiving.

- *Visualizing another's viewpoint.* You can use visualizing to help understand how the other person might view an action you view as provocative. By taking your partner's perspective you may gain insight into your own contribution to the conflict. Also, you can visualize how she or he might receive your angry messages.

Use problem solving skills

An important skill in managing anger is to discipline yourself to be problem-centred rather than self-centred when negative events happen inside or outside of your primary relationship (Ellis, 1977). Since, in the next chapter, I review cooperative approaches to solving problems, I only mention the topic briefly here. Anger can act as a stimulus for identifying and defining problems (Lerner, 1985). When difficulties occur in your life you can translate them into problems that require addressing rather than occasions for blame and recrimination (Deffenbacher, Thwaites, Wallace & Oetting, 1994). Possess a positive and constructive orientation to problems rather than a negative and destructive one. However badly your partner may behave or fate may treat you, these are problems for you too if you remain unhappy about them. Skills of rational problem solving include: confronting the problem rather than avoiding it; resisting impulsiveness and generating alternative approaches; carefully assessing the predicted consequences of each alternative; and choosing your preferred solution.

SOME ACTION SKILLS FOR ANGER

Following are some suggestions for what you can actually do to prevent, express, manage and repair damage from your anger.

Keep your temper

In addition to using thinking skills, there are a number of things you can do when you tune into your early warning systems that you are in danger of losing your temper. For example, you can breathe slowly and regularly. You can delay your response until less agitated: for instance, by using counting to ten or to a hundred strategies. You can remove yourself from the situation and take 'time out'. Also, you can engage in 'cooling off' activities, like going for a walk or taking a bath or 'letting off steam activities', like running or playing a competitive sport.

Use preventive assertion

Sometimes you can prevent or lessen anger by being assertive. Below are examples where people's failure to be assertive contributes to their anger.

- *Failure to disagree.* There may be occasions when you are angry because you are too timid about sharing your thoughts and feelings.

> Paul and Barb usually do what Paul wants. Paul
> is very positive about initiating and stating his

wants and wishes. Barb is very inhibited about stating what she wants. She resents Paul because she thinks he is too domineering and should know what she wants without having to be told.

• *Failure to make requests for behaviour change.* There may be instances when you disapprove of another's behaviour and either bottle up your anger or let some out indirectly, for instance through cynicism and gossiping. Until you have made a genuine effort to change another's behaviour you can collude in situations causing resentment.

Rita and Vera are partners. Rita does not like lending Vera money. Every time Vera asks, Rita grudgingly lets her have the money and then nags Vera until she gets repaid. Rita gets furious with Vera both because of her continual requests and also because Vera is poor at meeting repayment deadlines. Rita could prevent her anger if she made it clear to Vera that she wanted no more loan requests. If she backed up her words by not lending money, it is possible that, after a period of adjustment, Vera would stop asking her.

Chapter 15 reviewed assertive ways of disagreeing and making requests for behaviour change. Turn back to that chapter if you would like further suggestions for how to be assertive in those areas.

Express anger assertively

Alberti and Emmons (1990) observe: 'Remember that anger and aggression are not the same thing! Anger can be expressed assertively' (p. 140). Assuming you decide it is worth conveying anger how do you go about it? Though not always easy, try to use tact and diplomacy in your verbal messages. You can use the FFR (feedback, feeling, request) format mentioned in Chapter 15. Give specific feedback about what bothers you; state your feeling as an 'I' message; and let your partner know what you want. Also, beware of put-downs, defensiveness and playing the victim. Below are examples of expressing anger aggressively and assertively.

Veronica to Ted

Aggressive anger
You're doing it again. What's wrong with you? My father is much smarter than you. Shut your bloody gob.

Assertive anger
When you call my father an interfering bastard, I get damn angry. Please stop it.

You can accompany your assertive verbal messages with appropriate voice and body messages. For instance, speak in a firm voice without shouting and emphasize words like 'damn angry' and 'stop'. Also, make good eye contact and avoid threatening gestures.

Relax yourself

Mention has already been made of how you can try to counteract angry feelings by visualizing the tension leaving your body and visualizing a restful scene. In addition, focusing on your breathing and taking a series of regular slow deep breaths can often help you to become more relaxed. If anything, emphasize exhaling: for instance, 'Breathe in ... out ... out ... in ... out ... out'.

Progressive muscular relaxation is another method by which you can work to dissipate your anger. The term 'progressive relaxation' refers to the progressive cultivation of the relaxation response (Jacobson, 1938). You may use progressive muscular relaxation in conjunction both with visualized relaxation and also with other thinking skills, for example coping self-talk (Deffenbacher, Story, Brandon, Hogg & Hazaleus, 1988). Relaxation skills can help you to deal with unpleasant and counter-productive aspects of heightened emotional arousal. The desired consequences of this are that you think and act more rationally.

The first step in physically relaxing yourself is to find a quiet space where you will be uninterrupted. You may use a mattress, a recliner chair or a comfortable chair with a headrest. If possible wear loose fitting, comfortable clothing and remove items such as glasses and shoes. Your arms should be either by your side if you are lying down or on the arms of your chair if seated. Your legs should be uncrossed and your eyes shut.

Progressive muscular relaxation involves you in tensing and relaxing various muscle groups. There is a five tension-relax cycle that you go through for each muscle group (Bernstein & Borkovec, 1973). These are: (1) *focus*, focus attention on a particular muscle group; (2) *tense*, tense the muscle group; (3) *hold*, maintain the tension for five to seven seconds; (4) *release*, release the tension in the muscle group; and (5) *relax*, spend 20 to 30 seconds focusing attention on the letting go of tension and further relaxing of the muscle group. Following are 16 muscle groups for progressive muscular relaxation: right hand and forearm; right biceps; left hand and forearm; left biceps; forehead; eyes, nose and upper cheeks; jaws and lower cheeks; neck and throat; chest and shoulders; stomach; right thigh; right calf; right foot; left thigh; left calf; and left foot. Progressive muscular relaxation requires regular practice to gain its full benefits. When learning the technique, you should practise for at least 15 minutes daily for a week.

At times brief muscular relaxation approaches may assist you to manage anger. For example, you can tense and relax four composite muscle groupings: arms and hands; face and neck; chest and trunk of body; and legs and feet. Another option is to tense and then relax all your muscles simultaneously, accompanied by inhaling and then exhaling a deep breath.

Manage stress

Stress can come from both within and without. Both sources can contribute to anger. Develop awareness of your early warning signals of stress and listen to them. If all else fails, at least heed your final warning signals of a nervous breakdown. Also, become more aware of what stresses you. Such awareness may help you not only to prevent and manage your anger but also to avoid taking it out on other people.

Each of you has an optimal level of stress or a particular level of stimulation at which you feel most comfortable. At this level you experience stress without distress (Selye, 1974). Beneath this level you may be insufficiently stimulated or bored. Above this level you are likely to experience physiological and psychological distress. Body reactions include hypertension and proneness to heart attacks and ulcers. Feelings of distress may include shock, depression, frustration, anger, disorientation and fears of insanity or nervous breakdown. If the heightened stress is prolonged or perceived as extremely severe, you may feel you are in a state of excessive stress or crisis.

Below are two examples of people whose stresses make them more prone to anger. Kim has allowed herself to develop an excessively stressful lifestyle. Art is reacting to external pressures. However, in both examples there is an interaction between internal and external sources of stress.

> Kim is a high pressure foreign exchange dealer. She is always on the go both professionally and personally. She lives on her nerves and burns the candle at both ends and in the middle. When things go wrong, she gets tense and irritable. She is like a tightly stretched rubber band just waiting to break out in anger.
>
> Art has just received a promotion at work. He now has to supervise 15 people. While pleased at the promotion Art still needs to develop the skills of being a good supervisor. He feels under pressure because of his promotion and is very irritable when he gets home. Art does not sleep well and his appetite is poorer than usual.

Some of the skills of managing stress are peculiar to the specific situations in which people find themselves. For example, as Art develops supervisory skills he is likely to feel less under stress. Other skills are more general: for example, possessing good thinking skills. Further skills of managing stress include: muscular and visualized relaxation; developing adequate recreational outlets; staying physically fit; keeping in touch with nature (my favourite!); developing your support network of helpful people; and improving your managing problems skills. Sometimes the most effective way to manage anger is to analyse the broader context of stresses in which it occurs. There may be choices that you can make and skills that you can develop for dealing with stresses outside a relationship that will free you to be less angry, more relaxed and happier within the relationship.

Handle aggressive criticism

Below are five verbal strategies for dealing with aggressive criticism. You need to accompany your verbal messages with appropriate voice and body messages. Also, use self-talk that assists you to stay calm and in control of your emotions. You are a person in your own right who does not allow herself or himself to be overwhelmed by another's criticisms and feelings. The strategies may be used in combination as well as singly.

1. *Reflective strategy.* This strategy allows your partner to vent their strong feelings and shows you have understood both their feelings and their reasons. For example, 'You feel mad at me because you think I am not pulling my weight in doing the household chores.' Often people stay stuck in anger like broken records because, rightly or wrongly, they consider they are not being heard. Reflecting another's anger does not mean that you automatically agree with them.

2. *Deflective strategy.* The object here is to blunt the thrust of the aggressive criticism by agreeing with part of it. This strategy is especially useful where you actually do agree with part of the criticism. Examples of this are: 'You have a point, I am rather untidy at times' or 'I'm not always as considerate as I would like to be.'

3. *Enquiry strategy.* Following on from either a reflective or a deflective response or from both responses, you may then use an enquiry: 'Please be more specific about what I've done to upset you?' The enquiry may defuse the aggressiveness of the criticism since it shows you are willing to allow your partner to elaborate their position. Sometimes you can use a *negative enquiry* that gives your partner permission to air misgivings: 'Have I behaved insensitively to your feelings?' (Dickson, 1982, p. 88). With both forms of enquiry, you may obtain information to clear up misunderstandings. However, sometimes an enquiry ignites rather than defuses anger: people can become threatened when asked their reasons for anger.

4. *Feedback strategy.* After showing that you have heard your partner's criticism you may choose to give feedback both about the criticism and the manner in which it was given. For example: 'I feel very uncomfortable when you criticize me so harshly. The reason that I am so late in picking you up was that I was in a traffic jam on the way over.' Sometimes when another person attempts to talk you down, calmly and firmly repeat your position at the same time as acknowledging that they feel differently.

5. *Deferral strategy.* Often you have a choice as to whether to back off now and react to criticism at a later date. Backing off does not mean backing down. Rather you husband your resources for when you can be most effective. You may say something like: 'I've

heard what you're saying (if necessary specify). I would like some time to think about it.' Alternatively, if it becomes clear that you disagree, you might say: 'It's obvious that we disagree. I think we both need some time to think about it. Could we fix a time to discuss it again?' Deferral strategies are not intended to avoid issues. Rather they allow either or both parties to cool down and then deal more rationally with the matter.

Apologize and take corrective action

Defensiveness is probably more dangerous than anger in close relationships. If you are defensive you risk fanning the flames of one another's anger. However, if you are open, capable of acknowledging hurtful behaviours when pointed out and willing to change them, you not only defuse those situations but also make it easier for your partner to behave likewise. By your honesty and actions ill-will can get transformed into goodwill.

If you have been unreasonably aggressive, you will likely have hurt your partner and diminished their self-esteem. When cooler, you may feel genuine remorse and shame. In addition, you may wish to diminish the suffering and pain you have caused him or her. A skill of repairing your relationship is to make a genuine apology (Lazare, 1995). A good verbal apology restores balance by acknowledging that you have broken a norm or relationship rule: for example, 'I'm sorry that I was so rude about your father last night.' You may add an explanation for being so aggressive: for instance, 'I had drunk too much' or 'I've been overworking.' Your partner may perceive a good verbal apology as a pseudo apology unless your voice and body messages also indicate genuine regret. Before, during or after an apology you can physically reach out to your partner by touching his or her hand, arm or shoulder.

Sometimes, you can make amends through your actions alone. Lazare (1995) observes 'in long-term close relationships, an unsolicited gift or favor may completely supplant the verbal apology – every other dimension of the apology may be implicit' (p. 43). You can also mend fences through offering some sort of compensation or restitution: for example, 'Please let me know if there is anything I can do to make it up?'

You are likely to damage rather than restore your relationship if you apologize and then repeat the same aggressive behaviour. Corrective actions speak louder than crocodile tears.

Forgive and move on

After an angry outburst, your partner may apologize to you. Assuming the apology is genuine, he or she is attempting to restore the damage done to your self-esteem. By offering an apology, your partner acknowledges wrongdoing and places himself or herself in a vulnerable position. Assuming you choose to accept the apology, you can still acknowledge your pain: for example, 'I felt very hurt by your remarks about my father, but I accept your apology.' If you do not accept genuine apologies and forgive, you risk alienating your partner. Also, your failure to reward honesty may cause your partner to be defensive in future. In addition, you risk torturing yourself by holding long-standing grudges. Sometimes your partner may not have the inner strength to verbally apologize, but will take corrective action. Again, the best policy may be to forgive and move on in your relationship.

HELPING ONE ANOTHER TO MANAGE ANGER

In a close relationship based on assumptions of teamwork and equality you can help one another to manage anger. Some anger in your relationship is likely to be a fact of life. You can each take responsibility for managing anger constructively rather than destructively. The following are some ways in which you may work together as a team to manage anger.

• *Possess realistic relationship rules.* Together establish realistic rules for expressing and managing anger in your relationship. The following rules may be helpful.

> 'Each of us tries to become aware of and openly locate our anger in ourselves.'
> 'Neither of us tries to control the other through the use of threats or physical violence.'
> 'Each of us attempts to avoid hurting the other by aggressive put-downs and emotional withdrawal.'
> 'Expression of anger in our relationship is a signal to explore our own thoughts, feelings and actions and not just those of the other person.'
> 'If either of us has been aggressive, we openly acknowledge this when calmer.'

• *Develop accurate and caring models of one another.* Each of you attempts to move beyond a superficial personification of yourself and your partner to develop a more accurate understanding. Try to understand one another's past experiences, burden of previous hurts, fears, vulnerabilities, trigger points, stresses, defences and ways of showing and avoiding showing anger. In addition, acknowledge and appreciate one another's strengths and positive qualities.

• *Use listening and showing understanding skills.* Ways in which you can use listening and showing understanding skills include the following. First, by tuning into your partner and helping him or her to express angry feelings that he or she may have difficulty either acknowledging and/or getting out into the open. Second, by showing you clearly understand your partner's feelings and reasons for getting angry. Third, by helping one another analyse and deal with the material underlying the anger. This kind of analysis may entail helping articulate unmet preferences and unstated requests in the here-and-now of your relationship, working through hurtful there-and-then experiences prior to your relationship, and dealing with current there-and-now stresses outside your relationship. Offering informal counselling to one another is another way of looking at this process. A risk here is that you focus exclusively on your partner, when exploring your contribution to his or her anger might also be fruitful.

CHAPTER HIGHLIGHTS

• Anger represents a hostile feeling of displeasure which can be demonstrated by verbal, voice, body, touch and action messages.

• Incorrect stereotypes are that males express anger and females suppress it and that physical violence is exclusively a male problem. However the outcomes of male physical violence are more severe and, probably, its incidence is greater.

• Positive uses of anger include: being a guide to a clearer definition of self; a signal that something is wrong; a motivator: a call for attention; and a curb for unwanted behaviours.

• Partners are likely to be less angry if each can accept one another's separateness and difference and develop a capacity for forgiveness.

• Feelings associated with anger can be positive and life-affirming as well as negative and destructive. Usually other feelings, such as hurt, are associated with anger.

• Own responsibility for creating your anger or 'anger-ing'.

• Use the STC frameworks to analyse the contribution of your thoughts and thinking skills deficits to your anger.

• You may be inhibiting both your angry and your loving feelings and need to get more in touch with both. In addition, develop skills of tracking your level of anger arousal.

• Use coping self-talk before, during and after provocations to calm you down, coach you and affirm your strengths.

• Relinquish anger-engendering childish demandingness by identifying, disputing, and restating unrealistic into more realistic rules.

• Choose to perceive more accurately by: identifying your tricks of the mind, reality testing your perceptions, stopping aggressive and switching to kinder perceptions, perceiving assertion accurately and perceiving your own and one another's anger accurately.

• Explaining the cause of your anger by blaming another has numerous negative consequences. Look for how you contribute to your anger and can achieve desirable outcomes.

• Realistically predict the consequences of showing caring, getting angry and acquiring and maintaining anger-management skills.

• Set realistic goals for yourself and your relationship that are neither too high nor too low. If anger prone, strive to adopt a more accepting philosophy of life.

• Visualizing skills for managing anger include: mental rehearsal, visualizing the tension leaving your body, visualizing a restful scene, visualizing the opposite and visualizing another's viewpoint.

• Use problem-solving skills to address anger-engendering provocations.

• Skills for keeping your temper include: delaying responding, controlled breathing, time out and engaging in cooling off and letting off steam activities.

• You can prevent or lessen anger by being assertive early on: for instance, disagreeing or requesting behaviour changes.

• Use appropriate verbal, voice and body messages to express anger assertively.

• Progressive muscular relaxation and brief muscular relaxation procedures, often accompanied by visualized relaxation, can calm you down.

• Managing stressful situations well outside your relationship can prevent your importing anger into it.

• Strategies for handling aggressive criticism include: reflective, deflective, enquiry, feedback and deferral.

• When you have caused unnecessary pain through anger, you can apologize and take corrective action. When your partner has caused unnecessary pain, consider forgiving him or her and moving on in your relationship.

• Skills for helping one another to manage anger include developing: realistic relationship rules, accurate and caring models of one another, and listening and showing understanding skills.

EXERCISES

EXERCISE 16.1
ASSESS MY ANGRY FEELINGS

Instructions

Answer the following questions on your own. Then, if appropriate, discuss with your partner, another or others.

1. To what extent is managing anger a problem for you?

2. To what extent do you get angry with yourself rather than with your partner (or another)?

3. How good are you at tuning into your angry feelings?

4. What are the other feelings, for instance hurt or anxiety, that you experience when you are angry?

5. What physical reactions, for instance tension, do you experience when angry?

6. How confident a person are you and to what extent does this affect your proneness to anger?

7. To what extent do you consider you are less of a person because you have angry feelings? If so, please explain.

8. How good are you at tuning into positive feelings about your partner (or another) that might prevent or soften your anger?

9. What messages do you send when you feel angry?
- verbal messages
- voice messages
- body messages
- touch messages
- action messages

10. Have you ever been or do you consider you have the potential to be physically violent when angry? If so, please elaborate.

EXERCISE 16.2
DEVELOP MY THINKING SKILLS FOR MANAGING ANGER

Instructions

This exercise focuses on four thinking skills for managing anger. Do each part of the exercise on your own. Then, if appropriate, discuss and practise with your partner, another or others.

Part A
Use coping self-talk

1. List your main anger-engendering self-statements. If you find this difficult, keep a daily record of your anger-engendering self-statements in a diary or worksheet.

2. Identify a specific situation in your relationship with your partner (or another) where you consider that your anger is harmful. Write down:
a. your goals in this situation, and
b. at least one calming, coaching and affirming self-statement for each of before, during and after the situation,

3. For rehearsal and use-in-emergency purposes, write out on a reminder card the coping self-talk statements you find most helpful.

4. Implement your coping self-talk skills to manage anger in the situation and evaluate the consequences for yourself and others.

Part B
Choose realistic personal rules

Think of a recent situation in your relationship with your partner (or another) where you felt and behaved in an inappropriately angry fashion.

1. Perform an STC analysis by identifying:

> **S** – the situation or provocation
> **T** – your thoughts: focus on identifying both realistic and unrealistic rules
> **C** – your feelings and physical reactions and how you acted

2. Dispute each of the unrealistic rules you identified.

3. Restate each unrealistic into a more realistic rule.

4. List any changes you anticipate might result from your revised rules in:
• how you might feel
• how you might physically react
• how you might act
• how your partner (or another) might feel
• how your partner (or another) might physically react
• what your partner (or another) might think
• how your partner (or another) might act.

5. Cassette-record your restated rules and play them back to yourself at least once a day for the next week.

Part C
Choose to perceive accurately

1. Choose a situation in your relationship with your partner (or another) in which you felt angry, possibly without due cause.

2. Specify how you felt before, during and after the situation?

3. State your original interpretation of how the situation arose?

4. Now generate as many different interpretations of how the situation arose as you can.

5. Evaluate each of these different interpretations and choose the one with the 'best fit' for explaining how the situation arose.

6. Assess the ways in which, for yourself and your partner (or another) the emotional and behavioural consequences of your 'best fit' interpretation would differ from those of your initial interpretation.

Part D
Use visualizing to become more forgiving

1. Find a quiet place where you can be uninterrupted. Sit in a comfortable chair and after you read each instruction close your eyes.

2. Think of a person about whom you are holding on to some anger from the past.

3. Visualize a restful and relaxing scene. Evoke not only the sights, but the sounds, smells and other sensations that make this such a calm and peaceful scene for you. Stay in this scene for at least two minutes.

4. Visualize a clear picture of a person towards whom you feel anger. Then do each of the following visualizations. Spend at least two minutes on each and take note of your reactions.

a. Visualize characteristics of the other person that you like.

b. Visualize one or more happy times in your relationship that you both enjoyed.

c. Visualize good things happening to that person, the sort of things that make her or him happy.

d. Visualize your saying to the other person that you love her or him and value your relationship.

5. After doing the above visualizations, review which ones, if any, helped you to feel more accepting and forgiving of the other person. Repeat these visualizations a number of times to gain the full benefit from them.

EXERCISE 16.3
DEVELOP MY ACTION SKILLS FOR MANAGING ANGER

Instructions

First complete this exercise on your own. Then, if appropriate, discuss and practise with your partner, another or others.

1. Assess your strengths and deficits in each of the following action skills of managing anger.

Keeping your temper
Using preventive assertion
Expressing anger assertively
Relaxing yourself
Managing stress
Handling aggressive criticism
Apologizing and taking corrective action
Forgiving and moving on

2. If appropriate, identify one or more of your managing anger action skills deficits and develop a plan to change how you act. In your plan, specify:

a. your goals, including a time frame,

b. the steps you intend taking to attain each of your goals, and

c. how you will monitor your progress.

EXERCISE 16.4
GROUP DISCUSSION: MANAGING ANGER SKILLS

Instructions

This is intended as a group exercise, though it may be done individually or in pairs. For each part:

1. spend 10–15 minutes answering the question in groups of three or four,

2. each sub-group shares its answers with the whole group and

3. then the whole group lists the six most important points or skills from most important to least important.

Part A
Feelings associated with anger

Examine your own feelings and list the six most important feelings people in the group have that are associated with or underlie anger in close relationships.

Part B
Identify anger-engendering thoughts

Examine your own thoughts and list the six most important kinds of thoughts people in the group use to fuel anger in close relationships.

Part C
Skills deficits for managing anger

Examine your own actions and list the six most important action skills deficits people in the group use to manage anger in close relationships.

Part D
Skills strengths for managing anger

List the six most important action skills strengths that people can use to manage anger in close relationships.

SEVENTEEN
Solving Relationships Problems Skills

In the animal kingdom, the rule is eat or be eaten;
in the human kingdom, define or be defined.

Thomas Szasz

CHAPTER QUESTIONS

- *What are relationship problems?*

- *Can conflict be productive as well as destructive?*

- *What is the association between conflict and relationship satisfaction?*

- *What are collusive, cooperative and competitive approaches to solving relationship problems?*

- *What are some interactive patterns that sustain relationship problems?*

- *How can partners cooperate to increase the exchange of caring actions?*

- *What is the CUDSAIR seven-step model for cooperatively solving relationship problems?*

- *How can partners gain greater emotional acceptance of relationship problems?*

This chapter focuses on managing conflict in relationships by using problem-solving skills. Partners can use the relating skills described so far in this book to create emotional climates where problems are less likely to flare up in the first place and more likely to be solved amicably in the second place. However, partners may find some problems more difficult to solve and hence become in conflict. The word conflict comes from the Latin roots *com-*, together and *fligere*, to strike. Dictionary definitions of conflict emphasize words like 'fight', 'struggle', 'antagonism' and 'sharp disagreement'. These dictionary definitions have three elements: first, a difference or disagreement; second, the disagreement is severe; and third, there is ill-will.

Conflicts are inevitable in ongoing relationships. Partners can enter relationships with differences in: their socio-economic and, possibly, cultural backgrounds; sex-role expectations; self-worth; ability to tolerate stress; tastes and preferences; beliefs and values; interests; social and family networks; and capacity to change and grow. With continued closeness problems can become widespread and cumulative. Also, familiarity can disinhibit partners about expressing negative feelings to loved ones. Add to these factors, partners' deficits in relating skills, including those of solving relationship problems, and the inevitability of conflict becomes even more obvious.

Relationship problems

Problems are perplexing or difficult questions that require some form of solution or resolution. Relationship problems can vary in severity, duration and frequency. They have the potential to generate more heat than light. In addition, what may seem minor issues from outside may possess symbolic meanings to either or both partners that can create huge rows. Consequently problems are not just matters of difference, but of perceptions and interpretations.

Table 17.1 List of relationship problems

Difference problems

Accommodation – location, nature of, use of space,
    decoration, furniture and fittings
Caring – amount, how partner shows caring
Companionship – amount, activities, friends in common
Decision-making – gender roles, power imbalance, style
Driving – back-seat driving, route finding, map reading
Emotional expressiveness – quantity, quality
Household activities – cleaning, cooking
Intimacy – quantity, quality
Money – earning, saving, budgeting, spending
Parenting – having a family, raising a family
Personal space – amount, what you and your partner do,
    personal friendships
Physical appearance – clothes, fitness
Relatives – parents, in-laws, other relatives
Scheduling daily activities – meal times, sleep
Sex – amount, activities
Substance abuse – alcohol, drugs
Trust – honesty, reliability
TV – amount, switching channels
Values – politics, religion
Work – balance with home, dual careers

Change problems

Ageing parents, death of parents
Becoming bored
Developing different interests
Drifting apart
Moving house
Partner becomes more confident and assertive
Partner joins work force/obtains further education
Sex-role changes – feminism, men's movement

Crisis problems

Infertility
Infidelity
Physical violence
Serious financial loss
Serious health problems
Serious mental disorders
Severe substance abuse
Unemployment
Unwanted pregnancy

As illustrated in Table 17.1, difference, change and crisis are three main categories for relationship problems. Problems of difference reflect dissimilarity in partners' wants, wishes and preferences. Sometimes difference problems possess underlying themes, such as variations in culture, sex-role expectations and wishes for closeness or independence.

Problems of change reflect alteration or variation in individual partners and hence in their relationship. Change and impermanence are part of life. Ideally, partners develop in roughly the same ways and at roughly the same rate. Also, they help one another adjust to and accommodate their individual changes and development. However, harmonious development cannot be guaranteed. As one partner develops, he or she may feel constricted and become out of touch with the other. In addition, couples cannot escape the increased questioning of traditional roles and values arising from technological change.

Problems of crisis reflect potential turning points in relationships. Apparently, the Chinese use two symbols for the concept of crisis: those for danger and opportunity. In this sense, all relationship problems are crises that partners can use for the good or ill of themselves and their relationship.

Another way of looking at relationship problems is in terms of the problematic skills that can ignite, sustain and improve or worsen them. For example, if partners possess good problem-solving skills, they stand a better chance of avoiding serious and long-standing conflicts than if they possess poor skills. Thus a relationship problem has two dimensions: the problem itself and the problem solving skills each couple possesses.

Productive and destructive conflict

The negative effects of conflict stemming from relationship problems scarcely need cataloguing. Conflicts can cause immense psychological pain which can last well after relationships end. Relationships which offered promising opportunities for both partners can founder because partners possess insufficient skills to surmount their problems. In Chapter 1, I provided statistics on the high level of breakdown and distress in British and Australian marriages. Unhappy homes, where parents' energies are diverted both in fighting each other and also sometimes displacing their frustrations on to their children, can adversely affect those reared in them. Parental unhappiness or divorce can contribute to children's delinquency, aggression, disobedience, conduct problems, social withdrawal, depression, anxiety and bed-wetting. In addition, children may learn poor relationship problem solving skills for their own lives. On a more subtle level conflicts can fester in relationships contributing to withdrawal and distance where previously there was happiness and closeness.

Conflict over relationship problems can be good as well as ill. The course of conflict may be productive rather than destructive. It is very easy to state the negative aspects of conflict. To redress the balance, I now state four positive aspects of relationship conflict.

• *Greater trust.* Conflicts can build trust. Partners who relate despite problems, as well as solve problems together, may feel that their relationship is much less fragile than those who have not had such experiences.

• *Increased intimacy.* Problems can be viewed as vehicles for increased intimacy. An important aspect of intimacy is the ability to give and receive honest feedback. A fuller sharing of self can occur where partners can reveal and solve problems and disagreements rather than inhibit or suppress them.

• *Increased confidence.* Partners who solve relationship problems effectively may gain in confidence. They know that their relationship is strong enough to withstand conflict. Each may feel better for being able to say what they think and feel. Problems are confronted rather than allowed to fester. Each partner may gain a firmer sense of her or his identity as well as greater knowledge of one another. Both may gain valuable practice in solving relationship problems effectively.

• *Creative solutions.* The course of productive conflict can be viewed as a process of mutual problem-solving. Creative solutions which protect both parties' interests, sometimes called 'Win-Win' or 'No-Lose' solutions, may be the outcome of this process. The opposite of a 'Win-Win' solution is a 'Lose-Lose' one, in which neither partner's interests are protected. In a 'Win-Lose' solution only one partner gets what she or he wants.

Relationship satisfaction and conflict

Relationship satisfaction refers to each partner's subjective evaluations of one another and of the relationship. Relationship satisfaction can be contrasted with relationship adjustment which refers to the extent to which processes characteristic of functional and harmonious relationships are present. Sabatelli (1988) observes that 'the well adjusted relationship has been conceived of as one in which the partners frequently interact with one another, seldom disagree on important marital issues, communicate openly with one another, and resolve disagreements in a mutually satisfactory manner' (p. 894). My premise for this book is that good relating skills characterize well adjusted relationships and, as such, are highly associated with relationship satisfaction and stability.

Are conflict and relationship satisfaction incompatible? Arguing is one of the activities most characteristic of marriage and that more conflict is found in marriages than any other kind of relationship (Argyle, 1991). However, some couples report high levels of both satisfaction and conflict (Argyle & Furnham, 1983). Avoiding conflict by 'sweeping problems under the carpet' and emotional withdrawal either indicate dissatisfaction or, possibly, a brittle pseudo-satisfaction. Perhaps the critical consideration is how skilled partners are at solving their relationship problems rather than whether or not they have them in the first place. The results of an Australian study investigating 33 couples in the early years of marriage support this proposition. Partners high in relationship satisfaction after two years of marriage were less likely to manipulate one another, avoid dealing with conflict, behave coercively and engage in destructive patterns such as demand-withdraw than couples low in relationship satisfaction (Noller, Feeney, Bonnell & Callan, 1993).

PROBLEM-SOLVING STYLES AND PATTERNS

The best part of married life is the fights.
The rest is merely so-so.
                                        Thornton Wilder

Collusive, cooperative and competitive styles

Collusion, cooperation or competition are the three predominant styles partners can use for solving relationship problems. These styles correspond to the threefold distinction between nonassertion, assertion and aggression described in Chapter 15. In reality, partners may have mixed styles; a profile consisting of different mixes of collusion, cooperation and competition. Partners may adopt their predominant styles as individuals or couples. However, they may also differ. For example, one partner may collude to avoid open conflict with a competitive mate.

Where only one of the partners begins solving a problem with a cooperative style, the risk is that he or she does not maintain it in the face of continued competition or avoidance. The cooperative partner may require considerable inner strength to counter, and hopefully prevail over, the skills deficits of collusive or competitive partners. As relationships mature, the ideal is for both partners to become more skilled at solving relationship problems cooperatively.

Following are brief descriptions of collusive, cooperative and competitive styles for solving relationship problems, presented from the standpoint of partners as individuals.

- *Collusive.* Here you are unassertive. You collude in avoiding or submerging problems in your relationship. You may wish to keep the peace for fear of the psychological discomfort of confronting problems. You may deceive yourselves as to your motivation for colluding and insufficiently acknowledge your anxieties about conflict. A collusive problem-solving style can mean you give way to your partner much of the time. Collusion should not be confused with rationally accepting important differences or ignoring unimportant behaviour.

- *Cooperative.* Here you relate to your partner on the basis of respect. You work as a team both to prevent unnecessary conflicts and also to arrive at mutually satisfactory solutions to real conflicts. You acknowledge your contribution to problems. You strive to perceive your partner in balanced ways and to act with tact and diplomacy toward her or him. You do not attempt to impose your wishes on your partner. You seek solutions that maximize the gains and minimize the costs for one another and your relationship.

- *Competitive.* Here you view the problem as one in which there are scarce resources. Consequently, there has to be a winner and a loser. The loser is not going to be you. You adopt an 'I win-You lose' approach to the conflict and do all in your power to get your way. Your tactics may include manipulation, not telling the whole truth, not admitting mistakes and sending aggressive verbal, voice and body messages. The risks of such an approach include not arriving at the best solution and your partner feeling violated. Though you may have won in the short term, you still may pay a high price for your victory.

Table 17.2 depicts collusive, cooperative and competitive joint problem-solving styles, presented from the standpoint of partners as couples. As mentioned above, partners' problem-solving styles do not always match. The statement of cooperative style characteristics may seem idealized. Nevertheless, the list of characteristics represents a goal towards which partners can strive.

Table 17.2 Characteristics of collusive, cooperative and competitive styles of solving relationship problems

Collusive	Cooperative	Competitive
Nonassertive	Assertive	Aggressive
Collaborative	Collaborative	Individualistic

Insufficient commitment to relationship	Strong commitment to relationship	Insufficient commitment to relationship
De-selfing	Self-loving	Selfish
Mutual caution	Mutual caring	Mutual antagonism
Peace as goal	Problem resolution as goal	Power as goal
Problems partially addressed or avoided	Problems addressed	Problems personalized
Muted communication	Clean communication	Manipulative and/ or coercive communication
Debilitating anxiety	Manageable anxiety	Debilitating anxiety
Feelings expressed too weakly (verbal, voice and body messages)	Feelings expressed appropriately (verbal, voice and body messages)	Feelings expressed too strongly (verbal, voice and body messages)
Diluted perceptions	Balanced perceptions	Negative perceptions
Solutions insufficiently offered and considered	Solutions tactfully offered and rationally considered	Solutions aggressively offered and rejected or imposed
Problem partially solved or submerged	Problem solved or contained	Problem unsolved, escalated or waiting to re-erupt
Partial win/lose outcome	Win-win or no-lose outcome	Win-lose or lose-lose outcome
Post-conflict unease	Post-conflict satisfaction	Post-conflict distress

Interactive patterns and games

Many who write about relationship problems view the maintenance of conflicts in terms of interactive patterns (Christensen & Heavy, 1993; Litvinoff, 1993), systems (McKay, Fanning & Paleg, 1994), dances (Lerner, 1985, 1989; Tavris, 1989) and games (Berne, 1964). Circularity is the common feature of all these approaches. Partners become stuck in repetitive cycles of automatic and mutually reinforcing damaging behaviour. Each partner's actions become dependent on the other's with every action being a reaction.

Conflicts as interactive patterns

Interactive patterns between partners can be viewed as systems. A system is a set or arrangement of connected parts to form a whole. Family discord is frequently viewed in systems terms (Goldenberg & Goldenberg, 1995). It is possible to view discord between marital or cohabiting partners likewise: for instance, the collusive and competitive joint problem solving styles may be seen in systems terms. Partners are mutually trapped by their characteristic responses to one another's differences – each partner's behaviour being related to the other's. The cooperative joint problem-solving style is harder to view in rigid systems terms, since this style assumes that partners are rational choosers.

Though there are many couple interactive patterns or systems, two common ones are demand–withdraw and blamer–placater (Christensen & Heavy, 1993; Jacobson, 1989; McKay, Fanning & Paleg, 1994). In demand–withdraw, the more one partner demands emotional closeness, the more the other partner withdraws. Pursuer–distancer is another way of viewing the demand–withdraw pattern. In general, women are more demanding and men more withdrawing, a sex difference found to be 'more likely than the reverse in non distressed couples, clinic couples prior to therapy, divorcing couples and dating couples' (Christensen & Heavy, 1993, p. 122). In about 70 per cent of heterosexual distance–closeness patterns women want more closeness, and in the other 30 per cent men want more closeness. Although anxiety plays a large part, there can be something empowering about being the distancer–you have the power over the person wanting closeness. Male and female homosexual couples are more likely to have issues around distance and around closeness, respectively. The withdraw role in a demand–withdraw pattern can either be collusive, in the interests of keeping the peace, competitive, demonstrating passive-aggression, or possibly both. In the blamer–placater interactive pattern, the placater wants to avoid conflict and so always makes the necessary accommodations to the blamer. The blamer and the placater adopt competitive and collusive problem solving styles, respectively.

Conflicts as playing games

Eric Berne, the founder of Transactional Analysis, regarded playing games as one of six ways in which people structure time. A psychological game is a set of covert or ulterior as well as overt interpersonal transactions which lead to a predictable outcome or payoff. Frequently, these payoffs involve negative feelings or 'rackets' such as anger and depression. Berne observed that though the 'incidents' in games may appear to be adventitious, 'careful scrutiny reveals that they tend to follow definite patterns which are amenable to sorting and classification, and that the sequence is circumscribed by unspoken rules and regulations' (Berne, 1964, p. 17).

Each game has a motto or name by which it can be recognized. For example, 'If it weren't for you' is the name of a marital game. In IWFY a women marries a domineering man hoping he will restrict her activities so that she can avoid anxiety-evoking situations. However, when he restricts her, instead of thanking him for carrying out her intentions she complains about the restrictions. Her complaining makes him feel uneasy and gains her all sorts of advantages over him. An outside-the-marriage variant of IWFY is 'If it weren't for him', which she plays with her lady friends. Berne regarded all games as 'substitutes for the real living of real intimacy' (Berne, 1964, p. 18). Games are also inferior substitutes for cooperatively solving relationship problems.

COOPERATING TO INCREASE THE EXCHANGE OF CARING ACTIONS

If necessary, what can you and your partner do to try and improve your relationship satisfaction? You can show more caring for one another (Babcock & Jacobson, 1993; Beck, 1988; Margolin, 1981; Stuart, 1980). Partners in distressed relationships reciprocate more uncaring actions than those in satisfied relationships. Successful couples keep their relationships rewarding both by maintaining existing caring behaviours and by initiating new ones. They also enhance their relationship in other ways: for instance, by livening up sex and developing common interests. Exchanging a high number of caring actions both prevents and contains conflicts: preventing them, because happy people are less likely to pick unnecessary fights, and containing them by creating good will. However, increasing your exchange of caring actions is definitely not a substitute for developing communication skills for cooperatively solving relationship problems.

Partners in unhappy relationships may be well advised to take a systematic approach to increasing their exchange of caring actions. Partners can become habituated to one another's caring actions so that they lose their reward value. Couples who start with a narrow initial range of caring actions are especially vulnerable to erosion of mutual rewardingness. Also, partners may take for granted and not show appreciation for caring actions that they still value.

Increasing the exchange of caring actions can be viewed in six steps.

1. Become aware of the importance of exchanging caring actions.
2. Acknowledge existing caring actions.
3. Make wish lists for additional caring actions.
4. Agree upon willingness lists.
5. Implement your agreement.
6. Review progress and make further agreements.

1. *Become aware of the importance of exchanging caring actions.* Though it may seem obvious, you may need to become more aware that partners are more attractive to one another if they are caring rather than uncaring. This basic point can easily get lost in the heat of a conflict. You may also need to remind yourself that how you act influences how your partner reacts. Stuart (1980) observes that a basic principle of social interaction is that: 'POSITIVE ACTIONS ARE LIKELY TO INDUCE POSITIVE REACTIONS, FIRST IN THE ATTITUDES OF OTHERS, AND THEN IN THEIR BEHAVIORS' (p. 194).

Humans tend to reciprocate negative or uncaring actions more quickly than positive or caring ones, on a tit-for-tat theory. Nevertheless, if you maintain caring actions, chances are good that such actions will soften your partner's attitude. In turn, this softening of attitude may result in both an increase in their caring actions and a decrease in their uncaring actions towards you. Furthermore, if you both agree that insufficient exchange of caring actions is a problem in your relationship, the fact that each of you now makes an effort to please can help rebuild trust.

2. *Acknowledge existing caring actions.* Partners in unhappy relationships tend to overemphasize one another's uncaring actions. Conversely, they often misperceive, take for granted, or fail to show appreciation for one another's caring actions. Both of you may need to become more aware of the caring that already exists in your relationship. You can share your perceptions of existing caring actions in two main ways. First, each of you can make a list of your own caring actions. What do you do that pleases? What do you say that pleases? This process can help partners discover for themselves not only the caring actions they currently offer one another, but also how much or little care they show. Listing your own gaps in caring may be less threatening than having them pointed out by your partner. These lists of 'my caring actions towards you' can be exchanged and discussed. Second, each partner can make a list of the other's actions that she or he perceives as caring. Here it is important not to spoil your positive feedback with negative 'hooks' – for instance: 'I like it when you rub my back, but you could do it less clumsily.' These lists of 'your caring actions towards me' can be exchanged and discussed. Refrain from hostile criticism during this discussion.

3. *Make wish lists for additional caring actions.* Each of you now answers the question: 'What caring actions would I like you to do for me which you are not currently doing?' The actions on your wish list must be specific and stated in the positive. For example, 'Not to be such a messy person' is neither specific nor stated in the positive. 'Not leaving your dirty socks on the bedroom floor' may be specific, but it is not stated in the positive. 'Put your dirty socks into the laundry basket' is both specific and stated in the positive. It is important that you include some small caring actions that are not necessarily in your areas of major conflict, to allow your partner to take some easy first steps. In addition, try to make some of these actions the sort that can be performed almost daily – for example, 'Ask me how my day has been when I get home from work'. You may list the caring actions that you want in any area of your relationship: for example, companionship, sex, money, household chores and so on. You can also numerically rate the caring actions on your wish list: for instance, 1, nice; 2, better; and 3, great (McKay, Fanning & Paleg, 1994). Take care in making your wish lists. Be tactful: keep in mind that your purpose is to influence the other person to become more caring towards you, not to humiliate them. When both of you have had enough time to make your wish lists, exchange them.

4. *Agree upon willingness lists for performing caring actions.* Your goal here is to make an agreement in which you both state that you will perform some additional caring actions for the other for a specified time period, say the next two weeks. Each of you should feel free to choose which additional caring actions from your partner's wish list you put on your willingness list. If necessary, clarify each other's requests. Sometimes both of you may make the same request: for example, 'Spend more time talking to me.' Much of the time each of you is likely to be agreeing to different requests.

A choice in making agreements or contracts is whether they should be quid pro quo ('If you do this, I'll do that') or based on good faith ('My actions are independent of yours'). Good faith contracts are preferable in personal relationships since they make each of you responsible for your own actions. You can always review your partner's actions at the end of the agreement. The number of items on your willingness lists can be unequal – though avoid large imbalances, if possible. Following is a simple good faith contract made between Scott and Madeleine, both of whom wanted to improve their stormy relationship.

During the next week

Scott agrees to:

1. Have a happy talk period for at least ten minutes each evening when both of us are home.
2. Go out to dinner together at a restaurant we both like.
3. Give Madeleine a cuddle at least once a day.
4. Phone home when I am leaving the office late.
5. Empty the garbage daily.
6. Return Madeleine's library books.

Madeleine agrees to:

1. Have a happy talk period for at least ten minutes each evening when both of us are at home.
2. Go out to dinner together at a restaurant we both like.
3. Give Scott one body massage.
4. Have sex at least once.
5. Keep books and magazines off the living room sofa.
6. Mow the lawn.

Each person should have a written copy of the agreement. The agreement can be signed and countersigned if you think it will help you to keep it. Each should post the agreement in a place where they are likely to be frequently reminded of its terms – for instance, on a bedroom door or on the refrigerator.

5. *Implement your agreement.* Changing your pattern of behaviour from uncaring to caring may be difficult. If necessary, make a plan for how you are going to stick to your agreement. Caring verbal messages need to be accompanied by caring voice and body messages if they are to have the desired effect. For example, you do not say 'I love you' when you are deep in reading the newspaper. For the sake of your relationship, take a few risks in becoming more caring. Your taking some risks may make it easier for your partner to reciprocate. If you wish to perform further caring actions outside your willingness list, feel free to do so.

A skill of implementing your agreement is to acknowledge and reward one another's attempts to be caring by saying, 'Thank-you', 'That's great', 'I like that, or 'I appreciate your saying/doing that'. A fundamental psychological principle is that people are more likely to repeat actions that are rewarded than those going unrewarded. Possibly in the past each of you may received fewer rewards because you did not apply this principle adequately.

6. *Review progress and make further agreements.* As an individual, monitor your and your partner's efforts to become more caring. Also acknowledge what each of you achieves. When your contract expires, hold a joint review session in which each of you goes through everything you tried. Questions to ask in such sessions include: 'Was it noticed?', 'Was it appreciated?', 'How valuable was it?', 'What was it like for the giver?' and 'Could you do it in future?' Fine-tune your agreement or make it a stepping stone to another. Partners can add or subtract items both from their wish lists and their willingness lists. Also, you can indicate the importance of items, if not done so already. Even without agreements, develop skills of monitoring and reviewing how caring you are towards your partner and taking corrective action, if necessary. In addition, develop the skills of helping your partner to be more caring towards you: for instance, by making specific, tactful requests for caring actions and by saying 'Thank you'. Also, be careful not to sabotage your partner's attempts to be more caring by denying that he or she can do anything right.

CUDSAIR: THE SEVEN-STEP MODEL FOR COOPERATIVELY SOLVING RELATIONSHIP PROBLEMS

To jaw-jaw is better than to war-war.

Don't interrupt me when I am interrupting!
Winston Churchill

Couples may already use good caring, companionship and intimacy skills with one another and still have problems. Such couples are likely to have a credit balance of goodwill in their relationship bank account to draw on when problems occur. Other partners may need to increase their exchange of caring actions to reduce ill-will debit balances and increase goodwill credit balances before addressing major long-standing problems. Since relationship problems are inevitable, inevitably couples require good skills for solving them.

I now present CUDSAIR, a systematic seven-step model for cooperatively solving relationship problems. Each of the steps of CUDSAIR represents a cluster of skills – in fact, implementing the model involves almost all the sender and receiver skills described in this book. The model represents a framework of skills that partners can strive to use when difficulties and disagreements occur between them. Following are the seven steps in the CUDSAIR model.

1. Confront the problem.

2. Understand one another's perspective.

3. Define the problem.

4. Search for and assess solutions.

5. Agree upon the preferred solution.

6. Implement the solution.

7. Review implementing the solution.

Frequently, the seven steps of this confront–understand–define–search–agree–implement–review model overlap. Table 17.3 gives an overview of the central task and illustrative skills involved in each step of the model. Though not indicated in the table, partners require the values espoused in this book – commitment, compassion, gentleness, courage and mental cultivation – to remain focused on the task and avoid hurtful aggression.

Table 17.3 The CUDSAIR seven-step model for cooperatively solving relationship problems

Task(s)	Illustrative skills
Step 1 Initiate the cooperative problem-solving process.	**CONFRONT the problem** Owning the existence of the problem, deciding whether or not to confront, keeping calm, picking a proper time and place, asserting that the problem exists, inviting cooperation in problem-solving.
Step 2 Defuse emotions, clarify positions, clear up misunderstandings.	**UNDERSTAND one another's perspective** Expressing feelings, reasons and requests assertively, owning responsibility for your contribution, sticking to the issues, using honest positives, using listening and showing understanding skills, turning a deaf ear to negative statements, admitting to and altering misperceptions.
Step 3 Arrive at a mutually acceptable definition of problem.	**DEFINE the problem** Avoiding unfair fight tactics, identifying common ground, identifying hidden agendas, identifying specific actions that sustain the problem, stating the problem clearly and simply.
Step 4 Generate and assess solutions.	**SEARCH for and assess solutions** Generating solutions, assessing solutions rationally.

Step 5 Agree upon a win-win or no-lose solution and state it clearly.	**AGREE upon the preferred solution** Making compromises and concessions, stating agreements clearly.
Step 6 Back up words with action, build and maintain trust.	**IMPLEMENT the solution** Keeping your word, avoiding over-reacting to non-compliance.
Step 7 Ensure solution works in best interests of both partners.	**REVIEW implementing the solution** Renegotiating rather than breaking agreements, modifying and changing agreements when necessary, returning to earlier steps of the CUDSAIR model if new problems emerge.

CUDSAIR provides an easily comprehensible and memorized model for solving relationship problems. Sometimes conflicts can be handled in a more informal way. However, on other occasions, you will need to be systematic. Even when only one of you starts by adhering to the model, you may influence the conflict management process constructively. Unfortunately, in conflicts, some partners are so prone to defensive thinking that a model that assumes you are both fairly rational can have limited practicality.

Step one
Confront the problem

> Brett and Debbie had been dating for two months and thought each other special. However both were aware of tensions in their relationship over how much time Debbie spent with her parents. They avoided talking directly about this problem for fear of hurting and then losing each other.

> Natalie was getting increasingly steamed up because Sid was not doing his share of cleaning the flat. She kept her resentment to herself until one evening she blew her stack and said a whole lot of things she later regretted.

Some of you, like Brett and Debbie, may find it easier to avoid than to confront relationship problems. Others, like Natalie, may collect trading stamps and one day cash them in by going for your partner's jugular vein. There are many skills of confronting relationship problems in ways that are likely to initiate rational rather than destructive processes.

When you become aware of a problem, you may still choose whether or not to confront it openly. Considerations here include what will be gained and whether the problem is important enough to either or both of you to bring it out into the open. Tavris (1989) observes: 'Couples who are not defeated by rage and the conflicts that cause it know two things: when to keep quiet about trivial angers for the sake of civility, and how to argue about important ones, for the sake of personal autonomy and change' (p. 248). Assuming that the conflict is not so obvious that your partner cannot ignore it and also that you decide to bring it into the open, the following skills may help.

- *Keeping calm.* Even if you have had a flare-up, use anger management skills to calm yourself down. While you want your partner to take notice of you, you wish to avoid being unnecessarily threatening. Shouting and screaming is likely to alienate your partner and consolidate her or his unwanted behaviours.

- *Picking a proper time and place.* Choose a proper time to raise the issue that there is a problem between you. It is probably not a good time to initiate problem-solving when either of you are rushing off to work, when you have visitors, or when you have both arrived home tired after a hard day. A good time may be after a meal when both of you have more energy. Also agree on a suitable place to discuss your problems that is quiet and comfortable and free from interruptions and distractions. Kitchens and lounges are probably better locations than bedrooms for raising and solving problems.

- *Asserting that the problem exists.* Confronting a relationship problem involves assertion. Use 'I' messages and clearly state the existence of the problem. Be civil: get the problem-solving process off to a good start by using tact and diplomacy rather than off to a bad start by using sarcasm and blaming. You can neutrally state the problem as a difference – 'You want to see more of your mother and I want us to spend more time together' – rather than personalize it – 'There you are, off to your wonderful mother again.' If your partner still resists owning that the problem exists, you can persist in your assertion until your partner recognizes that this is a problem for her or him as well as for you. For instance, look at your partner directly and use repetition and emphasis to make your point.

- *Inviting cooperation in problem solving.* Some differences may be resolved quickly and amicably once they are out in the open and discussed. If this is not the case, try to enlist your partner in cooperating to solve the problem. In essence you say: 'We have a problem in our relationship. Let's see if we can cooperate to solve it for our mutual benefit.' Both of you then need to set aside sufficient time and energy for dealing with it.

Step two
Understand one another's perspective

Jack and Lizzie are unhappy in their marriage.
When they argue neither of them closely listens

> to the other. Instead they shout, finger point and make comments like 'You *never* think of anyone but yourself' and 'You have *always* been selfish.'

Partners can agree that, at the start of discussing a problem, each of you takes turns in having uninterrupted 'air time' to state your perspective. During your air time the only talking that your partner should do is to reflect and ask you to clarify your perspective. Each of you is more likely to listen once safe in the knowledge that you will have your turn. If your partner interrupts, you have a number of choices including: pausing; saying something like 'Please let me finish, you have had (will have) your turn'; and putting out your arm with your palm facing them – a standard body message requesting silence.

Making the effort to try to understand each other's perspective is critical to solving relationship problems for a number of reasons. First, you may discover that your so-called problem is based only on misunderstandings and misperceptions. It need not exist in future. Second, making the effort to listen indicates one another's commitment to solving your problem cooperatively. You show respect for one another. Third, trying to understand one another may take some of the emotional steam out of the conflict. Often, when partners feel they have been heard and understood, they calm down and become less aggressive, thus helping one another to think more rationally. Finally, trying to understand one another's perspective helps both of you to start identifying the real issues in the conflict, rather than focusing on imaginary issues.

Following are some sender skills of understanding one another's perspective.

- *Expressing feelings, reasons and requests assertively.* Focus on stating your perspective rather than on analysing your partner. Beck (1988) writes: 'As your problem-solving sessions unfold, you will make more progress if you *focus on what it is that you want to achieve, rather than on what your partner does wrong*' (p. 325). Share your feelings in an open, yet tactful, way. Use reason to support your points. Provide specific feedback so that your partner knows what actions you would like changed. Avoid sending general negative messages that poison the atmosphere and lead nowhere (emotional farting): for instance, 'You're a fool' or giving dirty looks. Where appropriate, translate complaints, such as, 'You're not affectionate enough' into specific requests. If necessary, turn back to the section on assertively requesting changes in behaviour in Chapter 15. Do not expect your partner to read your mind. Also, avoid communicating as though you have a monopoly of the truth and wish to impose your definition of the problem on your partner.

- *Owning responsibility for your contribution.* When partners become mad at each other, they both view themselves as victims of each other's behaviour. However, if you can communicate some insight into how you may have contributed to the problem, you may help your partner to become less defensive and aggressive. An example of a conciliatory statement might be: 'It's true that I have been irritable lately'.

• *Sticking to the issues.* Focus on the current issues. Avoid dragging in irrelevant past history and indulging in personal attacks. Do not put your partner down by means of hurtful voice and body messages. Relationship problems are often over highly sensitive issues. Your partner is more likely to tune out to you, if your voice and body messages belittle her or him. Stuart (1980) observes: 'AS A GENERAL RULE, COUPLES SHOULD BE TAUGHT TO USE BOTH NONVERBAL AND VERBAL MESSAGES WHENEVER THEY WISH TO EXPRESS POSITIVE FEELINGS BUT TO RELY HEAVILY ON WORDS WHEN THEY WISH TO COMMUNICATE NEGATIVE FEELINGS' (p. 213).

• *Using honest positives.* Be prepared to give positive as well as corrective feedback to your partner. Honest positives are things you genuinely like about your partner and her or his specific actions (Kasssorla, 1984). Your partner is more likely to listen to you if you do, since you are less likely to be perceived as doing a 'hatchet job' on him or her. Also, if your intentions toward your partner are positive, clarify them. For instance, you might truthfully say: 'I really do want to spend more time with you, but I'm worried sick about making enough money to pay our bills.'

Following are some receiver skills of understanding one another's perspective.

• *Using listening and showing understanding skills.* Use good attending behaviour. Sometimes you can lessen emotional distance by putting your arm around your partner or holding hands. Listen to and observe voice and body as well as verbal messages. Help your partner to share their perceptions of the conflict. Use restatements and reflections to show that you have understood. Pay particular attention to tuning in accurately to your partner's feelings: this, above all, may help her or him to feel understood by you. When something your partner says is unclear, tactfully request clarification – for instance, 'I think I hear you saying ..., but I'm not altogether certain?' Where appropriate, show your support and agreement. At the end of your partner's initial statement of his or her perspective, you can summarize to check you have understood it properly. Using checking and summarizing skills prevents your making unwarranted assumptions and inferences.

• *Turning a deaf ear to negative statements.* Admiral Horatio Nelson used to turn his blind eye towards anything he did not want to see. Similarly, when listening your partner's perspective, you may be wise to turn a deaf ear to some less than flattering remarks about you. See negative remarks as symptoms of hurt and anger and strive for the inner strength neither to 'tune out' to your partner nor to retaliate. Where possible, focus on the cause of the relationship problem rather than upsetting yourself by choosing to become side-tracked by your partner's personal attacks. However, look after yourself. If the abuse persists, you can change your tactics by challenging it or by leaving the situation.

• *Admitting to and altering misperceptions.* In light of any significant new information, update your perspective of your partner and the problem. Where you have misunderstood your partner's actions and intentions, let her or him know this. Also, if wrong, say you are sorry.

Step 3
Define the problem

Dave and Josie were both in their early 20s and had been seeing each other for over a year. The moment they became engaged their previously happy relationship became full of conflict. Whereas previously they made decisions easily, now they argued over practically everything: which restaurants to go to, what films to see and so on. One evening when they were trying to become reconciled, Josie redefined the conflict. She admitted that getting engaged symbolized the loss of her autonomy. Josie was panicking because she felt trapped. Once she identified her hidden agenda Josie and Dave were able to work through her underlying fears. They are now happily married with two children.

In step two each partner may offer his or her own definition of the relationship problem. Conflicts can become extremely destructive when partners compete to define the problem on their terms. Both of you risk repetitively stating your positions and getting increasingly frustrated and resentful. The task of step three is to try and arrive at a mutually acceptable definition of your problem. In step three, the sender and receiver roles that partners adopt are less clear than in step two. Consequently, the risk of destructive arguing is greater.

Following are some skills for defining problems.

• *Avoiding unfair fight tactics.* Unfair fight tactics are competitive put-downs that show a lack of respect for your partner (Bach & Wyden, 1968, Steiner, 1981). Such tactics are manipulative and coercive power plays designed to influence another's definition of you, themselves and the problems between you. Unfair fight tactics include the following.

Mindreading and ascribing negative motives
Unnecessarily attacking psychologically vulnerable spots
Engaging in overkill and coming on far too strong
Monologuing and dominating the conversation
Using threats that engender insecurity
Providing misleading information
Feigning moods

> Sending threatening body messages – for instance, finger pointing, eyes blazing, punching, or scratching.
>
> Sending threatening voice messages – for instance shouting and screaming
>
> Unnecessarily dragging in third parties' opinions to support your own
>
> Using guilt-engendering tactics, such as playing the victim and tears
>
> Emotional withdrawal and sulking
>
> Playing games, such as feigning cooperation, yet always frustrating the search for mutually acceptable definitions of your problem

• *Identifying common ground.* Even where relationship problems are not based on misunderstandings, partners may still have considerable common ground. Avoid polarizing problems into a simple 'good guy–bad guy' format which obscures areas of agreement. Identify and acknowledge any common ground. An important way you can both acknowledge common ground and defuse emotions is to acknowledge your own mistakes and hurtful behaviours.

• *Identifying hidden agendas.* Try and deal with the real rather than the surface agendas. For instance, if a spouse suspects his or her partner is having an affair, picking on him or her in a whole range of other issues is not the best way of trying to define and solve the problem. Ideally both of you should be able to communicate your needs, including those that are unmet, simply and clearly. Being allowed to say 'I want', 'I need' and 'I prefer' without recrimination can contribute to identifying the real agendas in a conflict.

• *Identifying specific actions that sustain the problem.* Focus on the specific actions of yourself and your partner that maintain the conflict. In short, focus more on *how* the problem is being sustained rather than on who started it or why it arose.

• *Stating the problem clearly and simply.* The end product of step three is a simple statement of the problem. Avoid personalizing the problem unnecessarily. Where possible, move from defining the problem in 'you-me' terms to defining the problem as an 'it'. You and your partner may find it easier to address a relationship problem with some detachment if you define it neutrally as a shared problem.

> Having raised three children, Angie wanted to return to the workforce. Her husband Rod was unhappy about Angie going back to work because he was already under pressure with his job and did not want any extra work at home. Once they became calmer, they both agreed to define the problem as how to get the

housework done. Rod admitted he had changed his position from not wanting Angie to have a job once they agreed to define the problem in a way that allowed the preferences of both of them to be met.

Step 4
Search for and assess solutions

Take the example of Rod and Angie just given. Having defined the problem as an 'it', they can now cooperate to search for mutually acceptable solutions. Such solutions might include: getting a smaller house, paying someone to clean the house, eating out more, getting more take-away meals and so on. Searching for alternative solutions is often best done in two distinct stages: first, generating solutions and, second, assessing them rationally. Generating solutions is a creative process that can be inhibited by prematurely assessing emerging solutions.

Following are some skills of step four.

● *Generating solutions.* Generating solutions is a creative process. The objective is to generate a range of options, among which there may be some effective ones. Sometimes it helps to brainstorm. The object of brainstorming is to discover ideas. The rules for a brainstorming period include avoiding criticism and evaluation of ideas and coming up with the greatest quantity possible. Whether you brainstorm or not, offer solutions constructively and tactfully: for instance, 'One solution might be to …' as contrasted with 'I think we should …' – the latter wording setting up a potential conflict.

● *Assessing solutions rationally.* Assess solutions on the basis of what is best for both of you. If you have brainstormed, agree on which solutions seem feasible and assess the possible consequences of each of them. Each of you needs to state your reactions to possible solutions as preferences rather than demands (Ellis, 1995). Provide logical reasons for your preferences. Also, be prepared to acknowledge if some of your reasons are more emotional than logical – such reasons may still be important. If necessary, ask your partner for her or his preferences among proposed solutions and the reasons for them.

Step five
Agree upon the preferred solution

Craig and Janet both hated doing the dishes. Also, they disliked their kitchen sink being full of dirty dishes. After reviewing other solutions, they agreed that they would buy a dishwashing machine. Their agreement included details of how they would share the dishwashing until the machine arrived, how they would go about purchasing the dishwasher, and how they would share the dishwashing once the machine was installed.

Agreeing upon a preferred solution to a relationship problem involves two stages: reaching the agreement; then, stating it clearly. Following are some skills of step five.

• *Making concessions and compromises.* If you ask many couples what makes for a successful relationship, they often answer 'give-and-take'. Some relationship problems, such as the example of Rod and Angie given earlier, lend themselves to 'win-win' solutions for both partners. However, many relationship problems are not so straight-forward. Sometimes, as with Janet and Craig, the best you can achieve in a 'no-lose' solution where neither party feels violated. When assessing solutions, you may be faced with choices as to whether or not to modify your position. In such circumstances, making realistic trade-offs and compromises can be a useful skill. Acknowledge and show appreciation of any concessions made by your partner. Also, if necessary, remind her or him of any concessions that you make.

• *Stating agreements clearly.* Unclear agreements are more likely to be broken than clear ones, if only through misunderstanding. Agreements vary according to the nature of the conflict. For instance, if like Janet and Craig, your conflict has been about household chores, your agreement will include who is to do what and when. Often it is desirable to put agreements in writing. Writing out your agreements helps you to verify that they are clearly understood and to avoid future conflicts over the terms of the agreement. Written agreements can also be posted in places where they serve as reminders to implement them.

Some agreements involve planning how to implement them. Craig and Janet's agreement specified who was responsible for purchasing the dishwasher and how this task was to be performed. Another example is that of Julia and Andy, who finally agreed to spend their 16 day vacation by motoring around both the north and south islands of New Zealand. They then needed to plan how best to go about this. Julia and Andy's agreement included who was to plan which aspects of the vacation by what time.

Step 6
Implement the solution

Craig and Janet had agreed that, within 14 days, Craig would investigate the different options for purchasing a dishwasher within a stipulated price. After 14 days, Janet politely asked Craig if he had collected the information about purchasing their dishwasher. Craig said he had not due to pressures in his job, but would do so in the next seven days. At the end of this period, Janet again asked for the information. Again Craig replied that he had not

> had time to visit different shops to find out
> what the dishwasher options were. On hearing
> this, Janet, feeling very let down and annoyed,
> said, 'I can't trust you to do even the simplest
> of things.' Craig replied angrily: 'Get off my
> back. If it's so important to you, why don't you
> do it yourself?'

Following are some skills of implementing agreements.

• *Keeping your word.* Relationship problems are not solved unless agreements are kept.
It is critical to back up your agreements by your actions. Never agree to do anything
unless you have sufficient commitment to keep your word. If partners do not keep their
sides of agreements, the anger and hurt attached to the initial relationship problem may
be rekindled and, possibly, worsened. In addition, couples can ignite problems if either
or both of them keep agreements with bad grace – obeying the letter of the agreement
but not its spirit.

• *Avoiding overreacting to non-compliance.* If, for some reason, your partner does not
keep her or his side of an agreement, try and find out why. She or he may still think the
agreement is a good one and want to stick to it. There may have been unexpected
complications that have made adhering to the agreement difficult. Assuming your
partner wants to adhere to the agreement, your goal is to achieve willing adherence
rather than to alienate her or him.

Step 7
Review implementing the solution

> Chris and Alex had an agreement that, every
> other week, each would have first priority on
> the use of their car for personal activities.
> However, Alex started playing for her club's
> tennis team and said she would like to have
> the car most Saturday afternoons during the
> summer. Consequently, Chris and Alex
> decided to review their agreement.

Following are some skills for step seven.

• *Renegotiating rather than breaking agreements.* If, for whatever reason, you cannot live
within an agreement, renegotiate rather than break it. Breaking your agreement is a
breach of trust. Furthermore, your partner may consider this gives her or him similar
rights. This may further damage your relationship.

• *Modifying and changing agreements when necessary.* Agreements are not meant to be
set in concrete, but to work in the best interests of both partners. Some solutions may
turn out to be inadequate when they are implemented. Frequently, only fine tuning of

initial agreements is necessary. However, on other occasions, either or both of you may discover that the preferred solution has major weaknesses. Possibly, you have another reasonable solution available from your earlier search for alternatives. Otherwise you need to generate and assess further solutions.

• *Returning to earlier steps of the CUDSAIR model if new problems emerge.* Sometimes, partners find that another problem emerges in addition to or instead of the original one. In such instances you can return to the earlier steps of the CUDSAIR problem solving model.

Some further points about using the CUDSAIR model. First, the spirit with which you approach using the CUDSAIR model can be far more important than the detail. For instance, genuine compassion plus skills deficits like 'you' statements and interruptions may be far preferable than going through the motions of skilled problem-solving without real commitment to your partner. Second, the CUDSAIR model is not meant as a straitjacket. Couples develop idiosyncratic styles of solving relationship problems. Adjust the CUDSAIR model to incorporate positive aspects of your personal styles. Third, partners can monitor and assess their cooperative problem-solving skills and, if necessary, change and develop them. Fourth, if you find the CUDSAIR model helpful in solving one relationship problem you may be more motivated to use it for solving future relationship problems.

GAINING EMOTIONAL ACCEPTANCE OF RELATIONSHIP PROBLEMS

In Chapter 16, I mentioned some skills by which partners can manage anger by becoming more accepting and less demanding of one another. Partners can also learn to become more accepting and less demanding about the presence in their relationship of 'problems that are not easily amenable to compromise and accommodation' (Koerner, Prince & Jacobson, 1994, p. 381). Couples who find accommodation and compromise difficult include severely distressed couples, older couples with long-standing patterns of negative interaction, highly disengaged couples, and couples who are incompatible and highly polarized about basic issues (Jacobson, 1992).

Jacobson and his colleagues have developed an approach to marital therapy called Integrative Behaviour Couple Therapy (IBCT) that attempts the promotion of *change* along with the fostering of *acceptance* (Christensen, Jacobson & Babcock, in press; Jacobson, 1992). This approach adds 'emotional acceptance work' to the more traditional interventions of behaviour exchange (increasing the exchange of caring behaviours) and communication problem-solving training. Emotional acceptance work can soften partners' perceptions so that they themselves are more prepared to change as well as make them more serene about aspects of their partner not amenable to change. Given that women are usually the demanders in the demand–withdraw interactive pattern, emotional acceptance work may be particularly important in preventing and treating their distress and depression (Koerner, Prince & Jacobson, 1994).

There are four types of interventions used in emotional acceptance work. First, partners are encouraged to join empathically around the problem. In this intervention 'therapists guide couples to incorporate a reformulation of the problem which emphasizes the vulnerability the problem evokes in each of them, instead of clinging to a blaming and accusatory stance' (Koerner, Prince & Jacobson, 1994, p. 382). The problem is defined in terms of partners' reactions to their differences rather than in terms of their differences. Second, partners are helped to turn the problem into an it. Earlier in this chapter I mentioned that it is easier for partners to obtain detachment from relationship problems if they avoid unnecessarily personalizing them. Sometimes IBCT therapists encourage emotional distance by tactics such as humour and putting the problem into an empty chair.

Third, therapists attempt to foster emotional acceptance through building partners' tolerance of one another's negative behaviour. Partners can be helped to see positive features in one another's negative behaviour. Presenting negative behaviours in the context of family of origin history can also lead to a softening of perceptions. For example, a spouse may be more understanding of her husband's defensiveness, even when she is only mildly critical of him, once she understands this behaviour in the context of how he protected himself when growing up in a highly critical family. Fourth, without devaluing the importance of showing caring to one another, acceptance is fostered by encouraging greater self-care. Therapists attempt to stop partners from becoming over-focused on unmet needs in their relationship by encouraging them to explore alternative sources of satisfaction.

I end this chapter on cooperatively solving relationship problems with some words of wisdom from theologian Reinhold Neibuhr:

God, give us the serenity to accept what cannot be changed,
the courage to change what should be changed,
and the wisdom to distinguish one from the other.

CHAPTER HIGHLIGHTS

* Conflicts and problems are inevitable in ongoing relationships.

* Difference, change and crisis are three main categories for relationship problems.

* Problems of difference reflect dissimilarity in partners' wants, wishes and preferences.

* Problems of change reflect alteration or variation in individual partners and hence in their relationship.

* Problems of crisis reflect potential turning points in relationships.

* Conflict can be productive as well as destructive. Positive aspects of relationship conflict include: greater trust, increased intimacy, increased confidence and finding creative solutions.

* Conflict may be compatible with relationship satisfaction if couples are skilled at solving relationship problems.

- Partners as individuals and as couples may adopt collusive, cooperative or competitive problem-solving styles. Partners' problem-solving styles may not match.

- Conflicts may be viewed as interactive patterns or systems in which partners' responses become inter-related. Demand–withdraw and blamer–placater are two common interactive patterns.

- Conflicts may also be viewed as games in which partners have ulterior motives for not addressing relationship problems directly.

- Partners in unhappy relationships can increase their exchange of caring actions by: (1) becoming aware of the importance of exchanging caring actions; (2) acknowledging existing caring actions; (3) making wish lists for additional caring actions; (4) agreeing upon willingness lists for performing caring actions; (5) implementing their agreement; and (6) reviewing progress and making further agreements.

- Couples can use the seven-step CUDSAIR (confront–understand–define–search–agree–implement–review) model for cooperatively solving relationship problems.

- Skills for step one, confront the problem, include: owning the existence of the problem, keeping calm, picking a proper time and place, asserting that the problem exists and inviting cooperation in problem solving.

- Skills for step two, understand one another's perspective, include: expressing feelings, reasons and requests assertively, sticking to the issues, using honest positives and using listening and showing understanding skills.

- Skills for step three, define the problem, include: avoiding unfair fight tactics, identifying common ground and hidden agendas and stating the problem clearly and simply.

- Skills for step four, search for and assess solutions, include: generating solutions and assessing them rationally.

- Skills for step five, agree upon the preferred solution, include: making compromises and concessions and stating agreements clearly.

- Skills for step six, implement the solution, include: keeping your word and avoiding overreacting to non-compliance.

- Skills for step seven, review implementing the solution, include: renegotiating rather than breaking agreements and modifying and changing agreements, when necessary.

- The spirit in which couples use the CUDSAIR model to solve relationship problems can be more important than adhering to its detail.

- Partners can be helped to gain greater emotional acceptance of relationship problems.

- Four types of interventions used in emotional acceptance work are: empathic joining around the problem; turning the problem into an 'it'; building greater tolerance of one another's negative behaviour; and enhancing self-care.

EXERCISES
EXERCISE 17.1
IDENTIFY RELATIONSHIP PROBLEMS
Instructions

This exercise assumes that you are in a relationship. First each partner completes Part A of this exercise by herself or himself. Then partners do Part B together.

Part A
Identify relationship problems on your own

1. Turn to the list of relationship problems in Table 17.1 and, using the following scale, rate each problem.
Does this problem characterize your relationship?

    Not at all   1   2   3   4   5   6   7   8   9   Very much

2. Using the scale below rate overall how satisfied you are with your relationship?

    Not at all   1   2   3   4   5   6   7   8   9   Very much

Part B
Share and discuss with your partner

1. You and your partner share and discuss your ratings of relationship problems in each of the following categories:
Difference problems
Change problems
Crisis problems

2. Can you identify any common themes running through your problems, for instance one partner wanting more closeness and the other partner wanting more distance?

3. What do you think of the overall level of satisfaction in your relationship?

4. Currently are there any important problems in your relationship that you might solve together?

EXERCISE 17.2
MY AND OUR STYLES FOR SOLVING RELATIONSHIP PROBLEMS
Instructions

This exercise assumes you are in a relationship (though you can answer some of Part A without being in one). Each partner completes Part A of this exercise by herself or himself. Then partners do Part B together.

Part A
Identify problem solving styles

Turn to Table 17.2.

1. From the standpoint of your style as an individual, assess the degree to which you solve relationship problems by being:
Collusive
Cooperative
Competitive

2. From the standpoint of your partner's style as an individual, assess the degree to which she or he solves relationship problems by being:
Collusive
Cooperative
Competitive

3. From the standpoint of you and your partner as a couple, assess the degree to which together you solve relationship problems by being:
Collusive
Cooperative
Competitive

4. Are there any underlying interactive patterns in your relationship conflicts, for example, demand–withdraw or blamer–placater?

5. Can you identify any games that you and your partner play that interfere with solving relationship problems? If so, please elaborate.

Part B
Share and discuss

1. You and your partner share and discuss your answers to each of the questions in Part A of this exercise.

2. Specify what, if anything, from doing this exercise you have learned that you can use to improve your skills of solving relationship problems:
a. as individuals,
b. as a couple.

EXERCISE 17.3
INCREASE OUR EXCHANGE OF CARING ACTIONS
Instructions

This exercise assumes that you are in a relationship. Whether or not your relationship is unhappy, experiment to see if you can improve it by completing the following parts of the exercise.

Part A
Assessment

Work through the procedures described in the text for acknowledging existing caring actions and for making wish lists for additional caring actions.

Part B
Make an 'If...then...' statement

Together make an 'If...then...' statement.
If we agree upon the following willingness lists for performing caring actions (partners write out two copies of their willingness lists, keeping one and exchanging the other) and implement our agreement,
then these consequences (specify) are likely to follow:
a.
b.
c.
d.

Part C
Implement and review your increased exchange of caring actions

Implement your agreement. Review how you implemented your willingness lists. If necessary, fine-tune your agreement and/or use it as a stepping stone to a further agreement. Assess the positive and negative consequences of it for yourself, one another and for your relationship of increasing the exchange of caring actions. What, if anything, have you learned that may help increase the satisfaction and stability of your relationship in future?

EXERCISE 17.4
USE THE CUDSAIR MODEL FOR SOLVING A RELATIONSHIP PROBLEM
Instructions

This exercise assumes you are in a relationship. Complete Part A on your own and Parts B and C with your partner.

Part A
Assess my and my partner's skills in solving relationship problems

Turn to Table 17.3 and, for each of the CUDSAIR model's seven steps, assess
1. your skills strengths and deficits,
2. your partner's skills strengths and deficits.

Part B
Share and discuss

1. You and your partner share and discuss your answers to Part A of this exercise.

2. What skills do you need to develop, both as individuals and as a couple, to improve how you solve relationship problems cooperatively?

Part C
Use the CUDSAIR model

1. Choose a problem that you identified when completing Exercise 17.1 or another problem in your relationship that both of you wishes to solve.

2. What have been your attempted solutions to the problem to date? What have been the consequences of your attempted solutions? So far, what have been your skills strengths and deficits in trying to solve the problem?

3. Pick a proper time and place for a problem solving session.

4. During your problem-solving session systematically proceed through the following steps of the CUDSAIR model:
Step 2 Understand one another's perspective
Step 3 Define the problem
Step 4 Search for and assess solutions
Step 5 Agree upon the preferred solution

5. After your problem solving session, proceed through the remaining steps of the CUDSAIR model:
Step 6 Implement the solution
Step 7 Review implementing the solution.

6. Either at the end of step 5, or at the end of step 7, or at the end of both, review how well you, individually and as a couple, have used the skills of each step of the CUDSAIR model.

EXERCISE 17.5
GROUP DISCUSSION: SOLVING RELATIONSHIP PROBLEMS SKILLS

Instructions

This is intended as a group exercise, though it may be done individually or in pairs. For each part:

1. spend 10–15 minutes answering the question in groups of three of four,

2. each sub-group shares its answers with the whole group,

3. then the whole group ranks the six most important problems, mistakes or skills from the most important to the least important.

Part A
Relationship problems

List the six most common relationship problems that partners encounter.

Part B
Mistakes in solving relationship problems

Examine your own skills for solving relationship problems, and list the six most important mistakes you make when trying to solve relationship problems.

Part C
Solving relationship problems skills

List the six most important skills that partners can use for solving relationship problems.

EIGHTEEN
Develop Your Relating Skills

Yes! to this thought I hold with firm persistence
The last resort of wisdom stamps it true;
He only earns his freedom and existence;
Who daily conquers them anew.

J.W. von Goethe

CHAPTER QUESTIONS

• *How can you monitor your relating skills?*

• *How can you maintain your relating skills?*

• *How can you develop your relating skills still further?*

This chapter focuses on how you can maintain and develop your relating skills. For the remainder of your life you are faced with the possibility of making good or poor relating skills choices: choices that help you achieve your goals or choices that cause you trouble. Maintaining relating skills requires daily vigilance. In addition, for the sakes of others and yourself, you can develop your skills still further.

Monitor your relating skills

Exercise 18.1 at the end of this chapter asks you to reassess your relating skills in the light of reading this book. Hopefully, you have completed some, if not all, of the exercises. Also, you will probably have tried to develop many of the skills by practising them in your daily life. Take your time over the exercise. Accurate assessment is vital in pinpointing deficits. Once deficits are clearly identified, you have made considerable progress in doing something about them. You may wish to complete Exercise 18.1 periodically in future to monitor your skills.

MAINTAIN AND DEVELOP YOUR SKILLS

Once you have acquired some relating skills strengths, how can you keep them? There are numerous pressures on you not to maintain relating skills. Some pressures are internal and come from yourself. For instance, when you have recently learned skills strengths, you may still feel the pull of long-established deficits. You may give up too easily because you have insufficiently learned that maintaining relating skills, for instance in times of conflict, involves inner strength and toughness. You may play the comparison game whereby, because your partner or someone else fails to use good skills, this legitimizes you in relinquishing them too.

Some pressures not to maintain your skills are external. Relatives, friends and colleagues may reward deficits rather than strengths: for instance, you may be more comfortable for them if nonassertive. The media constantly bombard you with messages conducive to superficial relationships. Additionally, the notion of people working hard in their relationship skills has still to gain widespread acceptance. Personal excellence gets left to individuals to develop as best they can.

Whether the pressures are internal, external or both, it is easy to backslide and transfer relating skills strengths into deficits. However, where possible, you can go in the other direction. Below are some suggestions for maintaining and developing your relating skills.

- *Keep viewing relating in skills terms.* This book emphasizes the importance of viewing relationships in skills terms and emphasizes that relating skills represent choices that can be well or poorly made. Because many of you have not been brought up to see your relationships in skills terms, you may lose both this perspective and its benefits: namely, a set of skills 'handles' you can develop to relate better. The relating skills approach assumes that you are personally responsible for making specific choices conducive to your happiness and fulfilment. Consequently, the approach keeps relationships out of the realm of magic and firmly in the realm of practicality.

- *Clarify your values.* Some people approach their relationships as though the others involved are objects to be manipulated or conquered rather than as persons worthy of respect. Others treat themselves like objects and scarcely allow themselves enough time and energy to relate well. Neither group places sufficient value on affirming others and themselves through the quality of their relationships. Both groups need to confront themselves with the consequences of their choices. You are more likely to commit yourself to developing your relating skills if you set a high value on the personal growth of yourself and others. If you value other goals more, such as making money or sexual conquests, this is likely to interfere with attaining your full humanity. Reassess and clarify your values. It is a contemporary tragedy that large numbers of people are neither fully committed to their own development, nor that of their partners, nor that of their children. A realization of more fundamental values, sometimes with the aid of religion, can release many people become more caring and compassionate.

- *Nurture altruism.* Being an effective person involves both inner and outer listening. You require inner responsiveness to your significant feelings and physical reactions. In particular, strive to keep in touch with your and your partner's altruistic feelings. Inevitably, you will need to draw upon your reserves of inner strength to maintain and develop your love (King, 1963). If you lose touch with your own altruistic feelings, it is easy to become negative and cynical about your partner. In doing so, you can stifle both your own and their altruistic feelings. The more you lose touch with your altruistic feelings, the more vulnerable you are to worsening your relationship by behaving aggressively rather than assertively. As your own and your partner's level of antagonism rises, it can become progressively more difficult to use good relating skills.

• *Discipline your thinking.* In Chapter 2, I mentioned the importance of mental cultivation. American President Abraham Lincoln is reported to have said 'Most folks are about as happy as they make up their minds to be'. Discipline your thinking. When the going gets rough, discipline your thinking even more. Make thinking choices that support rather than oppress you and others. Develop your skills of 'straight' rather than 'crooked' thinking.

Throughout this book, I have given numerous examples of people using good and poor thinking skills. Disciplining your thinking empowers you with the ability and flexibility to act effectively. When you catch yourself acting ineffectively, you can analyse what thinking skills deficits mediate your actions and change them. Instead of thinking from outside to inside and reacting to other people's behaviour, you can think from inside to outside and take charge of your life.

Think realistically about maintaining and developing your relating skills. Expect difficulties and set-backs. However, think and tell yourself that you can use your recovery skills to get back on track. You can choose not to turn isolated lapses into ongoing relapses. Where necessary, you can use your thinking skills to retrieve situations. Also, if you have previously used recovery skills to good effect, remember you can do so again.

• *Remember positive consequences.* Become aware of and remember the positive consequences of using relating skills. You are more likely to repeat behaviours perceived as rewarding than those perceived otherwise. Sometimes the rewards are obvious: for instance, your partner's happiness. Sometimes the rewards are more subtle: for instance, the gradual growth of trust in a relationship. On other occasions, the rewards may come from minimizing negative consequences: for instance, ending a relationship with minimal damage to the self-respect of both parties. Below is a vignette illustrating the assessment of positive and negative consequences to maintain relating skills strengths.

> Ray was a married man with three teenaged girls. As he worked on his tendencies to be violent in getting his way in his family, he felt he was losing some of his power. However, when he listed the positive consequences of treating his wife and family with more respect and moderation, he realized the importance of continuing to curb his temper by using his managing anger and conflict skills.

• *Work with your partner.* A number of times I have emphasized the importance of partners working together in various relating skills areas, for instance facilitating intimacy, encouraging one another's assertion and managing anger. When you use relating skills strengths, your example encourages your partner to reciprocate. By helping one another work through specific difficulties, either in your lives as individuals or as a couple, you show active concern for each other's welfare. By using relating skills daily, you raise your chances of staying rewarding to one another – you increase the good times and decrease the bad times. Furthermore, you help one another stay out of destructive cycles of blame and recrimination.

You can set aside a special weekly or monthly time to discuss your relationship. Your relationship session need not be a grim affair. Rather a 'you-me' talk session provides a chance to catch up with one another. Also, you can sort out problems and misunderstandings as they emerge rather than later, by which time they may have become more serious.

• *Co-counsel.* Co-counselling is an approach to working together. You can co-counsel either with your partner or with someone else. The latter has risks if your partner disapproves of sensitive material being discussed with third parties. In co-counselling you have joint counselling sessions on a regular basis. You decide who starts as 'counsellor' and 'client'. The 'counsellor' gives the 'client' air time to examine his or her relationship concerns and skills and supports this exploration by showing active understanding. The first person's air time may last for 10 or 15 minutes, longer if necessary. Afterwards you reverse roles. When you have both had your individual turns to talk, together hold a sharing and discussion session. Co-counselling with a spouse or partner has much to recommend it. It can help maintain communication as well as provide a regular opportunity to use and improve your relating skills.

• *Practise daily.* When relating, there is no such thing as not using skills. Whenever you are with someone, you are practising whether you like it or not. You can either practise good skills or poor skills or a mixture of the two. Here I refer to practising your relating skills strengths. The old saying 'practice makes perfect' is unrealistic. Better to say 'practice makes competent'. By practising your skills conscientiously, not just in crises but all the time, you are likely to improve them. You can become more confident and also more flexible in applying your skills. Often you face a very important gap between learning a skill and putting it into practise. Psychologists call overcoming this gap 'transfer of training'. However, transfer of training can go beyond maintaining a skill to improving it with continued practise.

• *Develop your support network.* People, as individuals and as couples, exist in support networks of varying degrees of adequacy: family, friends, work colleagues, clubs, church and so on. In addition, you can obtain access to voluntary or professional helpers. Develop a support network that contains people who use and reward the relating skills you wish to maintain and develop. Specific networking skills include: identifying suitable people and organizations to partake in your support network, knowing how best to access them, using them when necessary and being prepared to contribute so the flow of support is two way.

• *Participate in peer support groups.* You may choose to meet on a regular basis with a group of other people to work on your relating skills. Being in a support group has the advantage of enabling you to practise your skills, observe others' skills and obtain feedback. Peer support groups can be specifically focused on discussing relationships and helping one another with problems in them. Alternatively, within the context of another focus – for instance a women's group, a men's group, or a bereavement group – you can work on the relating skills pertinent to that group's main task.

• *Attend workshops and training courses.* No hard and fast distinctions exist between training courses and workshops. However, if anything, training courses are spread over a longer period, say a month or more, whereas workshops are ordinarily relatively intense experiences lasting from a day to a week. Means of finding out about relating skills workshops and training courses include: contacting counselling services – for instance, the local branch of Relate in Britain or of Relationships Australia; seeking information from professional associations in psychology, counselling and social work; and looking in newspapers, relevant journals and newsletters. In all instances look before you leap. Since acquiring good relating skills requires much work and practice, avoid courses and workshops offering miracle cures. Table 18.1 provides a checklist for assessing training courses and workshops.

Table 18.1 Checklist for assessing training courses and workshops

---

1. What are the course or workshop's goals?

2. What are the training methods that may be employed during the course or workshop?

3. What is the pertinent training and experience of the trainer or trainers?

4. What is the size of the course or workshop and is there a screening process prior to entry?

5. When does the course or workshop start? How long is each session? Over what period will the course or workshop continue? Where will it be held? Are the facilities adequate?

6. What, if any, is the fee for the course or workshop and are there any additional expenses that may be incurred?

• *Undergo professional counselling.* Either individually or as a couple, you may need the services of a professional counsellor to help improve your relating skills. Usually, on training courses or workshops, there is little chance for trainers to spend much time on individual problems. Also, you may be so lacking in confidence that you prefer a safer environment. Group counselling may be desirable either instead of, concurrently with, or after individual counselling. Counselling groups tend to be comprised of a leader and around six to ten members. They provide a more sheltered environment for working on emotional and relationship issues than that found in many training groups and workshops. All the items on the Table 18.1 checklist are relevant to assessing counselling groups.

Choosing a counsellor can be a difficult process. Counsellors differ greatly in their personalities, knowledge, skills and theoretical orientations. A counsellor reflecting this book's approach would be one combining existential–humanistic and cognitive–behavioural theoretical orientations. Put in lay person's language, a counsellor who: believes in the concept of relating skills; focuses on thinking and action skills as well as on feelings; and consistently encourages personal responsibility and self-help. Look for a counsellor with whom you feel comfortable and who both supports and challenges you to attain more of your potential. If dissatisfied, be prepared to change your counsellor.

You may not be immediately aware of a suitable counsellor. You may find the name of someone appropriate by asking a helping service professional: for instance, a psychologist, social worker, doctor or priest. You could look up the relevant occupational listings in the phone book. Also, you could contact a citizen's advice bureau. In addition, you could make enquiries to relevant local, regional and national associations, such as Relate (Britain) and Relationships Australia.

- *Avoid burnout.* People who have a combination of difficult environments and of poor skills in looking after themselves and managing relationships tend to be excellent candidates for burnout, if not breakdown. Freudenberger (1980) defines burnout as follows: 'To deplete oneself. To exhaust one's physical and mental resources. To wear oneself out by excessively striving to reach some unrealistic expectation imposed by one's self or by the values of society' (p. 17). If punch-drunk with exhaustion you may lack the energy to use good relating skills. You may be cranky, irritable and possibly highly abusive. Your perceptions of others get coloured by your own distress and you are more likely to be disappointed in them. In Chapter 16 I mentioned some skills of managing stress: for instance, relaxation skills and developing adequate recreational outlets. Feelings of exhaustion, being excessively stressed and having insufficient resilience can have numerous causes both within and outside your relationships. Consequently, you may require a wide variety of skills to deal with them adequately. Where possible, prevention is far better than a cure.

- *Read relevant literature.* Reading relevant books and articles is a further way to maintain and develop your relating skills. For this purpose, I have provided a 40 book annotated bibliography at the end of this book, plus numerous further references. Also, you can use this book as an ongoing resource. One approach is to go through the whole book every now and then as a refresher. Another approach is to target particular skills and then focus on specific chapters and relevant exercises.

POSTSCRIPT

The stark truth is that many, if not most, close relationships end up in hatred, pain or mutual recrimination. Frequently innocent parties, such as children, get hurt in the fall-out. Also, many work settings are characterized by considerable hostility. Each person possesses his or her own past pain and present skills deficits. However, the challenge of close relationships is to affirm yourself and others, despite these adverse factors. The answer to the challenge of relationships is to strive to use, maintain and develop your relating skills. Whatever progress you make, however slight, is a triumph, because you are choosing to increase your own, other people's and the world's store of happiness. As I wished you in this book's preface: GOOD LUCK AND, ABOVE ALL, GOOD SKILLS!

CHAPTER HIGHLIGHTS

• You can regularly monitor your relating skills strengths and deficis.

• There are numerous internal and external pressures on you not to maintain relating skills.

• Keeping viewing relating in skills terms helps you to own personal responsibility for maintaining and developing your skills.

• Reassess and clarify your values and place a high value on personal growth in the context of effective relationships.

• Nurture both your own and your partner's altruism.

• Discipline your thinking as a basis both for acting effectively and for dealing with difficulties and set-backs.

• Remind yourself of the positive consequences of skilful relating and the negative consequences of unskilful relating.

• Work with your partner to maintain and develop your skills. You can set aside special times to discuss your relationship.

• You can use co-counselling with either your partner or a third party to work on your relating skills.

• You cannot avoid practising relating skills so endeavour to practise daily your strengths rather than your deficits.

• You can develop a network that will support you in maintaining and developing your skills.

• Peer support groups can also help you maintain and develop your relating skills.

• You can improve your skills by attending well-led training courses and workshops.

• Either as an individual or as a couple you may undergo personal counselling. Take care in selecting your counsellor and, if necessary, be prepared to change him or her.

• Where possible, use skills that prevent excessive stress and burnout.

• Reading relevant books and articles is a further way to maintain and develop your relating skills.

EXERCISES
EXERCISE 18.1
MONITOR MY RELATING SKILLS
Instructions

First do this exercise on your own. Then, if appropriate, discuss with your partner, another or others.

Monitor your relating skills strengths and deficits by filling out the worksheet below. Focus on thinking skills as well as action skills. For more information about specific skills areas, turn to the relevant chapters.

Skills area	My evaluation
Disclosing skills a. My strengths b. My deficits	
Listening skills a. My strengths b. My deficits	
Showing understanding skills a. My strengths b. My deficits	
Managing shyness skills a. My strengths b. My deficits	
Choosing a partner skills a. My strengths b. My deficits	
Trust skills a. My strengths b. My deficits	

Caring skills

a. My strengths
b. My deficits

Intimacy skills

a. My strengths
b. My deficits

Companionship skills

a. My strengths
b. My deficits

Sexual relating skills

a. My strengths
b. My deficits

Assertion skills

a. My strengths
b. My deficits

Managing anger skills

a. My strengths
b. My deficits

Solving relationship problems skills

a. My strengths
b. My deficits

Additional tasks

1. Write a paragraph summarizing your relating skills strengths.

2. Write a paragraph summarizing your relating skills deficits.

3. Identify the main relating skills deficits on which you want to work. Refer back to the relevant chapter for suggestions and exercises on how to improve specific skills.

LIVERPOOL HOPE UNIVERSITY COLLEGE

EXERCISE 18.2
MAINTAIN AND DEVELOP MY RELATING SKILLS
Instructions

First do this exercise on your own. Then, if appropriate, discuss with your partner, another or others.

Below are listed a number of different methods whereby you can maintain and develop your relating skills. Using the worksheet below, assess whether and how you might use each method.

Method	My assessment of whether and how I can use each method
Viewing relating in skills terms	
Clarifying my values	
Nurturing altruism	
Disciplining my thinking	
Remembering positive consequences	
Working with my partner	

Co-counselling
Practising my skills daily
Developing my support network
Participating in peer support groups
Attending workshops and training courses
Undergoing professional counselling
Avoiding burnout
Reading relevant literature
Other methods not mentioned above

Questions

1. What do you consider the most useful methods for you to maintain and develop your own relating skills?

2. How can you and your partner work together to maintain and develop your relating as a couple skills?

EXERCISE 18.3
GROUP DISCUSSION: DEVELOP YOUR RELATING SKILLS

Instructions

This is intended as a group exercise, though it may be done individually or in pairs. For each part:

1. spend 10–15 minutes answering the question in groups of three or four,
2. each group shares its answers with the whole group,
3. then the whole group ranks the six most important points or skills from the most important to the least important.

Part A
Risk factors in maintaining skills

List the six most important risk factors that cause or contribute to partners not maintaining their relating skills.

Part B
Maintaining and developing relating skills

List the six most important skills partners can use for maintaining and developing their relating skills.

Annotated Bibliography

For those with an appetite for further reading and practice, I now provide a 40-book annotated bibliography on relating skills. The books are easy reading rather than written mainly with an academic audience in mind. I list the books alphabetically by author's name. I have not grouped books by area because many of the books cover more than one area. To avoid repetition, I do not include books cited in the Annotated Bibliography in the next section on Further References.

Alberti, R. E., & Emmons, M. L. (1990). *Your Perfect Right: A Guide to Assertive Living* (6th ed.). San Luis Obispo, CA: Impact Publishers. 247 pages.
This is possibly the leading self-help book on assertion. The authors make the threefold distinction between assertive, non-assertive and aggressive behaviour. They emphasize that much assertion is non-verbal rather than just verbal. The book is devoted to showing you how to think and behave assertively as well as help others deal with the new assertive you. The book contains a 35-item assertiveness inventory.

Argyle, M. (1991). *Cooperation: The Basis of Sociability*. London: Routledge. 276 pages.
Leading British social psychologist Michael Argyle asserts that cooperation is central to human existence. His interesting and scholarly book consists of four parts: the study of cooperation; the origins of cooperation – its evolution, cultural differences, and childhood origins; cooperation in different relationships – working groups, the family, and friendships; and personality and social interaction.

Argyle, M., & Henderson, M. (1985). *The Anatomy of Relationships: And the Rules and Skills to Manage Them Successfully*. Harmondsworth: Penguin Books. 359 pages. This book explores the structure and essential features of different types of social relationships – friendship, courtship, marriage, family, neighbours and work. It identifies formal and informal rules governing different relationships as well as variations associated with age, sex and social class.

Beck, A. T. (1988). *Love is Never Enough: How Couples Can Overcome Misunderstandings, Resolve Conflicts, and Solve Relationship Problems Through Cognitive Therapy*. New York: Harper & Row. 415 pages.
This book, by the founder of Cognitive Therapy, describes the power of negative and biased thinking in couple relationships. Beck shows how couples can improve their relationship by identifying and modifying their maladaptive automatic thoughts and underlying beliefs.

Berne, E. (1964). *Games People Play: The Psychology of Human Relationships*. New York: Grove Press. 192 pages.
Eric Berne, the founder of Transactional Analysis, wrote this best-selling book about how people sabotage their relationships through ulterior interpersonal transactions. The book consists of three parts: analysis

of games, a thesaurus of games and beyond games. The chapters in the thesaurus of games cover: life, marital, party, sexual, underworld, consulting room and good games. Berne gave each game a catchy title.

Bolton, R. (1986). *People Skills: How to Assert Yourself, Listen to Others, and Resolve Conflicts*. East Roseville, NSW: Simon & Schuster Australia. 300 pages.

Bolton acknowledges that effective communication is not something that has come easily to him. The popular self-help book consists of four parts: introduction; listening skills; assertion skills; and conflict management skills, including a six-step collaborative problem-solving method. The book ends with an afterword on training for improved communication.

Butler, P. E. (1992). *Self-assertion for Women* (rev. ed.). San Franscisco, CA: HarperCollins. 264 pages.

Butler's book shows women how to be more assertive expressing positive and negative feelings, setting limits and taking initiatives. She focuses on self-talk as well as on verbal and nonverbal messages. The book contains chapters on self-assertion in professional life and in female–male relationships.

Colliver, A. (1992). *Choosing to Love: Creating Trust and Commitment in Your Relationship*. Sydney: Random House: Australia. 223 pages.

Colliver admits his own difficulties in the area of commitment. This is a book about male fear of commitment and how to deal with it. The book's first part, entitled 'Identifying the fear of commitment', examines the predictable plot, triggers, experiencing and causes of the fear. Part two, 'Dealing with your fear of commitment', looks at changing your behaviours and attitude. Part three, 'Dealing with another's fear of commitment', reviews taking care of yourself. The book's final chapter focuses on choosing to love.

Comfort, A. (1993). *The New Joy of Sex*. London: Mitchell Beazley. 224 pages.

Comfort, a human biologist, starts this edition's preface by saying that he first wrote this book nearly 20 years and over eight million copies ago (I'm green with envy!). The book begins by discussing advanced lovemaking and the implications of AIDS. Then there are a series of excerpts divided under the following main headings: ingredients, appetizers, main courses, sauces, venues, and health and other issues. The book is amusingly written. Needless to say, the standard of artwork is very high – naughty, but nice.

Dickson, A. (1982). *A Woman in Your Own Right: Assertiveness and You*. London: Quartet Books. 171 pages.

Reprinted numerous times, this popular book describes the assertive woman and then describes how you can become one. Dickson covers such topics as your rights, body language, saying no, the compassion trap, confrontation and compliments, expressing feelings, expressing and dealing with anger, and assertive approaches to money and sex.

Dorwick, S. (1991). *Intimacy and Solitude*. Melbourne: Mandarin. 320 pages.

Highly recommended – I found this book very useful when writing my chapter on intimacy skills. The book's main theme is the more comfortable you are with yourself, the less you need other people and the more easily you can embrace them. The book consists of five parts: (1) self: is that who I am?; (2) women and men; (3) knowing yourself; (4) intimacy: knowing the other; and (5) desire: the language of your inner sphere. In 1993, Dorwick brought out a companion volume entitled *The Intimacy and Solitude Self-therapy Book*.

Egan, G. (1977). *You and Me: The Skills of Communicating and Relating to Others*. Monterey, CA: Brooks/Cole. 346 pages.

Egan's book is intended for people who wish to improve their interpersonal self-awareness, skills and assertiveness in small human relations training groups. Its six sections are: introduction and overview; the skills of letting yourself be known; the skills of listening and responding; the skills of challenging; the skills of effective group participation; and putting it all together.

Ellis, A. (1977). *Anger: How to Live With and Without It*. Melbourne: Sun MacMillan Australia. 282 pages.

Albert Ellis, the founder of rational emotive behaviour therapy, takes the position that you are responsible for creating your anger because of difficulties in relinquishing childish demandingness. He encourages you to dispute your self-angering beliefs and shows you ways to think, feel and act your way out of disturbing yourself with anger.

Ellis, A. (1988). *How to Stubbornly Refuse to Make Yourself Miserable About Anything, Yes Anything!* Sydney: Pan Macmillan. 215 pages.

Everyone is at risk of crooked thinking. This entertaining self-help book presents Ellis's views on emotional disturbance and on the importance of scientific thinking. Ellis presents a series of chapters showing you in simple language 'how to' take and maintain more control over your thoughts, feelings and actions. The book contains a number of self-help exercises.

Fromm, E. (1956). *The Art of Loving*. New York: Bantam Books. 118 pages.

This slim volume is a classic. Fromm asks whether or not love is an art. Love is an active process involving care, responsibility, respect and knowledge. Fromm reviews different kinds of love: brotherly, motherly, erotic, self-love and love of god. Also, he writes about love and its disintegration in contemporary Western society and the practice of love.

Glasser, W. (1995). *Staying Together: A Control Theory Guide to a Lasting Marriage*. New York: HarperCollins. 133 pages.

Late in 1992, after 46 years of marriage, William Glasser's first wife Naomi died. In this book Glasser, the founder of reality therapy, applies control theory to selecting a partner and maintaining a long-term relationship. He presents as a case study himself and his new wife, Carleen, whom he married in July 1995, assessing their potential compatibility on the basic needs of survival, love, power, freedom and fun.

Gordon, T. (1970). *Parent Effectiveness Training: The Tested New Way to Raise Responsible Children*. New York: Wyden. 338 pages.

This book's relevance extends beyond parenting to couple relationships. Gordon's book focuses on three main skills: active listening; sending 'I-Messages' and avoiding put-down 'You-Messages'; and a 'no-lose' method for resolving conflicts that gets to the real problems and eliminates the need for power.

Hendrix, H. (1988). *Getting the Love You Want: A Guide for Couples*. Melbourne: Schwartz & Wilkinson. 253 pages.

Hendrix has developed a theory of marital therapy called imago relationship therapy. This book is in three parts. Part one, 'The unconscious marriage', chronicles the fate of most relationships: attraction, romantic love and the power struggle. Part two, 'The conscious marriage', explores how to satisfy unmet childhood needs in positive ways. Part three, 'Exercises', provides a ten-week step-by-step course in relationship therapy.

Johnson, D. W. (1993). *Reaching Out: Interpersonal Effectiveness and Self-actualisation* (5th ed.). Sydney: Prentice-Hall International. 387 pages.

This textbook book integrates theory and practical experience to develop effective interpersonal skills. Topics include the importance of interpersonal skills, self-disclosure, developing and maintaining trust, expressing feelings verbally and non-verbally, listening and helpful responding, resolving conflicts, confrontation and negotiation, managing anger and stress and barriers to interpersonal effectiveness. The book contains exercises and comprehension tests.

Jourard, S. M. (1964). *The Transparent Self: Self-disclosure and Well-being*. Princeton, NJ: Van Nostrand. 200 pages.

This is the classic and seminal book on self-disclosure. The book consists of five parts: self-disclosure as a psychological fact; the importance of self-disclosure in human experience; role of authenticity in helping others; the role of 'inspiration' in wellness; and a new way of being for nurses. The book ends with a technical appendix for psychologists.

Kaplan, H. S. (1987). *The Illustrated Manual of Sex Therapy* (2nd ed.). New York: Brunner/Mazel. 181 pages.

Dedicated to Aphrodite, this user-friendly manual is divided into three main parts. Part one, 'Basic issues', covers the nature and causes of sexual dysfunction and sexual evaluation. Part two, 'The sexual exercises', consists of two chapters on sensate focus, an erotic technique used for many dysfunctions, and six chapters on erotic techniques used for specific dysfunctions. Part three, 'Conclusions', discusses the role of psychodynamics in sex therapy. The book is liberally and well illustrated.

Kotzman, A. (1989). *Listen to Me Listen to You: A Practical Guide to Improving Self-esteem, Listening Skills and Assertiveness*. Melbourne: Penguin Books. 160 pages.

Kotzman asserts that low self-esteem is a common problem. Her book consists of three parts. Part one, on self-esteem, focuses on how to develop a firm sense of your intrinsic worth as a person. Part two, on reflective listening, is a simple and clear summary of some of the skills involved. Part three, on self-assertion, introduces some of the values and skills of assertiveness training. The book ends with a list of Kotzman's favourite books and tapes.

Lazarus, A. A. (1985). *Marital Myths: Two Dozen Mistaken Beliefs that Can Ruin a Marriage (or Make a Bad One Worse)*. San Luis Obispo, CA: Impact Publishers. 168 pages.

Lazarus exposes 24 marital myths, grounded in Western English-speaking cultures, prevalent in his psychological practice. Examples of marital myths are: 'Husbands and wives should do everything together' and 'You should make your spouse over into "a better person" '. Lazarus analyses each myth to show that they are illusions capable of leading partners to impossible dreams and unrealistic expectations.

Lazarus, A. A., Lazarus, C. N., & Fay, A. (1993). *Don't Believe It For a Minute: Forty Toxic Ideas that are Driving You Crazy*. San Luis Obispo, CA: Impact. 179 pages.

Owing much to the work of Albert Ellis, this book tries to debunk 40 common misbeliefs – for instance, 'You're better off when you control other people' - that can lead to depression, anxiety, anger and guilt. The book contains a 40-statement beliefs questionnaire. The authors' treatment of each toxic belief follows a standard format: an example, an analysis of why the belief is toxic, a series of corrective self-statements that can act as antidotes and lastly a positive counter-belief.

Lerner, H. G. (1985). *The Dance of Anger: A Woman's Guide to Changing the Patterns of Intimate Relationships*. New York: Harper & Row. 239 pages.
Lerner's book looks at how women can use their anger constructively rather than by remaining stuck in circular dances in which the behaviour of one partner maintains and provokes the behaviour of another. She examines anger up and down the generations as well as in couples and family triangles. The book ends with a call for women to address not only personal problems inside the home, but also the societal institutions that keep women subordinate and de-selfed outside the home.

Lerner, H. G. (1989). *The Dance of Intimacy: A Woman's Guide to Courageous Acts of Change in Key Relationships*. New York: Harper & Row. 255 pages.
Lerner asks whether the pursuit of intimacy is women's work. This book aims to help women become more knowledgeable about the dynamics of change so that you can develop and redefine yourself in key relationships to increase significantly your capacity for intimacy. Every act of change requires a move towards greater selfhood, or self-focus. The book addresses issues of distance, difference and overcoming dysfunctional patterns that block genuine intimacy. Lerner investigates mother–daughter as well as couple and triangular relationships.

Lewinsohn, P. M., Munoz, R. F., Youngren, M. A., & Zeiss, A.. M. (1986). *Control Your Depression* (rev. ed.). New York: Prentice-Hall Press. 241 pages.
Part one and part three of this book are entitled 'The concepts' and 'Looking toward the future', respectively. Part two, entitled 'The strategies', describes self-help skills for controlling depression including: learning to relax, engaging in pleasant activities, learning how to develop and use social skills and constructive thinking. The book contains questionnaires – for example, a pleasant events schedule, assertion questionnaire and social activities questionnaire – and self-monitoring forms.

Litvinoff. S. (1991). *The Relate Guide to Better Relationships: Practical Ways to Make Your Love Last From the Experts in Marriage Guidance*. London: Vermilion. 256 pages.
Topics covered in this book include: myths about love and perfect relationships, compatibility before and after marrying, discovering whom you are marrying, sex roles, talking, listening, managing feelings, managing change, managing problems and crises and building a good sex life. Litvinoff draws upon the experience of numerous Relate (former British National Marriage Guidance Council) counsellors (only five males out of 46 counsellors acknowledged!) and liberally illustrates her book with case examples. Throughout the text there are tasks, quizzes and talking points to encourage you and your partner to build knowledge and skills.

Litvinoff, S. (1992). *The Relate Guide to Sex in Loving Relationships*. London: Vermilion. 227 pages.
This book consists of four parts: you and sex; sex in loving relationships; problems; and improving your sex life. Again Litvinoff uses the experience of Relate counsellors and sex therapists (one male out of 17!) who share their experience of clients to provide case vignettes. Throughout the text there are tasks, quizzes and talking points.

Litvinoff, S. (1993). *The Relate Guide to Starting Again: How to Learn From the Past to Give You a Better Future*. London: Vermilion. 256 pages.
The topics in the first part of this book, entitled 'The end of a relationship', include the decision whether or not to break up, coming to terms with loss, assessing what went wrong, and your children. Part two, entitled 'Working on yourself', focuses on building your happiness, confidence and independence and on challenging your self-defeating interactive patterns. Part three, entitled 'Starting again', covers developing a new social life, starting a new relationship well and family network issues. Again Relate counsellors (three males out of 25 this time!) provide insights and case material. The book includes tasks and quizzes.

Masters, W. H., Johnson, V. E., & Kolodny, R. C. (1986). *Masters & Johnson on Sex and Human Loving*. London: Pan Macmillan. 598 pages.

Written at the level of the intelligent layperson by eminent sex researchers Masters and Johnson, this is undoubtedly the best general book on sex I know – authoritative, comprehensive, thorough, well written and humane, if occasionally slightly outdated. Following are the 20 chapter titles: perspectives on sexuality; sexual anatomy; sexual physiology; birth control; childhood sexuality; adolescent sexuality; adult sexuality; gender roles; loving and being loved; intimacy and communication skills; sexual fantasy; solitary sexual behaviour; heterosexuality; homosexuality and bisexuality; the varieties of sexual behaviour; coercive sex – the varieties of sexual assault; increasing sexual satisfaction; sexual dysfunctions and sex therapy; sexual disorders and sexual health; sexually transmitted diseases. The book contains an epilogue on the future of sexuality.

McKay, M., Fanning, P., & Paleg, K. (1994). *Couple Skills: Making Your Relationship Work*. Oakland, CA: New Harbinger Publications. 280 pages.

The authors state that this book is for couples, married or not; heterosexual, gay or lesbian; young or old. The book consists of four parts: basic skills, for instance listening, expressing feelings and reciprocal reinforcement; advanced skills, for instance changing cognitive distortions and problem solving; anger and conflict, for instance coping with your own and your partner's anger; and understanding and changing what goes wrong, including coping with your defences and intervening in your couple system. You can use the book for making unilateral changes in your relationship, that in turn influence your couple system, as well as for working together.

Montgomery, R. & Evans, L. (1983). *Living and Loving Together: A Practical Step-by-step Manual to Help you Make and Keep Better Relationships*. Melbourne: Viking O'Neill. 234 pages.

This purposes of this self-help manual are to support marital and relationship enrichment and therapy. Written in straightforward 'how-to' language, the book focuses on skills such as levelling and listening, sexual relating, fight control, solving relationship problems, changing how you behave and coping with kids.

Powell, E. (1991). *Talking Back to Sexual Pressure: What to Say…to Resist Persuasion…to Avoid Disease…to Stop Harassment…to Avoid Acquaintance Rape*. Minneapolis, MI: CompCare Publishers. 254 pages.

This book is aimed at all people – regardless of age, sex or sexual orientation – who want to resist sexual pressure. The book is in four parts. Part one, 'How to become assertive about sex', focuses on breaking the silence, understanding assertiveness, and taking charge of your thoughts. Part two, 'How to respond to persuasion', reviews standing up to verbal pressure and speaking up to avoid disease and pregnancy. Part three, 'How to cope with intrusion and force', includes suggestions for resisting sexual harassment and avoiding acquaintance rape. Part four, 'How to speak up for society', examines searching for and changing the broader influences that cause sexual pressure.

Rogers, C. R. (1961). *On Becoming a Person: A Therapist's View of Psychotherapy*. Boston: Houghton Mifflin. 420 pages.

Carl Rogers, the founder of person-centred therapy, acknowledged this book as certainly his most popular and thought it had spoken to people all over the world. Written in a comfortable and personal writing style, the book comprises seven parts; speaking personally; how can I be of help?; the process of becoming a person; a philosophy of persons; the place of research in psychotherapy; what are the implications for living; and the behavioural sciences and the person. The book is a basic reference in the area of listening skills.

Rogers, C. R. (1973). *Becoming Partners: Marriage and its Alternatives*. London: Constable. 247 pages.
In this book Rogers explores, by means of interviews, heterosexual marriage and its alternatives. He identifies patterns of growth and threads of permanence and enrichment that can occur within initial marriages, in subsequent marriages, and in other less conventional types of 'marriages'. As well as allowing partners to speak for themselves, Rogers comments on each relationship, his own marriage and on marital relationships in general.

Steiner, C. M. (1981). *The Other Side of Power: How to Become Powerful Without Being Power Hungry*. New York: Grove Press. 256 pages.
Steiner was a leading associate of Eric Berne. This three-part book is about power and power abuse. Part one, 'Control', examines the American power dream, control in your everyday life, obedience, power-lessness and understanding myths about power. Part two, 'People's power plays', examines manoeuvres to control others and how to avoid being controlled. Part three, 'Giving up control', reviews letting go and how to fill the control vacuum.

Tavris, C. (1989). *Anger: The Misunderstood Emotion* (rev. ed.). New York: Simon & Schuster. 383 pages.
This book uses research evidence to explore myths about the biological basis of anger, suppressing anger and its effects of health, expressing anger and getting it out of your system and gender differences in anger. Tavris explores the role of anger in marriage and in seeking justice. The book's final chapter is on strategies for living with anger and getting beyond it.

Wellings, K., Field, J., Johnson, A. M., & Wadsworth, J. (1994). *Sexual Behaviour in Britain: The National Survey of Sexual Attitudes and Lifestyles*. London: Penguin. 464 pages.
This book provides information from responses provided by nearly 20,000 Britons randomly selected to represent the views of the whole population. Separate chapters examine the age of earliest sexual experiences, numbers of partners, frequency of intercourse, sexual orientation, alternatives to intercourse, moral convictions and awareness of risk reducing practices. Differences in patterns of behaviour are described by gender, age, marital status, geographical region and social class.

Zimbardo, P. G. (1977). *Shyness: What It is, What to Do About It*. Reading, MA: Addison-Wesley. 263 pages.
Zimbardo, a Stanford University psychology professor, has conducted extensive research into shyness as well as writing about it. The book is in two parts. Part one, 'Understanding shyness', examines what shyness is, the personal world of the shy, the causes of shyness, growing up shy and shyness in relation-ships. Part two, 'What to do about it', reviews understanding your shyness, building self-esteem, developing social skills, helping others to overcome shyness and preventing shyness in society.

Further References

Ainsworth, M. D. S., Blehar, M. C., Water, E., & Wall, S. (1978). *Patterns of Attachment*. Hillsdale, NJ: Erlbaum.

Alden, L. E., & Wallace, S. T. (1995). Social phobia and social appraisal in successful and unsuccessful social interactions. *Behaviour Research and Therapy, 33*, 497– 505.

Allport, G. W., Vernon, P. E., & Lindzey, G. (1951). *A Study of Values* (rev. ed.). Boston: Houghton Mifflin.

Allyn, E. (1992). *The Men of Thailand 1993 Guide to Gay Thailand* (4th ed.). San Francisco, CA: Bua Luang Publishing Co.

Alpert, R., & Haber, R. N. (1960). Anxiety in academic achievement situations. *Journal of Abnormal and Social Psychology, 61*, 204–215.

Altman, I., & Taylor, D. A. (1965). Interpersonal exchange in isolation. *Sociometry, 28*, 411–426.

Altman, I., & Taylor, D. A. (1979). *Social Penetration: The Development of Interpersonal Relationship*. New York: Holt, Rinehart and Winston.

American Psychiatric Association (1994). *Diagnostic and Statistical Manual of Mental Disorders* (4th ed.). Washington, DC: Author.

Argyle, M. (1983). *The Psychology of Interpersonal Behaviour* (4th ed.). Harmondsworth: Penguin.

Argyle, M. (1984). Some new developments in social skills training. *Bulletin of the British Psychological Society, 37*, 405–410.

Argyle, M. (1992). *The Social Psychology of Everyday Life*. London: Routledge.

Argyle, M., & Furnham. A. (1983). Sources of satisfaction and conflict in long-term relationships. *Journal of Marriage and the Family, 45*, 481–493.

Australian Bureau of Statistics (1995). *Australian Demographic Statistics: December Quarter 1994*. Canberra: Australian Bureau of Statistics.

Australian Institute of Family Studies (1993a). Divorce Trends. *Family Matters, 35*, 28–29.

Australian Institute of Family Studies (1993b). Families and the labour force. *Family Matters, 36*, 38–39.

Babcock, J. C., & Jacobson, N. S. (1993). A program of research on behavioral marital therapy; Hot spots and smoldering embers in marital therapy research. *Journal of Social and Personal Relationships, 10*, 119–135.

Bach, G. R., & Wyden, P. (1968). *The Intimate Enemy*. New York: Avon.

Bandura, A. (1986). *Social Foundations of Thought and Action: A Social Cognitive Theory*. Englewood Cliffs, NJ: Prentice-Hall.

Batson, C. D. (1990). How social an animal? The human capacity for caring. *American Psychologist, 45*, 336–346.

Beall, A. E., & Sternberg, R. J. (1995). The social construction of love. *Journal of Social and Personal Relationships, 12*, 417–438.

Beck, A. T. (1976). *Cognitive Therapy and the Emotional Disorders*. New York: New American Library.

Beck, A. T., & Emery G. (1985). *Anxiety Disorders and Phobias: A Cognitive Perspective*. New York: Basic Books.

Beck, A. T., & Freeman, A. (1990). *Cognitive Therapy of Personality Disorders*. New York: Guilford.

Beck, A. T., & Weishaar, M. E. (1995). Cognitive therapy. In R. J. Corsini & D. Wedding (eds.). *Current Psychotherapies* (5th ed., pp. 229–261). Itasca, IL: Peacock.

Bem, S. L. (1974). The measurement of psychological androgyny. *Journal of Consulting and Clinical Psychology, 42*, 155–162.

Bem, S. L. (1981). Gender schema theory: A cognitive account of sex typing. *Psychological Review, 88*, 354–364.

Bennett, W. J. (Ed.) (1993). *The Book of Virtues: A Treasury of Great Moral Stories*. New York: Simon and Schuster.

Berg, J. H., & Derlega, V. J. (1987). Themes in the study of self-disclosure. In V. J. Derlega & J. H. Berg (eds.). *Self-disclosure: Theory, Research and Therapy*. (pp. 1–8). New York: Plenum.

Berne, E. (1964). *Games People Play: The Psychology of Human Relationships*. New York: Grove Press.

Berne, E. (1972). *What Do You Say After You Say Hello?* London: Corgi.

Bernstein, D. A., & Borkovec, T. D. (1973). *Progressive Relaxation Training: A Manual for the Helping Professions*. Champaign, IL: Research Press.

Bloom, D. E. (1986). Women and work. *American Demographics, 6* (7), 19–23, 44.

Bowlby, J. (1979). *The Making and Breaking of Affectional Bonds*. London: Tavistock.

Bruch, M. A. & Pearl, L. (1995). Attributional style and symptoms of shyness in a heterosexual interaction. *Cognitive Therapy and Research, 19*, 91–107.

Buber, M. (1970). *I and Thou*. New York: Charles Scribner.

Butler, P. E. (1981). *Talking to Yourself: Learning the Language of Self-support*. San Francisco: Harper & Row Publishers.

Buunk, B. P. (1995). Sex, self-esteem, dependency and extradyadic sexual experience as related to jealousy responses. *Journal of Social and Personal Relationships, 12*, 147– 153.

Callan, V. J., Gallois, C., Noller, P., & Kashima, Y. (1991). *Social Psychology* (2nd ed.). Sydney: Harcourt Brace Jovanovich.

Carkhuff, R. R. (1987). *The Art of Helping* (6th ed.). Amherst, MA: Human Resource Development Press.

Castles, I. (1993). *Australia in Profile: Census of Population and Housing 6 August 1991*. Canberra: Australian Bureau of Statistics.

Chelune, C. J. (1976). Reactions to male and female disclosure at two levels. *Journal of Personality and Social Psychology, 34*, 1000–1003.

Christensen, A, Jacobson, N. S., & Babcock, J. A. (in press). Integrative behavioral couple therapy. In N. S. Jacobson & A. S. Gurman (Eds.). *Clinical Handbook for Marital Therapy* (2nd ed.). New York: Guilford.

Christensen, A., & Heavy, C. L. (1993). Gender differences in marital conflict: The demand/withdraw interaction pattern. In Oskamp, S., & Constanzo, M. (eds.) *Gender Issues in Contemporary Society* (pp. 113–141). Newbury Park, CA: Sage

Colebatch, T. (1994). Top jobs for women soar 23 per cent in five years. *The Age*, 17 December, p. 7.

Cozby, P. (1973). Self-disclosure: A literature review. *Psychological Bulletin, 79*, 73–91.

Dalrymple, T. (1995). The uses of resentment. *Psychology Today, 28* (2), 30–32.

Deffenbacher, J. L., Story, D. A., Brandon, A. D, Hogg, J. A., & Hazaleus, S. L. (1988). Cognitive and cognitive-relaxation treatments of anger. *Cognitive Therapy and Research, 12*, 167–184.

Deffenbacher, J. L., Thwaites, G. A., Wallace, T. L., & Oetting, E. (1994). Social skills and cognitive-relaxation approaches to general anger reduction. *Journal of Counseling Psychology, 41*, 386–396.

Derlega, V. J., & Chaikin, A. L. (1975). *Sharing Intimacy: What We Reveal to Others and Why*. Englewood Cliffs, NJ: Prentice-Hall.

Deutsch, M. (1973). *The Resolution of Conflict: Constructive and Destructive Processes*. New Haven: Yale University Press.

DeVoe, D. (1990). Feminist and nonsexist counselling: Implications for the male counselor. *Journal of Counseling and Development, 69*, 33–36.

Dorwick, S. (1993). *The Intimacy and Solitude Self-therapy Book*. Melbourne: Mandarin.

Dryden, W. (1991). *A Dialogue with Arnold Lazarus: 'It Depends'*. Milton Keynes: Open University Press.

Eakins, B. W., & Eakins, R. G. (1978). *Sex Differences in Human Communication*. Boston: Houghton Mifflin.

Easteal, P. (1994). Violence against women in the home: How far have we come? How far to go? *Family Matters, 37*, 86–93.

Egan, G. (1994). *The Skilled Helper: A Problem-management Approach to Helping* (5th ed.). Pacific Grove, CA: Brooks/Cole.

Ekman, P., & Friesen, W. V. (1969). Nonverbal leakage and cues to deception. *Psychiatry, 32*, 88–105.

Ekman, P., Friesen, W. V., & Bear, J. (1984, May). The international language of gestures. *Psychology Today*, 64– 69.

Ekman, P., Friesen, W. V., & Ellsworth, P. (1972). *Emotions in the Human Face*. New York: Pergamon Press.

Ellis, A. (1980). Overview of the clinical theory of rational-emotive therapy. In A. Ellis & R. F. Grieger (eds.). *Rational-emotive Therapy: A Skills-based Approach* (pp. 1–31). New York: Van Nostrand Reinhold.

Ellis, A. (1987). The impossibility of achieving consistently good mental health. *American Psychologist, 42*, 364–375.

Ellis, A. (1995). Rational emotive behavior therapy. In R. J. Corsini & D. Wedding (eds.). *Current Psychotherapies* (5th ed., pp. 162–196). Itasca, IL: Peacock.

Erikson, E. H. (1963). *Childhood and Society* (2nd ed.). New York: W. W. Norton.

Feather, N. T. (1994). Values and national identification: Australian evidence. *Australian Journal of Psychology, 46*, 35–40.

Feindler, E. L., Marriott, S. A., & Iwata, M. (1984). Group anger control training for junior high school delinquents. *Cognitive Therapy and Research, 8*, 299–311.

Frankl, V. E. (1963). *Man's Search for Meaning: An Introduction to Logotherapy*. New York: Washington Square Press.

Frankl, V. E. (1969). *The Doctor and the Soul: From Psychotherapy to Logotherapy*. Harmondsworth: Penguin.

Frankl, V. E. (1988). *The Will to Meaning: Foundations and Applications of Logotherapy*. New York: Penguin Books.

Freedman, J. L. (1978). *Happy People*. New York: Harcourt Brace Jovanovich.

Freud, S. (1936). *The Problem of Anxiety*. New York: W. W. Norton.

Freud, S. (1949). *An Outline of Psychoanalysis*. New York: W. W. Norton.

Freudenberger, H. J. (1980). *Burnout: The High Cost of High Achievement*. London: Arrow Books.

Friday, N. (1973). *My Secret Garden: Women's Sexual Fantasies*. London: Quartet Books.

Gendlin, E. T. (1981). *Focusing* (2nd ed.). New York: Bantam Books.

Glasser, W. (1984). *Control Theory: A New Explanation of How We Control our Lives*. New York: Harper & Row.

Glasser, W., & Wubbolding, R. E. (1995). Reality therapy. In R. J. Corsini & D. Wedding (eds.) *Current Psychotherapies* (5th ed., pp. 293–321). Itasca, IL: Peacock.

Goffman, E. (1963). *Stigma: Notes on the Management of Spoiled Identity*. Harmondsworth: Penguin Books.

Goldenberg, H., & Goldenberg, I. (1990). *Counseling Today's Families*. Pacific Grove, CA: Brooks/Cole.

Goldenberg, H., & Goldenberg, I. (1995). Family therapy. In R.J. Corsini, & D. Wedding (eds.). *Current Psychotherapies* (5th ed., pp. 356–385). Itasca, IL: Peacock.

Goldsmith, L. (1988). Treatment of sexual dysfunction. In Weinstein, E., & Rosen, E. (eds.). *Sexuality Counseling: Issues and Implications* (pp. 16–34). Pacific Grove, CA: Brooks/Cole.

Goldstein, A. P., & Keller, H. (1987). *Aggressive Behavior: Assessment and Intervention*. New York: Pergamon Press.

Good, G. E., Dell, D. M., & Mintz, L. B. (1989). Male role and gender role conflict: Relations to help seeking in men. *Journal of Counseling Psychology, 36*, 295–300.

Gourlay, P. (1995). Sexuality education. *Family Matters, 41*, 39–42.

Hall, E. T. (1966). *The Hidden Dimension*. New York: Doubleday.

Harrison, M. (1993). *Family Law and Marriage Breakdown in Australia*. Australian Family Briefings, No. 2. Melbourne: Australian Institute of Family Studies.

Haskey, J. (1986). One-parent families in Great Britain. *Population Trends, 45*, 5–13.

Haskey, J. (1988). Mid-1985 based population projections by marital status. *Population Trends, 52*, 30–32.

Haskey, J. (1993). Lone parents and married parents with dependent children in Great Britain: A comparison of their occupation and social class profiles. *Population Trends, 72*, 34–44.

Haskey, J. (1995). Trends in marriage and cohabitation: The decline in marriage and the changing pattern of living in partnerships. *Population Trends, 80*, 5–15.

Heath, S. (1995). Many marriages appear doomed: Study. *The Sunday Age*, 23 September, p. A10.

Henderson-King, D. H., & Veroff, J. (1995). Sexual satisfaction and marital well-being in the first years of marriage. *Journal of Social and Personal Relationships, 11*, 509–534.

Hendrick, S., & Hendrick, C. (1992). *Liking, Loving and Relating* (2nd ed.). Pacific Grove, CA: Brooks/Cole.

Henley, N. M. (1977). *Body Politics: Power, Sex and Nonverbal Communication*. Englewood Cliffs, NJ: Prentice-Hall.

Ho, D. Y. F. (1985). Cultural values and professional issues in clinical psychology: Implications from the Hong Kong experience. *American Psychologist, 40*, 1212–1218.

Ho, D. Y. F. (1995). Internalized culture, cultrocentrism, and transcendence. *The Counseling Psychologist, 23* (1), 4–24.

Holland, J. L. (1973). *Making Vocational Choices: A Theory of Careers*. Englewood Cliffs, NJ: Prentice-Hall.

Hutson, T. L., Surra, C. A., Fitzgerald, N. M., & Cate, R. M. (1981). From courtship to marriage: Mate selection as an interpersonal process. In S. Duck & R. Gilmour (eds.). *Personal Relationships 2: Developing Personal Relationships* (pp. 53–88). New York: Academic Press.

Ivey, A. E. (1994). *Intentional Interviewing and Counseling: Facilitating Client Development in a Multicultural Society*. Pacific Grove, CA: Brooks/Cole.

Jacobson, E. (1938). *Progressive Relaxation* (2nd ed.). Chicago: University of Chicago Press.

Jacobson, N. S. (1989). The politics of intimacy. *The Behavior Therapist, 12* (2), 29–32.

Jacobson, N. S. (1992). Behavioral couple therapy: A new beginning. *Behavior Therapy, 23*, 493–506.

Jacobson, N. S., Gottman, J. M., Waltz, J., Rushe, R., Babcock, J., & Holtzworth-Munroe, A. (1994). Affect, verbal content, and psychophysiology in the arguments of couples with a violent husband. *Journal of Consulting and Clinical Psychology, 62*, 982–988.

Jourard, S. M. (1971). *Self-disclosure: An Experimental Analysis of the Transparent Self*. New York: Wiley.

Kaplan, H. S. (1974). *The New Sex Therapy: Active Treatment of Sexual Dysfunctions*. Harmondsworth: Penguin Books.

Kassorla, I. C. (1980). *Nice Girls Do*. New York: Berkley Books.

Kassorla, I. C. (1984). *Go For It!* New York: Dell.

King, M. L. (1963). *Strength to Love*. New York: Harper & Row.

Kinsey, A. C., Pomeroy, W. B., & Martin, C. E. (1948). *Sexual Behavior in the Human Male*. Philadelphia, PA: W. B. Saunders.

Kinsey, A. C., Pomeroy, W. B., Martin, C. E., & Gebhard, P. H. (1953). *Sexual Behavior in the Human Female*. Philadelphia, PA: W. B. Saunders.

Koerner, K., Prince, S., & Jacobson, N. S. (1994). Enhancing the treatment and prevention of depression in women: The role of integrative behavioral couple therapy. *Behavior Therapy, 25*, 373–390.

Kruger, A. H. (1970). *Effective Speaking: A Complete Course*. New York: Van Nostrand Reinhold.

Kwee, M. G. T., & Lazarus, A. A. (1986). Multimodal therapy: The cognitive-behavioural tradition and beyond. In W. Dryden & W. Golden (eds.). *Cognitive-Behavioural Approaches to Psychotherapy* (pp. 320–355). London: Harper & Row.

Lake, T. (1981). *Relationships*. London: Michael Joseph.

Lazare, A. (1995). Go ahead say you're sorry. *Psychology Today, 28* (1), 40–43, 76, 78.

Lazarus, A. A. (1984). *In the Mind's Eye: The Power of Imagery for Personal Enrichment*. New York: Guildford.

Lazarus, A. A. (1989). *The Practice of Multimodal Therapy: Systematic, Comprehensive and Effective Psychotherapy*. (rev. ed.). Baltimore, MA: The Johns Hopkins University Press.

Lazarus, A. A. (1992). Multimodal therapy: Technical eclecticism with minimal integration. In J. R. Norcross & M. R. Goldfried (eds.). *Handbook of Psychotherapy Integration* (pp. 261-263). New York: Basic Books.

Lazarus, A. A. (1995). Multimodal therapy. In R. Corsini & D. Wedding (eds.), *Current Psychotherapies* (5th ed., pp. 322-355). Itasca, IL: Peacock.

Margolin, G. (1981). Behavior exchange in happy and unhappy marriages: A family cycle perspective. *Behavior Therapy, 12*, 329–343.

Maslow, A. H. (1962). *Toward a Psychology of Being*. Princeton, NJ: van Nostrand.

Maslow, A. H. (1970). *Motivation and Personality* (2nd ed.). New York: Harper & Row.

Maslow, A. H. (1971). *The Farther Reaches of Human Nature*. Harmondsworth: Penguin.

Masters, W. H., & Johnson, V. E. (1970). *The Pleasure Bond*. New York: Bantam Books.

May, R. (1975). *The Courage to Create*. New York: Norton.

May, R., & Yalom, I. D. (1995). Existential psychotherapy. In R. J. Corsini & D. Wedding (eds.), *Current Psychotherapies* (5th ed., pp. 262–292). Itasca, IL: Peacock.

McCabe, M. P. (1994). Childhood, adolescent and current psychological factors associated with sexual dysfunction. *Sexual and Marital Therapy, 9*, 267–276.

McDonald, P. (1988). Families in the future: The pursuit of personal autonomy. *Family Matters, 22*, 40–47.

Meichenbaum, D. H. (1983). *Coping with Stress*. London: Century.

Meichenbaum, D. H. (1985). *Stress Inoculation Training*. New York: Pergamon Press.

Meichenbaum, D. H. (1986). Cognitive-behavior modification. In F. H. Kanfer & A. P. Goldstein (eds.). *Helping People Change: A Textbook of Methods* (3rd ed., pp. 346–380). New York: Pergamon Press.

Meichenbaum, D., & Deffenbacher, J. L. (1988). Stress inoculation training. *The Counseling Psychologist, 16*, 69–90.

Moir, A., & Jessel, D. (1989). *Brain Sex*. London: Mandarin.

MORI (1982). *Neighbours and Loneliness*. London: Market and Opinion Research International.

MORI (1983). *Survey*. London: Market Opinion Research International.

Muehlenhard, C. L., Koralewski, M. A., Andrews, S. L., & Burdick, C. A. (1986). Verbal and non-verbal cues that convey interest in dating: Two studies, *Behavior Therapy, 17*, 404–419.

National Committee on Violence Against Women (1991). *Position Paper*. Canberra: Australian Government Printing Service.

Nelson-Jones, R. (1984). *Personal Responsibility Counselling and Therapy*. Milton Keynes: Open University Press.

Nelson-Jones, R. (1986). Toward a people-centred language for counselling psychology. *The Australian Counselling Psychologist, 2*, 18–23.

Nelson-Jones, R. (1995). Lifeskills counselling. In R. Nelson-Jones, *Counselling and Personality: Theory and Practice* (pp. 412–451). Sydney: Allen & Unwin. (Australian edition only)

Nelson-Jones, R (1996). The STC's of lifeskills counselling. *Counselling, 7*, 46–49.

Nelson-Jones, R., & Dryden, W. (1979). Anticipated risk and gain from negative and positive self-disclosures. *British Journal of Social and Clinical Psychology, 18*, 79–80.

Nelson-Jones, R., & Strong, S. R. (1976). Positive and negative self-disclosure, timing and personal attraction. *British Journal of Social and Clinical Psychology, 15*, 323–325.

Nelson-Jones, R., & Strong, S. R. (1977). British students' positive and negative evaluations of personal characteristics. *Journal of College Student Personnel, 18* (1), 32–37.

Noller, P., Feeney, J. A. Bonnell, D., & Callan, V. J. (1994). A longitudinal study of conflict in early marriage. *Journal of Social and Personal Relationships, 11*, 233–252.

Novaco, R. W. (1977). Stress inoculation: A cognitive therapy for anger and its applications to a case of depression. *Journal of Consulting and Clinical Psychology, 45*, 600–608.

Oakley, A. (1972). *Sex, Gender and Society*. London: Temple Smith.

Patton, W., & Mannison, M. (1995). Sexual coercion in dating situations among university students: Preliminary Australian data. *Australian Journal of Psychology, 47*, 66–72.

Pease, A. (1981). *Body Language: How to Read Others' Thoughts by Their Gestures*. Sydney: Camel.

Pietromonaco, P. R., & Rook, K. A. (1987). Decision style in depression: The contribution of perceived risks versus benefits. *Journal of Personality and Social Psychology, 52*, 399–408.

Pistole, M. C. (1995). College students' ended love relationships: Attachment style and emotion. *Journal of College Student Development, 12*, 417–438.

Powell, J. J. (1967). *Why Am I Afraid to Love?* London: Fontana.

Powell, J. J. (1969). *Why Am I Afraid to Tell You Who I Am?* London: Fontana.

Rapee, R. M. (1993). Recent advances in the treatment of social phobia. *Australian Psychologist, 28*, 168–171.

Reissman, C., Aron, A., & Bergen, M. R. (1993). Shared activities and marital satisfaction: Causal direction and self-expansion versus boredom. *Journal of Personal and Social Relationships, 10*, 243–254.

Rogers, C. R. (1951). *Client-centered Therapy*. Boston: Houghton Mifflin.

Rogers, C. R. (1959). A theory of therapy, personality, and interpersonal relationships, as developed in the client centered framework. In S. Koch (ed.). *Psychology: A Study of Science*. (Study 1, Vol. 3, pp. 184–256). New York: McGraw-Hill.

Rogers, C. R. (1980). *A Way of Being*. Boston: Houghton Mifflin.

Rogers, S. M., & Turner, C. F. (1991). Male–male sexual contact in the USA: Findings from five sample surveys, 1970-1990. *Journal of Sex Research, 28*, 491–519.

Rogoff, B., & Morelli, G. (1989). Perspectives on children's development from cultural psychology. *American Psychologist, 44*, 343–348.

Rokeach, M. (1967). *Value Survey*. Palo Alto, CA: Consulting Psychologists Press.

Rokeach, M., & Ball-Rokeach, S. J. (1989). Stability and change in American value priorities, 1968-1981. *American Psychologist, 44*, 775–784.

Roscoe, G. (1994). *The Triple Gem: An Introduction to Buddhism*. Chiang Mai, Thailand: Silkworm Press.

Rubin, Z. (1970). Measurement of romantic love. *Journal of Personality and Social Psychology. 16*, 265–273.

Sabatelli, R. M. (1988). Measurement issues in marital research: A review and critique of contemporary survey instruments. *Journal of Marriage and the Family, 50*, 891–915.

Satir, V. (1972). *Peoplemaking*. Palo Alto, CA: Science and Behavior Books.

Schwartz, S. H. (1992). Universals in the content and structure of values: Theoretical advances and empirical tests in 20 countries. In M. Zanna (ed.). *Advances in Experimental Social Psychology* (Vol. 25, pp. 1–65). New York: Academic Press.

Schwartz, S. H., & Bilsky, W. (1990). Toward a theory of the universal content and structure of human values: Extensions and cross-cultural replications. *Journal of Personality and Social Psychology, 53*, 550–562.

Seligman, M. E. P. (1991). *Learned Optimism*. Milsons Point, NSW: Random House Australia.

Selye, H. (1974). *Stress without Distress*. Sevenoaks, Kent: Hodder and Stoughton.

Sharkin, B. S. (1993), Anger and gender: Theory, research, and implications. *Journal of Counseling and Development, 71*, 386–389.

Shaver, P. R., & Hazan, C. (1988). A biased overview of the study of love. *Journal of Social and Personal Relationships, 5*, 473–501.

Simonton, O. C., Matthews-Simonton, S., & Creighton, J. L. (1978). *Getting Well Again*. New York: Bantam Books.

Slade, P. D. (1994). What is body image? *Behaviour Research and Therapy, 32*, 497–502.

Solomon, M. R. (1986, April). Dress for effect. *Psychology Today*, 20–28.

Speilberger, C. (1988). *State-Trait Anger Expression Inventory: Research Edition*. Odessa, FL: Psychological Assessment Resources, Inc.

Spindler, G. D. (1963). *Education and Culture: Anthropological Approaches*. New York: Holt, Rinehart and Winston.

Steck, L., Levitan, D., McLane, D., & Kelley, H. H. (1982). Care, need and conceptions of love. *Journal of Personality and Social Psychology, 43*, 481–491.

Steiner, C. M. (1974). *Scripts People Live*. New York: Bantam Books.

Stuart, R. B. (1980). *Helping Couples Change: A Social Learning Approach to Marital Therapy*. New York: Guilford Press.

Sullivan, H. S. (1953). *The Interpersonal Theory of Psychiatry*. New York: W. W. Norton.

Super, D. E. (1980). A life-span, life-space approach to career development. *Journal of Vocational Behavior, 16*, 282–298.

Szasz, T. S. (1973). *The Second Sin*. London: Routledge & Kegan Paul.

Taylor, D. A., & Altman, I. (1966). *Intimacy-scaled Stimuli for Use in Studies of Interpersonal Relationships*. Bethesda, MD: Naval Medical Research Institute.

Teague, A. (1993). Ethnic groups: first results from 1991 Census. *Population Trends, 72*, 12–17.

Teasdale, J. D., & Dent, J. (1987). Cognitive vulnerability to depression: An investigation of two hypotheses. *British Journal of Clinical Psychology, 26*, 113–126.

Tillich, P. (1952). *The Courage to Be*. New Haven, CT: Yale University Press.

Timnick, L. (1983, September). When women rape men. *Psychology Today*, 74–75.

Tinsley, H. E. A., & Eldredge, B. D. (1995). Psychological benefits of leisure participation: A taxonomy of leisure activities based on their need-gratifying properties. *Journal of Counseling Psychology, 42*, 123–132.

Tokatlidis, O., & Over, R. (1995). Imagery, fantasy and female sexual arousal. *Australian Journal of Psychology, 47*, 81–85.

Trotter, R. J. (1986, September). The three faces of love. *Psychology Today*, 46–50, 54.

Veroff, J., Douvan, E., & Kukla, R. A. (1981). *The Inner American*. New York: Basic Books.

Walster, E., & Walster, G. W. (1978). *A New Look at Love*. Reading, MA: Addison-Wesley.

Watson. O. M. (1972). *Proxemic Behaviour: A Cross-cultural Study*. The Hague: Mouton.

Watters, W. W., Askwith, J., Cohen, M., & Lamont, J. A. (1985). An assessment approach to couples with sexual problems. *Canadian Journal of Psychiatry, 30*, 2–11.

Winnicott, D. W. (1986). *Home is Where We Start From: Essays by a Psychoanalyst*. London: Penguin Books.

Wolpe, J, & Wolpe, D. (1988). *Life Without Fear: Anxiety and Its Cure*. Oakland, CA: New Harbinger Publications.

Yalom, I. D. (1980). *Existential Psychotherapy*. New York: Basic Books.

Zilbergeld, B. (1978). *Male Sexuality*. New York: Bantam Books.

Zimbardo, P. G. (1977). *Shyness! What It is, What to Do About It*. Reading, MA: Addison-Wesley.

Name Index

Subject Index